GAMBLING ON DEVELOPMENT

STEFAN DERCON

Gambling on Development

*Why Some Countries Win
and Others Lose*

HURST & COMPANY, LONDON

First published in the United Kingdom in 2022 by
C. Hurst & Co. (Publishers) Ltd.,
New Wing, Somerset House, Strand, London, WC2R 1LA

Distributed in the United States, Canada and Latin
America by Oxford University Press, 198 Madison Avenue,
New York, NY 10016, United States of America.

A Cataloguing-in-Publication data record for this book
is available from the British Library.

ISBN: 9781787385627

www.hurstpublishers.com

Printed in Great Britain by Bell and Bain Ltd, Glasgow

CONTENTS

ACKNOWLEDGEMENTS

This was a book I had to write. Much of the material evolved over many years via numerous presentations to students, fellow academics, development experts, public servants or just interested listeners, and across four continents. Some of these talks excited listeners and encouraged me to work further on clarifying my thoughts. Others got me into trouble on Twitter, or they led to whispered warnings from peers that I was being disrespectful to senior academics. Years of encouragement by friends and colleagues persuaded me to write this book, nevertheless.

I could not have gone down this path without decades of absorbing the much more careful work of many of my academic colleagues in international development across the world. I hope I have not offended any. My colleagues and generations of students at the University of Oxford deserve an extra thank-you as I learned more from them than they learned from me.

My main thanks have to go all my colleagues at the Department for International Development (DFID), now defunct and submerged in the Foreign, Commonwealth and Development Office. Some senior officials at DFID (you know who you are) took a gamble on me when they first appointed me their chief economist in 2011. It was a life-changing experience, and I learned so much, among other things about the relative futility of much of my academic work, although fortunately not all research has to have immediate utility. Senior DFID staff freed me to roam across their department and the world. Their generosity allowed me to fully appreciate how central the interaction of economics and politics is in any country, including the UK. The decade that followed my first appointment was unique, and professionally I have never been happier than during that period.

Forgive me if I don't list at length all those I should, but that is simply out of fear that I would forget and therefore offend someone. But I would like to call out a few people, nevertheless. Ranil Dissanayake commented insightfully on the entire manuscript, and Sabra Ledent was an astounding content editor. And, not least, I hail my father, whose optimism was always infectious, although that other infectious scourge of our time, Covid-19, took him away while I was drafting the early chapters of this book. I dedicate this work to him for his undying support of whatever I chose to do.

PREFACE

A decade or so ago, I came to a realisation. I needed to radically rethink how development comes about. By then, I had one foot in academia—as an Oxford professor—and one in government—as a senior UK government official, serving as chief economist and the most senior technocrat in the UK's Department for International Development (DFID). My moment of truth came not long after I first flew into Beijing and then travelled around China—the farthest east I had ever ventured, despite having already visited forty-odd developing countries.

I never saw in China the extreme deprivation I had seen Burkina Faso, Ethiopia, or India in earlier years. Even if not precise, the statistics don't lie: in the 1980s China was the country with the largest number of people living in such deprivation. More than 700 million were subsisting on incomes and consumption levels that could reasonably be described as reflecting the most extreme forms of poverty.[1] But by the time I was travelling around China, more than half a billion of Chinese had risen from those depths.

Half a billion is not a manufactured or a pie-in-the-sky statistic. Although the economic growth figures produced by China over the years goose-stepped in line with its development plans, the speed and scale of Chinese poverty reduction were never planned in the same way. However, the changes were clearly on view in carefully collected statistics and also on the ground. Most lives were not ones of affluence or leisure, but the China of ten years ago—and today—

was definitely not a country in the grip of large-scale extreme poverty. Across much of Asia, this change is also under way. In some places, such as Singapore, the Republic of Korea, and Taiwan, the process started well before it began in China.

A lot has been written about what happened in China and how it came about. Some experts argue that China and other East Asian states serve as an example—a recipe even—of how to promote development. Fundamentally, say the experts, the steps that these countries followed are exactly what needs to be done: invest in growth as a state, preferably export-led growth, and encourage the emergence of a dynamic private sector to drive not only growth but also job creation. Meanwhile, also invest in health, education, and basic social protection. Policies that promote economic growth and development are key. Most important, these good policies could be introduced into other countries.

I admit that I quite happily bought into this perspective for a long time—that there is a clearly defined recipe for success, and refining and applying it to other countries are all that is required. The task of the academic is to improve this recipe using ever better evidence. When travelling in China, I realised that, no matter how successful it and other countries had been, no single policy recipe can be refined and spread around the world. And when China's progress took flight, China did not have a clear recipe either. Those in power took a gamble, committed to it, but did not know where it would end.

African dreams and reality

Studying what was happening in China—and, before that, in India, Vietnam, and Bangladesh—was energising. Even if India and Bangladesh did not follow the apparent Chinese recipe, their fast growth and subsequent decline in poverty demonstrated that change was possible. Not that these places were more interesting or fascinating than the African countries I had travelled and worked in earlier. I am an Africanist at heart, and I feel more at home in somewhere like Addis Ababa than in most parts of the world. But by the 1990s, I had seen too much stagnation and lack of change.

The late 1980s and 1990s had at times been especially depressing for those of us working in and on Africa.

I was living in Tanzania when the Berlin Wall fell in 1991. However, Tanzania felt very far from Eastern Europe's path towards economic and political change. The country was still in the grip of chaotic attempts to stabilise its economy, with empty shops and a flourishing black market in dollars, and still reeling from two decades of attempts to build the African version of the socialist-controlled economy in a one-party state. I spent my days quietly waiting for research interviews with government officials, who never turned up because they were barely paid and in any case felt little responsibility to do their jobs. They spent their days minding their own business, whether that was dealing in goats or in hard currency.

Throughout the 1990s, Tanzania's economy ever so slowly improved. As time went on, I also felt that change was possible across much of Africa. I had learned early on that one cannot work in international development without being an optimist. The end of the Soviet Union heralded a sense among some of us working in Africa that the 1990s would be Africa's time. Maybe not the 'end of history' as the political scientist Francis Fukuyama suggested in 1992, but I definitely believed this was the start of something better.[2]

It was tempting to blame the lack of progress in Tanzania on corruption or the failings of the one-party state. However, such generalisations are not enough to explain development failings; if anything, these problems are symptoms, not causes. Corruption wasn't invented in Africa even if it was no doubt mucking up the economy and undermining development in Tanzania. Every part of the world, every civilisation, has struggled with corruption. Simplistically blaming Tanzania's problems on a political system doesn't hold either. Not only China but also many other successful Asian countries such as Korea had one-party states or authoritarian regimes during much of their periods of rapid progress, while others, including India, held largely free and open elections but lagged behind for a long time. Nevertheless, at that moment in the early 1990s it seemed that there was an opening, a possible breakthrough, in Tanzania as in other African countries. The pressure for elections would surely lead to more accountability in Tanzania and across the continent, and that would lead to more development.

By 1992 I had ended up in a teaching post at Addis Ababa University, where clearly things could only get better. Ethiopia had just come out of its vicious decades-long civil war with the defeat of a ruthless regime backed by the Soviet Union and its allies. The victorious rebel army had marched from the north where it had its roots and power base, clearly intending to launch something new, even though it was by no means clear what. Working with Ethiopian and other researchers, I learned from my studies in rural villages across the country how deep the deprivation was. I ended up fulfilling the Ethiopian government's first rigorous attempt to measure the scale of extreme poverty. I estimated that close to half the population was living in conditions of abject hardship, even though the benchmark I used was in no way enough for a decent life. Indeed, it is fair to say that more than four out of five people in Ethiopia lived in extreme deprivation.

With the end of the Ethiopian civil war it was hoped that peace would launch a new period of change and progress across the country and on the continent as a whole. But then in 1994 the Rwandan genocide reared its ugly head. I had been in Rwanda only a few years earlier, cautiously optimistic that the forthcoming democratic elections could sow the seeds of peaceful change. In the meantime, I did not see the genocide coming. And I was not alone. For many of us, it dashed our hopes that peace and open politics would bring rapid prosperity on the continent.

This was the Africa in which I matured as a researcher and as a person: still full of hope and possibility. In the following decade, this continent, with its perpetual ups and downs, changed, but ever so slowly. Conflict was raging in some countries, while other economies had only just stabilised. Political systems seemed to change, but in too many places the change only ensured that everything stayed the same. Improvements in people's lives were barely evident in the data we researchers collected and analysed, even though we looked hard for them.

Unbalanced progress

Overall, it's no wonder that researching and travelling in Asia fed my optimism: there life could change, and speedily, for many people, even if by no means all. Countries with very low average incomes saw their economies take off and grow quickly. Indeed, by 2018 India, Indonesia, Bangladesh, and Vietnam reached GDP levels several times higher than those in 1990. China stood out because figures suggested a tenfold increase.[3] This increase in incomes was not just for the rich: poverty went down dramatically in these countries as well. Extreme poverty[4] was probably lower by about 1 billion people across these five countries in 2018, starting from levels of about 1.4 billion in 1990, despite their populations in total growing by another 1 billion over this period. Progress had been made across a broad range of indicators, including health, nutrition, and education.

African countries saw some meaningful progress as well. In Ghana and Ethiopia, average incomes doubled and tripled, respectively, between 1990 and 2018, and the total number of poor people began to decline. But in several other countries, income growth was far less substantial, and the number of poor people continued to increase steadily in Angola, the Democratic Republic of Congo (DRC), Nigeria, and Madagascar. Nigeria and Angola had higher GDP per capita in 1990 than Bangladesh, Vietnam, China, or India, but subsequently showed little improvement in poverty and deprivation indicators. Nigeria now has more extremely poor people than any other African nation; it may even have surpassed India (which has a population more than four times larger) as the country with the largest poor population in the world.[5]

With the turmoil of the coronavirus pandemic, there are calls for global support for and solidarity with those countries left behind. Now is the time to learn the right lessons from progress and failure in recent decades. Why has there been so much divergence? Why did some countries with broadly similar circumstances a few decades ago end up with different outcomes, not least in terms of the most extreme forms of deprivation? To answer these questions, in this book I dig into the development experiences of a diverse set of countries in Asia and Africa, relying on my first-hand experience in these countries and knowledge of the in-depth research on them. I will ask who gambled on what and why. And, then, whether that bet paid off.

INTRODUCTION

When I wrote this book, Covid-19 was ravaging the economies and societies of poor and rich countries alike. What would happen next was uncertain, but what was certain was that political leadership worldwide would be tested for a long time to come. Leaders in better-off countries were invariably using terms invoking what had been lost, promising to 'build back', albeit 'better'.[1] For some of the fastest-growing economies in recent times such as China and India, as well as Ethiopia, Rwanda, Bangladesh, and Ghana, the general tenor was about the need to find ways to resurrect their earlier fast growth and strides in development. For many of the other countries struggling on the eve of the crisis, such as Lebanon and Nigeria, as well as much poorer and rather stagnant countries such as Sierra Leone and Malawi, it was hardly about building back because the recent past was dismal. Instead, populations were hoping for a way out of the growth and development traps in which their countries found themselves.

In fact, expectations were high, and politicians everywhere were scrambling to take the initiative. With finance from both East and West more constrained and global cooperation under duress, pressure to ensure that even the poorest countries would find economic recovery models consistent with climate goals was not making matters simpler. Meanwhile, development experts, practitioners, and others were tossing out prescriptions for what developing countries should or could do. And this is what worried me and why I wrote this book. Often those espousing or considering solutions lack a basic understanding of what has been going on in recent decades, even some of those prescribers most passionate about international development.

For one thing, the 'developing world' is no longer clearly defined in terms of living standards, poverty, health, or other development statistics. Today, some economies and societies with both the highest and lowest rates of economic growth and development progress are equally described as 'developing'. For another, during my years working as an academic at the University of Oxford and in the UK government department devoted to international development, I have been struck by how large the gulf is between the narratives on development challenges and solutions and the actual practice of development that has led to progress on the ground. This gulf, found both in academic circles and within international or nongovernmental organisations concerned with development, is worth bridging because too much poorly thought-out advice and international aid are being doled out. This book, then, can contribute to development being 'done better'.

Finally, I want to move on from the endless talk and writing about what needs to be done as if there were a silver bullet that would enable countries to pursue successful development. Those of us in the development community are told to 'focus on the Sustainable Development Goals', 'get economic policies right', 'commit to green growth' or 'build institutions so you can develop'—in fact, everyone seems to have their own recipe for development. And yet most of these recipes come with few instructions about how to prepare the dish—that is, how to make development happen in a practical sense—and with few explanations of why reasonably sensible steps are taken in some places but not in others. This book, then, is about how and why development has come about *here* and not *there*—that is, the failures and, especially, the recent successes.

Why successes and failures? The core argument

Why did I change my mind about how development comes about after spending some time travelling in China? It was not simply because China is a growth and development success story, at least in terms of moving from a desperately poor country with high levels of deprivation to one that has grown quickly and eradicated the most extreme forms of poverty. Rather, my trip convinced me that the development community is learning the wrong lessons from its success.

What China did no doubt worked for its take-off. I suspect no other country can pull it off in the same way. Indeed, if this state-led model was to work anywhere, it was bound to be in China: no other country of any scale has exceeded its two-thousand-year history as a centralised state, with its well-oiled bureaucratic machinery and centralised taxation. And yet success in China came about only from the 1980s onwards. So what made the difference in a way that has more in common with other successes? It was the shift in China after 1979 towards a fundamental commitment by its leaders to growth and development—indeed, they staked their own political legitimacy as a one-party state on offering their citizens better living conditions through growth and development. It was a gamble, no doubt, and it could have backfired, either economically or politically.

This example leads to my core argument.

First, so much attention is paid to the specific blueprints for development, and yet successful countries appear to have pursued a relatively diverse set of economic and other policies. Countries that have achieved their development goals have achieved broadly reasonable macroeconomic stability, invested in infrastructure and in health and education, managed their natural resources prudently, provided a reasonable investment environment for private sector growth, allowed the market to play a central role but with a broadly supportive state, focused on international trade, and avoided specific firms or families cashing in to an extreme extent on connections to the state. Moreover, specific programmes have helped to further reduce poverty. The group involved is broad: with the usual suspects such as the Republic of Korea, Taiwan, Thailand, Malaysia, and Indonesia, as well as more nascent successes in the last few decades, such as India and Bangladesh, or Ethiopia and Ghana. However, these countries have at times pursued a rather diverse set of policies and priorities. There is no one, cost-free path to development. Even some broadly successful countries have embraced policies that were costly to their economy. Crucially, learning from mistakes is intrinsic to success—and having structures that make this feedback loop possible is no doubt critical.

Second, a better understanding is needed of why some countries implemented sensible economic and other policies, while others never did, despite often claiming they would as part of arrangements with international funders. Even though both sets of countries adopted the same rhetoric, those that were far less successful did not appear to take actions consistent with growth and development. It would be naive to suggest that these nations and their leaders simply did not know what to do—it was not just a question of ignorance or lack of good advice. Understanding why the rhetoric was followed by action in some places and not in others is at the centre of understanding how development works.

Third, successful growth and development requires the presence of a development bargain—that is, an underlying commitment to growth and development by members of a country's elite (the people within the fabric of society, the economy, and politics who make decisions or can disproportionately influence them). Three conditions need to be satisfied:

Durable political and economic deals among the elite, to start with on peace and stability. Long horizons are required for growth and development; conflict and instability shorten horizons in political and economic decision-making.

A mature, sensible state. Few people studying development would claim that the state does not play a role in it, but there are huge differences in how much the state takes on in the quest for development. This is true even in successful cases, as well as in failures. Success requires finding a balance between what the state should do and what it can do—and local circumstances will dictate what this is.

Ability to learn from mistakes and correct course. There is no recipe for finding the right way of igniting and sustaining growth: it is a gamble. Success is not guaranteed, errors will be made, and confidence in leaders will at times be eroded. Stability may be threatened as some in the elite gain less or even lose. The need to correct will test the economic and political deal. Nevertheless, finding ways to correct course is essential for success, which will depend on mechanisms to hold to account those entrusted with implementing the deal.

The development bargain

The idea of a development bargain is not simply a restatement of 'good institutions matter', as in a shared set of laws, informal norms, or understandings that constrain economic or political behaviour. No doubt they do matter—how could anyone disagree?—but understanding change doesn't simply follow from what some researchers appear to call for: reduce political, legal, and societal structures to their historical roots. Even successful countries have quite diverse histories. In fact, several of the success stories described in this book did not necessarily have strong institutions at the time of take-off—just think of Bangladesh, with its volatile rent-seeking politics and, in all respects, seemingly a 'basket case', as Henry Kissinger famously called it. Even China, after the nationalist and Maoist eras of the preceding half-century, hardly had strong institutions to deliver the kind of take-off it achieved post-1979. The political and economic elite have much more agency than is usually allowed by the historical approach to institutions.

A development bargain is just one of many possible deals among the elite. Any stable elite bargain is not just a political deal, but also an economic deal about access to and distribution of the resources of the state and the economy. In a development bargain, this economic deal is centred around pursuing growth and development. It needs to provide the basis for peace and stability, and it determines the extent to which the state apparatus is best used in pursuit of economic progress.

Development isn't just a 'one-term' political programme. How this consensus, this bargain, is obtained or sustained manifests itself in varying forms from place to place and period to period. One thing is clear: when those in the political and economic elite move towards longer-term growth and development, they are making a bet that may not pay off. The elite tend to gain from the status quo—that is, the political system and the economy are built to serve them. Elites that move towards growth and development, with the long-term perspective that it requires, tend to gamble that restraint and lower gains in the short term may pay off later. Vested interests are bound to be affected, and the risks to their own position are obvious. The elite are thus gambling on development.

A development bargain does not simply consist of specific development goals or targets, such as a public signing of the Sustainable Development Goals. It is much more than that, even if far less specific: it is an implicit contract among those who can make development happen. This contract can take different forms. For example, in China the Communist Party sought legitimacy post-1979 by demonstrating progress in growth and food security and setting up systems of party discipline to hold officials to account to deliver these outcomes. In Ethiopia, something similar was part of its recent story of growth and development. But the subsequent conflict between erstwhile partners in the political and economic deal demonstrates just how hard it is to sustain a development bargain. By the late 1990s, India had achieved a broad cross-party and economic leadership commitment to ever so gradual liberalisation of the economy, which would have been out of the question in earlier years. And Ghana saw a repeated commitment to the peaceful transfer of power through elections for stability's sake, learning from the disruption to growth and development in preceding decades.

These four examples also show that the use of the term 'elite' here does not imply that all countries need a form of authoritarian leadership to take off. And yet members of the elite, as the economic, political, technocratic, and bureaucratic powers that be, are instrumental: how they act matters, rather than simply the political system in which they operate or however they achieved their elite status.

How does change actually come about?

Here are two of the hardest questions to answer: How is a development bargain achieved and sustained? When will an elite gamble on a future of growth and development, putting their own positions possibly at risk? In each country, the answers differ. In later chapters of this book, I document not only the challenges that many of the laggard countries must overcome, but also the sources of hope in countries that have taken at least baby steps towards development.

And what role does international cooperation and aid play in a development bargain? The power of elites is interwoven with international structures and rich countries' own economic and political elite bargains. These bargains often make it much harder for national development bargains to emerge, although the vast divergence in fortunes across the developing world means that local responsibility still matters at least as much. In this, aid matters. Effective aid is a bit like learning to dance the tango: if both partners are passionate and committed, they can learn to do it, and with practice they will improve. But dancing the tango with a partner who is not committed is doomed to failure. So it is with aid. Without this commitment, development aid is at best a tricky endeavour. Later chapters in this book are devoted to the question of what can be done.

Organisation of this book

The book is divided into three parts. In part I, chapter 1 sets the scene by comparing and contrasting how the views and advice of well-known development thinkers fit in with the divergent experiences of countries as they seek development and growth. Each thinker provides a different lens, together offering a competing framework of what explains success and failure in development. All in all, however, they don't provide a sufficient explanation for some of the more recent success stories. Chapter 2 then develops the idea of the development bargain and how politics and the economy interact. It introduces the key features of the development bargain in its diversity across different contexts. Using simple data, chapter 3 provides a snapshot of what has happened developmentally in recent decades, highlighting successes and failures.

Part II describes in zoomorphic terms the diverse experiences of countries with development bargains. The chapters are based on places where I have spent time and on people I have met, sometimes giving me hope or at times leaving me in despair. Chapter 4 offers some examples of three countries—China, Indonesia, and India—

in which a development bargain has recently emerged, even if in different ways.[2] Chapters 5 to 10 take a closer look at the nature of elite bargains in fifteen countries through the framework of the development bargain. These chapters delve into what is behind not only the failings of the Democratic Republic of Congo (DRC), for example, but also the apparent unlikely successes of Bangladesh, Ethiopia, and Ghana. I highlight as well where a development bargain may be on the horizon—such as across East Africa—or where at least a bargain seeking stability is emerging, as I observed in Somaliland and, despite its current challenges, in Lebanon.

Across these countries, I highlight the kinds of economic policies that followed a bargain among the elite, why the policies appear to have been chosen, and how they have helped or hindered progress in development and growth. The narrative winds through Ebola in Sierra Leone, corruption scandals and maize market mismanagement in Malawi, beer factories in the DRC, constitutional reform in Kenya, relief programmes behind enemy lines in South Sudan, business meetings in Somaliland, and the unlikely success of growth in Bangladesh and Ethiopia. It also describes the pressure of trying to be East Asian when in Africa and much more, and is threaded with accounts of conversations with prime ministers, vice presidents, and civil servants, as well as with ordinary working men and women and small business owners.

Part III highlights what I have learned about successful development, about how development can be enhanced in even some of the worst settings (locally as well as by international actors), and where research and academia fit in. In short, it features what can be done to help more countries achieve successful development bargains, improve them, and support their sustainability. Chapter 11 takes a critical look at the usual global development discourse, whether from the United Nations or from Washington and Beijing, and how aid fits into it. Chapter 12 makes the case for aid fostering and supporting development bargains—it's messier and complex, but with more chance for success. I recognise that many will not want to ignore poor people in countries without development bargains. Chapter 13 concludes by exploring what can be done to support populations living in poverty even in such settings, despite little chance for real development progress. This part also highlights the most important role for global cooperation: engaging in pragmatic international policies that increase the likelihood of successful development and allow countries and the leading elites in them to gamble on long-term development, despite all the challenges faced.

Despite the grim picture I paint of the experience of some countries, I remain hopeful. So many countries that seemed to be basket cases only a few decades ago have improved dramatically, even if not yet reaching living standards that people deserve. The lives of billions of people are better now than I thought they would be, despite the odds. Political and economic leaders, intellectuals, academics, and citizens in general in those failing places that risk staying further behind would do well to learn the lessons from these successes—and dare to gamble on development.

PART I

1

DEVELOPMENT THINKERS AND THEIR THOUGHTS

It was 8 September 2012, and the evening newspaper in London milked the leak for all it was worth. Reportedly, the new UK secretary of state for international development had said when appointed, 'I didn't come into politics to distribute money to people in the Third World!'[1] Moreover, she admitted to never visiting any of the countries receiving aid from the UK. Even though she always denied her protest, it was enough to put the entire UK Department for International Development (DFID) on full alert for her arrival. The question was what do with a new boss in charge of spending £11.5 billion a year on international development who clearly did not know much about it. An email then went around asking for ideas on what the new secretary of state should read.

Meeting her for the first time was memorable. Her facial expression spoke volumes when the policy director handed her a pile of books on development, saying that perhaps she should read them over the weekend. Without thinking, I said, 'I could also give you a tutorial on all these books.' And I did the next week. Over the course of about two hours, we discussed the books, and how they were different or alike, as well as the effects of the views in them on developing country governments, aid agencies, and international organisations.

This was an important assignment: I could shape her thinking and decision-making. In the UK, just as across the world, politicians and senior public servants can hardly be expected to be on top of the latest research on and happenings in economic growth and development worldwide or even in their own country. And yet they must be able to make good, consistent decisions on what policies to promote and how to spend their department's budget. In the UK ministers do not have the luxury of bringing in an army of trusted personal advisors. Instead they must rely on the UK civil service, a strongly independent body but one that is bound through a strict civil service code to give the best possible advice. And that day she had to rely on me, an academic who had stumbled into the civil service less than a year earlier, to induct her into international development thinking.

Not only in politics but also in most of life's choices, people need frameworks to help them make decisions. In psychology, these frameworks are called mental models—the concepts, stories, and views that reveal how the world works.[2] Politicians are no doubt shaped by their own worldviews and ideology, but in making decisions they also need a clear causal model of what is and is not possible. Because this minister's mental model of how the world of development works was somewhat empty, I was asked to help shape it, keeping in mind that in the UK civil servants advise, ministers decide.[3] I was, however, determined at least to make the new appointee aware of the grand and exciting opportunity she now had as the secretary of state for international development.[4]

The pile of books presented to the minister had been chosen because of their broad appeal—all were best-sellers—and because of their influence on the development and aid community. They were not chosen because someone, let alone me, had decided the views they espoused were right or in line with official UK views. Hence, the authors included best-selling academics and thinkers such as Amartya Sen, Jeffrey Sachs, Bill Easterly, Paul Collier, Jim Robinson and Daron Acemoglu, Esther Duflo and Abhijit Banerjee, Joseph Stiglitz, Dambisa Moyo, Angus Deaton, Ha-Joon Chang, and Dani Rodrik.[5] Yes, plenty of white males (although not all), and all were economists. By now, five have a Nobel Prize,[6] and I suspect one more is to come. Women, key authors from development studies or political science and other high-quality thinkers were surely missing, but the list was intended to reflect those who appeared to have had the most influence over the debates on economic development, including those that took place in political circles in Whitehall. As for this author, in the next chapter I offer my own understanding of how development comes about—that is, my own mental model of development.

The rest of this chapter gives a sense of the dominant thinking on why countries and poor people lag behind and what to do about it, based on what I told the minister. Later in this chapter, I will come back to these authors because each offers a different framework, both for the main problems surrounding international development, and also for how to overcome them. But first what follows is a brief introduction from the perspective of development economics on why countries or people may be poor.

A quick guide to the economics of poverty and development

Recent decades have seen much research and thinking on what holds countries and people back. But even mainstream development thinking, as reflected in the best-selling books, offers a range of answers. At the risk of not giving credit to the nuances of all this work, a few diagnostic statements allow me to differentiate between quite a lot of it, not least its implications for what can be done, if anything, to boost poor countries and people. Here, then, I offer in the form of four propositions competing diagnoses of what the core problems are.

Proposition 1: 'Countries and people are poor because they are poorly endowed'. All economists agree that markets matter. Since well before Adam Smith, they have understood that prices, set through the market mechanism, are key to achieving functioning economies. There are limits to how much a government can tinker with all this. Still, few economists have ever subscribed to the view that markets should just be left to get on with it and all will be well in society.

In fact, this point touches on what is likely a big misunderstanding about economists, not least those working with developing countries.

Some people claim that economists don't care about fairness. This misunderstanding comes from a misreading, or at least an incomplete reading, of the most basic economic theories. What economists call the first welfare theorem says that if markets are perfectly competitive so that anyone can enter a market, no one can hide what they do, and no one hinders this free market, the result will be the most efficient possible allocation of all resources—labour, capital, land, and technology. However, the fine print, wilfully ignored by some, says that those in such a system will be rewarded in line with what they had to start with: their labour, their endowments, the opportunities they were given, the power they had. So, because this is a world with rather big differences in the birth lottery—such as where you were born, who your parents are, and other factors determining your starting position—the market allocation can hardly be called fair. Markets really matter for efficiency, but it doesn't mean countries shouldn't do anything to seek fairness in outcomes or opportunities.

All this leads to a straightforward, almost tautological explanation of poverty: people or countries are poor because they were poor to start with. Much justification for large-scale social spending by governments as well as for development aid depends on this explanation. When resources are spent on boosting poor countries' or poor people's endowments—by building infrastructure, improving health, upgrading education, providing finance for small business— those countries and their populations will be able to reap bigger rewards from their efforts. A poor person may not have much to start with, but once receiving a good education and enjoying better health, or accessing some capital to buy a cow or the stock needed for a small shop, he or she can begin to make a bit more money and take a step towards making a decent living.

This simplest expression of why people or countries are poor— they were poor to start with—is not as innocent as it may seem. It appears to let markets off the hook: they just reward what anyone has to offer in view of what they have. After all, there is inequality to start with, and the economy just reproduces this inequality. If anyone doesn't have enough, don't blame the economy. Instead blame whatever process in history or society caused some to have a lot and others to have little. There's no need to interfere with the market; just set the past right.

Proposition 2: 'Market failures are costly for poor people and may trap them in poverty'. Market 'failures'—imperfections in the functioning of the market system—are an essential feature of any economy, and no simple set of instruments exists to avoid them, especially not the practice of laissez-faire.

What are examples of market failures? Perfect markets assume no oligopolies or monopolies: no firm is powerful enough to set the prices, and scale of operations does not offer any advantages. Perfect markets also assume no moral hazard: for example, a bank can easily be assured that anyone taking a loan will use it for the intended purpose. And perfect markets assume no negative externalities: a deal between two firms does not affect anyone not included in the deal, such as the households who must contend with any pollution generated as a result of the deal. Market power, entry constraints, and the presence of scale economies, moral hazard, and negative externalities such as pollution are common examples of market failure. Many economists view these imperfections as substantial enough to be highly costly to the economy and society itself. They open the door for interventions by the state to correct market outcomes, assuming this can be done.

Many authors, such as Joseph Stiglitz and Abhijit Banerjee, have linked market failures to poverty, claiming that some market failures especially hurt the poor and exacerbate their lack of initial wealth and endowments.[7] So the markets are not off the hook. Instead, their ingrained imperfections are a central cause of the plight of the poor and may end up trapping the poor in poverty. The differences between the rich and poor in access to capital in the credit market are a good example. A smart woman from a poor family will find it far harder than a not very smart woman from a better-off family to get a bank loan to pay for her education or to raise the capital for setting up a business. Banks will ask for collateral that neither she nor her family will have. But this will not be as much of a problem for someone from a better-off family. Without this constraint on raising capital, she will be able to get a better job through a college education or succeed as an entrepreneur.

Two people alike in ability will therefore end up with different earnings because banks don't hand out loans based on future income. Instead, faced with the deeply rooted problems of imperfect information or enforcement in the market system, banks ask for collateral. In this way, the market exacerbates the poverty of the woman from the poor family, who ends up earning less throughout her life because she was unable to go to college or start her own business.

The cost of market failures to the economy and society is huge. Poor people end up being trapped in low-return activities, with little chance of growing rich and leaving their poverty behind: they are in fact trapped in poverty.[8] And this would be true even if they were just as smart and entrepreneurial as a richer person, who was able to pursue an education or start a business and so earn more throughout life. In short, there are inequalities to start with, but markets reward people differently.

Proposition 3: 'Growth traps stem from market failures that are costly for poor countries'. This proposition offers a big-picture version of essentially the same ideas. The first two propositions offer explanations for why in a society one person may not be able to do as well as another. Likewise, countries may lag behind because they're unable to build up infrastructure or the educational levels of their population due to a low international credit score arising from market failures. Or they may not be able to compete against large international companies because of the way international markets work.

Long-standing conditions at work in a country, such as poor human or physical capital, are exacerbated by market failures. The result is long-term divergence between most developing countries and the world's richer economies. Two market failures feature prominently. The first one is externalities, particularly from human capital. For example, Paul Romer has suggested that education doesn't just boost the incomes of the educated; the externalities from higher levels of human capital also boost productivity across the economy through ideas and innovation.[9] The other market failure is economies of scale across the economy. For example, Paul Krugman and others have pointed out the importance of agglomeration effects—that is, the increasing returns from setting up firms in the same locality.[10] Firms can then take advantage of proximity through better-functioning product and input markets: it is easier to make sales, bring down transport costs, and hire or buy inputs.

Both kinds of market failures may explain why poor countries would find it hard to catch up because they are latecomers in these growth processes, leading to a growth trap. Countries with low education levels may find it hard to have the same growth and innovation dynamic as those with highly functioning education systems to start with. Countries that came late to manufacturing will find it hard to attract firms because firms tend to take advantage of the agglomeration effects in other locations with established firms. For example, sixty years ago, when the port areas of Singapore and Mombasa were likely almost similar, it was Singapore that first attracted new firms, while Mombasa missed the boat. As increasing returns benefit the early starter, Mombasa and other African ports have faced ever higher hurdles to catch up and so have persistently experienced lower economic growth, diverging ever more from Singapore's growth.

Proposition 4: 'Growth traps stem from failures in states and their governance'. Other authors have linked persistence in differences in growth performance to features of states and societies, both theoretically and empirically. In particular, instead of focusing on different levels of financial or human capital, they highlight a very different kind of capital—the fabric of society and institutions as they have evolved through history, such as the nature of the rule of law and the political system.[11]

Research has emphasised a whole slew of features.[12] Some investigators have focused on the failure of the preconditions for a market economy, required for proposition 1 to be valid. Such preconditions are well-defined property rights and contract enforcement through a functioning court system, among other features of the rule of law. Others have looked at the political system per se—such as whether a country is a democracy or an autocracy.

And especially when trying to explain why countries have lagged behind, researchers have pointed to conflict and the factors that may be associated with it, such as ethnic diversity, wealth inequality, or the presence of natural resources worth fighting over. Then there are factors such as religion or colonisation history, which may have influenced growth either directly or indirectly through the rule of law. Broadly speaking, researchers have emphasised the links between an economy, politics, and society, and how geographical or historical factors may have shaped them.

. . .

There is no doubt that among all the plausible factors driving growth under propositions 3 and 4, many are likely to have been true at the same time. Which ones matter most has long been the main differentiating factor. The problem is that researching growth empirically across countries is difficult, and many bunfights are still breaking out over which approaches are acceptable and whether any of this work reaches the standards required for science.

While it may be conceptually highly plausible, proving the causal growth impact of specific initial conditions empirically is highly disputed: correlations are easy to find, but they do not mean causation. Indeed, it is not only difficult to measure properly the possible explanatory factors under proposition 4, but also always hard to argue that anything in the present or in history is truly a random act. This makes the statistical work conducted by even the biggest research names often controversial. It also means that the evidence base to distinguish between the explanations for growth differences between countries remains contested.[13]

Which propositions are most convincing and which factors matter most within each are nevertheless relevant to a person's mental model about development. Various authors—especially those who wrote the best-sellers—have long argued about which of these propositions offers the right frame for looking at growth and development differences. And they have extended their arguments to which specific failures of markets or governance matter most and how any of these factors may change, including the role played by foreign aid. Because their views are generally quite nuanced and there is not enough space here to do them full justice, I offer only a brief summary, much like the one I gave my minister, with apologies for the shortcuts taken.

Best-selling development thoughts: A short summary

Policy-makers are often drawn to simple, easily communicated mental models about how the world works. It goes like this: poor countries and people lack resources, and so just by transferring financial resources to them, problem solved! It's no wonder one often hears such a mantra from supporters of development aid. In its simplest form, it is often a rallying cry for redistributing resources through aid from rich countries to poor countries. These resources can then be spent on strengthening the health, education, or the financial asset base of the poor—that is, the resources can be used to build poor people's human and physical capital.

In many ways, it is more subtle than that: even if a person were to believe that the world is more consistent with proposition 2—that market failures are really costly for the poor—and even proposition 3—that similar factors drive overall growth differences—building up the asset base of poor people and countries remains a way of improving their lot. If it is poverty that is locking them out, building up their assets—whether in education, health, financial capital, or infrastructure—would allow poor people to be more productive and take advantage of opportunities, even if the fundamental failures of markets are not addressed. Even with a more sophisticated mental model, then, the advice offered on what to do about poverty remains really simple—almost a silver bullet—and easy to campaign around: give lots of aid. This is almost all anyone needs to know to understand Jeffrey Sachs's *The End of Poverty*.

And yet not all thinkers more inclined to embrace proposition 2, and especially 3, would agree that this is the way to go: the poorly functioning markets must work better if a country is to see progress. Not just cash but also reforms of how economies function are required. For some thinkers, these changes will be mainly domestic, as Paul Collier calls for in *The Bottom Billion*. For others, market failures are important, but they need to be attacked internationally, says Joseph Stiglitz in his *Globalization and Its Discontents*, or through strong state intervention, as Ha-Joon Chang suggests in his work.

Those thinkers who tend to veer towards proposition 4 differ from the others by suggesting that states will not spend their new-found resources on the right people, that fiscal resources or outside aid will be misused, and that reforms will never be enacted. The problem, then, is never the cash, but the way these states are governed. Daron Acemoglu and James Robinson encapsulate such a view in their influential book *Why Nations Fail*, which links these present-day problems to the historical factors messing up politics and the economy. William Easterly's *The White Man's Burden* goes even further: those trying to fix these economies, such as the World Bank and aid organisations, are to blame by making things worse. And Angus Deaton and Dambisa Moyo, each in very different ways, share quite a lot of this viewpoint.

In short, each author has quite a different way of thinking (and different advice) about development and what holds countries back, or at times what makes them successful. What follows further explores these authors' arguments.

Development made easy: Aid as a silver bullet

Jeffrey Sachs published *The End of Poverty* in 2005, the first of those in the pile of books offering a grand vision of development. Although Sachs discusses many reasons for what keeps countries poor, two big drivers of the gaps and lower growth of certain countries jump out. First, some countries suffer from widespread poverty because they are facing a geographical and climatic challenge that leads to serious health problems, such as malaria or other tropical infectious diseases. Markets are not going to easily overcome such diseases. Second, global credit market failures are notoriously locking poor countries out of building the capital they need to invest in health or other economic or social infrastructure. What's the solution? Big buckets of aid to deliver a 'big push'—that is, pumping knowledge and finance into these countries through development support, especially around health. Or to quote Bono, the Irish pop star, who wrote the foreword to Sachs's *The End of Poverty*: 'The wealth of the rich world [and] the power [...] of knowledge ... make the end of the poverty a realistic possibility by [...] 2025.'

(Very) small steps to development

Perhaps like his music, Bono's quote now sounds very much as though it's from another age. Still, the notion that achieving development through spending on the poor lives on. For example, much of the work by Abhijit Banerjee and Esther Duflo is in that spirit, not least as on display in their book *Poor Economics*. So is much of the work of their intellectual sisters and brothers, who find it is possible to achieve large-scale reduction and even 'graduation' out of poverty through careful spending of public resources. But their approach to spending resources is fundamentally different from the views of Sachs and his supporter Bono. Instead of the confidence expressed in *The End of Poverty* that the main constraint to overcoming poverty is resources (because one knows how to use them), the authors of *Poor Economics* contend it is knowledge (because the understanding of how to use resources well is limited).

Starting from proposition 2—that market failures affect the poor most and keep them stuck in poverty—books such as *Poor Economics* offer a multi-step prescription, not just for how to strengthen the poor's asset positions but also for how often small, specific interventions can help overcome these market failures. Or as Banerjee and Duflo put it: 'If we resist lazy, formulaic thinking that reduces each problem to the same set of general principles [...] then we will be able to construct a toolbox of effective policies.'[14] Financial resources matter, they say, but the key to alleviating poverty is to identify (through careful research and evaluation) what works and what doesn't, and direct resources towards the best things able to nurture development, which are by no means self-evident. They radically reject the need for a grand vision as in propositions 3 and 4 or, indeed, as Sachs appears to promote it. Development will be achieved by lifting the veil of ignorance bit by bit, one intervention at a time, leading to an approach often labelled a marginalist view of development.

Gloom and doom

William Easterly's *The White Man's Burden*, first published in 2006, seems to be the antithesis of Sachs's book. It is firmly in the proposition 4 camp. Easterly suggests that states and their governance are to blame for growth traps. He also thinks aid has no role in them. Just the subtitle pretty much sums up his thinking: *Why the West's Efforts to Aid the Rest Have Done So Much Ill and So Little Good*. Of course, this is not the best statement to present to the newly appointed head of a government department that spends £11.5 billion a year on development aid. But that doesn't mean the book isn't worth reading. Easterly, a long-standing World Bank economist turned rogue, sees corrupt and failing states and institutions everywhere, supported by aid and, in later work, by foreign development experts. All would be different if only these countries had democratic elections, property rights, and the rule of law, as they are known in the West. Markets wouldn't do badly at all if only they were allowed to work. There is nothing to 'fix' here; markets wouldn't 'fail' so badly if it weren't for government failure.

In short, then, Easterly finds that aid has done more harm than good, and no one should deceive themselves into believing that some outside expert knows how to solve the development challenges of these countries. When reading his work, I could not help feeling, as a development practitioner, that Easterly was telling those of us trying to contribute to development that we are doomed whatever we try—that is, there is little to do despite all the misery.

This is a rather sobering thought for anyone involved in development work, but it is not unique; other versions of this view abound. For example, Angus Deaton's book *The Great Escape: Health, Wealth, and the Origins of Inequality* (2013) documents the massive improvements in living standards, such as in health, over the last century, telling a great story of success in development. But when it comes to development aid, Deaton reiterates Easterly's views: perhaps through spending on the development of medicines and vaccines or through trade outsiders can do good, but they shouldn't try to use aid as a vehicle for change in these countries. It just feeds corruption and bad governance and makes everything worse.

Zambian Dambisa Moyo goes further in her book *Dead Aid: Why Aid Is Not Working and How There Is a Better Way for Africa*. Large-scale aid is crippling African economies and leads to governments begging for more, she observed in 2010. Instead, free market solutions should be central. Beyond perhaps aid for humanitarian crises, she sees no role for aid or outsiders—nor frankly for governments, beyond getting out of the way. Let's just trust the market, especially global capital markets, the former Goldman Sachs advisor goes on to suggest.

Not all of her readers were impressed, especially philanthropist and entrepreneur Bill Gates, who declared that Moyo's book was promoting evil. Maybe that view was a bit strong, even if Moyo's argument relies on some pretty dodgy evidence, but having an African say this bluntly made some observers think. And for many more, it confirmed the beliefs they had long had. Easterly and Deaton put the failures squarely on developing countries, but, along with Moyo, they also lay the blame on the richer countries for messing up the poor countries through aid and for their well- and less well-intentioned involvement in these countries.

Failing global markets and values

Moyo's deep belief in global capital markets puts her at odds with all the other authors, and not least with Joseph Stiglitz. Besides being a brilliant academic, a worthy recipient of a Nobel Prize, he gained global recognition among development practitioners from his spat with the International Monetary Fund (IMF)—a spat that erupted while he was serving as chief economist of the World Bank. During the Asian crisis in 1997, when several East Asian and Southeast Asian economies were facing a macroeconomic crisis, Stiglitz pushed hard against the one-solution-fits-all and let-the-capital-and-other-markets-just-work approaches that the IMF of that time appeared to espouse. Arguably and with hindsight, it is rather unsurprising that someone like him, who had built his enormous academic reputation on his study of market failures in financial and other markets, would take this stance, but it was still shocking at the time.

In his book *Globalization and Its Discontents*, Stiglitz recognised, in line with proposition 3, that market failures abound, but the real failing is not trying to fix them, especially in global markets. Globalisation was not designed to work for the poor. One need look only at the failings in international trade or intellectual property rights that don't give poor countries a chance. For Stiglitz, the international system of multilateral organisations—such as the World Trade Organization, the World Bank, and not least the IMF— is to blame for its inaction on these matters. The right response is to reform the system. At the same time, support poor developing countries by giving them plenty of aid so they can move ahead and fix their own market failures.

With his anti–global institutions views and seemingly interventionist attitude, Stiglitz is an unlikely hero for more 'leftist' thinkers. But they have a more much negative view of the role of the market and a much more expansive view of the scope and scale of government intervention—that is, they want not just to fix market failures but also intervene more extensively and direct the economy towards specific sectors and activities. Cambridge University economist Ha-Joon Chang, writing in *Bad Samaritans: The Myth of Free Trade and the Secret History of Capitalism*, is a case in point. For Chang, governments can shape their countries' economic destiny in a directed way and 'do a Korea' in which strong government institutions use extensive protectionism and other measures to drive the emergence of an industrial comparative advantage. Stiglitz doesn't go this route. Contrary to many who see him as their standard-bearer, Stiglitz still strongly believes in the role of the market, as would befit a former chair of the US Council of Economic Advisors under President Bill Clinton.

Stiglitz's belief that the way ahead is to reform the various global development institutions is not quite the same position of another author critical of the way globalisation has evolved. In *The Globalization Paradox: Democracy and the Future of the World Economy* (2011) and subsequent work, Dani Rodrik sees much in the way global markets work that conflicts with social inclusion and democracy. His answer to this, however, is not to expect much from lofty attempts to reform the global system. Rather, start from recognition that each country needs to find an economic and societal strategy that fits its values. It is the only way to keep trade, as a basis for global wealth creation, firmly consistent with values such as democracy.

Traps from which one can escape

In his books, starting with *The Bottom Billion: Why the Poorest Countries Are Failing and What Can Be Done about It*, Paul Collier locates the key challenges squarely in the countries that stayed behind, but with recognition (and much sympathy) that these troubles are hard to overcome. Collier does not strive for nuance. His diagnosis covers aspects of propositions 3 and 4—but with boundless optimism and confidence that, despite the presence of market and governance failures, his policy ideas can drive success.

In Collier's narrative, geographical and historical endowments interact in ways that muddle the politics of the economy, leading to lack of growth and impoverishment. Many African countries are blessed with abundant natural resources, but that blessing creates incentives for those in power to show little interest in using that abundance to build a productive economy. After all, why should they bother when they enjoy access to the revenue from oil, copper, or other minerals? This winner-takes-all attitude to power fosters conflict and corruption, compounded by historical boundaries that forced different ethnicities and nations in uncomfortable cohabitation within these countries. Hence violence and distrust are widespread, undermining the chances for an economy to develop. Even if a country tries to follow a different path and avoid these traps, conflict and poor governance in neighbouring countries will often spill over and affect the chances to develop. Within the global economy, countries facing these challenges within or outside their borders have ended up lagging behind because firms tend to invest where there are other firms and also in good economic neighbourhoods, exploiting the economies of scale that this entails.

Collier pushes for strong support for the afflicted countries— from trade preferences to ample finance and expertise, and even at times military intervention to help reduce the risks and increase the returns to investing in such settings. In doing so, he walks a fine line between Sachs's push for large aid and Easterly's gloomy prediction that it will all be wasted. Meanwhile, he recognises that aid, just like natural resources, creates incentives for the political elite to cash in, but that, with much careful effort, it can be used properly and beneficially.

It's institutions, stupid

Other authors have questioned the notion that good policies with outside support are a sufficient condition for change because such efforts are constrained by deeper institutional and historical forces. Daron Acemoglu and James Robinson encapsulate this historical view in their influential book *Why Nations Fail*. They argue that failing nations do not have inclusive economic and political institutions that favour growth, innovation, and development. 'Institutions', as used here, refers to the set of economic and political rules created, implemented, and enforced by a state and followed by its citizens. Put differently, these are legal frameworks as well as more informal norms. They may include freedom of expression, the rule of law, protection against unfair competition, and protection of minorities or the vulnerable. But such frameworks do not just emerge. Rather, they are shaped by history, and in turn they determine today's economic, social, and political incentives to act in particular ways. On that basis, some societies (such as Britain) were able to build up prosperity and accountability, while others (such as Sierra Leone) are not on such a trajectory.

Why Nations Fail is a sobering read. In the authors' analysis, the reasons why nations have failed are deep ones, and they are not quickly rectified by impulsively enacting a policy or a financing package. Even if one doesn't buy Sachs's naive optimism around aid, Acemoglu and Robinson offer far less of the pragmatism of, say, Rodrik or Collier. It is a deeply pessimistic agenda for change or how change may be supported if history is to blame: countries appear to be told to 'buy yourself a better history' or citizens appear to be cautioned to 'wait for your moment'.

My advice to the boss

Fundamentally, all these authors agree on 'what success would look like'. They also agree on what is needed for success—growth in which private firms and markets create decent jobs and opportunities and in which social sectors such as health and education provide people with the skills and health they need to take advantage of emerging opportunities. All these thinkers know that poor countries lag behind in their assets and endowments, and they need to invest in infrastructure, health, and education. They also need the social, economic, and political institutions that help markets and society function in a broadly inclusive way. Where all these thinkers disagree is on where to start, who should act, and at what level. Is it about the role of the global system, or is change especially needed within countries? Can change happen quickly, or is it in the end historical predestination? And can outsiders help, or are they a nuisance?

I suggested that my boss look at the books of these thinkers, even if only for inspiration, but treat none as a blueprint. She could be emboldened by Collier's advice and optimism that change is possible; Banerjee and Duflo's admonishment to find ways, using the discipline of evidence, to strengthen the assets of the poor and contribute to fixing markets that currently fail for the poor; Easterly's and Deaton's counsel to acknowledge that development is a messy process and one may well make things worse; and Acemoglu and Robinson's assertion that understanding why countries seem to function as they do relies on better understanding the history of those countries. I also advised her to be careful in assessing simplistic solutions to development challenges. After all, it's not as though a country like Britain, an outsider, can just send aid and expect it will drastically change lives for the better everywhere. Indeed, development is hardly a matter of spending money or finding a silver bullet, thereby allowing technocrats to easily engineer success in a foreign country as long as the cash or some wizardry is available. Her organisation should ensure that if it tries to make a difference, it does so with a thorough understanding of these societies, economies, and politics. In the end, what is going on in these other countries will determine the success or failure of their own development efforts and any support outsiders may give.

Making development politically attractive

So what did the secretary of state conclude? Which view did she find compelling? That is between advisor and minister, but a few hints may help. By the time I gave the tutorial to my minister, Sachs's views calling for big buckets of aid seemed a bit dated, even though they had been published only seven years earlier, and politicians and the press were asking critical questions on whether aid was effective.[15]

Sceptical policy-makers found the Banerjee and Duflo marginalist view of development attractive because it was more critical of the view that all is well in aid spending. Its emphasis on specific evidence from experiments and on spending only on 'what works' played well in an institution that often faced accusations that aid was wasted. The scientific-technocratic demeanour of these authors attracted some policy-makers because it was hard to object to. After all, who dares to argue with hard evidence? For others, this was the main weakness of the approach: it appeared to keep its distance from power and politics, solving small problems and rarely favouring big policy or institutional reform.

And politicians like big-picture ideas; arguably, they need them to place small things within a broader framework and to process broad trends and challenges. Although Paul Collier had in the past been praised in public by Prime Minister David Cameron, by the time I was presenting these books to my boss in London, Cameron had said in a recent interview that Acemoglu and Robinson's *Why Nations Fail* was his favourite book. More scepticism towards aid was, then, the order of the day.

A good UK civil servant knows how to take a hint, and so my colleagues and I began to consider how that book could be used in DFID's policy-making. After all, whatever my minister thought, the prime minister's views had to be taken seriously and reflected in actionable programmes. Even before his election in 2009, Cameron, in a speech on development, had referred to countries being pulled out of poverty by 'a golden thread that starts with the absence of war and the presence of good governance, property rights and the rule of law, effective public services and strong civil institutions, free and fair trade, and open markets'. My colleagues and I hoped that *Why Nations Fail* offered the grammar needed to turn this 'golden thread' of nouns into at least a comprehensible paragraph for use in policy-making.[16]

The urge for silver bullets

The problem with an agenda built around 'the golden thread' or *Why Nations Fail* is that telling a country to 'buy yourself a better history' is not that easy. Advising countries 'to try to be like Britain in the nineteenth century' may go down well with conservative prime ministers such as David Cameron or Boris Johnson at No. 10 Downing Street in Britain, but it is hardly an agenda to go global with.

Indeed, it was hard to be good civil servants and act on either the 'golden thread' or the more eloquent *Why Nations Fail*, as our political masters asked us to do. For example, well-defined individual property rights are one of the features of inclusive institutions that these authors seemed to favour. However, because protection of these rights evolves over time, just rolling out some programmes to establish property rights is bound to be tricky. Nevertheless, a signal was received from No. 10 advisors that we should pursue this.

Moreover, they sought the help of Hernando de Soto, the author who achieved some fame for his book *The Mystery of Capital: Why Capitalism Triumphs in the West and Fails Everywhere Else* and who spearheaded such property rights programmes. In that book, land and other property rights are hailed as the solution to poverty—that is, the silver bullet that would turn failure into success, unlocking the trillions in assets of those in the informal sector and leading to huge growth and improvement in poor people's lives.[17] De Soto delivered an eloquent presentation. At some point, however, it turned awkward when he was asked repeatedly what the UK could do to promote this agenda, and his only response was 'hire me and my firm'. The deeper problem was the evaluation of such programmes, including those he had promoted in his home country, Peru, and elsewhere.

The truth was the programmes had proved weak in fundamentally transforming the lot of the poor in the way he described. Although no doubt an occasional study found that some of these programmes improved the welfare of the poor using mechanisms de Soto had suggested, the evidence was by no means clear-cut.[18] This suggests that individual property rights for the poor are at best just one part of the larger picture of development. They are no silver bullet.

* * *

All the books discussed in this chapter offer useful insights and are worth reading because each offers a lens through which to see the big picture of development problems, and they should mostly be taken seriously. Where do I come down myself? How does my mental model of development differ from those of the authors discussed in chapter 1? Four ways stand out. First, the primary challenges that developing countries must overcome reside within those countries, not in global markets. Like Stiglitz and Rodrik, I acknowledge that the present global markets do not make it easy for a poor country to succeed on the development front. And yet many rather poor countries have succeeded in recent decades, while others also poor to start with failed. Thus global challenges are not enough to explain failure. Second, although sensible economic policies are needed to nurture growth and development, as Collier and others explain, the essential constraint lies more in how countries are shaped, ruled, and managed by those with the power to do so and less in the details of specific economic policies. Third, although historical foundations play a role in explaining the economy and politics of today (as argued by Acemoglu and Robinson), the choices made by today's political and economic elite matter a great deal. Outcomes are hardly historically predetermined: progress in development has emerged in unlikely places through the actions of those with the power to make a difference. And fourth, I am not an aid sceptic like Easterly, Moyo, and Deaton, but, unlike Sachs, I think aid should not be a core concern in debates about development because putting aid to good use is hard or even at times counterproductive unless an elite bargain that is consistent with development is present or emerging.

Overall, I think they all miss the boat on one thing: a clear explanation of why a diverse set of countries have changed for the better in recent decades and why others have not—the subject of this book. Chapter 2 introduces the development bargain, and its key features, in its diversity across different contexts. Using simple data, chapter 3 provides a snapshot of what has happened developmentally in recent decades, highlighting successes and failures. I explain how, in countries that have thrived economically and otherwise, the primary factor driving success is the emergence of a development bargain. The stage is then set for part II, where I explore the experiences of a contrasting selection of countries.

References

Acemoglu, D., and S. Johnson. 2007. 'Disease and Development: The Effect of Life Expectancy on Economic Growth'. *Journal of Political Economy* 115 (6): 925–85.

Acemoglu, D., and S. Johnson. 2014. 'Disease and Development: A Reply to Bloom, Canning, and Fink'. *Journal of Political Economy* 122 (6): 1367–75.

Acemoglu, D., and J. Robinson. 2012. *Why Nations Fail*. London: Profile Books.

Acemoglu, D., S. Johnson, and J. A. Robinson. 2005. 'Institutions as a Fundamental Cause of Long-Run Growth'. *Handbook of Economic Growth* 1: 385–472.

Banerjee, A., and E. Duflo. 2011. *Poor Economics*. New York: Public Affairs.

Banerjee, A. V., and A. F. Newman. 1994. 'Poverty, Incentives, and Development'. *American Economic Review* 84 (2): 211–15.

Barro, R. J., and J.-W. Lee. 2015. *Education Matters. Global Schooling from the 19th to 21st Century*. Oxford: Oxford University Press.

Besley, T., K. Burchardi, and M. Ghatak. 2012. 'Incentives and the de Soto Effect'. *Quarterly Journal of Economics* 127: 237–82.

Besley, T., and M. Ghatak. 2010. 'Property Rights and Economic Development'. *Handbook of Development Economics* 5: 4525–95.

Bloom, D. E., D. Canning, and G. Fink. 2014. 'Disease and Development Revisited'. *Journal of Political Economy* 122 (6): 1355–66.

Chang, H. J. 2008. *Bad Samaritans: The Myth of Free Trade and the Secret History of Capitalism*. New York: Random House.

Collier, P. 2006. *The Bottom Billion: Why the Poorest Countries Are Failing and What Can Be Done about It*. Oxford: Oxford University Press.

Deaton, A. 2013. *The Great Escape: Health, Wealth, and the Origins of Inequality*. Princeton, NJ: Princeton University Press.

De Soto, H., 2000. *The Mystery of Capital: Why Capitalism Triumphs in the West and Fails Everywhere Else*. New York: Basic Books.

Durlauf, S. 2009. 'The Rise and Fall of Cross-country Growth Regressions'. *History of Political Economy* 41 (Suppl. 1): 315–33.

Easterly, W. 2006. *The White Man's Burden: Why the West's Efforts to Aid the Rest Have Done So Much Ill and So Little Good*. Oxford: Oxford University Press.

Field, E., 2005. 'Property Rights and Investment in Urban Slums'. *Journal of the European Economic Association Papers and Proceedings* 3: 279–90.

Krugman, P. 1991. 'Increasing Returns and Economic Geography'. *Journal of Political Economy* 99: 483–99.

———, and A. Venables. 1995. 'Globalization and the Inequality of Nations'. *Quarterly Journal of Economics* 110: 857–80.

Moyo, D. 2009. *Dead Aid: Why Aid Is Not Working and How There Is a Better Way for Africa*. London: Allen Lane.

Payne, G., J. Mitchell, L. Kozumbo, C. English, and R. Baldwin. 2015. *Legitimate Land Tenure and Property Rights: Fostering Compliance and Development Outcomes*. London: DAI.

Rodrik, R. 2011. *The Globalization Paradox: Democracy and the Future of the World Economy*. Oxford: Oxford University Press.

Romer, P. 1986. 'Increasing Returns and Long-Run Growth'. *Journal of Political Economy* 94 (5): 1002–37.

Sachs, J. 2005. *The End of Poverty: How We Can Make It Happen in Our Lifetime*. New York: Penguin Press.

Sen, A. 1999. *Development as Freedom*. Oxford: Oxford University Press.

Stiglitz, J. E. 1989. 'Markets, Market Failures, and Development'. *American Economic Review* 79 (2): 197–203.

———. 2002. *Globalization and Its Discontents*. New York: Norton and Norton.

World Bank. 2015. *World Development Report 2015: Mind, Society, and Behavior*. Washington, DC: World Bank.

2

THE DEVELOPMENT BARGAIN

They all wore sharp suits. About thirty people were in the cramped room in Kinshasa in the Democratic Republic of Congo (DRC). It was July 2013, and I had been invited to meet the economic advisor to the prime minister. President Joseph Kabila was in power, but few would ever see the president himself, not least foreign visitors, because he was generally occupied with matters of state or, as some suggested, playing the computer games to which he was reportedly addicted. As a senior official in the UK Department for International Development, I would typically meet with ministers of finance or central bank governors. Often, I would try to meet senior economic advisors as well because they were more involved in technical economic analysis, which I always found interesting. That way, I could learn about the real challenges they were facing, and perhaps offer my own experiences from other countries. This meeting, though, felt different. Of the more than two dozen senior economic advisors on hand, ten were lined up to make a presentation on aspects of the government's grand development plans.

The advisors covered weighty matters such as the need to seek macroeconomic stability, stimulate private sector growth through regulatory reform and effective credit markets, target revenue mobilisation and tax reform, reinvigorate health and education systems to raise the quality of care and learning, encourage smallholder agriculture through developing value chains and links to new agro-industrial zones across the country, and more. They were eloquent and well trained in France, Belgium, or Canada. And what they presented was really good—much of it based on the best advice the World Bank and other international agencies could give. In a typical African country, such an army of senior economic advisors was rarely hired to advise, let alone be allowed to develop such careful plans.

But then the DRC isn't a typical country, and I knew as much. Walking out of the long meeting, I felt I was coming out of a play performed by committed character actors. They put on a good show, but I was sure that not a single plan of those woven into the dialogue would ever be implemented. They probably all knew it, too, but no doubt had worked on these plans with the utmost sincerity. In fact, I would have been happy to bet that literally nothing of any importance related to growth or development would be implemented in the coming months or even years in the DRC.

Only a few months later, I was sitting in Ethiopia with a smaller, somewhat more senior group, consisting of junior ministers as well as the minister of finance and a few of the prime minister's economic advisors. One could call them technocrats—that is, experienced economists and public administrators hired more for their expertise than just for their political loyalty. We were discussing what progress had been made in implementing the Growth and Transformation Plan (GTP I, 2010/11–2014/15) and how its strengths and weaknesses could be addressed in the next plan, scheduled to launch in two years. Although the proposals were far less polished in the global policy language of economics and at times not quite convincing, I had no doubt they would do all they could to implement them—as they had done rather successfully thus far with GTP I, as well as the highly successful five-year plan that had ended in 2010. I was also certain that anything I said would be weighed in due course and then either dismissed or incorporated. The performances of these Ethiopian officials were totally convincing, even if the economic script was imperfect. Moreover, as I had worked by then with Ethiopian academics and policy-makers on and off for two decades, my sense of the situation didn't surprise me, and it stood in contrast to the earlier spectacle in the DRC. The facts speak for themselves: in the fifteen years up to 2019, Ethiopia grew by more than 7 per cent in per capita terms, three times faster than the DRC.[1] The Ethiopian state and the politics that controlled it were trying to grow and develop. The DRC's simply were not.

Development blueprints and bargains

This chapter looks at the kinds of things that are instrumental in moving countries towards growth and development and the kinds of things that prevent other countries from doing so. Most economists are interested in what needs to be done—the policies, the specific investments, the spending choices. The list of things that appear to nurture growth is rather long and less precise than sometimes suggested. Indeed, this chapter argues that a rather wide range of economic policies and public investments appears to drive decent growth and development. But if the range of choices is so large, why are there so many failures? In all countries, sensible policy choices tend to coincide with less sensible ones, extracting a cost in terms of overall growth and development. For example, public spending on infrastructure projects not on the list of priorities may be needed to manage ethnic tensions or ensure that a peace deal is sustained. Unfortunately, in many of the countries that have lagged behind in recent decades, the reasons are often not that worthy, and many policy choices are made for reasons other than growth and development, such as to serve the interests of those in control of the state or certain parts of the economy. And without benign forces to correct the worst excesses, failure beckons.

What matters for success? A development bargain. Its emerging presence in Ethiopia and absence in DRC made the difference in relevance between my meetings there. The defining feature of a development bargain is a commitment by those with the power to shape politics, the economy, and society, to striving for growth and development. This shared commitment is what, above all, more successful countries appear to have in common, despite disagreements over important details, including those on economic policy-making. It transcends simple definitions of political systems. It also transcends the strength of the state and how much leadership it takes on. In fact, in the most successful cases the state does not take on more than it can handle. In this chapter, the concept and features of the development bargain receive a closer look. In part II of this book, I use the development bargain framework to explore successful and failing countries during recent decades.

In search of a recipe for successful economic growth

What kinds of economic policies should a country adopt to achieve consistently high growth leading to development? About fifteen years ago, a group of eminent economists and policy-makers from across the globe set out to answer this question in a report from the Commission on Sustainable Growth and Inclusive Development. Michael Spence, a Nobel Prize winner in economics, was the lead author.[2] Published in 2008, *The Growth Report* offered an eclectic view of why the authors thought a set of very diverse economies had been able to grow in a sustained way for twenty-five years (since 1950) at 7 per cent or more per year while in the process partly or entirely converging with the living standards of richer Western and North American economies. Some economies caught up early on, such as first Japan and then Hong Kong and Singapore, as well as the Republic of Korea and Taiwan—all high-income countries for at least the last few decades. Botswana and Malaysia made the most of their natural resources, starting in the 1960s. Thailand, Indonesia, and China, still low-income countries in the 1970s, are of most relevance here because of the widespread poverty they faced during that period.[3] Besides China, the eight Asian countries on the list are often called the East Asia miracle countries.

Despite the geographical proximity of many of the successful countries, those reading *The Growth Report* in search of a recipe for their fast progress were disappointed. Indeed, the report is now often remembered just for its conclusion that the development community doesn't know the recipe for growth—only some of its ingredients. It took me much longer to appreciate this common-sense statement, especially when later trying to convey to students the secrets of economic policy-making. To achieve accelerating growth and development will require bold policy moves, but without a recipe success is not guaranteed: it always will be a gamble.

Some of the ingredients for growth

There appear to be many routes to successful take-off and catch-up growth when starting poor.[4] All the successful countries took some similar steps, but they did not have so much in common in terms of precise economic management and policies.

Macroeconomic stability surely was important, as the Growth Commission report argued, but how it was achieved in successful countries varied. For example, some countries on the way up actively manipulated their exchange rate regimes—Hong Kong and, later, China may have fallen in that camp—while others stuck to more orthodox approaches. At times, this posed difficulties, and several countries underwent macroeconomic crises, even having to seek help from the International Monetary Fund (IMF).

The successful countries all had high levels of investment. For some, such as Botswana, this involved the wise use of natural resources. Others were helped by high private savings rates, such as in East Asia where, more than elsewhere, much of what people earn is saved rather than consumed (this practice still puzzles economists). Public investment by the state mattered everywhere, in health, education, or safety nets, but not in equal measure. Given the experience of these countries, it is hard to be prescriptive about the optimal sectoral economic or social policies. Or about which public investments to prioritise, such as investing first in infrastructure or in education and health systems.

The Growth Report noted that all the successful countries trusted markets to provide signals and the impetus for the reallocation of capital and labour from less productive private sector firms to more productive ones, most of the time. They also had a credible and capable state, but the extent to which the state involved itself in the economy differed. All these countries sold to global markets when they could, taking advantage of opportunities, but some states worked harder than others at engineering these opportunities through protecting or supporting their firms initially through industrial policy, such as trade or exchange rate policies. Indeed, how they used markets differed, from adopting more liberal policies (as in Hong Kong and Taiwan), to early intervention (as in the Republic of Korea) and supporting private conglomerates so they could compete globally, and to using state-owned enterprises to work with foreign firms to absorb technological capabilities (as in China).

Beyond this, the report was somewhat vague. Some authors pushed for a narrower set of commonalities in policy-making for success, especially when focusing on the East Asian examples in *The Growth Report* list.[5] Whatever some have tried to argue, it was not just free markets or the state taking control.[6]

Reading this report more than a decade later, one feels it is dated in some respects, not least in its rather unqualified focus on pursuing high investment for growth. How times have changed: climate change is now more than an afterthought. No doubt, if the report were rewritten in 2021, climate change would be far more integrated in its advice. Without changing fundamentally the quest for economic growth, it would advocate growth that is greener and less carbon-intensive.

Beyond this, I doubt any team of this calibre would agree differently on the ingredients for growth. Why then aren't more countries finding their own recipe? This question leads to my core argument.

The development bargain

The DRC plans I heard in Kinshasa covered much of the ground suggested by the Growth Commission, using terminology familiar to those who wrote many of the background papers for the commission's report. Still, there is no doubt I would not have been alone in expecting that, in practice, the follow-through would be too little, too late. Policy pronouncements are one thing; a systematic attempt to pursue them is another. Why so little faith? To put it simply: those in the DRC that can make it happen have little interest in seeing that these policies are pursued or are successful. Those with power have other objectives, which run counter to the pursuit of economic growth and development.

'Those with power' are the economic and political elite—the business leaders, the political establishment, military commanders, and often the public intellectuals and journalists, union leaders, and prominent academics—that is, those who in the end have the power and influence to drive decision-making about the economy and society. Sometimes it is a small group, such as in authoritarian regimes or one-party states. Sometimes it is very fluid, such as in more open societies. Or sometimes it is a particular ethnic group. Their power stems from a deal, called the elite bargain, that determines the allocation of power and resources.[7] This bargain or agreement is typically informal and implicit: a shared commitment and not some kind of legally binding arrangement.

A development bargain is a specific form of an elite bargain, one of many possible ones. It is an agreement among those with power that growth and development should be pursued, even if they disagree about the policy details. Countries with a development bargain tend to have three features in common: (1) the politics of the bargain favouring development are real and credible, not just some vague official statement or pronouncement; (2) the capabilities of the state are used to achieve the goals of the bargain, but, importantly, the state avoids doing more than it can handle; and (3) the state possesses a political and technical ability to learn from mistakes and correct course.

Credible politics. The underlying commitment of the elite to growth and development has to be more than some general policy pronouncements or vision statements; it has to be a credible, lasting, shared political commitment. The bargain's continuation, even when power changes hands, is a critical element. Success is best judged by how much a country grows economically and develops over time, in terms as well of progress for the poorest.[8] The nature of the political system is by no means a necessary or sufficient condition for progress in this respect. As I describe later in this chapter, the pursuit of development has been observed across democracies as well as authoritarian regimes.

Capabilities of the state. Success does not depend simply on whether the development process is state-led or market-led. In all successful countries in the Growth Commission study, markets mattered. However, the state mattered as well, not in a singular way across all cases, but by typically doing what it could within its capabilities and constraints. Relevant factors here are the quality of public administration systems, including the technical skills of public servants, and how well policies and investment projects are implemented. Some countries already had very strong public administration systems, whereas in others they were much weaker. In some cases, the state led, but this worked only if its capabilities were sufficient to start with. In others, success required finding a balance between what the state should do and what it could do. At times, the state may have had to take on more or constrain its reach, depending on the context.[9]

Ability to learn from mistakes and correct course. Because a uniform recipe for success is missing, economic policy-making for growth and development carries serious risks of failure. It is a gamble and success is by no means guaranteed. All successful countries in the Growth Commission study had some mechanisms to correct course when growth and development were flagging. But resorting to such mechanisms requires the political elite to be willing to take advice and admit to and learn from mistakes. Otherwise, trust in the development bargain may be eroded, and even the country's stability may be threatened, for instance by those in the elite gaining least from the development bargain. As the Growth Commission report revealed, a relatively broad set of policies and actions may correlate with success, but at times certain policies will be inappropriate or other factors will derail the direction taken, even in successful countries. Those countries nevertheless learned from their mistakes and were willing, sooner or later, to correct policies when needed, aided by accountability mechanisms through party discipline, the ballot box or bureaucratic structures.

* * *

For each of these three features, there were three clear differences between Ethiopia and the DRC in 2013 when I met their teams, as well as more recently. First, in Ethiopia those in power were clearly focused on kick-starting fast growth and development. So much so, in fact, that the IMF was able to declare in 2019 that Ethiopia was the fastest-growing economy in the world of the previous decade, despite having no natural resources or fast-growing neighbouring economies. The IMF also complimented Ethiopia on its poverty reduction. In fact, growth and development had become a strong, clear-cut political objective in that period—part of a deliberate quest for legitimacy by the groups that controlled the state.[10] By contrast, the DRC had barely put together a stable political bargain by then. It was struggling not only with stability but also with the fact that most of those in the political sphere were bent on capturing rents from natural resources and other sources by legitimate or illegitimate means.

Second, in Ethiopia the state apparatus, with all its imperfections as far as capabilities go, was directed towards supporting its ambitious plans. In the DRC, the state largely had its eye on engaging in corrupt and even predatory behaviour towards firms and citizens.

Third, as for lessons learned and change of course, Ethiopia's leadership trusted some able technocrats and put them in powerful positions in the government, allowing them to take key decisions, especially when trying to manage tricky macroeconomic conditions.[11] In the DRC, there seemed to be a recurring and depressing sense of déjà vu, with little accountability and technocrats adding to the theatre of the state but not much more.

Why aren't the DRC or other countries that haven't succeeded practising better economic policy-making focused on growth and development? My simple answer: if success requires an elite bargain that favours growth and development, then failure suggests the lack of this bargain. What is it about these countries? How does a development bargain emerge in some places and not in others? This rest of this chapter looks at how development bargains emerge from among different possible elite bargains, but first I explore how elite bargains figure in understanding states and their functioning, and take a look at the economics underlying them.

States and the economics of elite bargains

Some economic historians date the emergence of countries as states to the time when 'elites organised themselves into a political system to manipulate the economy'.[12] An elite bargain is, then, the underlying agreement involved: how military, political, and economic power is distributed among leading groups. The elite bargain underlying countries is not just a political deal but also an economic deal— that is, an implicit agreement on who should gain or profit from the economic opportunities in a country in view of its assets such as land or natural resources. In this so-called rent-sharing deal, 'rent' is used in the economic sense, meaning the gains over and above the cost of keeping the country's assets intact.[13] It is in the end a deal about who can control or manipulate the economy. Hence, I use the term 'economic deal' instead of rent-sharing deal.

Understanding the emergence of states is also helpful to understanding states as they exist now, and this section develops the idea further. Because I am interested in what the elite bargain means for growth and development, here I address the underlying economic deal. In the rest of this section, I address three questions. First, why is the economic deal underlying states fundamental to understanding success or failure in development? Second, is an economic deal crucial for peace and stability? And, third, how do state structures as they emerge reflect these economic interests?

States as economic deals

Economic historians view the emergence of state structures as something like this. In a nascent state, turning marauding gangs into the elite requires identifying an alternative route to enrichment to replace the usual looting. The gangs may find that achieving a better-functioning economy—that is, putting the resources of that nascent state to use, whether land, people, assets, or natural resources—may be a good reason to stop looting and keep the peace instead. But the leaders of the gang will want something in return, and so they will seek to profit from this economic activity. That, in turn, will require that they sit down and bargain with each other to figure out how to share the profits from the assets and the opportunities in the new economy. This process defines who can become rich and how. These rules of the game are the economic deal underlying a state.

That said, it's not a pretty picture and not a pretty state. In its rawest form, this state-building exercise sees roving bandits replaced by stationary bandits, as Mancur Olson puts it.[14] Such states restrict activity and opportunity—in other words, while providing order and limiting violence, the elite restrict entry into the elite and limit access to trade or owning certain property.[15] This is not just a history lesson: many if not most modern states still have such features. Indeed, states tend to have rules on property and inheritance rights that may not only facilitate economic activity, but also limit equality of opportunity.[16] Rules or norms may limit access to certain activities, or there may be brutal ethnic or other favouritism. Taxation may be used to redistribute wealth, but not necessarily to the poorest. In short, different economic deals are possible in respect of both access to opportunities and the gains from them. Today, the raw features may have been largely removed, but most countries, including my own, still have structures and systems that limit access to both economic gains and politics.

The nature of the economic deal and the way it affects opportunities for growth and development are, then, a key aspect of understanding success and failure in development. Assessing an economic deal is not a matter of simply identifying the one 'good' deal—that is, the one set of simple conditions that will result in growth and development—and denouncing all other deals as leading to failure. But this is not necessarily the view held by other authors. For example, North, Weingast, and Wallis suggest that success is restricted to the system present in a few dozen countries, where liberal democracy and free markets offer political and economic competition with few or no constraints to entry.[17] However, it appears North and his colleagues were considering a different question—the conditions for long-term growth over decades, if not centuries, and not, as in this book, the conditions for take-off growth and progress in fighting the most extreme levels of poverty. Whether achieving long-term growth aimed at the GDP levels enjoyed by Western economies requires a combination of liberal democracy and free markets remains to be seen. History may offer examples consistent with this claim, but in view of China's continued rapid growth, a current Chinese foreign minister may well want to paraphrase his illustrious predecessor Zhou Enlai and declare, 'It is too early to say.'[18]

The economic deal as a source of peace

Max Weber famously defined a state as a group of people who have a monopoly on the use of violence across some territory.[19] Peace is the basis of social order, providing for political stability as well as for investment in economic activity. Peace and stability are also preconditions for development. They definitely mattered for those countries that have taken off in recent decades or have failed to do so.

But there's more. Peace and stability do not just make economic growth possible; the nature of the economic deal is an essential basis of peace and stability. Just as the emergence of states depended in part on an economic deal among those with the power to stop looting and promote peaceful economic activities, the same is true of peace deals in current times, especially when countries emerge from internal conflict. The nature of the elite bargain for peace and stability matters here—ending violence and distributing the gains from economic assets during peacetime tend to be intrinsically linked. As described in chapter 8, often for a peace deal such as that in South Sudan or Afghanistan, this is hard. At times, though, these deals can be surprisingly successful, such as in Lebanon and Somaliland.

Building a state to serve the elite bargain

Every elite bargain and its underlying economic deal need structures to serve and facilitate them.[20] State structures have two distinct roles: a legal role and a fiscal role. The first is no doubt some form of 'legal' capability—upholding the rules of the game that underwrite the elite bargain. What is key is a functioning army, the rule of law, and protection of property rights. This is not just in the interests of the elite (although no doubt they will ensure they are the first protected, or even benefit with impunity), but also in the interests of those engaging in the economy, so that they at least receive some clarity on the returns from and the obligations stemming from their economic activities (such as what taxes a trader must pay and what share of a harvest is owed to a sharecropper).[21]

However obvious, it is at times hard to take such protection for granted. For example, Mobutu Sese Seko, the notorious president of Zaire (now the DRC) from 1965 to 1997, received complaints about the large-scale corruption throughout his administration. He responded by explaining to a group of administration officials that they should listen to the people, and therefore if they had to steal, they should steal only a little and leave enough for the other public servants and the people.[22]

The second role for the state is its fiscal one—that is, raising taxes and putting them to use. Beyond security, the state will ordinarily use tax revenue to deliver public services or provide infrastructure. However, its fulfilment of that role should also not be taken for granted. For example, as described by Max Weber, history is rife with examples of patrimonial states, simply there to server the ruler, the patron. What public goods are provided serve only to strengthen the position of the ruler.

Such forms of a state have largely disappeared, but many or even most state structures are organised to serve mainly the elite and their economic deal. The state administration may appear to be a functioning bureaucracy and the courts may look like the textbook example of a justice system, but fundamentally they are there to serve the group in power. Patronage—such as giving privileged access to resources and services and also government or army jobs or other benefits—becomes a defining feature of those in power. Those receiving these benefits—the clients—are expected, by their participation in such an arrangement, to support the patron. Political scientists call these states clientelist: the patron is head of the state thanks to those clients who sustain his power.[23]

Most states have had or still have patrimonial and clientelist features, including many of those discussed later in the book. It may seem reasonable to expect that efforts to build stronger state capabilities, like the rule of law and accountability, would be an obvious way to get rid of such features.[24] Although formal structures and processes may be put in place, often as part of ongoing reforms, the underlying more informal practices persevere, even if conflicting with laws and rules. The public administration may look independent and may seem to be only following rules and regulations, but getting something actually done depends on whom one knows, or at least it helps. Hence formal and informal channels cross, restricting who has access to the state and to the delivery of services in a way accepted within the politics of the state.[25]

The emergence of development bargains

How does the development bargain fit into this discussion of the role of the economic deal in how states function? It is essentially one form of an elite bargain in which the economic deal is structured in ways consistent with growth and broad development, including widespread poverty reduction. More precisely, the development bargain is one possible elite bargain—one with plenty of room for imperfections, but with sufficient features to make take-off growth and development a possibility.

Box 2.1 Political bargaining and game theory

In the language of game theory, an elite bargain among those with power in society is an agreement that defines the nature of cooperation—a so-called cooperative equilibrium. As game theory understands it, it is a deal on the division of the gains (the pay-offs) from this political 'game'. If the deal among the elite is credible, so that it can be enforced, it will lead to limited violence, social order, and political stability. Some political scientists, especially those with close connections to international development, have begun using another term for this rent-sharing equilibrium: 'political settlement'. They often document in fascinating detail how day-to-day politics and decision-making around the economy reflect this underlying deal, not least in rather poor and conflict-affected societies.[26]

While history matters for the nature of the state today, current outcomes are not predestined. Nor are they self-evident. The agency of people does matter, here and now. Competition, contestation, struggle, deal-making, and deal-wrecking involve the actions and behaviours of various groups within society and the elite. In the language of game theory, players compete, take strategic actions, and do not just settle for cooperation. These actions will affect which outcome, which equilibrium, if any, is achieved—that is, the observed bargain. And many outcomes are possible, multiple equilibria, some better than others. A development bargain may be one of them, whereby through cooperation an economic deal among the elite emerges that is also good for growth and development. With returns from such a deal usually far in the future, it rarely is a foregone conclusion that all involved will stick to it: those cooperating will take a gamble. Or if the elite fail to cooperate, society may find itself able to settle only on a rather bad bargain, even if others may have been possible.

Some bargains may be more stable than others. Political players excluded from a current deal may take advantage of the instability of the political equilibrium—again, not necessarily leading to good outcomes. Alex de Waal and his colleagues have written about the political marketplace in Africa where the elite try to prevent newcomers from participating in deals among the elite, but political entrepreneurs can use techniques ranging from armed uprising and coups to promises of rents to dislodge those in power, and to replace them, or to simply claim a place within the elite bargain.[27]

This section begins by elaborating on how and why a development bargain may emerge. What would drive those with power in an economy, politics, and society to settle for a deal that favours growth and development? It then asks what helps or hinders this decision, focusing on political systems, but also on the underlying characteristics of countries, such as the wealth generated by natural resources. In later chapters, the relevance of these drivers and constraints is explored in more detail using specific cases.

Drivers of a development bargain

Development bargains do not just happen; they emerge and are shaped by people. Often, at any moment in time there may well be a small set of possible deals, some more in favour of development than others, but all still consistent with the elite's interests. The situation can, however, be quite fluid: minds may change, sometimes significantly, sometimes slowly, or sometimes not at all. What then drives these players in the elite towards a development bargain?

It may be tempting to follow historical hagiography to attribute the driving force to an enlightened leader. Singapore's Lee Kuan Yew, China's Deng Xiaoping, or, in more recent times, Rwanda's Paul Kagame and Ethiopia's Meles Zenawi have been seen in that light, more or less convincingly. No doubt they mattered, but to attribute a move towards a development bargain solely to their personal commitment is not likely enough. They would still have to gain and maintain the support of an elite bargain among those with the power to shape politics, the military, and the economy—rarely a simple matter. As the case studies in later chapters will highlight, Deng Xiaoping in China, Suharto in Indonesia, and Meles Zenawi in Ethiopia all played their role, but many others were involved in shaping the new development bargain that emerged. In short, leadership and the ideas of particular individuals may well have mattered significantly in certain countries, but serious risky political deal-making would always be part of the mix, as well as a competent group implementing the economic deal.

Three more drivers appear to be present as well: emergence from conflict or other extreme events; a quest by the elite in power to gain legitimacy; or the foresight that a better economic deal is likely to result from pursuing growth and development. They are briefly introduced here, and the examples are developed further in part II of the book.

As for the first driver, several development bargains appear to have emerged after a period of deeply challenging conflict and societal disruption. As described later in more detail, China's development bargain appeared not long after the disruption of the Cultural Revolution in 1966–76. And Indonesia's period of growth emerged from deep internal conflict in 1965–6, which ended a period of stagnation since independence. Other chapters will describe how Bangladesh experienced a violent war of independence in 1971–2 and a famine period soon after. The regime in Ethiopia that appears to have settled on a development bargain emerged first from a long period of civil war in 1991, but then faced a humanitarian crisis linked to a serious drought in 2001–2 and a political challenge in the elections of 2005. And Rwanda clearly moved to a very different bargain focused on growth and development after the genocide in 1994.

Qualitatively, in all these countries the emergence from conflict and disruption is part of the underlying narrative that may well have shaped the development bargain. It is also consistent with emerging research that shows that conflict may encourage cooperative behaviour at various levels of society,[28] and so the emergence of new forms of cooperation between the elite may well be possible. However, in many places conflict and disruption have occurred, either with neighbouring countries or internally, and no development bargain has emerged. In fact, although it does not help to explain conflict, the best predictor for experiencing conflict at present is past conflict.[29] It's no wonder, then, that those countries that manage to emerge from conflict with a development bargain will cherish this feat in their political narratives.

This finding leads, however, to a second likely driver of a development bargain: legitimacy-seeking behaviour by those in power. As developed in more detail in later chapters, they may use their attraction to growth and development as a mechanism for gaining broader legitimacy within the elite or in the wider society. Regimes that may lack legitimacy in the eyes of society or whose position has been challenged are candidates for this kind of behaviour. In China, the development bargain emerged after the Communist Party had fuelled turmoil across society during the Cultural Revolution, followed by the power struggles after Mao's death in 1976. It was a political gamble to avoid instability and dissent and rebuild support and political stability in new ways.

Legitimacy-seeking behaviour was evident in Indonesia as well. Suharto's rise to power was regarded by many as illegitimate because it was initially a power grab supported by factions in the military. Elsewhere, this kind of behaviour also may have been a quest for legitimacy by regimes representing only part of society or even the elite, such as those from particular ethnic groups. For example, after the end of the conflicts in both Ethiopia and Rwanda, power ended up in the hands of a leadership that clearly identified with one region or group (the Tigrayans in Ethiopia and the Tutsi in Rwanda). The emerging focus on development and economic growth observed in those countries may then be interpreted as a quest for legitimacy across the broader elite and society.

Finally, and possibly encompassing the first two drivers just described, a development bargain focused on development and growth may simply be an economic deal that delivers larger gains to all involved—whether political benefits or private financial profit. It makes sense that the elite would pursue such a deal for that reason. But this is not self-evident. Growth and broader development tend to require public and private investment now for later returns, meaning there are fewer resources to distribute in the short run. It also may require the elite to accept new entrants, such as dynamic entrepreneurs who accumulate wealth and who over time may challenge the incumbents in the elite. New institutions or organisations may then emerge. In short, moving to a development bargain is a serious gamble, and the outcome is not certain.

Over time, it may become clear that the risk was worthwhile, and the elite bargain may become more stable if it delivers results. For example, during the 1970s oil price boom, Indonesia used its new-found rents much more productively than, say, Nigeria, and the growth emerging helped solidify support for this route. Elsewhere, the Indian politicians favouring a more outward-looking and more market-oriented economy successfully used the economic crisis in the early 1990s to force the gamble. Over time, the benefits of this different elite bargain became clear, convincing in the process an ever-larger part of the relevant elite of the merits of an approach favouring growth with less narrow economic nationalism.

Each of these drivers does not self-evidently lead to one specific elite bargain. Multiple bargains are clearly possible, and not all will evolve into a development bargain. Some of these outcomes will be better for some parts of the elite across business, politics, or the military, and not others. For example, an economic deal among the elite focusing on growth will require some redistribution towards those with stronger economic interests in areas with opportunities for growth. It will also postpone consumption in favour of investment. The agency of the different movers and shakers will matter again. Leadership qualities will be required to make the deal—not just enlightened insights.

Do some factors hinder or help the process of moving towards a development bargain? In particular, does it matter what type of political system a country has? The rest of this section is devoted to answering these questions.

Do authoritarian or democratic political systems help or hinder?

As noted, political leadership plays a role in all of this. Substantial skills are needed to craft national narratives, build legitimacy, and persuade leading groups in society to choose the longer-term gains from growth and development over the immediate economic gains. And some examples of this kind of leadership—such as Lee Kuan Yew in Singapore, Meles Zenawi in Ethiopia, and Deng Xiaoping in China—were no doubt extremely skilful at undertaking these efforts.

That said, it is not just a matter of having a strong leader, or blaming the wrong leader. The blame for failure and even praise for success must be shared much more widely. Countries get the leaders their elites deserve.

In all of this, day-to-day politics and the political class play a central role. And yet I have said remarkably little about the political system required for the emergence of a development bargain. As a good former UK civil servant, I surely cannot suggest that anything other than regular free and fair elections is essential for a development bargain. Well, maybe I can. There are good reasons why the political system itself may not be essential to achieve take-off in growth and development.

Often, those assessing the difficulties of steering a country towards a development bargain are tempted to say that surely an authoritarian leader or state may find it easier to do so.[30] Usually, China is then mentioned, or the military dictatorship in the Republic of Korea between 1979 and 1988. As the argument goes, authoritarian rule makes it possible, if so desired, to delay the capture of immediate gains and move instead to a more growth-oriented set of policies. But this is too easy. Indeed, an authoritarian leader may not need to seek legitimacy at all, nor correct course when things go wrong. In fact, as too many failing countries reveal, authoritarian leaders can make an absolute mess of economic policies, driving countries into the abyss. Zaire (and later as the DRC) is an unfortunate example, as described in chapter 7.

If authoritarianism is no guarantee for growth and development, is democracy then one? Democratic countries may well choose a development bargain. Surely, if people have a choice, they would choose development and whatever it takes to raise living standards, and they would punish at the ballot box those not pursuing this goal. This simple narrative is definitely alive and well in Whitehall in London and other Western capitals.

Unfortunately, it is still remarkably rare that in countries with high levels of extreme poverty, elections, even when free and fair, are run on the issue of development agendas. They are often much more focused on regional, religious, or ethnic divides, inviting clientelist behaviour. Coming to power in elections may simply mean it is time for the winners to claim their share of the patronage—'It's our time to eat'[31]—which is not likely a good basis for a development bargain.

Because running in elections is expensive, the support of the elite is usually required. However, the bargain struck within the elite to win an election is by no means necessarily a development bargain. In Nigeria, political 'godfathers' use their money and influence to deliver votes for the candidates they adopt, creating obligations for candidates elected in this way. For example, Bola Tinubu, the former governor of Lagos, was instrumental in delivering elites of the South-West to candidate (now president) Buhari.[32] Many others did the same, and some suggest Buhari is indebted to the tune of billions, which need to flow back, one way or another.

And so it is not surprising that, especially for developing countries and for take-off growth, it is hard to find strong evidence that either autocracy or democracy is best.[33] Perhaps in the long run, democracy will matter. There is some persuasive evidence that democratisation may well result in higher long-term growth—even if this finding continues to be disputed.[34] As for take-off growth—that is, reaching higher growth from low levels of development—it is not so clear that a democratic or an autocratic system *necessarily* does better.

Constraints on the emergence or stability of development bargains

In practice, even with well-intentioned political actors, agreeing on and sustaining a development bargain are not easy. Development bargains are still economic deals between elites, and so the nature of the elite will matter, among other familiar factors such as the challenges of ethnic or religious divisions and the consequences of the spillovers from conflict. And then there is the wealth generated by natural resources.

Much has been written about the natural resource curse.[35] I'm not sure it is a curse—it could be a blessing, as Indonesia, Malaysia, and Thailand have shown. For them, the commodity price boom of the 1970s launched a period of fast growth and served as the basis for their development bargain. In many other countries, though, such as Nigeria and the DRC, it did not help in forging a development bargain. Indeed, as discussed in chapter 7, it is a key factor in why these countries are such a mess. The problem is not the economic management of natural resource wealth, even if its prices fluctuate. That is a technical problem; errors can be made but also corrected, and there is plenty of knowledge and experience to draw on. The problem instead is the political management of this wealth—that is, how to manage the elite's behaviour and expectations when there are natural resources. If there is plenty of natural resource wealth to divvy out to the elite, why try to forge a development deal with a longer horizon? Why seek legitimacy when popular support is not needed to reap the profits from natural resources? Or even if support is needed, it could be bought. Plenty of stories can be told—and later in this book you will hear them, including some about Nigeria and DRC, and also how Indonesia avoided failure.

No gloom and doom

This chapter has painted a picture of how elite bargains that favour development could come about. Part II gives more details of these and other examples, with considerable optimism—such as from Indonesia, India, Ghana, Bangladesh and, more tentatively, Rwanda and Ethiopia. The emerging development deals may not necessarily be in the style of Korea's or Singapore's, or similarly successful, but a far better growth and development experience than before is possible. Such an experience does not require perfect institutions or even a particular political system. It will not necessarily have to arise from a huge upheaval. Instead, it may be gradual by, for example, seeking legitimacy for self-interested economic deals among the elite that favour saving now for investment and growth. The result will be not only greater future benefits for the elite, but also development and progress for the whole population.

That said, success should never be taken for granted. Those in the elite, its leaders and its technocrats, are taking a gamble on development. Even with a strong shared commitment and a reasonably capable state with sensible technocrats, growth and development will not miraculously emerge or be sustained. In fact, it's hard to keep these elite bargains together to stay the course. Chapter 10, about Ethiopia, will show this. History or economic endowments conspire to make the journey hard. The examples discussed in this book are not unqualified successes, nor are they at all guaranteed to turn a country into a Korea or a Singapore in coming decades. That does not mean that one should not applaud the gambles taken by those with power in the countries highlighted.

All this also means there is no reason for gloom and doom. Rather than a pessimistic view of historical determinism, the picture painted here leaves room for change and for forces within society to seek and push for change for the better, even if it is more difficult in some places than in others. And it has happened in some surprising places. Gunnar Myrdal, an economics Nobel Prize winner in 1974, wrote Indonesia off as late as 1968,[36] not least because the state was controlled by various rent-seeking elites. This was not an unreasonable view because of the previous decade, but then from the 1970s onwards Indonesia underwent change on an unprecedented scale, as chapter 4 will discuss.

Leadership will matter, but not in the simplistic sense of one strong, authoritarian figure who is in charge of all key decisions. Political leaders (often more than one) must forge and sustain a coalition among the elite, and find ways of keeping the population onside, and not just in democracies. In the end, the leadership will gain its credibility from its delivery on promises, in the form of investment, growth, and development.

Beyond politicians, technocrats, including economists, can help with moving away from economic deals focusing on short-run gains towards one with a longer-term horizon. As later chapters will show, in successful countries it was often a small number of such technocrats, trusted by the leadership, who helped to change the structures of the economy for the better.

Even development aid and the experts that come with it could play a role and contribute to change. Not, though, in the way they usually work. There is little point in presenting the perfect textbook plans and even the evidence without thinking through the politics of change. Politics are too important for development in general to be left to political scientists alone. Treating advice and aid as something purely technocratic and detached from politics will limit their effectiveness, and it will often lead to their poor use. In part III I will return to this point. For now, however, a simple rule of thumb may suffice: judge advice and aid on the basis of how they will affect the economy and politics today and in the future. How will they change the odds of success? Will they strengthen those supporting a focus on growth and development? Will they strengthen those offering sensible economic advice? Will they give ammunition to those keen to capture more rents? Could they fuel more conflict? Will they actually make rent capture easier? Will they give elites an excuse to ignore certain groups or policies? What will matter is not just the immediate direct impacts of policies and programmes but also whether they increase the likelihood that a development bargain emerges, can be sustained and is, in the end, a gamble worth taking.

References

Acemoglu, D., and J. Robinson. 2012. *Why Nations Fail*. London: Profile Books.

Acemoglu, D., S. Naidu, P. Restrepo, and James A. Robinson. 2019. 'Democracy Does Cause Growth'. *Journal of Political Economy* 127 (1): 47–100.

Amsden, A. H. 1989. *Asia's Next Giant: South Korea and Late Industrialization*. Oxford: Oxford University Press on Demand.

———. 2001. *The Rise of 'the Rest': Challenges to the West from Late-Industrializing Economies*. New York: Oxford University Press.

Basuchoudhary, A., J. T. Bang, T. Sen, and J. David. 2018. *Predicting Hotspots: Using Machine Learning to Understand Civil Conflict*. Lanham, MD: Rowman and Littlefield.

Bauer, M., C. Blattman, J. Chytilová, J. Henrich, J. E. Miguel, and T. Mitts. 2016. 'Can War Foster Cooperation?' *Journal of Economic Perspectives* 30 (3): 249–74.

Besley, T., and M. Kudamatsu. 2008. 'Making Autocracy Work'. In *Institutions and Economic Performance*, edited by E. Helpman, 452–510. Cambridge, MA: Harvard University Press.

Besley, T., and T. Persson. 2011. *Pillars of Prosperity: The Political Economics of Development Clusters*. Princeton, NJ: Princeton University Press.

Birdsall, N., D. Ross, and R. Sabot. 1995. 'Inequality and Growth Reconsidered: Lessons from East Asia'. *World Bank Economic Review* 9 (3): 477–508.

Burton, M. G., and J. Higley 1987. 'Elite Settlements'. *American Sociological Review* 52: 295–307.

Chang, H. J., ed. 2003. *Rethinking Development Economics*. London: Anthem Press.

Cheeseman, N., E. Bertrand, and S. Husaini. 2019. *A Dictionary of African Politics*. Oxford: Oxford University Press.

Collier, P. 2006. *The Bottom Billion: Why the Poorest Countries Are Failing and What Can Be Done about It*. Oxford: Oxford University Press.

De Waal, A. 2015. *The Real Politics of the Horn of Africa: War, Money and the Business of Power*. London: Wiley.

Di John, J., and J. Putzel. 2009. 'Political Settlements Issues Paper'. Discussion paper, University of Birmingham, UK.

Evans, P. B. 1995. *Embedded Autonomy: States and Industrial Transformation*. Princeton, NJ: Princeton University Press.

Fukuyama, F. 1992. *The End of History and the Last Man*. New York: Free Press.

————. 2014. *Political Order and Political Decay: From the Industrial Revolution to the Globalization of Democracy*. New York: Macmillan.

Gould, D. J. 1980. 'Patrons and Clients: The Role of the Military in Zaire Politics'. In *The Performance of Soldiers as Governors: African Politics and the African Military*, edited by I. J. Mowoe. Lanham, MD: University Press of America.

Gray, H. 2016. 'Access Orders and the "New" Institutional Economics of Development'. *Development and Change* 47 (1): 51–75.

Johnson, C. 1982. *MITI and the Japanese Miracle: The Growth of Industrial Policy, 1925–1975*. Stanford, CA: Stanford University Press.

Khan, M. H. 2018. 'Political Settlements and the Analysis of Institutions'. *African Affairs* 117 (469): 636–55.

Melling, J. 1991. 'Industrial Capitalism and the Welfare of the State: The Role of Employers in the Comparative Development of Welfare States; A Review of Recent Research'. *Sociology* 25 (2): 219–39.

Myrdal, G. 1968. *Asian Drama: An Inquiry into the Poverty of Countries*. New Delhi: Kalyani Publishers.

North, D., B. Weingast, and J. Wallis. 2009. *Violence and Social Orders: A Conceptual Framework for Interpreting Recorded Human History*. Cambridge: Cambridge University Press.

Olarinmoye, O. O. 2008. 'Godfathers, Political Parties and Electoral Corruption in Nigeria'. *African Journal of Political Science and International Relations* 2 (4): 66–73.

Olson, M. 2000. *Power and Prosperity*. New York: Basic Books.

Perkins, D. H. 2013. *East Asian Development*. Cambridge, MA: Harvard University Press.

Pritchett, L., K. Sen, and E. Werker. 2017. *Deals and Development*. Oxford: Oxford University Press.

Rodrik, D. 1994. 'King Kong Meets Godzilla: The World Bank and the East Asian Miracle'. CEPR Discussion Paper no. 944, Centre for Economic Policy Research, London.

Stiglitz, J. E., and S. Yusuf, eds. 2001. *Rethinking the East Asian Miracle*. Washington, DC: World Bank.

Stokes, S. 2011. 'Political Clientelism'. In *The Oxford Handbook of Political Science*, edited by R. Goodin. Oxford: Oxford University Press.

Van Reybrouck, D. 2014. *Congo: The Epic History of a People*. London: HarperCollins.

Weber, M. 1919. *Politik als Beruf.* Munich and Leipzig: Verlag von Duncker and Humblot.

Whitfield, L., O. Therkildsen, L. Buur, and A. M. Kjær. 2015. *The Politics of African Industrial Policy: A Comparative Perspective*. Cambridge: Cambridge University Press.

World Bank. 2008. *The Growth Report*. Report of the Commission on Sustainable Growth and Inclusive Development. Washington, DC: World Bank.

Wrong, M. 2010. *It's Our Turn to Eat: The Story of a Kenyan Whistle-Blower*. London: Fourth Estate.

3

DEVELOPMENT TILL TODAY

MOSTLY UPS, SOME DOWNS

'Let me show you something at the back of my garden,' he said, waving determinedly while he slowly stood up. He was a slight, sickly man, probably in his mid-thirties but looking much older. We had just spent some time talking about him and his family, about the few good times and the many bad times. We had been sitting on a small bench next to his hut in the stunning Ethiopian Highlands just north of Debre Libanos, about a three-hour drive from Addis Ababa. It was 1993, and I was a young researcher on a field trip.

I don't recall his name—it may have been Mekonnen—but what he showed me I have never forgotten. He had been given a small parcel of land as part of a land redistribution scheme in his village in the 1980s. His part of the country had remained relatively peaceful despite the brutal war raging farther north. But he had suffered from poor health for much of the last decade, and his wife also looked frail and tired. Two of his children had died as infants, and his three remaining young children were just becoming old enough to help him tend his land. Only one had gone to school, but just for a few years. Overall, Mekonnen had little to show for two decades of working life—no radio, no bicycle. The rickety bench we sat on was among his few possessions.

At the back of his tiny vegetable garden, Mekonnen pointed to a simple earthen pot, turned upside down. Then, triumphantly, he took the pot away. Underneath it was a sapling, only about a foot tall. 'This', he said, 'will make me rich one day.' Despite all his hardship, he was still dreaming: of a better life, of becoming rich.

I looked at it in stunned silence because I recognised what it was—a small qat (chat) plant. It is a mild stimulant with amphetamine-like qualities grown in western and southern Ethiopia, as well as in Kenya. At that time, the end of war in Ethiopia had led to a huge demand for this crop. With prices high, farmers were increasingly turning from coffee and other crops to qat, making more money than ever before.

But standing there at the back of that garden, I tried very hard not to show my disappointment. I knew what Mekonnen probably also knew: he had no chance to make it big. He was living hundreds of kilometres from those areas where qat grows well, and at his high altitude it was too cold at night for qat to survive the winter. Even though the pot was intended to keep his sapling alive for now, its growth had already been stunted by the adverse circumstances. But I could see hope in his eyes, and the last thing I wanted to do was to quash it. I never returned to his village, so I don't know for sure what happened next—although I fear my guess is right.

I talked to Mekonnen early on in what became a twenty-year research programme conducted by Addis Ababa University aimed at understanding what keeps people poor and how they can get out of poverty. Dozens of men and women across rural Ethiopia patiently answered long lists of questions during my visits. Meanwhile, I learned a lot about the conditions in desperately poor rural Ethiopia at that time. Well over half the children were too short for their age owing to poor nutrition, and a quarter of adults were underweight for their height. A third of families had just one ox, even though a pair of oxen are needed to plough the land effectively. Whatever features are typically associated with deprivation, they were widespread in rural Ethiopia at the time.

One could argue for ever how to define extreme poverty, but sometimes it is obvious. Mekonnen was one of tens of millions of

Ethiopians at that time who were clearly living in extreme poverty. It is about having not enough food or having too little cash to spend on the basic necessities of life, or being in poor health, or being unable to keep children alive because of little to no access to good health care, or being unable to give children an education, or having no assets to build a better livelihood. As two Ethiopian researchers were told a few years later when talking at length to poor families across the country, 'It is a life of no thought for tomorrow' and 'We have neither a dream nor an imagination'.[1] For some, this may be true, but poor people are not all just the same, and not all just give up. I suspect it made meeting Mekonnen even more memorable for me. He still had a dream, but no way to fulfil it.

According to Nobel laureate Amartya Sen, poverty is the deprivation of a person's capability to live the life he or she has reason to value.[2] So how many people across the world are like Mekonnen, deprived and lacking this capability? Measuring the scale of global poverty and deprivation (the subject of the next section) is clearly difficult: it is not just defining what makes a person poor, as distinct from someone who is not poor, but also discovering a way to state one's findings on the scale of poverty in a country or across the world.

Measuring the extent of poverty

Great conceptualisation does not, unfortunately, make the measurement task much easier. Indeed, there could be reasons not to even attempt to measure the state of global poverty or development. Perhaps the data are bad, or it's just not possible to put a number on poverty. It may not be possible to capture the despair of Mekonnen's condition or his hope that cannot be fulfilled. Anything attempted may be too derivative and blatantly wrong.

This is a reasonable position, but I don't agree with it. Even if the data and the methods available are not perfect, it's worth a try. It is helpful to attempt to gauge what progress is being made and comment on the nature of the likely errors involved—not least if researchers are keen to understand whether and how the Mekonnens of the world could improve their lot. Or, as Tony Atkinson, one of the best and most sensible researchers on poverty and inequality, wrote, 'The estimates of global poverty are flawed but not useless.'

The rest of this chapter describes the changes in the extent of poverty and deprivation in recent decades in the developing world and identifies those countries where there appears to have been substantial progress or not.[3] The focus here is on the larger countries whose progress has contributed significantly to global progress. In subsequent chapters featuring country cases, each country is put in the context of the larger trends. The indicators used here are based on methods that most researchers engaged in measurement tend to agree are at least somewhat flawed. But because they are probably the best available, and quite robust, even those critical of these methods will nevertheless agree with the broad trends described in the rest of this chapter.

Twin peaks and the changing global distribution of living standards

The 'developing world' is no longer clearly defined in terms of living standards. Today, economies and societies with both the highest and the lowest levels of progress are equally described as 'developing'. Figure 3.1 charts the global distribution of the standard of living over the last few decades.[4] It is measured in terms of the value of the actual consumption of goods such as food, clothing, and other necessary or not so necessary items per person a day by region. Consumption also includes not just what is purchased in the market for cash, but also what is produced at home or on the farm or received from friends or even from the government.

Three observations are striking. First, in 1990 the global income distribution had two peaks (two modes), each showing a highly frequent standard of living (for each value, the height of the curve indicates how frequently this level of the standard of living is reached in each region and across the world). In the graph, those living in sub-Saharan Africa and Asia are distributed around the first peak, and those living in the Americas and Europe are distributed around the second peak, with its 15 times greater purchasing power. In 1990, then, it seemed still true that there was a distinction between the poor 'developing' world and the rich 'developed' world. But this had already been changing for a while: the 'valley' between the two distributions was considerably shallower than it had been in the 1970s and 1980s, suggesting that more and more Asians had managed to move towards a standard of living closer to that of some of their European and American counterparts. By 2000 and clearly by 2019, the Asian income distribution had moved steadily towards the European one, and the distinction between the rich and poor world had blurred. So no more twin peaks—just one peak in the global income distribution, even if the vast majority of Asians were still experiencing far lower purchasing power than Europeans.

The second observation is that the East Asia distribution (dominated by China with its 1.4 billion people in 2019) initially drove the shift in income distribution entirely. South Asia (dominated by India with its 1.37 billion people) nevertheless also shifted. Sub-Saharan Africa, however, remained centred around a much lower standard of living, having barely shifted throughout the 1990–2019 period. The Middle East and North Africa (as well as Latin America—not shown but part of the Americas) moved much less in relative terms. The large spread is a reminder of the large persistent inequalities in these regions.

Finally, Figure 3.1 illustrates how one can measure global poverty and what it implies. If these income distributions are constructed correctly—so that people across the world and between time periods can be compared in terms of their living standard—then a simple way to assess global poverty is to draw somewhere in this distribution a line indicating a reasonable level of consumption below which surely a decent life is no longer possible. The World Bank draws this line at $1.90 a day in 2011 international dollars.[5] Below this line, people live in extreme poverty. By design, as in these graphs, because all distributions are expressed in dollars with the same purchasing power in each year and across the globe, the same line can be used for each year. The graphs show clearly that, over the period depicted, less and less of the distribution fell below that poverty line, so that by 2019 the share of the global population living in extreme poverty was near 10 per cent, or only a quarter of what it had been in 1990.

Figure 3.1 Global income distribution by region, 1990, 2000, 2019

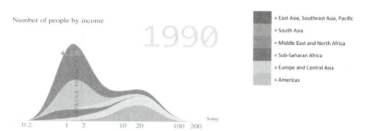

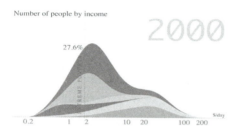

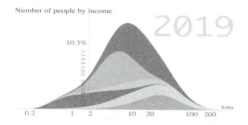

Source: Free material from www.gapminder.org.

Note: For each value, the height of the curve indicates how frequently this level of the standard of living is reached in each region and across the world. These data are produced using heroic assumptions, combining large-scale surveys and other data, but also correcting for price differentials over time and between countries, so that each dollar unit can acquire the same level of consumption goods across the world as assessed in 2011. The data allow for the fact that everywhere goods have become more expensive over time, and also that money goes further in terms of basic goods in some, mainly poorer, countries. This is related by the phrase 'expressed in 2011 international dollars'. The graphs use a log scale, meaning that for every unit on the axis values double.

Poor, absolutely speaking

It is reasonable to question this poverty line. After all, could anyone agree that once a person exceeds the $1.90 a day benchmark, all is well? This would suggest that almost no one in Europe or the US is poor. Of course, that preposterous suggestion is not what is meant. A standard should be relevant to the country under the microscope. Amartya Sen captured this well in the title of one of his articles, 'Poor, Relatively Speaking'. For assessments within countries, any benchmark ought to be defined relative to locally acceptable standards.[6] For example, in the UK, a country with relatively strong social protection systems, those considered too poor for a decent life would qualify for benefits such as housing as well as other benefits to sustain them.

Absolute deprivation still has relevance, not least when making global comparisons. Take, for example, someone in the UK whose only source of income is their benefits—someone the British would call poor. Simple calculations suggest that in 2020 such a person would have received about $20.50 a day in international dollars.[7] At that level of poverty line, about 78 per cent of the world's population would be poor.[8] In other words, some 'poor' people in the UK actually have greater purchasing power than more than three-quarters of the world's population. This finding puts in perspective repeated calls not to care about the poor globally if in rich economies there are plenty of poor at home. Indeed, this is not a 'like with like' comparison. Even so, in 1990, if one drew the line at $20.50, the share of the world's population below it would have been 87 per cent—and so again a substantial decline ever since. These figures suggest that at wherever level the line is drawn—at $1.90 or at ten times or more higher—global poverty has come down. The $1.90 figure just represents an extreme level of material deprivation—not for nothing is it called 'extreme poverty'.

Figure 3.2 offers an alternative way of looking at what has happened since 1990 by adding up the number of people below the $1.90 poverty line.[9] Again, the sheer scale of the progress is striking: from more than 1.9 billion people living in extreme poverty in 1990 to about 700 million in 2017—a huge change, not least taking into account that during that period the global population grew by more than 2 billion, from 5.3 to 7.6 billion. In 1990 almost 1 billion of the extreme poor lived in East Asia—the vast majority in China—but by 2017 this figure had declined dramatically, to about 30 million. Within this figure were declines of about 750 million in China, 85 million in Indonesia, and 40 million in Vietnam, accounting for the lion's share of the total reductions across East Asia. Until about 2005, the numbers of extreme poor had stagnated in South Asia, suggesting that poverty reduction was only just about keeping up with population growth. Since then, a declining trend is noticeable, dominated by India's measured poverty declines between 2004 and 2011—from about 38 per cent to 21 per cent of the population—or a reduction in the Indian poverty numbers of more than 250 million since 1990. Another 55 million decline in Pakistan and 25 million in Bangladesh contributed to more than halving the number of people

Figure 3.2 Total Population living in extreme poverty by region, 1990–2017

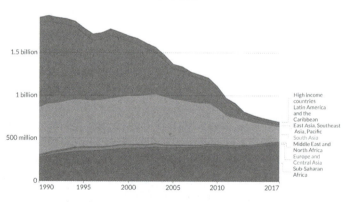

Source: Max Roser and Esteban Ortiz-Ospina (2013) – 'Global Extreme Poverty'. *Published online at OurWorldInData.org.* Retrieved from: https://ourworldindata.org/extreme-poverty [Online Resource].

Note: Extreme poverty is defined as living with per capita household consumption below 1.90 international dollars per day (in 2011 PPP prices). International dollars are adjusted for inflation and for price differences across countries. Consumption per capita is preferred welfare indicator for the World Bank's analysis of global poverty. However, for a number of countries poverty is measured in terms of income. An income basis is common among high-income countries and Latin American countries.

in extreme poverty since 1990, to less than 200 million by 2017 in South Asia.

The experience in sub-Saharan Africa was very different. The numbers in extreme poverty first went up and then at best stagnated after 2010—at about 410 million. Between 1990 and 2017, the share of the population in extreme poverty fell from about 55 per cent to 41 per cent, but the population more than doubled to over 1 billion. Because poverty in other parts of the world has been falling much more rapidly, the nature of poverty has changed globally. In its most extreme form, it is now increasingly an African phenomenon and no longer widespread across the whole of the developing world.

Within these figures lie large differences among African countries. Of the forty-seven countries usually included in sub-Saharan Africa, eighteen had a population of more than 8 million and a poverty rate of more than 20 per cent of their population in 1990.[10] Only Ghana and Ethiopia more than halved their poverty rates and had fewer people in poverty in 2018 than in 1990. By 2018, there were seven countries in which the number of people living in extreme poverty had more than doubled: Angola, the Democratic Republic of Congo (DRC), Kenya, Madagascar, Malawi, Nigeria and Zambia. Overall in sub-Saharan Africa, about 150 million more people were living in extreme poverty in 2018 than in 1990, with the largest increases in the DRC (plus 35 million), Nigeria (plus 26 million), and Madagascar (plus 13 million). The success of Ghana and Ethiopia is then even more striking. Most likely, Mekonnen's grandchildren will have better lives than he could give his own children.

Other deprivations

The implied changes of poverty across the world are fraught with methodological and measurement challenges.[11] One sensible way to assess whether the implied statements on broad changes in the standard of living are valid is by looking at dimensions other than just consumption or another monetary measure.

Some researchers have sworn by the need to develop alternative overall statements of deprivation by using a multidimensional index of other aspects of deprivation and poverty.[12] While having much merit, such an idea tends to lack intuitive simplicity when one is communicating to a broader audience. I prefer to simply offer other types of deprivation and ask whether they have changed in a way similar to that of extreme poverty over recent times. One obvious indicator, and one of the most basic dimensions of standard of living, is child mortality—that is, whether a child survives to age five. Mekonnen's family clearly suffered in this respect: two of his five children had died at an early age.

Figure 3.3 shows the scale of this kind of suffering across the world.[13] Across the better-off part of the world, child mortality, while still tragic, has become a rare occurrence because relatively few children in North America, Europe and Central Asia, the Middle East and North Africa, and Latin America and the Caribbean die before their fifth birthday. This finding reflects the great improvements in living standards as well as in medical science and public health practice. As of 1950, an estimated one in ten children in Europe died before the age of five. In 2019 this figure was less than one in two hundred.

Figure 3.3 Number of under-five deaths by region, 1990–2019

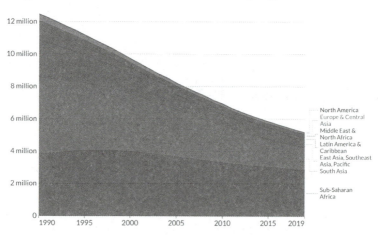

Source: Max Roser, Hannah Ritchie, and Bernadeta Dadonaite (2013) — 'Child and Infant Mortality'. *Published online at OurWorldInData.org.* Retrieved from: https://ourworldindata. org/child-mortality [Online Resource].
Note: The figure gives the number of children dying before reaching the age of five.

Under-five child mortality is therefore almost exclusively a phenomenon of the developing world. But the changes there are also remarkable. In 1950 one in three children in sub-Saharan Africa was expected not to survive to age five. Now the figure is well below one in ten, even if material living standards have not quite reached the European standards of the 1950s. As a result, even since 1990 there has been a steep decline in the total number of children dying across the world—indeed, by 2019 that figure was less than half of the more than 12 million who died in 1990.

Declines are evident in all parts of the world. The pattern over time is, however, strongly reminiscent of that for the extreme poor (figure 3.2). From 1990 to 2019, the fastest declines were experienced in East Asia and the Pacific; a delayed but also fast decline was experienced by South Asia to a lesser extent; and only small changes were seen in sub-Saharan Africa. There, the decline in the mortality rate for children barely exceeded the growth in population. Increasingly, just as for extreme (material) poverty, child mortality is becoming an African phenomenon. Even so, it hides differences within Africa. The DRC, for example, is one of the few countries where a higher number of children die now before their fifth birthday than in 1990. By contrast, in Ethiopia a quarter of a million fewer children died in 2019 in their first five years than they did in 1990.[14]

Women and children

For most if not all other dimensions of living standards, at least for those describing the more extreme levels of deprivation, similar patterns emerge. The fertility rate—the number of children born to a woman—is particularly striking. Often, high fertility is thought to be a major cause of deprivation and lack of development. Although there are no doubt families for whom their large number of children has proved to be a hardship, its relevance as a cause of global poverty is highly disputable. The fertility rate is nevertheless a helpful indicator of progress in development because it captures how several factors reflecting progress come together. In particular, in societies across the world fertility rates have tended to come down when incomes rise and poverty declines; when health care improves and children survive early childhood; when better child care and forms of old-age security such as basic pensions emerge; when education levels increase, especially for girls; when women begin to take on paid jobs; and more. In short, development thrives and opportunities for women increase. The fertility rate is therefore a rather useful indicator capturing multiple dimensions of development and declines in extreme deprivation, even though the exact combination of factors determining it differs among countries.

Globally and in developing countries, fertility rates have been coming down fast. Global population growth rates have been declining as well, but the world will still reach over 10 billion later in the twenty-first century because mortality rates have come down even faster. Across the developing world and African countries, positive trends in fertility rates are emerging. They indicate fast progress in the developing world, especially in East Asia and subsequently in South Asia, converging to levels seen in much richer countries, whereas slower progress is evident in sub-Saharan Africa together with quite some differentiation (figure 3.4). The fertility rate in China has been coming down dramatically, reaching European levels but at material living standards well below Europe's. Often, casual observers attribute this dramatic decline to the one-child policy in 1979, with its extensive monetary and other punishments for violators. But as these data reveal and more in-depth research has confirmed, this policy was not what brought down China's fertility rate.[15] If anything, the decline began largely before 1979, and in the decade after introduction of the policy relatively little changed. China's fertility rate fell in response to better health and education and greater access to it—in short, broader development. There was no doubt pressure on families to limit children, but that was just one factor in the broader progress made in reducing extreme poverty during this period.

In fact, none of the other Asian countries shown in figure 3.4 had such a draconian policy, and family planning was just one of the many factors that brought down fertility levels in those countries as well. Bangladesh's success is possibly most striking: a Muslim society that in 1970 had one of the highest fertility rates in the world, it is

Figure 3.4 Fertility rates: Children per woman in selected countries, 1970–2019

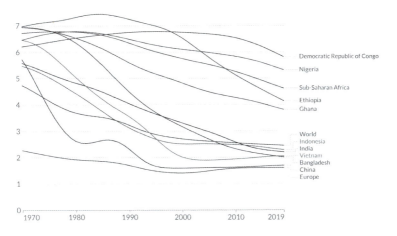

Source: Max Roser (2014) – 'Fertility Rate'. *Published online at OurWorldInData.org.* Retrieved from: https://ourworldindata.org/fertility-rate [Online Resource].

Note: Children per woman is measured as the total fertility rate, which is the number of children that would be born to the average woman if she were to live to the end of her child-bearing years and give birth to children at the current age-specific fertility rates.

now well below the global average and below the rates of other Asian countries that have made huge progress. Bangladesh reduced its fertility rate by two-thirds, from more than six children per woman in 1980 to close to two now, thanks to pro-poor and pro-women development, not a one-child policy.

The fertility rate in sub-Saharan Africa has also come down, from about seven to five children per woman, but by no means on the scale experienced in Asia (figure 3.4). Later in the century, sub-Saharan Africa's population, now about 1.1 billion, is likely to increase to about 4 billion, according to UN estimates—or to more than a third of the global population—and it is beginning to rival Asia's share of the world total.

Explaining patterns

This review of development indicators has illustrated some undeniable facts about development in recent decades. The developing world has made substantial progress in at least reducing some of the clearest manifestations of deprivation such as extreme material poverty and low child survival. Other indicators such as improving educational opportunities are reflected in outcomes, such as fertility rates, that point to progress across a range of dimensions. For countries with the largest populations living in deprivation by 1990, progress was clearly evident first in East Asia, notably China, and also elsewhere such as Indonesia and subsequently South Asia. There is nevertheless rising differentiation across the developing world—extreme poverty and deprivation are increasingly a factor in sub-Saharan Africa. Still, even in that region there are clear signs of differentiation: countries such as Nigeria and the DRC are on trajectories very different from those of countries such as Ghana and Ethiopia. This shows that considerable progress is also possible in the region.

'It's the economy, stupid'

These facts and figures are intended to provide context for the central question addressed by this book: Why is it that some countries and regions, each with a different history and different political and economic regimes, were more successful than others in climbing the ladder towards development? However, that context is not complete without answering another question: What did their economies have to do with making progress, or not? The simple answer is an awful lot, but not everything. Figures 3.5 and 3.6 make this clear, using estimates of GDP per capita.[16] GDP is an imperfect measure of standard of living itself: it does not capture anything about the distribution of incomes in any meaningful way, or many of the dimensions one may have reason to value. It does measure, however imperfectly, the total income generated in an economy, and in that sense it offers a measure of the value of goods and services that can be acquired by the citizens of a country.

Figure 3.5 shows the extent to which East Asia (including its largest economy, China) managed to improve its overall per capita income by more than six times its 1990 level, starting from levels similar to the average of those of South Asia and sub-Saharan Africa.[17] In doing so, it was able to converge with other parts of the world,

Figure 3.5 GDP per capita in 2017 international dollars by region, 1990–2019

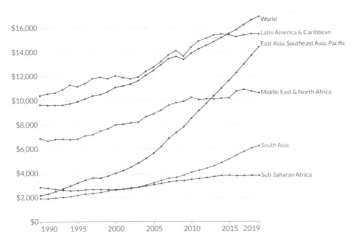

Source: Max Roser (2013) – 'Economic Growth'. *Published online at OurWorldInData.org.* Retrieved from: https://ourworldindata.org/economic-growth [Online Resource].

Note: These estimates of GDP per capita are expressed not in actual dollars, but in 2017 constant international dollars, thereby making them comparable over time and between countries in terms of purchasing power. The data for Latin America & Caribbean, East Asia, Southeast Asia & Pacific, and Middle East & North Africa exclude high-income countries.

such as the middle-income economies of the Middle East and North Africa as well as Latin America and the Caribbean regions. South Asia's rise is also notable, but it came later and at a slower rate, and yet it still reached levels three times those of 1990. Sub-Saharan Africa also improved, but by far less than the others.

This rise of East Asia should be viewed with caution to avoid a wrong impression. Even though it has a large population, its apparent huge economic power in per capita terms is still relatively modest. Per capita, East Asia has only reached the purchasing power of about a quarter of the per capita level of the US and a third that of the UK.

Figure 3.6 further depicts the progress in GDP per capita by some of the countries featured in this book. Indonesia and Nigeria started at higher levels in 1990 than the other countries shown, whereas Ethiopia was no doubt the poorest in 1990. The largest increases are evident for China, but Vietnam, India, and Indonesia

Figure 3.6 GDP per capita in 2017 international dollars for selected countries, 1990–2019

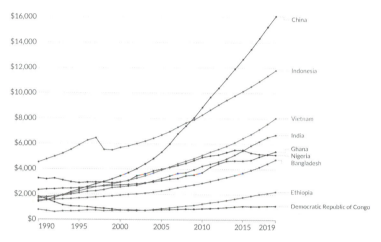

Source: Max Roser (2013) – 'Economic Growth'. *Published online at OurWorldInData.org.* Retrieved from: https://ourworldindata.org/economic-growth [Online Resource].

Note: These estimates of GDP per capita are expressed not in actual dollars, but in 2017 constant international dollars, thereby making them comparable over time and between countries in terms of purchasing power.

also saw considerable increases in GDP per capita. Moreover, each of these Asian countries saw its poverty and other indicators of deprivation improve strongly during this period. Meanwhile, the DRC's declining GDP has also contributed to its desperately poor outcomes across a range of indicators. But the relationship between GDP and these outcomes is more subtle. Growth in Bangladesh, another apparent success story across the different development indicators shown earlier, was higher than that of Nigeria from 1990 to 2017, but by 2017 its GDP per capita was still well below Nigeria's. In fact, Nigeria's GDP per capita approximates the GDP levels of Bangladesh or Ghana in 2019, but with dramatically poorer outcomes for its population.[18] Ethiopia's GDP per capita is considerably below Nigeria's and is only reaching the level of the DRC in 1990, but is performing far better on other development indicators.

High levels and fast growth of GDP per capita have no doubt made broader progress in development more achievable, but in themselves they are not sufficient. One may argue they are not necessary, and yet no societies appear to have achieved sustained reductions in poverty without substantial GDP growth. A diverse set of countries such as Ethiopia, Ghana, India, Vietnam, and Bangladesh have done so in recent times, apparently taking the steps required to join the ranks of China, Indonesia, and others who started this process of growth and poverty reduction earlier, and more or less convincingly. They are unlike countries, such as the DRC or Nigeria, which appear to have lagged behind—a phenomenon explored in the next part of this book.

Looking ahead

Before proceeding, a look ahead is useful in the form of three questions. First, if the current growth and poverty reduction patterns remain in place, what will extreme poverty look like across the world by 2030? Second, how has Covid-19 likely affected recent and future progress? Third, how is climate change likely to matter for these patterns?

What will extreme poverty look like by 2030?

Economic growth appears to be a key part of the kind of bargain in society that also drives a reduction in poverty levels, but the exact link between extreme poverty and economic growth depends on the local context. Using this locally specific link as well as likely changes in population, researchers have devised scenarios of what will happen over the next decade or so. In doing so, all of them tend to agree on one thing: the Africanisation of poverty will continue, driven largely by a small number of countries, even though other African countries will improve.

Figure 3.7 gives one such projection, up to 2030, and suggests that reductions in extreme poverty will continue in Asia, but the poverty levels in Africa will change little.[19] This projection by no means indicates that 'the development job is done' in Asia. Many people will still have living standards that by no means meet Sen's notion of a decent standard of living as one that offers 'the capabilities to live

Figure 3.7 Projection of number of people in extreme poverty by region, 2015–30

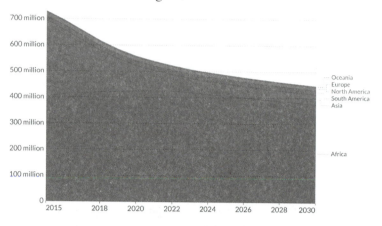

Source: Max Roser and Esteban Ortiz-Ospina (2013) – 'Global Extreme Poverty'. *Published online at OurWorldInData.org.* Retrieved from: https://ourworldindata.org/extreme-poverty [Online Resource].

Note: Number of people by region projected to be living in extreme poverty through to 2030. Extreme poverty is defined by the international poverty line of $1.90 per day (2011, PPP-adjusted). The projections are based on a business-as-usual scenario of recent socio-economic trends and medium future population scenarios.

a life one has reason to value'. Even so, enabling the vast majority of the population to move beyond the most extreme deprivation is still an important achievement for Asia. Meanwhile, no such overall optimism is present in sub-Saharan Africa. Its extreme poverty levels are predicted to remain close to what they are now—around 400 million. And they will be driven by countries such as Nigeria, which is projected to be the country with the largest number of extreme poor people throughout this decade, followed by the DRC and Madagascar. But there will be success stories, too; countries such as Ghana and (possibly) Ethiopia will continue to see fast reductions in the number of poor people.[20]

How much has Covid-19 derailed progress?

As I write this, the coronavirus pandemic is still raging worldwide. It appears that it did not hit many African countries as hard as could have been expected, but the worst may still be to come. In the richest economies, optimism has returned as vaccines are being rolled out. Nevertheless, the global slowdown and the various degrees of economic lockdown have led to large declines in economic growth across the world, affecting living standards. There's no doubt, then, that in many countries extreme poverty has increased.

The World Bank estimates that during 2020 more than 100 million people will have joined the ranks of the global extreme poor (see figure 3.2 to compare levels).[21] It is far too early to assess the impact of such an increase on other indicators such as child mortality because basic health services, such as infant vaccinations, were disrupted by the lockdowns. Even fertility rate declines may slow because education for girls was disrupted, and girls were married off younger as poverty increased.

It is likely that progress in development to 2030 and beyond will have slowed, but beyond this my own crystal ball is hazy. I nevertheless remain optimistic that progress in Asia may only be delayed and will not halt altogether. A strong recovery there is likely, boosting living standards again and allowing these countries to bring down extreme poverty, as shown in figure 3.7, even if a delay of five years or so occurs. In sub-Saharan Africa, where growth and development are progressing less persistently than before the crisis, economic recovery is likely to be slower, and development may stall at even higher levels of deprivation, but with exceptions. These exceptions are likely to include the countries that can sustain and strengthen their development bargain and gamble on growth and development when the pandemic peters out.

Climate and the future: The end of growth (as we know it)?

It is not possible to assess trends in poverty reduction without addressing the possible effects of climate change on poverty. A lot is often made of how the developing world and the poor will suffer most from climate change, necessitating urgent action. Although poorer people will find it much harder than the better-off to cope with the consequences of climate change, quantifying the additional hardship is difficult.

Most of the estimates follow the reasonable assumption that extreme poverty is currently affected by climate change mainly through disruptions linked to the increased intensity of extreme events such as storms, floods, and drought. Such shocks often have temporary effects but no longer necessarily permanent ones on extreme poverty because of better government responses such as the provision of safety nets. The estimates of the impacts of climate change on extreme poverty by 2030 are therefore relatively modest. Some researchers have suggested that if the effects of climate change intensify in number and speed, the extreme poverty reductions just described would be slower. One calculation projects that global poverty will decrease by less than what figure 3.7 implies. Because of the more intense effects arising from climate change, 62 million fewer people would escape extreme poverty, and the global poor would still number about 450 million.[22] However, such consequences would not be spread equally across the developing world. The largest increases in such a scenario are likely to be in sub-Saharan Africa (55 million), with Nigeria and the DRC the largest contributors. Still, the impact would then seem to be less than the pandemic's.

One reason for this seemingly modest impact is that climate models predict that the larger impacts will be evident more from 2040 or 2050 onwards rather than during the next decade. Poverty impacts over such a longer horizon are much harder to predict. But because the poor are no doubt the least able to cope and the most vulnerable, overcoming their persistent poverty in the next decade or so could affect substantially whether extreme poverty numbers increase in the second half of this century as a result of climate change. Populations in those countries that are already unlikely to see a reduction in extreme poverty will be most at risk of further deprivation because of a changing climate.

It may seem, though, there is a catch-22 here: unless their incomes increase considerably, large numbers of people, not least in sub-Saharan Africa, would remain extremely poor and more vulnerable. However, trying to move the poor out of poverty using known means, which include increasing economic growth to create the potential to achieve poverty reduction, could produce CO_2 emissions on a scale that would undermine the purpose of reducing poverty and make populations more vulnerable. China, the biggest success story in recent decades at least in terms of poverty reduction, offers a scary precedent. In 2019 it was responsible for about 29 per cent of global CO_2 emissions.[23] If other countries were to go its route, the consequences for the planet would be catastrophic.

There is no doubt some truth in all this, but also some spin. In particular, relative to the size of its population, China's yearly emissions are large (7.3 tonnes per capita), the same as across Europe in 2019 but still smaller than those in Japan (8.7 tonnes), and the US (15.6 tonnes). India's emissions are still only 1.9 tonnes per capita, and the average for Africa is only 1.1 tonnes per capita. In short, per person, the richer societies are still emitting vastly more than India and the developing world in general. There still is much more mileage in bringing down emissions in the rich world than there is in preventing emissions in poorer countries.[24]

More striking, even though North America and Europe only account currently for 15 per cent of the global population, they are responsible for 60 per cent of *cumulative* emissions—that is, the stock of greenhouse gases.[25] China and India, each with 18 per cent of the global population, have contributed cumulatively 13 per cent and 3 per cent, respectively. Other developing countries have contributed even less. It is no wonder, then, that countries with recent histories of poverty, including India and China, are tough partners at climate negotiations.

The truth, however, is that the planet cannot afford having the developing world emit at the levels of richer countries, let alone cumulatively account for a share of the stock of emissions their populations may warrant. Not only do rich economies need to move to net zero or even negative emissions—that is, to a level of emissions that is at least offset by the amount removed from the atmosphere such as through a country's forest cover—developing countries also need to do something similar in coming decades to keep climate change in check. Tougher, coordinated international action will no doubt be required to guide both the richest economies, with their fossil fuel–intensive lifestyles, and developing countries towards this low-carbon transition.

It is worth noting, however, that developing countries, including India and China, are succeeding in achieving higher living standards with far lower cumulative emissions per capita than all the 'rich' countries had achieved earlier. Yes, they continue to rely heavily on coal and other fossil fuels, but alternatives are becoming both plentiful and cheaper. And they have thus far used fewer carbon-efficient production technologies than currently have become cost-effective.

The good news therefore is that the need to combat climate change does not have to stifle the ambitions of poor countries to take off using the tried and tested methods of economic growth: alternative carbon paths consistent with growth are available. My focus in this book on growth or the lack of it can therefore be consistent with a concern for the planet.

* * *

To sum up, recent decades have seen remarkable progress in reducing extreme poverty and other indicators of deprivation. The most striking change has occurred in Asia, making extreme poverty increasingly an African phenomenon, and this is likely to remain the case in the future. Even there, though, some countries have been far more successful than others in development terms: sub-Saharan Africa is a region with diverse experiences. In part II, I explore some of these examples in more detail to find out why some countries have been successes, while others have lagged.

References

Alkire, S., and J. Foster. 2011. 'Counting and Multidimensional Poverty Measurement'. *Journal of Public Economics* 96 (7–8): 476–87.

Allen, R. C. 2017. 'Absolute Poverty: When Necessity Displaces Desire'. *American Economic Review* 107 (12): 3690–721.

Chen, S., and M. Ravallion. 2010. 'The Developing World Is Poorer Than We Thought, but No Less Successful in the Fight against Poverty'. *Quarterly Journal of Economics* 125 (4): 1577–625.

Crespo Cuaresma, J., W. Fengler, H. Kharas, H. K. Bekthiar, M. Brottrager, and M. Hofer. 2018. 'Will the Sustainable Development Goals Be

Fulfilled? Assessing Present and Future Global Poverty'. *Palgrave Communications* 4 (1): 1–8.

Deaton, A. 2010. 'Price Indexes, Inequality, and the Measurement of World Poverty'. *American Economic Review* 100 (1): 5–34.

Gietel-Basten, Stuart, Xuehui Han, and Yuan Cheng. 2019. 'Assessing the Impact of the "One-Child Policy" in China: A Synthetic Control Approach'. *PLOS One* 14 *(11): e0220170.*

Goodkind, Daniel. 2019. 'Formal Comment on "Assessing the Impact of the 'One-Child Policy' in China: A Synthetic Control Approach"'. *PLOS One* 14 (11): e0222705.

Harrell, S., W. Yuesheng, H. Hua, G. D. Santos, and Z. Yingying. 2014. 'Fertility Decline in Rural China: A Comparative Analysis'. *Journal of Family History* 36 (1): 15–36.

Rahmato, Dessalegn, and Aklilu Kidanu. 1999. 'Consultations with the Poor: National Report'. Paper produced for World Bank project: D. Narayan, ed., *Voices of the Poor* (2000). Washington, DC: World Bank.

Sen, A. 1983. 'Poor, Relatively Speaking'. *Oxford Economic Papers* 35: 153–69.

_____. 1999. *Development as Freedom*. Oxford: Oxford University Press.

Whyte, Martin K., Feng Wang, and Yong Cai. 2015. 'Challenging Myths about China's One-Child Policy'. *China Journal* 74: 144–59.

World Bank. 2020. *Poverty and Shared Prosperity 2020: Reversals of Fortune.* Washington, DC: World Bank.

PART II

A SHORT ZOOMORPHIC GUIDE TO PART II

'Our aim is to be a tiger economy,' the prime minister of the Democratic Republic of Congo (DRC) told his captive audience. The place was Kinshasa, the year was 2015, and Augustin Matata Ponyo, the stylish and articulate prime minister of the DRC, was opening an event.

Ponyo was not the first or the last leading African politician to invoke the Asian Tigers as the kind of economy he wanted for the continent. And yet there are no tigers in Africa—literally. Tigers— real ones or as a metaphor for a type of successful economy—are found only in Asia. What have become high-income economies— Singapore, Hong Kong, the Republic of Korea, and Taiwan—have been likened to tigers because of their fast growth for almost half a century, leading to almost unimaginable ten- or twentyfold increases in per capita GDP. Together, they account for only about 90 million people, more than half of them in Korea, but they have captured the imagination of onlookers. Although it is possible to use the development bargain framework to analyse their take-off in the 1950s or 1960s, and their evolution to high-income countries by the 1990s, they are experiencing little or none of the extreme poverty or deprivation at the core of this book. Instead, part II features those countries in which I have spent time, studying their inner workings and meeting key players in the economy and politics. And by 1990 those covered accounted for more than three-quarters of the world's extreme poor.

The success of the tiger economies launched a whole menagerie of animal metaphors to describe how politics and economics interact in countries, and over the years I have joined in their use. Beyond the tiger economies, there are the tiger cubs, such as Indonesia, Thailand, and Malaysia, while China has been called the dragon. However, when discussing other countries' experiences, not least across Africa, the diversity of experiences has meant I have had to expand on that menagerie. Mine is not quite based on science, but it is suggestive of the kinds of states and elite bargains described here.

In part II, I look at some of the successful and some of the failing developing countries of the last few decades, using the framework developed in part I. The discussion of each state is accompanied by a snapshot of its success or failure in development—that is, how well it did in achieving some of the common features of success such as economic growth, macroeconomic stability, investment in physical and human capital, and extent of poverty across some measures of deprivation. The key features of the underlying conditions for progress are described as well: the nature of the elite bargain, the extent to which it has maintained peace and stability, and what it has meant for the nature of the state—that is, its ability to foster development and correct course. In particular, I assess whether these countries gambled on growth and development and, if so, how.

Chapter 4 describes the three largest developing countries in the world, which account for almost 40 per cent of the world's population: China, the dragon; Indonesia, the largest of the tiger cubs; and briefly India, the peacock (the country's national bird). All three countries were very poor in the 1960s and 1970s, but their elite bargains, each quite different in practice, delivered substantial progress in growth and development and currently over a billion fewer extreme poor. And yet these countries are still work in progress, especially Indonesia and India.

Many governments and states in the developing world resemble the hippopotamus—large and unwieldy and, when in a river, mostly hidden from sight. As the saying goes, 'One can only see the hippo's ears.'[1] The ears represent the formal state structures—a parliament, courts, government procurement offices, a revenue authority. But beneath them, just like the vast body beneath the tiny hippo ears on the surface of the river, are the invisible and yet clearly well-known informal structures and links along ethnic lines, personal connections, business interests, and other alliances. Most of the large and small decisions taken and favours extended emerge from these informal structures and not from the formal state. This kind of informal state is not just there to help run the country, but also to reward a group of people with jobs or contracts or access to resources. Most states in the world still have a hippo within them.[2]

Chapter 5 looks at Sierra Leone and Malawi, which have most of the features of a hippo state. Development seems to be on hold, keeping people poor and economies stagnant. Chapter 6 then examines three more states: Kenya, Uganda, and Ghana, still much like hippos but maybe evolving. They have clientelist structures, focusing on redistribution to those who are well connected. However, progress may be possible—as Uganda demonstrated during at least a decade straddling the 1990s, and as Ghana has revealed since it emerged from a deep crisis in the 1980s. In fact, these countries illustrate first-hand how states can evolve and not remain simply stuck in some equilibrium.

Some strongly clientelist states built on patronage appear to have an elite bargain that is stuck. Nigeria and the Democratic Republic of Congo fall into this category (chapter 7). Nigeria has state structures in which too many are aiming just to serve themselves or, at best, their fellow elite members. Oil hasn't helped. When rents are easily captured by the few, norms are created in the state and society that make it acceptable for those connected to steal from firms and individuals. In fact, because Nigeria has so many features of a predatory state, it most likely isn't just a hippo anymore. The DRC has been a hippo state for a long time, impoverished despite massive natural resource wealth. And it isn't on its way to becoming a tiger economy, whatever Prime Minister Ponyo may have wished for. A tigerfish economy seems more appropriate for the DRC, as well as for Nigeria.[3]

Chapter 8 turns to countries afflicted by conflict and war. Conflict tends to involve a breakdown of any elite bargain—that is, the equilibrium of many states is precarious. Afghanistan, a dramatic state failure of recent times, is featured first. Its hopes for peace are assessed, but they do not look good. South Sudan has seen its oil rents dry up, and its elite bargain since peace and independence in 2011 has increasingly descended into fighting over the scraps, turning it into a scavenger economy, hyena-like in its behaviour. Political and economic deals are at the core of turnarounds. In Nepal, politicians stepped back from continuing conflict, choosing the gradual change of the economic deal instead. In both Lebanon and Somaliland, after promoting peace as a business deal, economic deals emerged that made peace more worthwhile for the elite than conflict. The result is by no means a development bargain, but it is the first step towards something better.

Chapters 9 and 10 describe several countries that are genuine success stories, despite threats and the failings of their models. Chapter 9 turns to an unlikely success story, Bangladesh. The official national animal is the Bengal tiger, but a tiger cub seems a more appropriate metaphor for this country and its development story. Since the independence war in 1971, Bangladesh has come a long way, creating economic growth based on garment exports and remittances and producing a substantial reduction in poverty and deprivation. Success remains surprising: its elite bargain is still laced with clientelism and patronage, and the state is rife with corruption and inefficiency. This chapter argues that the secret of success lies in how the state was *not* used because of its low capabilities. For example, when garment manufacturing began to flourish as an export industry, the state did not try to capture all the rents. However, when nongovernmental organisations and foreign aid found ways to bring effective social services to ever larger numbers of people, the state promoted these efforts.

Chapter 10 finally sets its sights on Ethiopia and Rwanda. In the decade before Covid-19, Ethiopia was the fastest-growing economy in the world, thanks to a determined strategic gamble by those with power to develop the country. Rwanda has many similarities. Both countries had emerged from conflict with what could have become a hippo state serving those controlling the state because in each certain ethnic groups gained more power than all the others. Instead, an elite bargain took shape that sought legitimacy through a narrative of development, and the state worked hard at delivering it within its capabilities, even if much power remained concentrated in the hands of the victors. Because of their ruthlessness in suppressing opposition, and their stubborn determination to succeed, these states hardly fit the description of a cuddly animal—the fierce image of a lion is more appropriate. Ethiopia's success has been something of a miracle given its deep ethnic rivalries, but the recent return to widespread violence has put its gamble at risk.

Meanwhile, international development assistance and international financial institutions have played a role in all the countries featured in the following chapters—in both the successes and the failures. The use of aid in the emerging success stories, such as Bangladesh, Ghana, and Ethiopia, deserves more attention, as does international policy-making. These countries tell us more about not only how development efforts succeed, but also how international support could help in those efforts, thereby setting the stage for part III.

4

THE DRAGON, THE TIGER CUB,
AND THE PEACOCK

CHINA, INDONESIA, AND INDIA

'Did anything ever go wrong?' This was the question Sufian Ahmed, the Ethiopian finance minister, posed to Justin Lin, the Chinese academic and former World Bank chief economist. It was 2013, and I had assembled a small group of well-known academics for a retreat with some of Ethiopia's most senior economic policy-makers. We met in Bishoftu, an attractive small town built around volcanic lakes, an hour outside Addis Ababa. We were discussing what we could learn from countries' experiences of development across the world. We had just heard a short presentation on the economic policy changes in China in the early 1980s that had spurred its economy to grow quickly in the decades that followed.

To my surprise, 'No' was Professor Lin's resolute answer to the minister's question. It has become part of a rather simplistic narrative that any country can do what China did so long as it assigns the state a leading role, focuses on infrastructure investment, and creates special economic zones.[4] This flat-pack version of China's experience is now being exported, supported by ample finance from China's state-owned 'policy banks', such as the Export-Import Bank of China (EXIM) and the China Development Bank (CDB), and an army of Chinese contractors and willing manufacturers.

What happened as far as change in China is concerned is not in question. In fact, it is amazing and still surprising—and not for nothing did China become known as a dragon economy. The shift in economic direction began in 1979 with gradual liberalisation and a greater emphasis on market forces, but with continued state involvement. China also began to restructure its economy, which involved moving towards urbanisation and export manufacturing with the establishment of special economic zones. Clearly, then, China found a way to make policy choices that earlier had figured in the success of other East Asian countries such as the Republic of Korea and Japan, but it made the choices within the Chinese political and economic context. *How* China managed to move forward is often less understood and so is examined here. A better understanding of China's evolution enables a better understanding of how difficult it is for other countries to simply replicate China's progress. They can learn lessons from China, but not the ones usually promoted. Understanding how China's elite bargain for growth and development emerged and was implemented is central to those lessons.

This chapter looks as well at Indonesia, often called the tiger cub because it appeared to follow the Asian Tigers' example in the 1980s, although not quite with the same success. Nevertheless, during this period it managed to change from a country clearly staying behind to one with a much faster-growing economy and with substantial progress on the development front as well. Still, no one seeks to copy Indonesia, even though useful lessons can be learned. For example, even though it shifted over time towards growth and development, its elite bargain has long been much more fragile. Too many in the elite display rent-seeking and corruption tendencies, and state institutions lack the strength and commitment to keep these in check, compared, say, with what is possible in China. Even so, those with power have learned to avoid using the state too much as the main driver of growth and development—a useful lesson for others.

India receives a briefer look—although its path to development deserves its own book. Its state has had a habit of presenting its own success since independence in 1947 as more dazzling than the evidence would suggest, just as a peacock's feathers decorate what is otherwise not a very strong bird. My focus is on the pivotal period in the 1990s when the elite bargain did not change in itself but its outlook and focus did—a substantial course correction that began with a new economic deal. Economic growth and development then accelerated, at last. That is the most essential lesson from India, as its potential was never in doubt, but those engaging in the elite bargain, for better and for worse, lacked for too long a willingness to shift to a model in which growth and development held a more central position. It is a matter of debate whether this path is still beyond doubt, but the shift in the 1990s was nevertheless striking.

In this chapter, the development bargain framework described in chapter 2 is applied to all three countries, focusing on the actors in the elite, the nature of the political and economic deals underlying the elite bargain, and the factors that allowed the development bargain to emerge.

China's development miracle revisited

China is no doubt the most striking success story in economic growth and poverty reduction of the last four decades. Its turning point was 1979. Since then, its economy has grown spectacularly, reaching by 2019 a GDP per capita (in constant 2010 US dollars) twenty times higher than that in 1979.[5] Its success was especially remarkable because in the two decades prior to 1979 growth in per capita terms had been around 2.8 per cent a year, in contrast to the 8.5 per cent a year in the subsequent four decades. As documented in chapter 3, China also reduced poverty and in general saw its living conditions improve dramatically.

The period preceding 1979 was turbulent both politically and for ordinary Chinese. The Communist Party of China, which had been in power since 1949, seriously mismanaged a string of natural disasters between 1959 and 1961, and at least 30 million people may have lost their lives as a result. The Cultural Revolution disrupted economic and political life from 1966 to 1976. After the death of party leader Mao Zedong in 1976 and a relatively brief power struggle, the remnants of the leadership of this disruptive period lost their power. Their successor, the reformist Deng Xiaoping, managed to assert his leadership, and he became the architect of a new direction in the economy, starting at the end of 1978.

Some of the best-known reforms exemplify China's success. Farmers were allowed more control over the returns to agricultural land as part of the Household Responsibility System. Meanwhile, the government spearheaded large reforms in agriculture based less on central control and more on initiative at the local level. The Open Door Policy allowed the entry of foreign direct investment, boosting the kind of export-led manufacturing firms that other East Asian states had attracted. Chairman Deng also experimented with the establishment of special economic zones—later proven to be very successful—that gave local governments substantial autonomy to attract economic activity, including foreign investment, as well as boost urbanisation in these localities. From 1984, more economic liberalisation followed, including some tentative privatisation of state-owned enterprises.

In the meantime, the idea of a socialist market economy was taking shape. In 1993 China began to consolidate liberalisation and privatisation. Even though there were some reversals, growth continued unabated, goose-stepping in line with the official plans and further supported by large-scale public infrastructure investments.

Throughout, China's economic model managed to exploit its great but only natural resource: people. Industrial development and urbanisation pushed up the demand for labour, while allowing rural–urban migration, albeit implemented in a controlled way. All this contributed to structural transformation—that is, changes in the sectoral economic structure where production factors, including labour, were being used. And in line with basic economics, this change slowly but dramatically pushed up rural incomes and reduced the number of poor, lifting well over half a billion people out of extreme poverty. Combined with better health care, education, and other social provisions, this achievement offered a better basic quality of life for many and a development success story for the country at large.

How well does what happened in China since 1979 align with the three features of a development bargain? Quite nicely as it turns out. In the following sections, I will describe how the three features of the development bargain—political and economic deals, the appropriate role of the state in this context, and the role of learning and course correction—played out in China.

The political and economic deals from 1979

The change in economic direction in 1979 was not just the inspired choice of Chairman Deng. It is much better understood as the emergence of a new political bargain among those with power (the elite). The Communist Party of China had controlled the mainland since 1949. Effectively, its political and military leaders and those in the higher echelons of the economy and broader society became the elite in the way the term is used in this book. The political bargains— the deals they made with each other—shaped the direction of politics, the economy, and society.

Throughout the Cultural Revolution, political ideology took priority over the economy; economic growth and broader development were secondary. After Mao's death in 1976, an internal struggle ensued between the Gang of Four and their supporters, including Mao's widow, who wanted to continue this line, and those who feared that it posed an existential threat to the party and its dominance in the state. In the end it was settled in the form of a new political bargain, when the Gang of Four were sidelined in favour of those giving the highest priority to strengthening the economy. The political bargain could even be dated to December 1978, when during the third plenary session of the Central Committee 'Reform and Opening Up' became the driving slogan. It was the symbolic consolidation of a new political bargain—now a development bargain—in which economic growth was the core objective. Chairman Deng played a central role in its emergence, and that allowed him to personify what was essentially a deal within the party leadership. He became the 'architect' of the reforms that favoured economic development above all.[6]

In the new direction adopted in 1979, economic progress was central. But, of course, it had political objectives as well. Because of the turbulence in the preceding years, the party leadership no doubt understood, probably correctly, that its position might not remain unchallenged and so its main source of legitimacy would have to be growth and development.[7] Indeed, Karl Marx and the communist movement understood that to progress it must provide the people with better living standards. Under Chairman Deng, the focus shifted much more to the objectives rather than to the mechanism by which they were achieved, as reflected in his famous saying 'It doesn't matter whether a cat is black or white so long as it catches mice'.[8]

Mobilising state capabilities from below

The oft-repeated story of the economic history of China, the 'China model', goes something like this: Just as in China, development will come about in other countries when the state plays the leading role. It should establish special economic zones, packed with labour-intensive factories with a strong export orientation, and combine these with high levels of investment in public infrastructure.[9] Such restructuring will not just deliver growth but also rev up the urban industrial growth engine, which will absorb surplus labour. Combined with green revolution agricultural technologies, restructuring will lead to a large-scale reduction in poverty.

An export orientation, infrastructure, urban growth, and green revolution technologies are no doubt sensible ingredients for development beyond China. However, how China used the state requires more clarification than the simple suggestion that state-led development will always work.

China had had powerful public administration structures for several millennia. A high-quality public service had been built up, with officials accustomed to engaging in economically relevant activities, such as rule-based tax collection. After coming to power, the Communist Party of China was able to build on this state apparatus to run a centrally planned economy, inspired by politics and ideology. It could hardly be called a success, and a simple lesson emerged: even with strong state structures, state-led development does not always work.

From 1979, as part of the reforms by Chairman Deng, the party decided to exploit the market system rather than stop it. Years ago at a seminar at Tsinghua University, a Chinese scholar implored me to stop talking about the economic reforms of this period; they were first and foremost governance reforms, he said. This was still state-led development, but the Chinese state had to change fundamentally how it governed the economy.

Initially, the economic structure was not changed; what changed was who could make decisions. The Household Responsibility Model was not an end to the targets that agriculture should meet, but a transfer of agency to those who should make the micro-level decisions in agriculture—the farmers—instead of commune leaders or higher-ups. Similarly, the special economic zones were not just physical infrastructure or even 'one-stop shops' for customs or regulators. Rather, they were fundamentally governance reforms whereby local governments were given far more authority to handle business as well as urbanisation and infrastructure development—so long as the objectives were actually met. In the process, much scope for local private entrepreneurship was created, but again so long as it remained consistent with broad objectives.

For officials, however, it was not always clear what was expected. There may have been goals and targets, such as for output or growth, but far less guidance on how they should be achieved beyond some vague directions. The succinct nature of sayings such as 'capitalism with Chinese characteristics', as favoured by Deng Xiaoping and the Central Committee, may have sounded great, but what did they actually mean, along with the other utterances by the leadership? Indeed, as it turned out, thousands of study groups were set up to interpret these statements, explore what would and would not be allowed, and then try to put them into practice.[10]

Learning by doing, with Chinese characteristics

Despite its strong state and party, and new-found commitment to economic development, China had to find ways within its political and administrative set-up to learn and act more successfully than it had before 1979. It did this rather slowly and cautiously by 'crossing the river by feeling the stones', as Chairman Deng famously said. This was the hardest part.

Changing who can make decisions was one step. Creating space for experimentation in the economy was another. The success or failure of party officials was closely monitored in terms of achieving goals and targets, but less in terms of how they were achieved.[11] What is notable here is not that experimentation took place—all over the world governments engage in endless pilot programmes. More important is understanding how this experimentation was governed. Experimentation was encouraged and failure was acceptable, but failure stemming from incompetence or inaction was often penalised and punished.

Despite the way this period is represented, there was no certainty; the reforms undertaken by Deng and his allies were one big gamble. Indeed, the period of reform was not an endless stream of successes. Overall, yes, it was a success—it was, in fact, a most remarkable story of growth and development. But, unsurprisingly, many things did not go according to plan.[12] Indeed, at a small closed meeting I attended in 2019 in Beijing, a very wise and respected retired high-level technocrat who had worked with Chairman Deng admonished the young Chinese researchers present to study more the Chinese failures in this period than the successes. He reminded them that when starting the work on special economic zones, Deng himself drew four circles on a map and ordered that the new idea be tried out in all four. Today, Shenzhen is the one that comes to mind because it was a spectacular success, but few people would be able to name the three other zones—they were far less successful at first. As for the state planners, lessons were learned quickly from both successes and failures, and five years later 77 special economic zones were in operation.

So beyond a shared political commitment and smart use of its own state capability, China, especially in the early 1980s, had the means to correct course if matters went wrong and to learn quickly. Experimentation requires both administrative and political processes to respond to success or failure. The party appears to have had the mechanisms needed to remove those people and projects that did not deliver growth and development.[13] This was possible only because, in the end, those with power—the political and economic elite— were fundamentally committed to growth and development.

Lessons from China for other countries

If China has anything to teach the rest of the developing world, it is not why it took the measures it did or used the strong central state as it did. The lesson is the importance of its development bargain— that is, the Chinese state's deep commitment during the last forty years, and especially in the early period, to growing its economy and developing the country, even if the way the Chinese did it might not be to everyone's liking.[14]

A political deal to elevate the economy over ideology was central. In the case of China, it made it possible to successfully use instruments such as industrialisation by means of special economic zones or a heavy reliance on public infrastructure. After all, without a such commitment, growth from policy measures related to industrialisation or infrastructure was unlikely to be achieved, as ideological or other objectives would have diverted resources without much scope for correction or lesson-learning.

The need for a strong state to lead the economy is not a key lesson. It is not surprising that China, with its long history of a strong, centralised state bureaucracy, involved in central taxation and other policies, was able to muster such a strong state *capability* to find ways to steer and manage growth. Few other poor developing countries in the world have a state capability comparable to what China had at this early stage of economic development. The far more important lesson, then, is the need to use the state sensibly, in ways that suit the local reality, while recognising the state's capabilities, as China did. Vietnam was perhaps a successful pupil. Even so, it had to be far more pragmatic in how it implemented its plans, and it warmly welcomed outside investors and assistance (see box 4.1).[15]

Box 4.1 Vietnam, the quiet emulator

Vietnam has emulated some of China's progress, making it no doubt a success story in economic growth and poverty reduction. After the country's emergence from war in 1975, its economy did not recover for some fifteen years because of both global isolation and ideology-driven economic policy. GDP per capita barely increased in these years, leaving Vietnam with a GDP per capita that ranked it among the poorest countries in the world in the 1980s. After 1990, Vietnam managed to grow its GDP per capita 5.5 per cent a year by enthusiastically embracing global opportunities, as well as by high levels of public investment in infrastructure and social sectors. Extreme poverty and a slew of other development indicators improved quickly, making the country one of the development success stories around the turn of the century.

Vietnam probably comes closest to the kind of development bargain observed in China. By the mid-1980s, a strong Communist Party was leading the country, but it faced economic stagnation. Meanwhile, more and more neighbouring countries were managing to embark on a successful growth-oriented development journey. Launched in 1986, the Doi Moi economic reforms were a move towards overhauling the Communist Party of Vietnam, while retaining political control, but using economic growth and development as a vehicle for maintaining stability.

The underlying political bargain was based on a mixture of socialist legitimacy-seeking and self-preservation, with proud nationalistic fervour similar to that of its large neighbour. Smaller and poorer, Vietnam had to be more pragmatic than China. The state opened up its market and showed more willingness to attract foreign investors than China. Indeed, it was truly 'developmental', doing anything it could to spur growth, such as being supportive of foreign investors. Meanwhile, the state built up its capabilities quickly from low levels, while also working enthusiastically with development agencies, including the World Bank, as a means of correcting policy errors and improving its development indicators. In the process, it received large amounts of aid. The result? Not only has Vietnam now seen three decades of fast economic growth, but it also can report that extreme poverty, affecting more than half the population in 1992, has been all but eradicated. In fact, the latest estimates suggest that about 2 per cent of the population is currently living on less than $1.90 a day.

Meanwhile, those connected with the elite in politics and the economy have benefited from growth, though also from corruption. Some observers ask how this growth can be sustained without a trade-off with further cronyism and corruption, especially in view of the continuing role of state-run conglomerates. And they go even further, predicting regularly the demise of growth. Yet growth continues to be strong. It has remained at high levels, and over time both political stability and macroeconomic stability have tended to be managed reasonably well.

Another lesson is that the Chinese state found mechanisms that suited its circumstances to learn from its errors and correct them. With the benefit of hindsight, China often refers publicly to the reforms of the early 1980s as though there was no doubt about their likely success, just as Justin Lin seemed to imply at the event described at the opening of this chapter. In China, developing mechanisms to correct course involved experimentation with devolving initiative to lower levels of the state but with ambitious goals and targets. Such an approach needs more than strong leadership from the top. It also needs mechanisms for accountability, politically rewarding success in growth and development and applying corrective action when success did not follow, ending projects or careers.[16] However, this approach is often misunderstood, not least by the political entrepreneurs in other countries dreaming of an all-powerful one-party state.

Indonesia's frail development bargain

Indonesia offers a very different experience from that of China (or Vietnam), but one still consistent with the successful emergence and pursuit of a development bargain. The country declared independence from the Netherlands in 1945. Agreement was reached with the former colonial power in 1949 to recognise the independence of the country, which was then under the leadership of President Sukarno. The economy remained relatively stagnant in the first two decades of independence, with little growth in GDP per capita.[17] Political tensions, involving the increasingly powerful Indonesian Communist Party (PKI) and the army, led to large-scale violence in 1965–6. In 1967, President Sukarno was ousted by the increasingly powerful General Suharto, who would then rule for as president for 31 years. Unrest after the 1997 Asian crisis, which hit Indonesia hard in economic terms, led to Suharto's removal from power and to more democratic politics since then.

Indonesia has seen its GDP per capita grow since the civil conflict in 1965–6—on average, 3.7 per cent per capita a year for more than fifty years.[18] And yet despite what has seemed like smooth long-term growth, at each moment in time it has not seemed so smooth. In fact, Indonesia's growth has never reached the stable high levels achieved by China. Up to 1997, its economy had achieved 4.5 per cent annual growth over thirty years in GDP per capita terms, and since 2000 it has grown by 3.9 per cent a year. In 1997–8, the economy shrank dramatically, by almost 13 per cent. Overall, almost seven years of steady per capita growth were lost as a result.[19] In 1997, extreme poverty dramatically increased—by more than 40 million people— but this proved temporary, and a few years later extreme poverty numbers were back on their long-term declining trend.[20] Between the early 1980s and 2018, poverty declined by more than 100 million people to less than 6 per cent of the population, even though the population had during this period expanded by 120 million.

Overall, Indonesia could, in line with the report of the Growth Commission (described in chapter 2),[21] be considered a success in take-off growth and development over this fifty-year period. The development bargain that sustained it did look frail at times, and it was definitely tested and had to be recalibrated repeatedly. Still, a political bargain emerged that was broadly maintained throughout, while the state, far weaker and less capable than, say, China's, was used in Indonesia in a restrained way. Technocrats and other actors such as the International Monetary Fund (IMF) were enlisted sensibly to correct course when the path towards growth was derailed. The following sections discuss each feature of the development bargain as applied to Indonesia in turn.

The evolving political and economic deals: Legitimacy and rents

The 1965–6 civil conflict sent shudders through Indonesian society, including its elites in politics, in the military, and across society. The economy, already in decline in part due to naive nationalistic self-sufficiency policies by Sukarno, was strained further by the conflict. Meanwhile, the money printed to finance military expenditures led to hyperinflation. The economy bounced back in the late 1960s once stability had been restored. The situation continued to improve when the oil shock in the early 1970s, which presented the country with a windfall, was well handled, unlike in some other developing countries. Oil revenues were generally well spent, on productive investments and in other ways. Some of those investments complemented early attempts to ensure there was a conducive environment for more diversification in the non-oil economy, successfully providing the impetus to boost agriculture as well as to attract foreign direct investment to labour-intensive export manufacturing.[22]

No doubt, the neighbourhood effects of the fast-growing East Asian economies such as the Republic of Korea, Taiwan, Hong Kong, and Singapore, and subsequently China and Vietnam, played a role in inspiring and nudging Indonesian policy-makers to use macroeconomic and other policy levers to maintain competitiveness.[23] And although the aftermath of the Asian crisis in 1997 contributed to political and democratic change, Indonesia's economic ascent was merely interrupted, not halted. Indonesia was, then, not quite an unwavering success story in the absolute sense, but, compared with so many other developing countries, it was a success story nevertheless.

So what can explain the underlying elite bargain that made this shift in the 1970s possible and then helped maintain it and reshape it after the Asian crisis? No doubt the events in 1965–6, in which hundreds of thousands of people died in violent purges, had traumatised society. The restoration of order, the purging of communist sympathisers, and the stabilisation of the economy brought support to Suharto across many in the elite. Nevertheless, the way by which Suharto gained power was questioned widely.

One explanation for the elite commitment in Indonesia during the early period in the 1970s may well lie, therefore, in the need for the regime to gain legitimacy with the elite and the population in general. During Sukarno's tenure, the politics of an economic nationalist ideology dominated sound economic policy-making. Not only did it keep the country impoverished, but any benefits to the elite also dried up. Newfound stability aligned the military but also the business elite, not least because from the outset of Suharto's regime, results became more important than just ideas about markets or economic nationalism. These more pragmatic policies, such as the way oil revenues were invested and the opening up to foreign investment, delivered results directly and allowed new entrants, including some from the local elite (at times working with foreign investors to pursue economic activities that contributed to growth). In turn, the success of these investments reinforced a political bargain that favoured growth-oriented policies, offering opportunities and legitimacy, and not just in the eyes of the elite, because living conditions more broadly began to improve.[24]

Although the political and economic deals favouring growth offered some Indonesians a route to increasing their wealth through productive investment, it also proved helpful to those in the elite who were more interested in investing some of the returns from economic growth in 'directly unproductive activities'. This is the euphemism introduced by the economist Jagdish Bhagwati for corruption as well as more legal forms of rent-seeking behaviour, such as protectionist policies serving only the narrow economic interests of particular firms.[25] For example, this period saw the emergence of Pertamina, the vast state-owned company that holds much of Indonesia's oil and gas interests and has at various times since the 1970s bankrolled segments of the Indonesian elite more or less legitimately. Corruption was seemingly tolerated as well. One key player of the elite, Madame Tien Suharto, wife of the president, became notoriously known as Madame Ten Percent because she reportedly took a 10 per cent cut from all large-scale government projects.[26] Despite these shortcomings, excessive long-term harm to the economy was avoided—and that requires political commitment. Over time, it required even the removal of the Suharto family, which occurred after 1997, and a move to a gradually more accountable democratic system.

Overall, then, rather than a political bargain set in stone, in Indonesia an ever-evolving political and economic deal between old and new interests emerged, balancing new activities such as export manufacturing with old structures of rent-seeking. It was not a perfect development bargain, but one that more or less worked, and in the end with sufficient commitment to ensure growth and development progressed, despite excesses such as Madame Ten Percent. Two additional features, the nature of the state's actions in dealing with the economy and the way errors were corrected, were clearly part of this bargain.

A restrained state capability

The state present in Indonesia throughout its take-off phase and more recently does not look like China's. In Indonesia, the state acted, but it did so at times by stepping aside and even passing on responsibility to outside forces.

One could argue that the leadership and elite that sustained the political deal made a sensible choice in this respect, even when it moved increasingly towards growth. By no means did Indonesia have the strong and competent state that could align itself easily to act in a determined, persistent way to drive growth and development. For that, there was too much contestation, too many different interests at play in the state. So to achieve success, the state had to withdraw relatively soon from the economy, opening up and letting market forces play a bigger role. In many ways, this is what China and Indonesia had in common: a state that appears to act in a way suitable for the realities on the ground—not too much, not too little. In China, the state could do a lot effectively; in Indonesia, much less.

In Indonesia, economic policy choices were strongly contested politically. The state itself had a strong core of technocrats, who managed to strengthen themselves by linking with international networks and organisations, but they did not act outside the political imperatives. Political pressures were at times strong, such as for economic nationalism in the form of protectionism or limits on foreign investment, especially in the 1970s or in the early period of political liberalisation after the end of the Suharto era.[27] But there is no way all those policy stances, even with the benefit of hindsight, could be called optimal. Perhaps the secret here, in the use of the state for development, was that the state did not go too far either way. If the state had tried to lead too much, it might have led to an economy that was as flawed as the state oil company, Pertamina, or that gave even more power to Madame Ten Percent and similarly connected people.

Restraint through technocrats and the IMF

Some technocratic strengths inside the state, as well as public contestation, may well have helped avoid the worst excesses, while finding a route for economic policies that worked for Indonesia and its political elite. Nevertheless, throughout the decades macroeconomic instability risked derailing the development bargain, repeatedly requiring a course correction. The biggest crisis was no doubt the deep recession that followed the Asian crisis of 1997–8—almost seven years of growth were essentially lost. And it led to the demise of the Suharto regime. Looking back, even though much has changed since the Suharto era, the crisis may not have changed the underlying development bargain so much, as growth picked up, although it was slightly lower than in the first three decades after 1967. By then, too, many interests across the economy, politics, and society appear to have been interlinked with growth and even development concerns.

How to manage this crisis was not self-evident, nevertheless. And it was also not the first time that growth had been seriously undermined by macroeconomic pressures. Correcting policy errors or responding to external shocks does not simply require economic skills from technocrats but also political support. For many countries, such crises require the assistance of the IMF. When used well, the IMF offers not just a technical fix and financial support, but also a political mechanism for restoring macroeconomic stability. As an outside agency, it can be 'blamed' politically for unwelcome but necessary policy measures when internal politics cannot credibly create the conditions for such policies. In Indonesia, the close historical links of some Indonesian technocrats to the IMF paid off in restoring macroeconomic stability. Although the role of the IMF remains an issue for debate in Indonesia, no doubt it was used there as a means of keeping the underlying development bargain on track when internal mechanisms for course correction became politically harder.

Reformist India

Since the early 1990s, India appears to have joined the ranks of these decently fast growers as well. Between 1960 and 1991, its average growth in GDP per capita was 1.8 per cent, well behind that of other rising Asian stars. Observers suggested that this 'Hindu growth rate' reflected the Hindu religion's sense of contentedness or even fatalism.[28] More commonly, it became identified with the heavily regulated and controlled economy with its limited dynamism that had characterised India since independence—the so-called Licence Raj.[29] The period was associated with trade and production licences, strict restrictions on foreign investment, and extensive import and export controls through bans, tariffs and quotas, and price controls, as well as subsidised food rations, energy and seed subsidies for farmers, a host of specific welfare schemes, and quota systems for particular groups. Such measures were based on a strong belief in the ability of the bureaucracy to control and guide the economy. They had closely related political roots as well; they were intended to keep the elite bargain, in place since independence, as stable as possible.

The elite bargain as a balancing act

When India became independent in 1947, it was an amalgamation of states and regions, each with a different colonial history and powerful local elites. The independence movement had mobilised people across societal divides, each with huge expectations that it would be their tryst with destiny as well. While embracing democratic values, politics became highly clientelist: political leaders protected vote banks across caste, religious, and regional identities, as well as pursued support and finance from traditional wealthy business or farming families. The elite bargain, locally and federally, wasn't necessarily fragile, but it needed to be fed all the time, leaving little room for changing with the times and balancing interests to avoid as much as possible lighting the wick of potentially explosive communal, caste, religious, or regional conflicts. Protectionism and controls ensured the ongoing support of wealthy family conglomerates with oligopolistic powers in the market.

This approach worked, sort of, and the Hindu growth rate was, maybe, as good as it could get. Some progress was achieved, and Indian policy-makers prided themselves on, for example, boosting food production through the green revolution in the 1970s and 1980s, thereby offering India the self-reliance it aimed for. Still, high production never means that all can afford this food, and India's limited economic progress meant it had become the country with the largest number of extreme poor (succeeding China when its growth took off); more than half of its population was below the global poverty line in the 1980s, decades after independence. More accessible than most developing countries in the world, India became synonymous with persistent poverty.

A changing economic deal in the 1990s and politics followed

While travelling around India and studying its economy, I always felt that during this period it was a country with bottled-up dynamism. When the genie was let out of the bottle, the impact was fast but also persistent for several decades, even though India was never as successful as some of the East Asian countries. From 1991 to 2019, its per capita growth rate accelerated to 4.8 per cent, a development largely attributed to the liberalisation policies first started under Finance Minister Manmohan Singh and Prime Minister Narasimha Rao. Finally, those favouring more market-based allocations had won the upper hand in the political discourse, even though many of them, including Singh, had argued for such allocations for decades.[30] In the process, they overcame a strong industrial oligopolistic business lobby that for decades had benefited from strong protectionism and the Licence Raj. Some firms adjusted successfully—and so the billionaires Mukesh Ambani and Ratan Tata remain household names. The changes also led to a rapidly expanding middle class and a nascent consumer society.

Was the shift in the elite bargain in the 1990s a decisive step towards a development bargain? I would argue yes, within the constraints of what was possible amidst the country's complexities. What is remarkable, though, is how this shift emerged. It came out of economic crisis, and the skills and role of some key reform-minded technocrats, led by Finance Minister Singh, cannot be denied. They provided the basis for the shift in the political bargain as well.

These technocratic reformists did not waste the balance of payments crisis of 1991. They used the need for an IMF programme as justification for launching a home-grown reform agenda focusing on measures such as abolition of the licensing system, encouragement of foreign direct investment, some early privatisations, and gradual trade liberalisation. The surprise was not necessarily that these policy changes were implemented. After all, India had little choice but to seek support from the IMF and commit to opening up because it was only a few weeks away from having to default on its liabilities. The real surprise was that the IMF support led over time to a shift as well in the political and economic deal in the country that has continued.

The shift in attitude towards gradual liberalisation proved to be a pivotal moment and the start, in turn, of a shift in the political deal. Earlier dominant forces in politics and the economy had settled on a mixture of economic nationalism and ideology, leading to an inward-looking economy and a state heavily involved in endless regulation and controls. That model became increasingly unsustainable in the 1980s, culminating in the crisis of 1991. The move towards a more outward orientation and market-based growth policies proved enduring through its rather fast success but also because many incumbent beneficiaries of the previous model among the business elite found their balance sheets improving, too. A telling sign that a shift in the political bargain had taken place came when the Congress Party–led government lost power in 1998. Astonishingly, the governments between 1998 and 2004 led by the usually economic nationalist Bharatiya Janata Party (BJP) did not reverse these growth-oriented policies, but gradually became strong supporters of them, no doubt encouraged by willing party funders in the business community. Finance Minister Singh appeared to have already noticed the shift by 1995, when he said that he thought the economic reforms initiated by the Congress government (of 1991) were irreversible.[31] In hindsight, it is hard to understand why these shifts were so controversial until then.

Unfinished business

Debate is always raging in India, and the subject of how successful India has been in moving towards growth and development has not been left on the sidelines. India continues to have a rather controlled economy: there are important restrictions in some sectors, encouraged by business interests keen to protect entry, not least from abroad. This is still not a state set up to quickly and forcefully contend with those pressures holding back growth and development. It is still too much captured by clientelism, delivering for specific groups in return for electoral and financial support or engaging in basic rent-seeking and corruption. And it is still a brutal economy and society, with what seems to be a large welfare state, but with huge exclusions for some highly vulnerable groups, such as tribal or lower-caste communities. Poverty remains high.

Nevertheless, its progress and the shift in its trajectory cannot be denied. Its GDP per capita since the 1990s has been similar to that of Vietnam—often considered a development success. India's number of extreme poor has more than halved in the last two decades and, as suggested in chapter 3, is on track to decline further, even if Covid-19 and the devastation of the livelihoods of groups such as migrant labourers have set back this progress. Deprivations in other dimensions are declining as well—whether child mortality or the fertility rates of women—to levels not unlike those of Indonesia. India could not have done so without a shift in the way the state functioned, within its own capabilities. Health, education, and social safety nets, such as a legal commitment to providing rural work for some days to whoever asks for it (following the National Rural Employment Guarantee Act), may have their ongoing limitations, but no doubt are offering the poor more protection, making economic change more inclusive than in preceding decades.

In India, the attitudes of those engaged in the political bargain to achieve growth have no doubt shifted, and the result is higher growth as well as better development outcomes. It remains to be seen how sustainable those attitudes will be and whether the country will be able to go beyond this take-off stage towards the global growth power to which it aspires. The Indian peacock likes to show off its majestic feathers, but underneath it is for now still a rather lightly built, spindly bird.

* * *

Although China, India, and Indonesia differ greatly in terms of political systems, societal structures, and history, all three saw their economic growth accelerate at some point over the last half-century. For all three, too, this was made possible as part of a shift in the elite bargain towards growth and development. In each of these countries, this shifting elite bargain emerged as part of a crisis—in China amidst a crisis of legitimacy, in Indonesia after civil conflict, and in India within an economic crisis that had shown the underlying economic deal to be unsustainable.[32]

None is at present a success story of the magnitude of the Asian Tigers, which today are high-income countries—and it is too soon to tell whether the dragon, the tiger cub, or the peacock ever will be. However, it is fair to say that they have succeeded in accelerating their take-off with not only rising GDP per capita, but also substantial reductions in extreme poverty and other deprivations—and China most spectacularly so. Perhaps this achievement came at the cost of other things that, in the words of Amartya Sen, 'we have reason to value', not least the ability to live with freedoms that other societies take for granted. Indonesia and India are then perhaps less spectacular in terms of growth and basic development, but they have allowed these aspirations to be cherished.

Why can't other countries manage to come at least close to emulating the successes of even their most modest comparators? My thesis is that, fundamentally, the failing countries still have elite bargains that are generally not consistent with growth and development. Much has to do with the choices they made and the political deals that sustain their power. Moreover, an awful lot can go wrong in basic economic policy-making. Often ridiculous decisions are made with big appeals to some ideology, commonly with nationalistic origins, and at times even to Karl Marx. In practice, though, economic policy-making is rarely truly like Marx but more like the Marx Brothers. Or rules and regulations supposedly enacted to foster competitive markets are actually intended to enrich the president's siblings. And so leaders and elites stumble through attempts to steer economies and end up in the abyss, or they allow their cronies to capture vast parts of the economy and suck them dry. Unfortunately, there are too many cases from recent history, or today, to discuss this category comprehensively, but examples in the chapters that follow from Malawi, Sierra Leone, the Democratic Republic of Congo, Nigeria, and South Sudan will help make the point.

References

Acemoglu, D., and J. Robinson. 2012. *Why Nations Fail*. London: Profile Books.

Ang, Y. Y. 2017. *How China Escaped the Poverty Trap*. Ithaca, NY: Cornell University Press.

Bevan, D., P. Collier, and J. W. Gunning. 1999. *The Political Economy of Poverty, Equity, and Growth*. Washington, DC: Oxford University Press and World Bank.

Bhagwati, J. N. 1982. 'Directly Unproductive, Profit-Seeking (DUP) Activities'. *Journal of Political Economy* 90 (5): 988–1002.

Dinh, Q. X. 2000. 'The Political Economy of Vietnam's Transformation Process'. *Contemporary Southeast Asia* 22 (2): 360–88.

Lal, D. 1988. *Cultural Stability and Economic Stagnation: India c1500 BC–AD 1980*, vol. 1. New York: Oxford University Press.

Lin, J. Y. 2013. 'Demystifying the Chinese Economy'. *Australian Economic Review* 46: 259–68.

Maddison, A. 2001. *The World Economy: A Millennial Perspective*. Paris: OECD Development Centre Studies.

Mukherji, R. 2008. 'The Political Economy of India's Economic Reforms'. *Asian Economic Policy Review* 3: 315–31.

Nathan, A. J. 2001. 'The Tiananmen Papers'. *Foreign Affairs* 80 (1): 2–48.

Nee, V., and S. Opper. 2012. *Capitalism from Below: Markets and Institutional Change in China*. Cambridge, MA: Harvard University Press.

Pritchett, L., K. Sen, and E. Werker. 2017. *Deals and Development*. Oxford: Oxford University Press.

Rodrik, D., and A. Subramanian. 2005. 'From "Hindu Growth" to Productivity Surge: The Mystery of the Indian Growth Transition'. *IMF Staff Papers* 52 (2): 193–228.

Vuong, Q. H. 2014. 'Vietnam's Political Economy: A Discussion on the 1986–2016 Period'. Centre Emile Bernheim Working Paper, no. 14/010, Université Libre de Bruxelles.

World Bank. 2008. *The Growth Report*. Report of the Commission on Sustainable Growth and Inclusive Development. Washington, DC: World Bank.

Xu, C. 2011. 'The Fundamental Institutions of China's Reforms and Development'. *Journal of Economic Literature* 49 (4): 1076–151.

5

HIPPOS IN THE LAKE

DEVELOPMENT ON HOLD IN SIERRA LEONE AND MALAWI

'One can only see the hippo's ears' is an African saying alluded to earlier. Too often, the state one encounters looks like a hippo. Just like the hippo's ears, only the state's formal structures are visible: government departments, courts, and a parliament. Beneath them, like the vast hippo's body, invisible though apparent to everyone, are the ethnic, personal, business, and other links with politics. Power is balanced across these networks.

Most states have features like this, even well-off and successful countries. At times, the informal, invisible structures dominate, and delivering rents to those with connections is the goal.[1] It is too easy to call this corruption, as if it were exceptional behaviour, and as if to stop it, all that's needed is a well-structured judiciary, an anti-corruption commission, or a principled senior government official. Using the state to distribute to those who support those in power is an essential feature, not deviant behaviour. It was definitely present in the Republic of Korea when it took off and in Indonesia or India. It is widespread across the world, even in quite successful countries. That said, when it becomes more dominant than other features and layers of the state and the behaviour of the elite, it will halt any take-off. Overall, such states, like hippos, seems purposeless and directionless, floating in a lake but going nowhere. Development is on hold.

In Sierra Leone and Malawi, the state in recent times seems to have acted like this hippo. Their elite bargains are based on an apparent political bargain for short-term gains by those in the elite who control the state. It is an economic deal with far less interest in creating economic growth and development than in redistributing the gains from controlling the state to the groups that happen to be in control or support those in control. The state structures in both countries are built to serve this purpose through patronage and clientelism. Leadership transitions are possible through electoral processes, but, as described in this chapter, those processes appear to function mainly as a way of simply passing control of the patronage structures from one group to another.

Both Sierra Leone and Malawi have failed to take off in recent decades. Sierra Leone managed to settle its civil war less than two decades ago. But it's hard to say it took advantage of that return to peace to move to a development bargain. If anything, Sierra Leone appears to have settled back more or less into the kind of elite bargain that held sway before the civil war that tore the country apart. For Malawi, conflict is not an excuse—it has been remarkably peaceful for at least half a century. This chapter, however, is not about success or total failure. It is more about countries that appear to have settled into low-equilibrium elite bargains that hardly point them towards some form of take-off and development. No one should expect them to become another Singapore or Republic of Korea. But surely they could have done much better.

Sierra Leone and Ebola

'I don't understand why you aid donors care so much about the poor,' said the smartly dressed governor of the Central Bank of Sierra Leone. It was May 2015, and I was in Freetown at a dinner organised by the UK High Commissioner and attended by government officials, academics, business leaders, and civil society leaders. We were discussing what to do now that the Ebola crisis seemed to be on its way out. The recent global experience with Covid-19 may make the Ebola outbreak seem insignificant, but in early 2014 it was not. Ebola began to spread from Guinea into Sierra Leone and Liberia, leading to a large-scale crisis in West Africa and a global health scare.

It shouldn't have happened. In the early days of the crisis, when exploring how aid agencies could respond, I was told by Peter Piot, the celebrated Belgian virologist and member of the team who in 1976 first identified *Zaire ebolavirus*, that it actually is hard to catch. Once it is caught, however, the vast majority of patients die. A working vaccine was not available at the start of the crisis, so it was essential to provide the public with information on how to stay safe and then quarantine anyone with the disease. Tracing and tracking cases and their contacts proved to be both an important and a successful strategy, even in relatively poor settings. The development communicator, Hans Rosling, one of the public health experts involved, captured the situation well in a later interview: public health workers and data defeated Ebola.[2]

Unfortunately, the crisis got out of hand before it got better. In Sierra Leone, 3,956 people died, and the economy came to a standstill. A huge international support operation was launched across the larger region, but that did not prevent more than 11,300 dying. In Sierra Leone, the operation also involved thousands of British military. For some, the story is that valiant outsiders came to the aid of these poor unlucky nations and, working with governments, helped to overcome this tragic health crisis.

But there are other ways of looking at the situation. As a senior official in DFID, I had a front-row seat in observing what happened not only during the crisis and its aftermath, but also in the years running up to it. In 2013, on the eve of the crisis, Sierra Leone, just like Liberia and Guinea, was a poor country, but with a GDP per capita on a par with those of Ethiopia, Rwanda, and Uganda. Sierra Leone emerged from a civil war only in 2002, but these other countries had also recently experienced violent conflicts. As regards health outcomes, however, on the eve of the crisis Sierra Leone was one of the worst places on earth. For example, it had the highest infant mortality rate in the world: one in ten children born alive died before reaching age one—or more than double the rate in Ethiopia,

Rwanda, and Uganda. The rate had barely improved since the end of the war, while across sub-Saharan Africa much progress was being made in that very same period.

After the conflict, choices were made—with the resources the government had itself, as well as with the generous aid money it had received. State structures were rebuilt in line with textbook instructions on public administration. However, the aim was not to frugally strengthen health and education services or to build the economy, but to serve those in power. Whatever the political bargain was among the elite, it was not to foster growth or development.

What follows is a brief discussion of the health system on the eve of Ebola and the way political leaders proposed rebuilding after Ebola. It is followed by an explanation of how, despite elections, the political bargain that emerged was hardly one to serve development. This is not a complete analysis, but an illustration of what happened in one unsuccessful country in recent times.

Not quite a health system

I was aware that Sierra Leone had serious problems with its health system before I travelled to the country in 2015. Just before the Ebola crisis broke, one of my students had left a posting there out of disgust with the rampant corruption in the health ministry. Too many of the health officials she had to deal with cared far more about per diems than doing any work. But these examples were just symptoms of a deeper malaise in the health system. The procurement fraud, whereby seemingly open tenders were rigged in more or less sophisticated ways, was so bad that many of the leading aid agencies had stopped funding the health ministry in the period leading up to the emergence of Ebola.[3]

A ten-year-old internal DFID report I carried with me to Sierra Leone contained statements such as 'the state has never penetrated rural Sierra Leone to a degree that would enable it to deliver goods and services' and 'the state and its offices tend to be vehicles for the social and economic advancement of individual politicians, bureaucrats and their extended networks'. Researchers and investigators also found serious shortcomings, resulting in a health system with limited effectiveness, lacking protective equipment and other supplies, and suffering from low staff morale. It's no wonder patients had little trust in the system.[4]

Ebola showed that, just like the hippo, a state like Sierra Leone may end up complicit in the deaths of a lot of people—not on purpose but as a result of collateral damage. Indeed, there is little evidence that the government did much of anything when Ebola was first reported in February 2014 in the border areas. A carefully selected public health team, with appropriate political support, could no doubt have brought the situation under control—not easily but in good time.[5] Instead, the state had made no effort to build up basic health services in the years leading up to the crisis. It wasn't that the government had no money; since the end of the civil war, it had received more aid per capita or as a share of GDP than, say, Ethiopia or Uganda.[6] But with the public health system it had, and with the leadership and incentives one could observe, it had no chance.[7] In the end, huge outside support packages from international agencies, including support from the UK military, and a massive mobilisation of local community health workers were required to bring the epidemic under control at enormous cost. Much has been written about the lessons from the international response, which was by no means faultless.[8] Nevertheless, the underlying failure of the state in using its meagre resources, including aid, to build up a health system definitely played a role.[9]

An Ebola dividend?

The epidemic peaked towards the end of 2014. When it became clear by May 2015 that the spread of Ebola was being brought under control, it felt like the right time to check with the key interlocutors in Sierra Leone on a plan for support in the post-Ebola era, even though in the end another twelve months would pass before the country was Ebola-free. The dinner at the UK High Commissioner's house described earlier was meant to be an open and informal exchange. I was keen to promote the idea of an Ebola dividend for the informal workers in the urban sector and off-farm businesses in rural areas, who, studies had shown, were those most affected by the lockdown and movement restrictions. Most formal sector firms had been able to use credit lines or continue production with clear health restrictions, so it was likely they would soon be fully operational.[10]

At that dinner, I vaguely described some things that could be done—the usual list of cash transfers, grants for micro-enterprises, boosting local health centres, basic agricultural extension services— that is, the things with decent chances of success and impacts that a government usually includes in its efforts to reach and help the poor. So the comment by the governor of the Central Bank of Sierra Leone, 'I don't understand why you aid donors care so much about the poor', surprised me. Was he just being honest? If so, it was somewhat surprising in the context of our discussion. Or could I have misunderstood what he really meant? For example, maybe he was implying that, for the poor, boosting economic growth may be the best way to help them. Therefore, using resources to build essential infrastructure or reforming the port might be a better approach to recovery, which would intellectually be a reasonable point to debate. I fear, though, this interpretation was not correct: he meant it as it sounded, or maybe even worse.

His view echoed President Koroma's. In the end, all talk of a big Ebola dividend for the poor as part of a large aid package to help these West African economies recover quickly became bogged down because of a demand by the president. He would sign on to an aid package only if he was allowed to also sign a deal to build a $318-million shiny new airport with a loan from China (adding almost 20 per cent to the country's external debt), despite serious concerns by the International Monetary Fund (IMF).[11] It is true that accessing the country was not easy, but that was largely due to geography, and the newly planned airport was not going to change that—Freetown would still be accessible only by boat from the airport. The president nevertheless had set his heart on it, and probably boosting someone else's bank balance was on offer as well. He showed little interest in anything else that could be done for the population.

Although just an anecdote, I fear this episode is representative of how politics operate in Sierra Leone and how they affect the extent to which the state is willing to go to pursue development.

It illustrates the nature of the elite bargain, which in Sierra Leone meant focusing on sharing the gains from control over the state and state structures that serve it.

A democracy, hippo-style

Sierra Leone is not an authoritarian state, even though President Koroma had claimed to possess 'supreme executive powers'. He argued that his actions as president were laws in their own right and could not be wrong or illegal.[12] Such behaviour is not unlike that of other presidents elsewhere, even in some more sophisticated and richer countries.[13] And yet since the end of its conflict in 2002, Sierra Leone has had a very lively electoral system, with active popular participation. Democracy has been flawed, and elections have by no means been perfect, but irregularities have never been thought to take the form of active ballot stuffing or falsifying voting on election day.

Meanwhile, no matter what party has been in power, it has used the state as a mechanism to offer jobs, deals, and contracts to those in business and society on whom it depends for retaining power. President Koroma and his party did in Sierra Leone what every state receiving ample aid does, whatever its intentions: it took steps to look like a respectable state. As a natural resource–rich economy, it set up an excellent natural resource regulator, the Natural Minerals Agency, with sharply defined authority, and formed in the State House a multidisciplinary and multidepartmental negotiating team for natural resource contracts. On paper, and when meeting them in their offices, I found the team quite impressive, but when it came to crucial agreements, they were out of the picture. So it was in 2015. The Tonkolili mining project, covering the third-largest iron ore deposit in the world and the largest in Africa, had been licensed to London-registered African Minerals, but the company entered into bankruptcy proceedings. In a deal also involving the Sierra Leone state, the mine was then sold to Hong Kong–based Shandong.[14] The Natural Minerals Agency and the state negotiating team had to admit that despite their legal role in these matters, no one among them ended up seeing the details of the contract beyond a small cabal around the president (which no doubt captured the goodies (rents) on offer).

Maybe even more shocking, when fighting Ebola with huge international support, the respectable Office of the Auditor General documented in January 2015 that about 30 per cent of the $9.5 million mobilised locally by Koroma's government through donations could not be accounted for.[15] Moreover, whenever he could, the president had awarded all Ebola-related contracts to a small network of businessmen, each owning several companies and allegedly with close connections to the president's All People's Congress (APC) government. And yet nothing was done about it, despite the presence of a high-profile Anti-Corruption Commission. Koroma, however, had appointed Ady Macauley, with close links to his own APC, as its head, and so no significant prosecutions were carried out. When the APC lost the presidency again to the Sierra Leone People's Party (SLPP) in 2018, a commission of inquiry began to look into the behaviour of the Koroma presidency. But it has not delved into the impact of the Ebola crisis on people's lives—just the corruption involved. Although the inquiry has generated some great headlines[16] and is likely to bring some individuals to justice, it won't change the system. That would not be in the interest of anyone close to power.[17]

Meanwhile, it now appears that President Koroma's airport plans have been scrapped by the current president, Julius Maada Bio. He is going to build a massive bridge instead, connecting the airport to Freetown. The price tag is $1.3 billion.[18] Why do I think I know what will happen next?

Poor Malawi

Compared with Sierra Leone, Malawi is a haven of peace, with no conflict since it became independent in 1965. On the economic front, its GDP per capita is well below that of Sierra Leone.[19] Nevertheless, it has managed to build up its basic health care and primary education systems, and its infant mortality rate is only half that of Sierra Leone. Just like Sierra Leone, Malawi receives large amounts of aid—in 2018 around $70 per person. Still, it is one of the poorest countries in the world—only five countries were poorer in 2018 in terms of GDP per capita (Burundi, Central African Republic, Democratic Republic of Congo, Niger, and Liberia). Well over two-thirds of its population is estimated to be living on less than $1.90 per person per day.[20]

Since its independence in 1965, Malawi has managed to grow by only 1.5 per cent in per capita terms per year, with a GDP per capita of $237 in 2010 dollars in 1964 and $517 by 2018. Compared with that of most other poor countries in this period, this growth rate is very low. This period includes a span of one-party and increasingly authoritarian rule until 1993, after which a multiparty democracy emerged. And yet in terms of per capita growth, democracy has barely made a difference—until 1993 the growth rate was 1.4 per cent and afterwards just over 1.5 per cent. In the 1990s, in discussions of democratisation through political conditionality in foreign aid, Malawi was often hailed as a success story of this policy.[21] Although there is no doubt much more openness and debate in the country now,[22] the change in the political system has not altered the elite bargain in any way. In the end, the same kinds of people are in charge, with apparently the same incentives and interests.

What follows is a look at two aspects of the policies and politics of Malawi's agricultural sector—the agricultural inputs subsidy programme and the overall policies related to the maize market—to illustrate how the interests of those with power are leading to ineffective policy-making in this key sector for growth and development. As a landlocked country with almost no natural resources, Malawi is bound to find it hard to achieve rapid, high growth. However, it takes effort of a particular kind to achieve such poor performance, not least because conflict has been largely absent.

A brief introduction to Malawi's economy and politics

Unlike Sierra Leone, Malawi does not have natural resources, and so it has no shortcut to development by exploiting them to generate capital for investment. Often, though, natural resources hinder growth, not because they are technically or economically hard to manage, but because they tend to complicate the emergence of a development bargain. As discussed in chapter 2, when a country has ample natural resources, it has much less incentive to try to pursue economic growth in its productive sectors—that is, it faces rather huge political challenges in sustaining and managing any elite bargain. In any case, any progress in Malawi will have to come from using its land and workforce as productively as possible.

Unfortunately, Malawi is not an easy country to turn into a growth miracle, even with a much better development bargain. It is largely rural with less than 20 per cent of its population living in urban areas. Most people live off agriculture, and more than 80 per cent of exports are agricultural—the lion's share is tobacco. Most farmers are smallholders, many of whom mainly grow maize for sale, although there is a large-scale commercial farming sector as well. Added to the mix are Malawi's climatic conditions, which at times are erratic, with droughts and floods rather common.

Worldwide, agriculture is typically a relatively low-productivity sector and, at best, it tends to require slow, painstaking investments both at the farm level and along the value chains to drive growth.[23] In general, there is a limit to how much productivity can be increased in agriculture relative to, for example, manufacturing. No doubt, Malawi's agricultural productivity could rise considerably. However, it would over time have to rely on other sectors as growth engines, especially to create better earnings opportunities for people. Indeed, for this reason structural transformation and the gradual shift of labour from agriculture to other sectors, such as garments or other forms of manufacturing, are a key part of development. Nevertheless, starting by pursuing growth from agriculture is no doubt sensible in Malawi.

It would be unfair to say that Malawian policy-makers have not devoted any time to pursuing an effective set of development policies for agriculture that could be integrated into an overall economic strategy. Still, it seems to be largely a part-time activity when they are not playing the other two big games in town: getting a share of the 'loot' from being part of the groups in control of the state and cleaning up the mess these games tend to create, making any well-meaning technocrats permanent crisis managers when the economy has tanked again.[24] Much of the time, the first game is played at night, in the bars of the pleasant hotels around Lilongwe or at Lake Malawi, away from the prying eyes of accountants and auditors.

At times, matters can get rather spectacularly out of hand, as happened in 2013. In-fighting among those in an embezzlement scheme run by leading politicians and civil servants turned more dramatic when an accounts assistant of the Ministry of Environment was found with thousands of dollars in his car. The situation escalated rather unexpectedly when the budget director of the Ministry of Finance was shot a week later.[25] Soon afterwards, several prominent officials and politicians were found with substantial amounts of cash in their homes. Cashgate, as it has become known, then implicated more and more people, all the way up to President Joyce Banda, as well as many around former president Bingu wa Mutharika, who had died in office and who had belonged to another party, now in opposition.[26]

In many ways, aid may have incited these wrongdoers, but it also became their undoing. The problem for the Malawian elite bargain has long been finding the loot to share. Malawi's total revenue collection is about 17 per cent of GDP.[27] While impressive,[28] it goes mainly to creating a large number of government jobs and paying for government contracts. Because the country has no natural resources and little growth, the government's treasure chest barely grows. Aid money has therefore continued to constitute a big share of the country's financial resources (around 20 per cent of GDP in recent years), especially in the form of foreign currency. For those inside government, these extra resources become too tempting to ignore.

It was a set of UK-funded audits using a new electronic financial management system that first revealed the extent of the scandal. It found that a large portion of contracts were funnelled through businesses connected to a handful of families, many with close ties to the governing People's Party of Joyce Banda. About 25 per cent of funding in government procurement could not be accounted for. There were also strong indications of false accounting, overinvoicing, and fraudulent payments, as well as of collusion between those authorising payments and the firms involved. In all, plenty of evidence emerged of fraud for personal enrichment. A Germany-funded report highlighted that the fraud went back to Bingu's rule and to many politicians who are associates of his brother, Peter Mutharika, then president, or who even served in his government.[29]

Ironically, the most prominent person prosecuted was Justice Minister and Attorney General Ralph Kasambara, who allegedly ordered the shooting because he wasn't getting a big enough share of the cash. This elite bargain was apparently just a very unsophisticated rent-sharing deal that was struggling to remain stable. However, not all schemes are as unsophisticated as the embezzlement in Cashgate. Fraud is often carried out in totally legal ways, and ways possibly even more damaging for people and the economy. Here is where maize comes in.

The politics of maize and fertiliser subsidies

White maize is the main food staple across Malawi. It is used to prepare *nshima*, a dense porridge that consists of cornflour and water. More than 90 per cent of smallholder farmers grow maize to supply maize for urban consumers or for their own consumption.

Because of the importance of maize to Malawians, it is politically important. Usually, the politics of a main staple involve maintaining a balance between supporting producers in one way or another, while keeping food prices low for consumers. The economics of maize also involve taking steps to avoid distorting the very incentives to grow, store, and trade this crop, while keeping its price low.

Keeping food prices low means that growing maize is not going to make poor smallholder farmers well-off, although most depend on this route to better lives. In other parts of the world, such as South and East Asia, the green revolution had boosted yields in ways that allow food prices to remain low but still allow farmers to raise their incomes. A few decades ago, it became clear that nothing of this kind had happened in most of Africa. Part of the problem was that science had not delivered the huge opportunities for many locally grown crops as it had for rice in Asia or wheat across the world. White maize was, however, the exception, and new hybrid seeds suitable for East African farms came onto the market, offering to double or triple yields. And yet, just as for wheat in Asia, the higher yields would typically be achieved only in favourable climatic conditions and with the addition of fertiliser and other inputs.[30]

In Malawi, where these inputs are rather expensive and the price of maize is kept low, that was a problem. It would not be profitable for all farmers to use these new seeds and fertilisers. Meanwhile, the usual solution to such a problem—credit for inputs to be paid back after the harvest—would not work because profitability was not guaranteed. The solution finally adopted was a vast programme of input subsidies. The Farmer Input Subsidy Programme, or FISP, launched in 2006, offered inputs at huge discounts.[31]

Many agricultural experts applauded the programme, seeing it as, at last, a way to have their technology toolkit adopted. Politicians loved it because it directly benefited farmers and so ensured more support from farmers in the next election. But the World Bank and many other economists were more sceptical.

Conceptually, the programme made sense. Even though it might end up distorting market prices, boosting maize production by smallholders could, beyond just a contribution to GDP, improve the nutrition of farm households; raise farmers' incomes so they could spend more on other essential goods or on their children's education and health; lower food prices, thereby improving living standards; and lower food imports, thereby saving scarce dollars for use on other essential imports. By 2007, yields were more than three times those of 2005, although admittedly the 2005 harvest was a very poor one because the rains failed. The country also did not have to beg for food aid for 5 million of its 13 million population that year. A few years later, one of the FISP champions, Jeffrey Sachs, trumpeted the success in a *New York Times* article entitled 'How Malawi Fed Its Own People'.[32] Magic beans exist, it seemed.

Equipping farmers with fertiliser and modern seeds definitely made a huge difference in production, even if at times the size of the impact has been questioned. Although the yields of 2007 have not been repeated since, compared with the period from independence to 2005, yields have been about 68 per cent higher.[33] Whether the massive subsidy was required is less clear. Other countries in the neighbourhood also saw large yield increases in this period, linked not only to a big push to use fertiliser and modern seeds, but also to clement weather for maize.[34] Early studies declared the programme in Malawi an amazing success, but this finding is now much more controversial.[35]

The expensive silver bullet

The government had promised that the Farmer Input Subsidy Programme would not just boost the incomes of farmers but also unleash a growth dynamic that would in the end see the programme pay for itself through higher tax revenue.[36] However, its overall impact on growth and on food prices has been less than anticipated. The programme proved highly expensive and probably not the best allocation of resources.[37]

No doubt FISP boosted production and probably helped with rural poverty reduction.[38] The question is: at what price? In recent years, it has boosted agricultural spending in total recurrent public spending to more than 16 per cent (one of the highest shares in the world), but up to three-quarters has gone to pay for the input subsidy programme. Although many economists applaud high spending on agriculture, it has left precious few resources for any other spending that would produce a more diversified and dynamic agricultural sector. Surely, a more diverse set of crops, some of higher value, is essential to help people escape poverty. Likewise, because of the high climate variability, diversifying into other crops or activities would be sensible. Anyone looking at similar agricultural policies will not find one anywhere else in the developing world as narrowly focused as this 'silver bullet'.

Meanwhile, once adopted, agricultural input subsidies are almost impossible to reverse politically. From day one, FISP has not been a well-targeted transfer to the poor; it goes well beyond the poorest, until recently benefiting 1.5 million of the country's 3 million smallholder farm households. Why so extensive? As noted, smallholders are politically important voters. MPs, selected by geographical constituencies, generally find it hard to connect to their voters. Their inability to deliver much is no doubt partly responsible for the high turnover of MPs at elections. In 2014, only 27 per cent of standing MPs were returned; in 2019, 32 per cent.[39] So MPs have few incentives to strip voters of any direct benefits, whether well designed or not. The government technocrats who have to find ways to construct a sensible government budget despair at the cost. However, others in the system benefit: well-connected groups can take advantage of the huge system that must be set up outside competitive market processes to procure and distribute the inputs.[40] This arrangement leads to the other side of maize politics: how those with access to power can manipulate markets to their benefit, in the process wiping out any potential benefit from the fertiliser silver bullet policy.

Muddled markets

The cost of FISP is exacerbated by the bad policy and corruption in maize marketing. Maize markets in Malawi are among the most distorted and worst-functioning on the continent, although they please politicians and maize-related businesses. Government intervention in staple food markets has long been common worldwide, for better or worse.[41] It is hard for governments not to intervene: everyone buys or sells staple foods, and they look to the state to ensure that the deal they get is fair.

Trying to manage food markets is at the best of times an almost impossible job for governments—a job that usually ends up being quite costly. Across much of southern and eastern Africa over the years, food market policy became a hotbed of inefficiency as well as corruption and patronage.

In 1989 I visited Malawi's northern neighbour, Tanzania. At the time, I was a doctoral student with plans to write my thesis on these food markets. Farmers were paid little, but urban prices were still very high, and markets were undersupplied, all features linked to inefficient and corrupt control of grain marketing. In the years that followed, most countries in Malawi's neighbourhood tried with more or less success to liberalise their markets. Nowhere have they become perfect, but private traders, large and small, are now dominating food marketing, and the costs and distortions from government marketing agencies have become much lower. In countries in the neighbourhood such as Tanzania, Uganda, and Zambia, maize remains both economically and politically important, but it is one of many crops and activities. It's no wonder I was shocked when decades later I found in Malawi that practically nothing had changed.[42]

Malawian government agencies are tasked with securing sufficient maize supplies and offering farmers and consumers decent and stable prices, complementing FISP.[43] And yet the country's food prices remain among the most unstable in Africa.[44] In fact, Malawi sought food aid or other humanitarian assistance from 2013 to 2016, and again more recently. That situation brought me back to Malawi in 2015, keen to get to the bottom of the problems at the encouragement of the minister of finance, the respected economist Goodall Gondwe.

Gondwe knew that the country's maize policy was increasingly unaffordable but worried about the impact on food insecurity if government agencies were to stop their role in maize markets.

As the story goes, Malawi's inclement weather causes this food insecurity. Drought and floods are indeed quite common. Meanwhile, the perceived wisdom is that food markets function poorly or are at best run by speculators, and so the government must come to the rescue of poor consumers and producers. Government agencies buy maize at home and abroad, paying Malawian farmers well but selling to consumers at low and stable prices. However, subsidising consumers and producers is expensive, consuming what's left of the agricultural budget after the input subsidies involved in FISP are distributed.

Once one digs a bit deeper, it becomes clear, as plenty of research has shown, that this version of Malawi's food security narrative is helpful to politicians, but it's false. In fact, the country's maize policy is deliberate chaos. Three factors are at work. First, from the viewpoint of producers, policy uncertainty exacerbates the climatic risks. Prices are in practice not supported at a decent level, and farmers cannot plan on the basis of the pre-announced prices because they are rarely honoured. One of the government agencies may buy up grain for some time, but then run out of money and stop buying. Previously, when harvests were good, prices could fall even below those in neighbouring countries because export bans were regularly imposed.[45]

Second, prices for both consumers and producers are affected by the 'surprise' tactics of government agencies. They tend to dump supplies unexpectedly in certain locations, but not on the basis of any objective triggers beyond political expediency to enhance a party favourite's chances for election or to settle a score with private traders. For a while, consumer prices may be kept low through sales, but then they are allowed to shoot up again.

Third, Malawi hardly has a productive climate for investment in trade and storage by private traders. Why would they? If traders buy grain to store and sell later, they may suddenly face a price far lower than their costs of buying and storage. In fact, research has shown that Malawi has the highest measured seasonal variability in food prices across the continent—that is, the difference in prices just after the harvest and later on in the year is the highest in Africa.[46] The government often justifies its extensive interventions by calling private traders speculators. However, it is complicit by creating a situation in which legitimate traders are turned into speculators as they have to try to second-guess what the government will do. And it has made Malawi far more food insecure than it should be by killing off all private sector investment in competitive trading and storage of any scale without offering good prices to consumers and producers. Meanwhile, the government has forced more reliance on humanitarian support, while wasting massive fiscal resources on expensive imports. A small set of players, though, seem to make handsome profits, probably using their connections to the system through procurement fraud. For example, import tenders are issued with little notice, but connected traders are warned well in advance by insiders so only they can fulfil orders on time in neighbouring countries, with handsome profits.

In 2015, the minister of finance asked me write up an analysis of Malawi's food security problem and offer concrete ideas on what could be changed so he could take them to his cabinet (I doubt, though, anything I said was news to him). I was asked to get the minister of agriculture on board, which he would arrange. Finally, we agreed that because Cashgate was raging, it would be useful to add an angle on the risks of procurement fraud and some proposals for reform.

After some further correspondence, in early 2017 I met with Minister of Agriculture George Chaponda, who agreed with my proposals. They would reform the present ad hoc system into a rule-based one. It would include decent producer prices, a commitment to consumer stability within a broad range of prices in the neighbourhood and especially incentives for private traders and storage, and an end to the procurement games. All would be undertaken in the spirit of creating more transparency, certainty, and affordability. I was not the only one who had made such suggestions,[47] but I thought the minister had at least listened and made a commitment. The next step, then, was to go to the cabinet.

A few weeks later, Minister Chaponda was sacked. Six months later, he was arrested, and bin bags full of foreign currency were found in his house.[48] His alleged crime: procurement fraud in the purchase of maize. Court documents suggest he was in cahoots with a firm importing maize from Zambia in 2016, using exactly the same tactics I had described in my analysis.[49] The memory of my conversations with him on the topic, trying to explain how procurement fraud worked, still makes me cringe. Meanwhile, no one is displaying any urgency in trying to carry out even the most basic reforms of the system that most of Malawi's neighbours undertook decades ago.

This case of corruption in Malawi is only worth mentioning because of its limited sophistication. What was worse was that the most important damage to people and their livelihoods was inflicted by totally 'legal' but terrible policies in the maize market. This is not about ignorance: I'm pretty sure all involved were aware of the costs to the economy and to the people of such economic mismanagement. And yet during that period I met with Vice President Saulos Chilima, who told me, 'From now onwards it will be different.' He suggested that Malawi simply had to find ways to better implement the new policies being designed. 'It was just a human resource issue,' he added, and DFID should help train his officials. The 'lack of discipline' of Malawians was to blame for the corrupt system, he concluded.

But this is not an issue of 'capacity-building'—a favourite solution of donors and governments of this nature alike. No training workshop will change this. Surely, the problems go much deeper.

After intervention from the Supreme Court, Malawi's presidential elections of 2019 had to be rerun. The opposition candidate, Lazarus Chakwera, won overwhelmingly. He made encouraging noises of change, but many familiar faces from earlier times appeared in his cabinet.

Malawi isn't Sierra Leone, but that isn't good enough

In Malawi, politics have been reduced to a game of very basic distributive actions. Whether jobs for those connected, tailored advantages for certain businessmen or areas, or the politics of subsidised rations for particular constituencies or towns—all are signs of politicians and the state trying to capture rents for distribution to specific groups. In their zero-sum game, they treat the economy as a fixed asset to be captured and not something that should grow, even if only to ensure the scope for larger rents and development in the future. As a result, at times they seem content to suck all the potential out of the economy and the state.

That said, Malawi may not be perfect, but some may argue that the glass is definitely half full. Just look at the health and sanitation indicators. They have been doing well and are on a par with those of some of the more successful countries in the neighbourhood. For me, though, the glass is definitely half empty—this country is much poorer than it should be.

That said, it is not failing as badly as Sierra Leone seems to be. For comparison's sake, one only has to look at some of the requirements for moving towards a development bargain: peace and stability, an elite commitment in support of growth and development, and a state willing and able to act to support both. The scores of both countries are rather weak, but Sierra Leone is clearly the weaker. As for peace and stability, Sierra Leone may be stable at the moment, but it has enjoyed less than two decades of peace. Malawi, despite a relatively minor hiccup in recent years, is very peaceful and stable. As for the political and economic deals, both states appear to fail because their elite in business, politics, and society have conveniently remained in an elite bargain that serves them but without a commitment to growth and development. There is, then, no development bargain.

Finally, in terms of state capability, Sierra Leone has clearly failed in its willingness and ability to act, such as in developing services. Malawi could surely have done better, but at least its basic health and education services appear to function rather well, even if much of that is more attributable to outside support than a dedicated state. In both countries, political transitions have occurred over the last few years, and Julius Maada Bio in Sierra Leone and Lazarus Chakwera in Malawi are declaring that they seriously want change. Time will tell whether they can reconfigure the elite bargain, and I hope to be surprised.

In the next chapter, three other countries whose state structures resemble the hippo appear to be moving towards something much better. Even with all their imperfections, they show this is possible.

References

Africa Confidential. 2013. 'Shooting Triggers Reshuffle'. 54 (21): 9.
_____. 2016a. 'Iron Man'. 57 (20): 12.
_____. 2016b. 'Stuck at the Airport'. 57 (4): 12.
_____. 2016c. 'Unending Flow of Cashgate'. 57 (16): 4–6.
_____. 2017a. 'Mutharika's Uncertain Future'. 58 (20): 7–8.
_____. 2017b. 'Mutharika's Woes Look Terminal'. 58 (6): 10–11.
_____. 2018. 'A Bridge Too Far'. 59 (18): 12.
_____. 2019. 'Koroma's Record on Trial'. 60 (7): 6–8.
_____. 2020. 'Koroma Probe Risks Backlash'. 60 (21): 10–11.
Banik, D., and M. Chasukwa. 2019. 'The Politics of Hunger in an SDG Era: Food Policy in Malawi'. *Food Ethics* 4: 189–206.
Bratton, M., and N. van de Walle. 1994. 'Neopatrimonial Regimes and Political Transitions in Africa'. *World Politics* 46 (4): 453–89.
Cheeseman, N., E. Bertrand, and S. Husaini. 2019. *A Dictionary of African Politics*. Oxford: Oxford University Press.
Chinsinga, B., and C. Poulton. 2013. 'Beyond Technocratic Debates: The Significance and Transience of Political Incentives in the Malawi Farm Input Subsidy Programme (FISP)'. *Development Policy Review* 32 (2): 123–50.
Chirwa, E., and A. Dorward. 2013. *Agricultural Input Subsidies: The Recent Malawi Experience*. Oxford: Oxford University Press.
Clapham, C., ed. 1985. *Private Patronage and Public Power*. London: Frances Pinter.

Clarke, D. J., and S. Dercon. 2016. *Dull Disasters? How Planning Ahead Will Make a Difference*. Oxford: Oxford University Press.

Crawford, G. 2000. *Foreign Aid and Political Reform: A Comparative Analysis of Democracy Assistance and Political Conditionality*. New York: Palgrave.

Dabalan, A., A. de la Fuente, A. Goyal, W. Karamba, and T. Tanaka. 2016. *Pathways to Prosperity in Rural Malawi*. Washington, DC: World Bank.

Denning G., P. Kabambe, P. Sanchez, A. Malik, et al. 2009. 'Input Subsidies to Improve Smallholder Maize Productivity in Malawi: Toward an African Green Revolution'. *PLOS Biology* 7 (1): e1000023.

Dercon, S., and D. Gollin. 2014. 'Agriculture in African Development: Theories and Strategies'. *Annual Review of Resource Economics* 6: 471–92.

Dorward, A., E. Chirwa, V. Kelly, T. Jaynem, R. Slater, and D. Boughton. 2008. 'Evaluation of the 2006/2007 Agricultural Input Supply Programme, Malawi'. Food Security Collaborative Working Paper 97143, Department of Agricultural, Food, and Resource Economics, Michigan State University.

DuBois, M., and C. Wake, with S. Sturridge and C. Bennett. 2015. 'The Ebola Response in West Africa: Exposing the Politics and Culture of International Aid'. HPG Working Paper, ODI, London.

Ejeta, G. 2010. 'African Green Revolution Needn't Be a Mirage'. *Science* 327 (5967): 831–2.

Gilbert, C. L., L. Christiaensen, and J. Kaminski. 2017. 'Food Price Seasonality in Africa: Measurement and Extent'. *Food Policy* 67: 119–32.

Global Fund. 2015. 'Investigation Report of the Global Fund Grants to Sierra Leone'. GF-OIG-14-005, Office of the Inspector General, Global Fund, Geneva.

Harrigan, J. 2003. 'U-Turns and Full Circles: Two Decades of Agricultural Reform in Malawi 1981–2000'. *World Development* 31 (5): 847–63.

Jayne, T. S. 2012. 'Managing Food Price Instability in East and Southern Africa'. *Global Food Security* 1 (2): 143–9.

———, and S. Rashid. 2013. 'Input Subsidy Programs in Sub-Saharan Africa: A Synthesis of Recent Evidence'. *Agricultural Economics* 44: 547–62.

McArthur, J.W., and G. C. McCord. 2017. 'Fertilizing Growth: Agricultural Inputs and Their Effects in Economic Development'. *Journal of Development Economics* 127: 133–52.

Messina, J., B. Peter, and S. Snapp. 2017. 'Re-evaluating the Malawian Farm Input Subsidy Programme'. *Nature Plants* 3 (17013).

Ochieng. D. O., R. Botha, and B. Baulch. 2019. 'Structure, Conduct and

Performance of Maize Markets in Malawi'. MaSSP Working Paper 29, International Food Policy Research Institute, Lilongwe, Malawi.

Pieterse, P., and T. Lodge. 2015. 'When Free Healthcare Is Not Free: Corruption and Mistrust in Sierra Leone's Primary Healthcare System Immediately Prior to the Ebola Outbreak'. *International Health* 7 (6): 400–4.

Quiñones, M. A., N. E. Borlaug, and C. R. Dowswell. 1997. 'A Fertilizer-Based Green Revolution for Africa'. *Replenishing Soil Fertility in Africa* 51: 81–95.

Ricker-Gilbert, J. E., and T. Jayne. 2017. 'Estimating the Enduring Effects of Fertilizer Subsidies on Commercial Fertilizer Demand and Maize Production: Panel Data Evidence from Malawi'. *Journal of Agricultural Economics* 68 (1): 70–97.

Said, J., and K. Singini. 2014. 'The Political Economy Determinants of Economic Growth in Malawi'. Working Paper Series, Esid-040-14, Global Development Institute, University of Manchester.

6

KENYA, UGANDA, AND GHANA

READY FOR TAKE-OFF?

It was 30 December 2007, in Nairobi, Kenya. In the State House, President Mwai Kibaki had just been hurriedly sworn in for his second term. The State House, though, was not very stately; staff and journalists were running around while he spoke. The initial election results had pointed to another outcome, but with no official results published, the Election Commission had only minutes earlier declared Kibaki winner of the presidential election held three days previously. Meanwhile, outside smoke could be seen rising from the Mathare and Kibera slums, where ethnic Luo and other supporters of opposition candidate Raila Odinga were targeting Kikuyu supporters of the president. In the riots, killings, and looting that continued for weeks across the country, about 1,300 people died. And before peace was restored, much damage was inflicted, not only on property but also on Kenya's reputation as a stable business destination in Africa.

Ethnic tensions had been expected, even though the economy had been performing considerably better during Kibaki's first five-year term—GDP per capita had grown by an average of 2.6 per cent a year after two decades of stagnation. With this outcome in mind, I decided to use this election as an opportunity to study how voting may balance ethnicity and economic performance. My team collected data across the country in the weeks preceding the election.[1]

Just like all opinion polls, our survey data showed, contrary to the final results, that Raila Odinga would convincingly beat the incumbent.[2] Our data also revealed that three-quarters of the population would vote strictly along ethnic lines. So the Kikuyu and Meru voted for Kibaki, and the Luo, Kalenjin, and most Luhya voted for Odinga. Likewise, other groups lined up behind their candidates. This was not a matter of the poor not understanding the importance of voting for their livelihoods because, in fact, the wealthy and educated also voted along ethnic lines. In reality, the president's performance did not matter. Most voters gave Kibaki positive approval ratings on economic and government management for his term in office, but ethnic preference dominated all voting.

The crisis was resolved only after the violence made headlines across the world for weeks. In the end, high-level international attention and mediation put a stop to the impasse and violence.[3] By the end of February, Kibaki and Odinga had struck a deal,[4] but bickering continued until agreement was reached in April that Kibaki would serve as president and Odinga as prime minister, and the cabinet would be composed of representatives of all the main parties. Meanwhile, no senior leaders were ever held to account for their role in inciting the violence, however hard it was to deny their involvement. The International Criminal Court in The Hague brought charges against six very senior politicians, but after a few years the charges were dropped, including those against Uhuru Kenyatta, currently Kenya's Kikuyu president, and William Ruto, its Kalenjin deputy president.

The 2007–8 electoral crisis in Kenya erupted in the kind of ethnic violence so often identified with Africa. In truth, politics in many African countries have a strong ethnic dimension. Its roots are not simply a blind, deep-seated hatred or grievances, as though ethnicity is a long-time, hard-wired identity. Rather, it is largely a social construct, exploited historically by colonial rule as well as by present-day politicians.[5] The data bear this out. In studies in a range of African countries, the proportion of people that identify first and foremost by their ethnic group rather than by class or religion is typically (only) about a third, but it is substantially higher at election time.[6]

In Kenya, as well as across Africa and elsewhere, ethnicity is exploited to gain political power. However, to be credible as a strategy, it also requires finding ways to reward those who give their support, and so ethnic-based clientelism becomes the order of the day. In Kenya, clientelism has since independence come at a great cost. For all the benefits of Kenya's location and opportunities at independence, it has underperformed in growth and development. Indeed, the state and those that captured it served themselves and small groups belonging to their ethnicity far more than the people in general, and so the effectiveness of the state has been compromised.

This chapter takes a closer look at not just Kenya but also Uganda and Ghana—countries that also have struggled at times with the political deal needed for peace and stability, and where favouritism, patronage, and clientelism, at least partly built on ethnic politics, have prevailed for much of recent decades. But the picture that emerges is not a grim one because much that is positive can be said about what has been achieved and the opportunity that lies ahead. This is, then, not just a story about various failures, as the previous chapter's stories on Malawi and Sierra Leone were, but also one about how change is possible.

Kenya: The missed opportunity is finally arriving?

Kenya's economic performance since independence in 1964 can only be described as lacklustre, involving growth of about 1.5 per cent per capita a year on average. The country got off to a good start, with relatively solid annual growth of more than 3 per cent per capita on average until 1980. However, that period was followed by a dark economic one lasting more than two decades, when the economy on average shrank. Over the last decade, growth has climbed back to around 3 per cent per capita a year on average. Poverty and other indicators of deprivation increased during these decades of stagnation, although the last two decades have seen considerable improvement.[7] And yet more than a third of the population still lives in extreme poverty, even though in health and education outcomes Kenya ranks among the better performers in the region.

Despite its decades of economic stagnation, it would be unfair to call Kenya's performance an exceptional failure during that period when compared with sub-Saharan Africa as a whole or with neighbouring countries such as Tanzania, Sudan, Uganda, and Ethiopia.[8] Rather, it always seemed to have more potential. It had gained independence with GDP levels not very different from countries such as Thailand and Indonesia, and even by 1980 it was far better off than Vietnam. It also enjoyed a coastal location, servicing the neighbouring countries by means of its port and rail and road networks. It has maintained a dynamic private sector with strong links to Asia and an economy that has stayed relatively open and market-oriented.[9] And to a lesser extent than other countries, it had not been affected by ideologically inspired poor policy-making as in Tanzania, or by conflict as in Ethiopia or Uganda.

Ethnic politics holding development for ransom

Ethno-politics have seriously undermined Kenya's economic and development potential since independence. Soon after independence, President Jomo Kenyatta consolidated his power in the executive and built it as a source of patronage in the civil service and state-owned enterprises, mainly for his own Kikuyu support base. After he died in 1978, power passed to his vice president, Daniel arap Moi, who became a more autocratic leader until defeated by Kibaki in 2002. Because the interests of the Kikuyu lay in agricultural exports, economic growth had remained healthy until Moi's ascendance. Moi was part of the Kalenjin ethnic group, a poorer group dependent on food crop production, and this clearly played a role in Moi's efforts in the 1980s to promote food production at the expense of agricultural export interests to favour his own tribe.[10] Meanwhile, despite rather strong manufacturing capabilities[11] linked to firms owned by Asian families who had settled decades earlier, both leaders undermined their emergence because economic progress outside their control might have upset their own political game, leaving Asian interests largely focused on trade.[12] It's no wonder, then, that when possible growth engines are repressed, economic growth is quashed as well.

The most visible way in which politics undermined development was the endless corruption scandals, most likely just the hippo ears of the more systematic ways in which the state was enriching those in control. Two corruption scandals stand out.

One was the Goldenberg scandal. In its quest to get its hands on foreign currency, in the 1990s the Kenyan government offered incentives to sell gold on the international market through a government scheme rather than by smuggling. It would pay a vast premium in local currency for such gold exports by offering an exchange rate that was a third better than the official one. Such schemes are not uncommon in other countries to discourage smuggling from local gold mines, but Kenya has not much gold to mine itself. Instead, vast quantities were smuggled into Kenya from Zaire (now the Democratic Republic of Congo), clearly with the support of powerful political figures, to profit illegally from the subsidy scheme. Those accused later of involvement were largely family members and friends of President Moi, as well as political rivals, all of whom pocketed many millions of dollars between them.

The second case, the 1997 Anglo Leasing scandal, was a more classic procurement fraud surrounding a contract for printing passports and involving very senior politicians and officials. Millions of dollars in bribes were paid by a British firm to win the contract, thereby defeating the far more competitive bid of a French firm.

Corruption scandals come to mind in any contemplation of the nature of Kenyan politics. The scale reflects a political deal about using the state for profit. Ethnic politics add another dimension: the power to control the state derives from ethnic clientelism—that is, delivering for the tribe. This form of redistributive politics then leads to misallocation: resources are not spent where they are most needed or where the return to the benefit of development is the highest. Instead, resources are allocated according to the preferences of the political support base. In few other developing countries is the evidence so clear on the extent to which public resources disproportionately flow along ethnic lines, such as spending on road infrastructure or education.[13]

Post-2010: Is it now everyone's turn to eat?

'It is impunity that keeps Kenya back.' His voice booming, John Githongo stared straight at the assembled cameras. It was May 2008, and he was speaking as part of a public discussion in a small conference room in Nairobi. I was on the same panel, together with a few other colleagues from Oxford, presenting our research on electoral violence and the political challenges. There was no doubt why the cameras were there: to capture Githongo, who had recently returned from exile in the UK. From 2003 to 2005, Githongo had served as the permanent secretary of governance and ethics. He was brought in by President Kibaki to fight corruption, but when he dug into the Anglo Leasing scandal, he came up against powerful forces and left Kenya in fear for his life.

The impunity noted by Githongo penetrated all aspects of how politics operated in Kenya. For example, not one of the senior politicians implicated in the Goldenberg and Anglo Leasing corruption scandals was punished, and in the 2008 electoral violence, the International Criminal Court tried to bring prosecutions but in the end to no avail. Impunity applied as well to mismanagement of the state, which was riddled with fraudulent deals with connected firms, keeping the nation far poorer than it should have been. In the title of her book on Githongo's efforts to combat corruption, *It Is Our Turn to Eat,* Michela Wrong aptly caught the attitudes of politicians when capturing power.[14]

A few years earlier, there had been much more optimism. After ten years of multiparty but deeply divided democracy, the opposition to President Daniel arap Moi managed to unify behind Moi's former vice president, Mwai Kibaki, as presidential election candidate. He won convincingly as part of a coalition made up of leaders with different ethnic bases. Meanwhile, there was hope that with democracy would come more accountability. But that didn't quite happen. Not only did the coalition fall apart a few years later, but it also set the stage for further polarised political competition, pitching the Kikuyu Kibaki against the Luo Raila Odinga in 2007, resulting in post-electoral violence.

Some things have changed since then, however. The last decade and a half has seen faster economic growth than during the preceding four decades, albeit with much variability often linked to occasional political turmoil. The current government, led by Uhuru Kenyatta (Jomo Kenyatta's son) since 2013, appears to be more interested in manufacturing and development areas such as health and food security.[15] However, any optimism must be tempered because implementation has never been a strong suit of the Kenyan state. The results, then, are not that striking but still better than before—Kenya, just like the rest of East Africa, is outperforming most of sub-Saharan Africa.

And yet Kenya's economy has been performing well in recent years despite the state and politics, not because of it. The data hardly show a real acceleration of growth and development. Even though Kenya's macroeconomy remained quite stable before Covid-19, little private or public investment is occurring,[16] and the promised boost in manufacturing and a transformation of the economy are not materialising.[17] This would require a much more long-term horizon from politicians than currently on offer. Similarly, progress in poverty reduction is slow, and 18 million people, or more than a third of the population, are still living in extreme poverty. Nevertheless, the potential is there. Kenya's infrastructure and human capital are of somewhat better quality than those of most of its neighbours.[18] As long as one knows how to operate in Kenya, there are plenty of opportunities, and it remains the most dynamic economy in its East African neighbourhood.[19]

Another reason for hope is that 2010 saw approval of a new constitution. The move was an attempt to change at least some of the incentives for the most ruthless aspects of ethnic politics by devolving more powers to Kenya's 47 counties. Under the previously strong centralisation of power in the executive, political competition was an extreme form of 'winner-take-all'. With decentralisation, more resources are controlled at the local level because at least 15 per cent of revenue is now earmarked for services delivery at the county level. This change thus offers an opportunity for more results-based politics, with additional accountability at the local level. More likely, however, it will first decentralise patronage: a politician may fail to gain power in national elections, but as long as a local base exists, there will still be resources to control and distribute, unlike before. Now, there is a way for everyone to eat.[20]

Will these reasons for hope take the sting out of ethnic politics? It is obviously not the same as the emergence of an elite bargain promoting growth and development. Some observers suggest politics still use the same rulebook. The 2017 presidential election was a case in point. Perhaps more peaceful but hardly less eventful, in the end it led to Kenyatta's re-election after a rerun ordered by the Supreme Court.[21] As I write this, the jockeying for the 2022 elections has all the elements of ethnic polarisation.[22] I am more hopeful that the rulebook has begun to change: this decentralisation has affected the 'rules of the game', changing the underlying incentives for engaging in politics. Allowing 'everyone to eat' is clearly expensive, as new layers of management and delivery have to be created. Over time, however, it may lead to political competition that focuses more on outcomes in the economy and as a result of development.[23] On balance, therefore, I am hopeful that conditions are emerging for an elite bargain that favours growth and development.

For now, the State House, the president's residence, remains a fortress on a hill to be captured by those not in control and kept under control at all cost by the incumbent. Kenya's state structures remain neopatrimonial, built on patronage and clientelism, with coexisting informal norms and formal structures. It is not clear to what extent the state is relevant; the economy seems to perform well without and despite State House. The 2010 constitution and the Supreme Court intervention in 2017 suggest, however, that optimists like me should have hope because formal rules may constrain the informal and personalised drivers of clientelism that feed instability, and promote more effective government nationally and locally.[24] One day, the political stars may align to fulfil Kenya's potential. But for the moment the nature of Kenyan politics ensures that the country remains far too poor and the lives of its citizens remain far too hard.

Uganda: Diminishing development returns to presidential terms?

If in Kenya formal rule changes appear to have been used to find ways of resolving ethnic as well as personal rivalries, in Uganda they largely appear to have been used to keep the president in power as long as possible. In both cases, they may have contributed to stability. President Yoweri Museveni came to power in 1986 after his forces captured Kampala and put an end to a bloody regime and a civil war that had raged since 1981. Even though competing parties were banned, he stood for and won election in 1996, based on a new constitution that had both a term limit and an age limit. Both limits he managed to reverse, the two-term limit in 2005 and the age limit in 2017.

Sensible policy-making led to a remarkably successful period of growth, starting in 1986. One could give Museveni credit for allowing this, although it was not without self-interest. If in Kenya constitutional change may gradually dislodge the short-term horizon implied by patronage and clientelism, in Uganda the personal political manoeuvring by Museveni has had a more long-term horizon, almost as though he has always had in mind remaining president for life. Despite persistent clientelism and the question of Museveni's political legitimacy, this longer-term horizon has helped growth and development. He may have foreseen the need for good economic management and economic growth in view of the high cost of politics.

Since 1986, economic progress has never been spectacular, but it has continued to be solid in view of the preceding decade of conflict and decline. From 1986 to 2019, the economy grew persistently and with remarkable stability, averaging 2.7 per cent per capita a year. From 1986 to 2011, average growth of 3.1 per cent per capita a year was achieved. In short, GDP per capita doubled in less than a quarter of a century.

Development outcomes have also improved in Uganda. In fact, although in 1990 one in ten children born alive would not survive beyond age one—roughly equal to the average in sub-Saharan Africa and much worse than in neighbouring Kenya[25]—Uganda outperformed the rest of the continent and caught up with Kenya in 2018. By then, one in thirty children would not reach age one in Uganda, almost the same as in Kenya, compared with one in twenty in sub-Saharan Africa. Much progress has been made on other indicators as well: extreme poverty has fallen over the last two decades, from about 60 per cent of the population to about 40 per cent. Although still high, it is nevertheless a considerable improvement.[26] This is not a performance that elevates a country to the success category, and yet it is worth noting, not least to highlight how progress is still possible in a state built on patronage.

The cost of politics

It is a caricature to suggest that much of the politics in Africa is just about the presence of a 'Big Man', and then for this man to either loot the state or, on rare occasions, become an enlightened leader.[27] Even if much of President Museveni's story appears to be about a Big Man, maintaining control of the state is in practice hard work for him and his entourage.

After thirty-five years in power, Museveni is still a popular leader. He has been elected six times—first in 1996 and then in 2001 during the days of the 'no-party' democracy, when candidates could stand but no parties could be built up to challenge the incumbency of the president's National Resistance Movement (NRM). Since 2015, however, parties have been allowed to support presidential candidates as well. Even so, Museveni has won by handsome majorities.

Museveni does not leave anything to chance when it comes to getting elected—but merely stuffing ballot boxes is not his style. He and his supporters have, in addition, put a lot of effort into disrupting opposition politics, using violent harassment, arrests, legal constraints, and more to prevent opposition leaders from building up a party machinery and a large base. Nevertheless, it would be wrong to describe Uganda as simply a deeply repressive, security-led state. Public debate has continued to be relatively open, with freedom of expression, and building broad popular support remains important for the president.

Museveni's political skills appear to have been far more tested in keeping his own movement, the NRM, together. One of its strengths is its 'big tent' focus, bringing together elites from business and politics with various regional and ethnic backgrounds. But keeping the show on the road for decades and ensuring Museveni is the undisputed leader have proved to be expensive. Because of a very leaky NRM leadership and a quite open press, a lot more is known now about the cost of politics in Uganda. For example, MPs, despite being elected from his NRM, appear to expect payment for their votes in support of the president's policies. Reportedly, they were paid $3,000 each to vote for extending the presidential term limit in 2005, almost $2,000 each to vote for a controversial marriage and divorce bill in 2013, and at least $5,000 (some have suggested $30,000) each to halt a former prime minister from challenging Museveni for the NRM leadership in 2015. The price tag to remove the presidential age limit was allegedly up to $80,000 per MP.[28] Meanwhile, amassing the votes needed for election is also expensive: tens of millions were spent just on the campaign, and much more was paid to mobilise local NRM organisers.[29]

Given the usual perception of African politics, there is something remarkable about all this. Because Museveni is fully in control of the country's security services, he could have resorted to far more repressive ways of exercising power. The political deal he has settled on also involves considerable legitimacy-seeking behaviour in following (some) rules and, especially, in seeking popular approval.

For this to work politically as an elite bargain, an economic deal with a long-term horizon was needed—an economic deal that would ensure the resources were there to both pay for the rising cost of politics within Museveni's movement and keep people voting for him.[30] And this is where growth and development come in, not quite as part of a full-fledged development bargain, yet with aspects that at least look like it. How this was achieved is discussed next.

The role of economic management

Emmanuel Tumusiime-Mutebile, the imposing governor of the Central Bank of Uganda, spoke softly. It was 2015, and we were discussing the public finances of the country, which, as ever, were slightly precarious. I told him I was struck by how cautious the

Finance Ministry was about government spending, even though oil had been discovered a decade previously, and the country was moving closer to actual production deals. He said the government could not just assume that oil would flow soon. Meanwhile, to avoid derailing the economy, 'we will have to leave some money for the President for next year'.

Elections were looming in 2016, and the president would want to spend freely, even though it was absolutely clear he would win them. Mutebile wanted to avoid at all cost what happened in the 2011 election period when there was an explosion in spending, financed by his Central Bank, essentially through printing money. The resulting crisis led to the highest inflation rate in decades and other economic imbalances. In fact, only a year before our meeting Mutebile had publicly berated the president for making him do this.[31] He could do so only because the president owed him much.

Mutebile was one of a small group of excellent technocrats and civil servants who made possible Uganda's growth and development. A career civil servant and economist, he became the top official in the Ministry of Finance in 1992 before becoming governor of the Central Bank in 2001. With a few others, he was instrumental in enacting sound macroeconomic policies when it mattered most, in the 1990s. With security returning, this group stabilised inflation and cut export taxes and other harmful price distortions, thereby creating a market- and investment-friendly environment.[32] They also strengthened the influence and reputation of key ministries involved in growth and development, from the Central Bank to the Finance Ministry, thereby offering a valuable restraining factor in the public sector and avoiding derailment.[33] The fact that this has been sustained, with occasional bumps in the road, is remarkable.

Since the 1990s, the chosen route to a growing economy has been a strong commitment to market-based allocation—that is, without trade taxes or endless licences and without extensive government intervention. This commitment has at least removed some sources of the kind of patronage-based distortions one still observes in, for example, Malawi. Uganda's economic policy is in general strongly based on laissez-faire, allowing liberalised markets to provide incentives and giving the state only a limited role in the economy.

'Museveni is the last believer in the Washington Consensus,' I was told by the representative of the International Monetary Fund (IMF), who was surprisingly dismayed by Museveni's stance.[34]

This approach to growth has proved to be rather successful. From its days as a conflict economy plundered through misrule, Uganda has been able to gradually attract much new investment in many sectors, including foreign capital through the many Asian family firms with historical links to the country and region. An inventory of subsectors with growth potential found newer export products such as fish and cut flowers, as well as investments in plastics and metal products.[35] The northern city of Lira, for example, located in a once-backward, neglected region bearing the scars of conflict, is now a rather dynamic area with promising investments by small and medium-size firms in agricultural processing and value chains. Many of these growing or newer firms willingly support Museveni's NRM with financial resources, but there is little evidence they are bullied into doing so.[36] It is a great marriage of convenience.

The discovery of substantial oil reserves just over a decade ago has also not derailed the government's approach to growth. Rather than moving towards rapid exploration and cashing in quickly to buy off cronies, the president assigned some of his best government officials to negotiate a good deal for Uganda with the relevant French, British, and Chinese companies. Even though it took much longer than expected for oil to be exported and revenues to flow, most agree that Ugandan officials deserve credit for avoiding mostly what so often has been observed in other countries—natural resource discoveries leading to spending and corruption bonanzas.[37]

Uganda today is by no means an undisputed development success story, but it has come a long way. In the early 1980s, with political turmoil and conflict raging, few would have thought such progress possible. This is still a country with endemic corruption linked to patronage and expensive and exclusionary politics. Economic growth has been reasonably good, and development indicators have improved, even though not by as much as may have been hoped for. Nevertheless, a long-term political horizon favouring growth and development may emerge in places, even within political and economic deals that are also focused on rents and on maintaining political control.

Ghana: A development success story?

'This is the first time I've seen my husband cooking.' His two other wives laughed loudly when Ibrahim's senior wife shouted this at us. Ibrahim giggled when he translated her remark while the three of us were struggling to cook the butter squash, our gift to them, in the large pot over the open fire in the cooking area of the courtyard. I was travelling in northern Ghana with a colleague from DFID in 2012, and we were staying in his old friend Ibrahim's modest house in Gupanarigu, a village not too far from Tamale, the capital of northern Ghana.

Besides being a farmer, Ibrahim worked hard at many odd jobs, including putting the English he had learned at school and his personal charm to good use. It paid for his children's secondary education, for his phone, and for the nice colourful clothes his family were wearing. His children's lives were definitely much better than what his parents were able to offer him. He lived in a poorer part of Ghana, harsher in climate and farther away from the better-off cities in the south. But much has improved. Despite having failed to get a place in a teacher training course and being turned down for a government job in emergency management, Ibrahim has not allowed his ambition to be checked. Some more progress may still be in store for him because he was chosen on merit to be the local party organiser for the New Patriotic Party, which gained power in the 2016 elections and retained it in 2020.

Over the last two decades, Ghana has begun to fulfil the promise it had at independence. Independence hero Kwame Nkrumah was a better political strategist than economist. His quest for rapid industrialisation and state-run agriculture clearly failed, and by the time he was removed by a coup in 1966 the economy had shrunk considerably. More economic turmoil linked to mismanagement followed, and by 1983 GDP per capita was a third lower than it had been in 1960. It would in fact take until well into the twenty-first century for GDP per capita to recover to levels around independence.[38]

The turnaround since 1983 has been remarkable but not spectacular. Among African economies, it would be fair to say that Ghana crashed first, but managed to turn around its economy earlier than most. Until about 2007, it saw initially modest and somewhat disappointing growth rates of about 2 per cent per capita. In the last decade, this has accelerated to a much more solid level of 4.3 per cent per capita, partly but not exclusively helped by rents from the launch of oil and gas exploration.

Ghana's growth has delivered considerable poverty reduction. In fact, extreme poverty data suggest Ghana has done far better than Kenya. In the 1990s, the measured rates were rather similar. In 2015–16, Kenya's poverty rate remained high at about a third of the population, whereas Ghana's level reached 13 per cent of the population.[39] When it comes to non-monetary indicators, such as in health and education, Kenya and Ghana are at similar levels, both showing considerable progress in recent few decades.

Still, there is reason to consider Ghana more successful now than Kenya. This is not just a judgement on economic growth rates in the last decade. More important, it is Ghana's ability to find a political model that is less captured simply by ethnicity or even patronage, and shows signs of more results-based politics. Ghana found an economic model that matches its circumstances as well. And even though there is still plenty of patronage, clientelism, corruption, and inefficiency in the functioning of the state, the state may well be more and more in line with a development bargain.

A fickle democracy

From the 1960s to the 1980s, a large number of African countries turned into one-party states or succumbed to military regimes, often against the backdrop of the Cold War. Conflict and political instability were common. Most economies also collapsed in the 1980s, and pressure for multiparty democracy increased, not least with the demise of the Soviet Union.

Ghana experienced all of this, and much earlier than most. Nkrumah's one-party state collapsed in 1966 as a result of a military coup, and much turmoil followed. A further military coup by Jerry Rawlings in December 1981 brought military rule but stabilised politics. In 1992 multiparty democracy was restored. Rawlings became an elected president based on broadly free and fair elections. The ruling Provisional National Defence Council (PNDC) party set up in 1982 became the National Democratic Congress (NDC) party, with the president at the helm. Since then, elections have been held every four years.

But what makes Ghana different is not repeated elections. It is the way they are fought, the acceptance of the rules of the game by the participants, and the acquiescence of those defeated in the results.[40] Rawlings did not try to change the two-term limit, and his party accepted defeat in 2000 by John Kufuor's New Patriotic Party (NPP). That party in turn accepted defeat by the NDC in 2008. More recently in 2016, the sitting president, John Mahama, lost to the NPP's Nana Akufo-Addo. Transitions of power have been peaceful and rather dignified.

There is no doubt that the PNDC's move to multiparty democracy came not simply from deep love of that system of government, but had as much to do with the need for continued international finance to keep Ghana going.[41] Now, though, Ghana has begun to look more like many young but relatively stable democracies. Politics are still based on patronage and clientelism: power delivers jobs, contracts, and more, and even government officials estimate that billions are lost through procurement fraud and other misdemeanours.[42] As other examples have shown, such behaviour is not uncommon in election-based systems. However, three features of Ghanaian politics stand out. First, ethnicity, despite strong historical roots, is not the defining feature of how politics are conducted or voters behave, even if the two parties are relatively stronger among certain ethnic groups or regions.[43] Second, the voters are demanding, and they are clearly willing to vote according to actual or likely performance, for example, in contrast to voting by ethnic allegiance in Kenya.[44] Third, the voters are fickle: they want politicians to deliver, and seemingly rather quickly. It is clearly clientelism—people expect something from their MPs and presidents—and not just promises. Some have called this evaluative[45] or competitive[46] clientelism. In fact, it is a sign of an evolving but stable democracy. It is a political deal among the elite that appears to work for them and for the country. It offers stability and continuing elite access to the state, but with some accountability. And yet the deal still comes at an economic and development cost.

An economic model to restrain politics

Just as Museveni has Mutebile, Rawlings had Kwesi Botchwey, his finance minister until 1995. Even if market liberalisation and other features of IMF–World Bank stabilisation programmes of the 1980s were totally opposed to the leftist inclinations of the PNDC, he and his team were given a free hand to negotiate a deal that would give Rawlings access to the international finance that he, and Ghana, needed. Much has been written about the rights and wrongs of these programmes and the lessons that were or could have been learned. Ghana definitely was a good pupil, and it changed from a rather controlled economy, unstable and with much state intervention, to a market-based one. I have little doubt that it had to happen, but with the benefit of hindsight it could well have been done better, with more Ghanaian ownership, consultation, and an eye on the impacts on various poorer groups.

When viewed over a longer time frame, these changes were nevertheless fundamental. Reform towards a market economy, the aid to which it offered access, and Ghana's evolving democracy provided the basis for solid but not spectacular progress in growth and development. With patronage and clientelism rife, a move to a market-based economy definitely reduced the scope for capturing rents from the state. For example, price controls and the role of state-owned enterprises were vastly scaled back, removing their manipulation as a source of mismanagement or just profits for those connected, and thereby limiting potentially huge distortionary impacts. Such an approach offered a better internal mechanism for restraint and avoidance of derailment, unlike the attempts to control the economy that had preceded it.

Of course, this still left scope for a large hippo state as a source of rents, such as by means of procurement for the benefit of friendly companies, or just vast numbers of public sector workers appointed through patronage. Here, smart and trusted officials such as Botchwey played a key role too, not unlike the role played by Mutebile in Uganda or indeed the Indonesian technocrats around the same time (see chapter 3). Even if they could not halt patronage or other corrupt practices, they could ensure that progress was not fundamentally derailed. Their good relations with international financial institutions provided a stick and a carrot to ensure politicians remained relatively prudent in fiscal terms—the stick in the form of conditions from the IMF and the carrot in the form of access to financial assistance.

Progress without transformation

The changes delivered, up to a point. They restored growth, albeit at modest levels and only accelerating over the last fifteen years, but then with much volatility and partly linked to new oil and gas discoveries. Macroeconomic stability is always harder, and high inflation and balance of payments crises were recurring.[47] The nature of democracy and clientelism since 1992 played a role here, too. With a fickle electorate, growth alone wasn't enough—people had to feel this progress as well, and before the next election. So two factors played out together. On the one hand, there was a focus on tangible development outcomes—with notable successes, which politicians had to deliver. On the other hand, these successes led to fiscal electoral cycles of boom and bust and of debt and deficits. Meanwhile, Ghana's friends at the IMF often acted as the only restraining force on cyclical political excess, caused in part by responding to electoral clientelism.

What happened in 2015 is a good illustration of all these challenges. Oil had been discovered and production began in 2010. Combined with high levels of foreign direct investment (FDI), production pushed per capita growth rates up to 11 per cent in 2011. The fiscal deficit of the state then got out of hand because the state had spent any returns from oil for years to come. For example, faced by looming elections and fuelled by popular expectations of oil wealth, the NDC government tripled the civil servant wage bill, adding a few billion dollars to it.[48] International commercial finance was required, but it was expensive. More strikingly, much expensive domestic debt had been accumulated as well, so that by 2014 government debt had doubled in about five years to 70 per cent of GDP.

As so often before, Ghana appealed for help from the IMF. And in 2019 the IMF called Ghana 'one of sub-Saharan Africa's success stories'.[49] But it has been a star pupil since 1983. It probably is also the teacher's pet. Because it was one of the first reformers of both its economy and politics, it had to succeed. In 2015 Ghana asked for more programme and financial assistance, the sixteenth time it had received IMF support since the beginning of the 1980s. Since then, growth has been restored and the economy has stabilised, allowing the fiscally more prudent government of the NPP to correct the errors of its NDC predecessors.

Meanwhile, Ghana has continued to receive considerable aid. Shifting political incentives to deliver for development across the country makes it attractive to donors looking for more effective spending. Thus since 1983 Ghana has received ever year roughly $50 per capita in 2010 prices, even though its GDP per capita has tripled over this period.[50] This is typically somewhat higher than what Uganda receives per capita, and yet Ghana has twice the GDP per capita. As for Kenya, only in the last decade has it received similar amounts because it lost a large share in the 1990s. I would dare to call Ghana the first African development success story of the combined forces of government, international financial institutions, and development aid.

Yes, this is success, but still only sort of. There is little doubt that Ibrahim and the village he lives in have benefited considerably from all Ghana's progress. GDP per capita has tripled over the last forty years. Poverty has declined rather spectacularly. Ibrahim's children have access to ever better health care and more educational opportunities. The underlying political and economic deals have made this success possible, and yet fickle voters and political cycles ensure the horizons are very short. This is not an elite bargain

157

designed for long-term growth.[51] This is not an elite bargain for prudent macroeconomic stability. This is not a form of politics that can easily save or turn the emerging natural resource rents into long-term capital investment. Instead, it ends up consuming those rents too quickly. This is a politics and a state that are struggling to remain focused on delivering long-term projects.[52]

As a result, for many studying Ghana the economic scorecard of change since 1983 is rather disappointing.[53] Agriculture is still too important an employer and source of income. Industrial development is more limited than its promise. And in the urban economy, the informal service sector remains too large. Yet the country still falls in the success category. One cannot deny its progression on a range of indicators, surpassing that of most other sub-Saharan African economies. However, it remains to be seen whether the successful political bargain that brought stability, a functioning democracy, and signs of growth and development can also deliver a longer-term development trajectory over coming decades.

A glass half full, not half empty

It is easy to bemoan the shortcomings of the three countries discussed in this chapter. Each has politics laced with patronage and clientelism. They are neopatrimonial states with intertwined formal and informal structures. One can see their hippo ears, but otherwise a lot is hidden, such as corruption and inefficiency. They won't turn quickly into growth miracles in the image of the East Asian examples. Nevertheless, much is possible. Kenya, Uganda, and Ghana have features that have served and will serve them well in years to come.

Recall the simple framework for elite bargains in countries. They focus on the underlying political deal that at least should offer peace and stability, built around an economic deal for capturing rents and a state to serve this deal. Development bargains are a particular type of elite bargain in which all three facets focus on growth and development. Kenya, Uganda, and Ghana are no doubt imperfect elite bargains, still some way from a development bargain, but each has positive features that give hope. In Kenya, there has been progress towards using formal constitutional reform to take some of the sting out of ethnic politics, thereby setting up the possibility of more stability as well as of economic deals and state functioning that could be more accountable to development outcomes at the local level. A move towards a development bargain now seems more likely than before. Uganda's current regime offers much more stability than before—politically, and also economically. Despite endless imperfections in its political set-up, it has managed to direct the economic deal and the state more towards growth and development, however imperfect and even at the risk of becoming unstuck. And Ghana especially can be called a success. However imperfect its development bargain may seem, the political deal, which has seen functioning political transitions, and the underlying economic deal have shifted in the last few decades more towards development. Even if Ghana's underlying economic transformation is far from progressing quickly enough, it may be a full-blown success in the coming few decades. Both Uganda and Ghana also show how smart technocratic management, including that supported by aid, can offer pockets of excellence and progress, however imperfect both the state and politics.

In short, none of the three countries has found a clear, direct route towards the longer-term horizon required for more strategic capital investments or building a more supportive state. Such a horizon will be needed to accelerate and sustain growth because, in the end, investors, local or international, have to have confidence that putting their resources to use for the long term makes sense. Maybe this is asking too much of Kenya, Uganda, and Ghana: they need a development model consistent with the elite bargains that are possible. Multi-ethnic states or states with a history of patronage and clientelism may need some form of distributive politics to maintain stability and a state that refrains from taking on too much as capture looms. That said, all three states have shown that decent growth and good progress in development are possible, at least during some periods.

References

Africa Confidential. 2016. 'How the Next Election Will Be Won'. 57 (5): 1–3.

_____. 2017. 'The Seven Ages of Museveni'. 58 (21): 7.

_____. 2018a. 'Grafting against Corruption'. 59 (25): 12.

_____. 2018b. 'Hey Big Spender'. 59 (24): 1–2.

Arthur, P. 2009. 'Ethnicity and Electoral Politics in Ghana's Fourth Republic'. *Africa Today* 56 (2): 44–73.

Aryeetey, E., and A. Fosu. 2008. 'Economic Growth in Ghana: 1960–2000'. In *The Political Economy of Economic Growth in Africa, 1960–2000*, vol. 2, edited by B. J. Ndulu et al. Cambridge: Cambridge University Press.

Aryeetey, E., and S. R. Kanbur, eds. 2017. *The Economy of Ghana Sixty Years after Independence*. Oxford: Oxford University Press.

Barkan, J. D., and M. Chege. 1989. 'Decentralising the State: District Focus and the Politics of Reallocation in Kenya'. *Journal of Modern African Studies* 27 (3): 431–53.

Bates, R. H. 2014. *Markets and States in Tropical Africa: The Political Basis of Agricultural Policies*. Oakland, CA: University of California Press.

Berman, B. J. 1998. 'Ethnicity, Patronage and the African State: The Politics of Uncivil Nationalism'. *African Affairs* 7: 305–41.

Branch, B., N. Cheeseman, and L. Gardner. 2010. *Our Turn to Eat: Politics in Kenya since 1950*. Berlin: Lit Verlag.

Burgess, R., R. Jedwab, E. Miguel, A. Morjaria, and G. Padró i Miquel. 2015. 'The Value of Democracy: Evidence from Road Building in Kenya'. *American Economic Review* 105 (6): 1817–51.

Cheeseman, N., ed. 2018. *Institutions and Democracy in Africa: How the Rules of the Game Shape Political Developments*. Cambridge: Cambridge University Press.

_____, G. Lynch, and J. Willis. 2017. 'Ghana: The Ebbing Power of Incumbency'. *Journal of Democracy* 28 (2): 92–104.

D'Arcy, M., and A. Cornell. 2016. 'Devolution and Corruption in Kenya: Everyone's Turn to Eat?' *African Affairs* 115 (459): 246–73.

Dercon, S. 2008. 'Ethnicity, Violence and the 2007 Elections in Kenya'. University of Oxford, 8 January.

_____, and M. Bratton. 2008. 'Ethnicity and Violence in the 2007 Elections in Kenya'. *Afrobarometer Briefing* 48: 1–3.

_____, and R. Gutiérrez-Romero. 2012. 'Triggers and Characteristics of the 2007 Kenyan Electoral Violence'. *World Development* 40 (4): 731–44.

East African. 2014. 'Mutebile Lifts the Lid on Patronage and Electoral Financing in Uganda'. https://www.theeastafrican.co.ke/news/ea/Mutebile-lifts-lid-on-patronage-electoral-financing-in-Uganda/4552908-2523800-3b6vi9z/index.html.

Eifert, B., E. Miguel, and D. N. Posner. 2010. 'Political Competition and Ethnic Identification in Africa'. *American Journal of Political Science* 54 (2): 494–510.

Franck, R., and I. Rainer. 2012. 'Does the Leader's Ethnicity Matter? Ethnic Favoritism, Education, and Health in Sub-Saharan Africa'. *American Political Science Review* 106 (2): 294–325.

Hausmann, R., B. Cunningham, J. M. Matovu, R. Osire, and K. Wyett. 2014. 'How Should Uganda Grow?' HKS Faculty Working Paper Series RWP14-004, Harvard Kennedy School, Cambridge, MA.

Hyden, G. 2012. 'Big Man Rule'. In *African Politics in Comparative Perspective*, 97–116. Cambridge: Cambridge University Press.

IMF (International Monetary Fund). 2019. 'Ghana: IMF Program Helps Restore Luster to a Rising Star in Africa'. IMF Lending Case Study. https://www.imf.org/en/Countries/GHA/ghana-lending-case-study.

———. 2020. 'Kenya Country Report 20/156, Request for Disbursement under Rapid Credit Facility'. Washington, DC: IMF.

Kasekende, L., and M. Atingi-Ego. 2008. 'Restarting and Sustaining Growth in a Post-conflict Economy: The Case of Uganda'. In *The Political Economy of Economic Growth in Africa, 1960–2000*, vol. 2, edited by B. J. Ndulu et al. Cambridge: Cambridge University Press.

Kramon, E., and D. N. Posner. 2016. 'Ethnic Favoritism in Education in Kenya'. *Quarterly Journal of Political Science* 11 (1): 1–58.

Lynch, G., 2014. 'Electing the "Alliance of the Accused": The Success of the Jubilee Alliance in Kenya's Rift Valley'. *Journal of Eastern African Studies* 8 (1): 93–114.

Mwega, F., and N. Ndung'u. 2008. 'Explaining African Economic Growth Performance: The Case of Kenya'. In *The Political Economy of Economic Growth in Africa, 1960–2000*, vol. 2, edited by B. J. Ndulu et al. Cambridge: Cambridge University Press.

Ndulu, B. J., J. P. Azam, S. A. O'Connell, R. H. Bates, A. K. Fosu, J. W. Gunning, and D. Nijinkeu, eds. 2008. *The Political Economy of Economic Growth in Africa, 1960–2000*, vol. 2. Cambridge: Cambridge University Press.

Patey, L. 2015. 'Oil in Uganda: Hard Bargaining and Complex Politics in East Africa'. OIES Paper WPM 60, Oxford Institute for Energy Studies.

Reuss, A., and K. Titeca. 2017. 'Removing the Presidential Age Limit in Uganda: The Power of Cash and Coercion'. *Open Democracy*, 7 August.

Whitfield, L. 2018. *Economies after Colonialism: Ghana and the Struggle for Power*. Cambridge: Cambridge University Press.

Williams, M. J. 2017. 'The Political Economy of Unfinished Development

Projects: Corruption, Clientelism, or Collective Choice?' *American Political Science Review* 111 (4): 705–23.

World Bank. 2019. *Creating Fiscal Space to Deliver the Big Four While Undertaking a Needed Fiscal Consolidation.* Kenya Public Expenditure Review. Washington, DC: World Bank.

Wrong, M. 2009. *It's Our Turn to Eat: The Story of a Kenyan Whistle-Blower.* London: Fourth Estate.

7

NIGERIA AND THE DEMOCRATIC REPUBLIC OF CONGO

NOT ENOUGH OIL AND DIAMONDS?

Coming from Belgium, I grew up with 'De Kongo', as my parents' generation used to call it, and with Zaire, as it was called only in the news broadcasts. The country defined Africa for me and offered visions of Tintin in the Congo, of Congolese leader Mobutu Sese Seko, and of Nonkel Pater (Uncle Father) because most of my peers had an uncle or great-uncle working in the 'missions' in Zaire, as it was renamed in 1971, a decade after independence from Belgium. Later, as an academic, I consciously avoided working on Zaire's challenges or travelling there in the 1980s and 1990s. It had nothing to do with some national guilt. It's just that too many Belgians of an older generation whom I struggled to admire worked on those challenges.

So I never stepped foot in the country until, as a DFID official, I visited the UK Embassy there for several weeks in 2014. Kinshasa, the capital of what was now named the Democratic Republic of Congo (DRC), turned out to be more familiar than I expected. It was not just about the shape of the traffic signs and the frites with mayonnaise. I was surprised to recognise so much of Belgium in its surprisingly well-functioning dysfunctionality, the mood on the street and in the office being vibrant but also somewhat downcast. Certainly, it wasn't Belgium, and it was, of course, desperately poor. In fact, it has been predicted that by 2030 the DRC would be home to the second-largest number of extremely poor people—probably beaten to top spot by Nigeria.

As for Nigeria, it always feels rather unreal. For years I travelled there, with surprising access to senior officials at the State House, the centre of government, and presidential aides. I was always received courteously as an official from London, but my reception was infused with an incredible self-confidence in the righteousness of the way the country was being run, including its economy. It was as if, in their eyes, Wakanda, the fictional and amazing African kingdom depicted in the film *Black Panther*, was just around the corner or even already there. But if one peered behind the facade, all one could see was a chaotic state, seemingly not going anywhere or possibly going in all plausible directions at the same time.

Nigeria is not just a country characterised by both extreme wealth and the deepest abject poverty. It also has pockets of innovative entrepreneurship, of the highest intellectual sophistication, of bureaucratic excellence, and of inspiring artists and writers such as Chinua Achebe and Wole Soyinka. At times, it is vibrant with unbridled optimism. But it is also home to some of the worst forms of patronage, rent-seeking economic behaviour, absurd economic policies, ethnic political competition, poor or at times predatory and corrupt public administration, violence and conflict, and, too often, little hope.

This chapter only scratches the surface of why these two countries with such potential appear to be underperforming so spectacularly. History matters, no doubt, but so does the behaviour of the current political, military, and economic elite. Both countries have bountiful natural resources: oil and gas in Nigeria and diamonds and virtually any other natural resource in the DRC. The resources matter, but more important is the elite bargain on how to deal with them. The elite bargain is built on these resources, but the elite behave as though they have far more. And that behaviour holds back, as in Nigeria, or even destroys, as in the DRC, the economy. These, then, are hippo states but with predatory features. The state as a tigerfish is not far off in Nigeria and definitely present in the DRC, where it is living off little fish, with affluence for some at the expense of poverty for many.

Nigeria: A missed opportunity

'I don't know anything about economics,' he said at the outset of our meeting. In was 2016, and we were in London, in a tiny office in the government building I worked in at the time. I was meeting informally with Abba Kyari, chief of staff to Nigerian president Muhammadu Buhari, for what turned out to be an intense three-hour discussion of the economy of Nigeria. At the time, Kyari was the most powerful and trusted person in the administration of President Buhari.[1]

Kyari went on to tell me, 'I am a big fan of Jeremy Corbyn,' referring to the leftist leader of the UK opposition Labour Party, 'and the government should take control of the means of production.' His feigned ignorance of economics was not terribly credible, and his views may have seemed a little surprising for someone who, after his military career, had served as CEO of a commercial bank in Nigeria and on the boards of Exxon Mobile and Unilever in Nigeria. But, in fact, ideology did not really play a big part in Nigerian politics. Kyari was a pragmatist. His role for President Buhari was simply to hold the elite bargain together. And that was a big job. It entailed reining in the diverse, fractured, and somewhat bizarre coalition of influential forces from business and politics that formed the bedrock of the regime and that needed to stay inside the tent for the upcoming presidential election in 2019. His government was not trying to control the means of production. But it was trying to maintain control of who received rents from the economy. As with everything in Nigeria, politics are a business deal. Capturing government is a means of capturing markets. Perhaps this is best summed up as 'the government taking control of the means of production', but not quite in the way Karl Marx intended.

Actually, the most basic economic figures don't look that bad. Nigeria is a middle-income country, still richer than, say, Kenya, with almost double that country's GDP per capita.[2] Over the last two decades, Nigeria's economy has grown at quite decent rates, by almost 3 per cent a year per person. By 2013, it had become the largest economy in Africa, overtaking South Africa after it recalculated its GDP using more up-to-date methods and a little encouragement (the head of the National Bureau of Statistics probably did not understand my slight smile when he told me in 2013 that the only instruction the president had given him was to ensure that the recalculated GDP was larger than South Africa's). Even so, this has been a middle-income country for a while, and it has experienced solid growth in recent times.

Digging a bit deeper, one sees what is far less of a success story. In fact, since 2015 Nigeria's economy has been shrinking by almost 2 per cent a year. Similarly, between 1980 and 2000 the economy shrank by a third in per capita terms. And despite Nigeria being considerably richer than the countries discussed in the previous chapter, its indicators, such as health and extreme poverty, are considerably worse. For example, the rate at which infants die before they reach age one is twice that of Kenya, Uganda, and Ghana. With more than 50 per cent of Nigerians classified as extremely poor (based on internationally comparable data), its share is far higher than those of these three countries.

The politics of oil

It would be wrong to ascribe all of Nigeria's troubles to oil. The country had experienced political problems in early postcolonial times and arguably well before. Nigeria is a multi-ethnic country in which many groups and kingdoms with long histories were brought together within uncomfortable colonial boundaries. The Hausa, Yoruba, and Igbo, the largest ethnic groups, together make up more than two-thirds of the population. Although in modern-day Nigeria these groups vie for power mostly peacefully, it wasn't always like that. A long period after independence was blighted by coups and even a bloody civil war with widespread atrocities.

Meanwhile, oil has remained too important to the economy. Even with prices and production down, oil revenue presently accounts for more than 90 per cent of all export revenue—it's as though Nigeria doesn't make anything else that the world finds worth buying, despite its entrepreneurship. Periods of economic growth and decline or stagnation coincide with oil prices and production. Prices declined in real terms after 1980, stagnated from 1985 to 1999, showed fast growth from 2000 to 2014 (albeit with a two-year collapse in 2008–9 during the financial crisis), and languished in the doldrums after 2014. As for volume, in the 1980s oil production gradually recovered to the 1970s levels of around 2 million barrels a day, only to peak from 2000 to 2015, but then once again to collapse.

Any economy too dependent on one commodity to earn foreign exchange will struggle with economic stability. Solid macroeconomic management is needed for a country to remain attractive for investment in other sectors, but Nigeria has never managed to achieve such success for long periods of time. Although the economy has gradually expanded, Nigeria is, as noted, still barely exporting anything other than oil. This situation also has implications for the country's ability to keep its public services functioning and of high quality: in the last few decades, more than two-thirds of total government revenue has consisted of oil revenue.[3]

Oil has shaped the nature of Nigerian politics for a long time. When oil became important by the early 1970s, it was initially, as a sign of the times, largely used to promote home-grown industrialisation under policies for protectionism.[4] But that approach was soon changed. Oil wealth, being easy to generate, became a great prize for whoever could forge a strong enough bargain among military and civilian forces. Brief periods of civil rule were followed by repeated coups, mostly involving leaders from the economically weaker but militarily stronger north, and political competition focused on oil revenue allocation, with wild promises but little delivery.[5] These elite bargains were all relatively weak, and they ended up involving not only widespread patronage but also large-scale embezzlement of the easy wealth, with impunity.[6] During booms, life was easy, and officials claimed a new Nigeria had emerged, where during busts politics were about clinging to privilege and power and delaying change until it was someone else's time to eat.

That sequence has hardly changed, despite much hope in recent times. Since 1999, an election-based presidential system has been in place, and gaining power requires constructing a complicated and usually expensive elite bargain involving the different regions and the heads of the leading ethnic groups. Much hope had been pinned on the checks and balances that may emerge from that bargain and the scope for a more growth-oriented elite bargain to stick. Meanwhile, politics became a deal between the economically more dynamic southern elite and the politically powerful northern elite. During President Olusegun Obasanjo's tenure from 1999 to 2007, technocrats were given more power, not least in dealings with international organisations. It may have appeared that a new elite bargain, a coalition for growth, had emerged.[7] However, beyond some quick wins such as in telecommunications,[8] investments in essential infrastructure did not take off, nor was there a reversal in the pitiful levels of government expenditure on essential services such as health care. More fundamental economic and public sector reform, in particular of the notoriously leaky Nigerian National Petroleum Corporation (NNPC), never happened.

In the end, the economic deal underlying the coalition in power continued to require short-term pay-offs to its key supporters and benefactors, with little concern for long-term growth and transformation of the economy.[9] Politics remained a game of powerful godfathers—that is, those who have successfully accumulated wealth as well as built political capital and who woo and need to be wooed in an ever more complex web of fragile coalitions. When President Buhari came to power in 2015, the economy was already sliding again and has continued to do so ever since. It failed once more to transform and diversify, and so, when oil prices collapsed, Nigeria's economy collapsed.

Change seems as remote as ever. Re-elected in 2019, President Buhari presented a platform for fighting corruption that continued to appear empty. He may well have meant it—after all, he was paraded, without irony, at the UK prime minister's anti-corruption summit in 2016. But that hasn't stopped the leakage to the elite few. Indeed, many studying Nigeria will see less change in patronage than the president and his entourage would like to project.[10] Perhaps with the exception of Angola, nowhere are the stories of the diversion of state funds or the manipulation of contracts as juicy and murky as in Nigeria, and most of them are related to oil, directly or indirectly. Some stories hit the global press, such as the investigations in 2011 of military dictator Sani Abacha's oil minister, Dan Etete, and his role in dealings worth \$1.1 billion with two European oil companies, British-Dutch Shell and Italian ENI. Etete had already been convicted of money-laundering in France in 2007.

Most cases of diversion of funds are far more complex than the ENI corruption scandal, involving lucrative licences for oil exploration or commissions for arranging joint ventures. Many are within the law even if hardly above board, related to import licences for essential or luxury goods. In any case, a host of billionaires and many more millionaires have emerged among the elite from such dealings, with several having now turned into godfathers in their own right, controlling political financing. Meanwhile, with fun and games at the top, the rest of the state and much of the economy have to fend for themselves.

Infectious predatory behaviour at the local level

During my travels across the developing world, I am always keen to visit factories or other businesses. Whether in Lira in Uganda or Sialkot in Pakistan, talking about the challenges managers face gives a sense of a country's business climate. Skirting any discussion of politics, I just ask them about their own business and the challenges and aspirations in the market. Such discussions are hugely enlightening and help bring the numbers in my economic briefings to life.

In Kano, Nigeria's second-largest city and the main city in the north of the country, I met in 2013 one of my favourite entrepreneurs ever. Kano is special. It is home to a historical West African marketplace, the end point of the trans-Saharan trade route. An early Muslim state, Kano became part of the western African Sokoto Caliphate in the early nineteenth century, and it was one of the last large slave societies. It only became a British protectorate in the twentieth century. In recent times, Kano has had its ups and downs. When I visited, the business climate was poor. Once a proud manufacturing city of textiles and other produce, its infrastructure had crumbled and costs had soared. Boko Haram had only just recently committed atrocities in the city, and security was on everybody's mind.

My visit to the manager of Dala Foods was fascinating. It processes and blends tea and cereal-based drinks for the 'bottom of the pyramid' market by packaging them in single portions—for example, selling two teabags at a time. The company's hundred or so employees use simple but effective machinery for hygienic and safe packaging, some of it constructed on-site. As a young man, the manager had often travelled to Europe to find the right machinery, befriending guards at food-processing plants in order to sneak in at night to take pictures. These days, watching YouTube videos of famous brands and machinery has allowed him to make this industrial espionage legal, with the same effect. His work site was immaculate.

Still, one of his biggest complaints was the endless visits of health and safety officers, claiming he broke Nigerian food standard regulations and threatening to stop production. He knew full well what they were after, and so he could do little else but pay. This is the other side of Nigeria. The quest for gains and lucrative favours at the top sets a peculiar example for others working for the state. In other words, the big players grab the big loot, inciting those down the ladder to fight over the scraps. The resulting norm? It is acceptable to prey on citizens and firms to top up earnings or even simply a department's budget. It is then not necessarily corruption, but legal revenue mobilisation for one or other department implementing health and safety legislation. Make no mistake, however; even when such legislation was passed, no one believed it would be fully enforced—after all, the entire informal economy of food stalls and street kitchens would have to be banned. Instead, laws are made with the full knowledge that only firms that can pay the fine or the bribe will be targeted. The largest or connected firms will know how to protect themselves,[11] while the tiny informal sector ones are not worth the effort for the predators. Entrepreneurial firms, like Dala Foods, then take the brunt.

Too little oil

Why does Nigeria seem stuck in this zero-sum game, where all gain appears at the expense of others? Oil has much to answer for, but it cannot be blamed for all of it. Plenty of other countries have succeeded in using oil or other natural resources to build an economy aimed at long-term growth and development.[12] Natural resources give countries easy money, but to manage their revenues three things need to be done at the same time. First, those with power have to resist just consuming the revenue. Second, they should invest instead in diversification to help the economy limit its dependence on a natural resource such as oil, such as through infrastructure or other means. Third, they should establish sensible macroeconomic management of both the likely appreciation of the exchange rate, making imports cheap, and the instability stemming from fluctuating commodity prices.

Nigeria clearly has wasted many of its resources. In any case, it hasn't invested enough to change the structure of its economy, despite its repeated political commitments to doing so. And for macroeconomic management, the last decade has seen some of the worst examples, again. All of this, in the end, comes down to the politics of the elite bargain.

Since the fall of oil prices in 2013, Nigeria's exchange rate policy has complied with a rather striking set of rules: let currency markets work when oil revenues are high (resulting in appreciation), but stop markets from working when oil revenues are low (trying to avoid depreciation). The objective is simple: keep dollars and therefore imports as cheap as possible at all times. The incentives are obvious. In a society in which the lifestyle of the powerful elite is entirely based on imported goods, including the purchase of property or education overseas, maintaining a cheap dollar seems to be the appropriate political strategy. Those in the Louis Vuitton and Land Rover overseas sales offices will surely approve. And since much food and other essentials need to be imported, few will ask for a change in this strategy, as it keeps them cheap for all consumers— even though it stifles the incentives to produce these items locally, perpetuating the dependence on oil.[13]

But the problem is that Nigeria has too little oil to pay for this kind of elite bargain. In 2010, when prices were still high, Nigeria made about $54 billion from oil and gas, of which $38 billion ended up through royalties, rents, and taxes in the hands of the government. That may seem like a lot, but per Nigerian it was not so much: less than $340 per capita and $240 per capita in government revenue. These figures are quite a bit lower than the per capita figures for other natural resource exporters—such as Australia ($5,131), Saudi Arabia ($7,477), Gabon ($2,965), and Algeria ($1,206). Even South Africa receives more at $564 per capita.[14]

But, surely, $240 per capita in government revenue from oil is still a nice sum. For example, the World Health Organization suggested at the time that less than $50 per person could pay for decent basic health care, which was still lacking in much of Nigeria. However, for those controlling politics such a sum from oil would hardly keep the government's key supporters on board. Dividing these sums among, say, 100,000 of the government's most influential supporters in business, the civil service, the military, and society becomes more interesting for them: $382,000 per connected person in government revenue. Even by 2017, with much lower prices, $139,000 per connected person remained a tidy sum. Over the years, the elite bargain has focused on distributing these rents— unequally—entirely across those with connections. But because there isn't really so much oil and gas, little remains for broader development or public investment in the rest of the economy.

Nigeria seems stuck in an extreme form of distributive politics. And because it does not have the resources of a Saudi Arabia, after elite capture there is just nothing left to invest, which leaves the country much poorer than it should be. Downturns in commodity prices often become the right moments to reset and rethink the economy—Covid-19 is another moment. Nigeria has suffered plenty of downturns, but they did not lead to reform. If crises should not be wasted, no one told Nigerian politicians. In my many conversations with Abba Kyari, or in meetings with Vice President Yemi Osinbajo over the last five years, it was clear they understood that this short-term elite bargain still focusing on distributing today's or even tomorrow's revenue was stuck and unsustainable. Thus far, it hasn't quite shifted.

Hippos, tigerfish, and hyenas in the Democratic Republic of Congo

By some indicators, recent progress in the Democratic Republic of Congo looks promising. For example, since the end of the war in 2003 its economy has grown by 2.8 per cent a year. Also since then, extreme poverty has fallen by about a fifth, and children now have a considerably better chance of surviving past their first birthday. But these numbers don't tell the real story. At the time of the country's independence in 1960 from Belgium, GDP per capita (in 2010 US dollars) was estimated to be just over $1,000. By then, it was a middle-income country. In terms of GDP per capita, it was close to the median of all developing countries.

In 1974 the economy of what was now known as Zaire began to systematically collapse. For the thirty years that followed, GDP per capita declined every year, by on average about 5 per cent a year. By 2003 the Democratic Republic of Congo, as it had become, was among the five poorest countries in the world in terms of GDP per capita—and it still is.[15] Poverty was estimated to be a staggering 94 per cent in 2004, whereas more recent estimates have suggested 77 per cent. Fewer children survive beyond the age of one than in all but several other countries. Only Nigeria, with a population almost three times as large, will have more extremely poor people by 2030, according to the best estimates.

Conflict no doubt has played a role in the country's troubles, first the war in 1996–7 that brought Laurent-Désiré Kabila to power, and then the Second Congolese War, from 1998 to 2003, involving forces from Rwanda, Uganda, Angola, Namibia, Zimbabwe, and other countries, making it the 'Great African War'. This war brought devastation, and probably more than 5 million people were killed, directly or indirectly. Today, conflict persists, especially in the eastern DRC.

And yet persistent conflict is hardly the cause of the DRC's ongoing troubles. It is a consequence of an elite bargain built on predatory behaviour. And when the elite became too weak to plunder in an orderly fashion, the neighbours joined in. More stability may be in the wings, but the omens are not good. The DRC is a useful case study of the role of history and of how persistent institutions are shaped, but also how history does not have to be predestination. The outcomes today stem from choices by leaders and by those close to them in the elite. The roots of the decline and devastation lie no doubt in colonial times, even if those times are no excuse for some of the elite's behaviour afterwards, up to today. The rest of this chapter is devoted to looking not only at these roots, but also at the behaviour of the country's leaders. In view of its present condition, the DRC will, despite some positive signs, realise its potential only if those in power are willing to make a huge commitment to unlocking that potential. There are, unfortunately, few signs that this is happening.

The colonial roots

For most people, Belgian colonial times essentially consist of the brutal reign of King Leopold II (1865–1909), who founded and owned the Congo Free State. He literally ran it as his private estate (1885–1908), at first mainly for ivory and then increasingly, and brutally, for rubber.[16] In 1908, Leopold, broke and disillusioned, reluctantly ceded Congo to Belgium. The move followed one of the first human rights campaigns in history, largely fuelled by voices from Britain and the US, and even debates in the House of Commons protesting against the atrocities in the Congo Free State.[17] What followed as a Belgian colony was different, but just as in all other colonial regimes, it was not necessarily better.

A 'geological scandal' was how one of the early discoverers of copper in Congo had described the wealth of natural resources all concentrated in one country.[18] Congo has since provided the key minerals of the day, including the uranium of the Cold War and the coltan essential for today's mobile phones. Along the way, it also exposed the fundamental and persistent weakness of the Belgian state, founded on a coalition based on three forces: business interests, the church, and the royal family. With the royals out of the way, the other two forces muscled in. The roots of the current fractured state were sown during this period: the fast spread of business interests and of the missions, with the colonial state only essentially serving them, left Congo, just like Belgium, with weak central power.

Mining grew quickly. Some of the big companies then shaped Congolese history, such as Union Minière de Haut-Katanga (financed with Belgian and British capital), Forminière (financed with US capital and decades later sold to De Beers), and BCK (financed with Belgian–French capital). Union Minière especially became a state within the state, with its own private army and an organisation better than that of the colonial state. Big business did not just arrive in mining. In one of the largest land grabs in history, William Lever was granted 7.5 million hectares for the cultivation and harvesting of palm oil. In Congo, he became known, not as Lord Leverhulme, the enlightened philanthropist he was thought to be in the UK, but as a harsh employer who did not discourage forced labour on his plantations. In 1912 a bar of Sunlight soap produced from Congolese oil was presented to King Albert, the new Belgian king, by Lever Brothers. The firm later became one constituent part of the British–Dutch conglomerate Unilever.

With rapid urbanisation and structural transformation, Congo changed. By the 1930s, close to a half-million wage workers in a population of less than 10 million were working in mining, on plantations, in nascent manufacturing, and for the state and the army. The white population numbered about 20,000. Fast-forward another fifteen years—a second wave of structural transformation took place after World War II. With more investment and a more active colonisation policy, the number of whites grew to more than 80,000. But strikingly, by the end of the 1950s a staggering 40 per cent of the African male adult population was working for wages— more than anywhere else in Africa. Congo also became, for Africa, relatively urban. By the 1950s, 22 per cent of the population was living in urban areas—a high percentage for Africa, where by then the average was about 14 per cent, and higher than the average for Ethiopia today.[19]

Post-1945 until independence in 1960, some may have been tempted to call Congo a colonial development success. Indeed, when independence came, Congo was seemingly among the better-positioned developing countries, not unlike Ghana or Kenya. Its

GDP grew quickly, and it was a middle-income country at the time of independence. The first post-independence government inherited rather magnificent infrastructure: about 9,000 miles of railroads, 140 kilometres of quality highways, 40 airports or airfields, and 100 power plants, mostly hydroelectric. The country also had a modern industrial and mining sector, an educated blue-collar and small white-collar labour force, 300 hospitals for the local population as well as many more medical centres, and high literacy throughout its population of about 14 million. In short, Congo had some of the best development hardware in sub-Saharan Africa and improving human development outcomes. It was in better shape than, say, Indonesia— that other large tropical economy colonised by a small country, Belgium's northern neighbour, the Netherlands.[20] However, just like Indonesia, Congo was an extractive state, serving business interests at home and the small number of settlers.

Poor at colonisation, Belgium was terrible at decolonisation. Congo stumbled into independence in June 1960, with neither side prepared in any way. The colonial power had done nothing to encourage institutional development. In fact, it had repressed any emergence of such development. The state had remained weak, even if it gradually strengthened in the post–World War II period. Economic and business interests and the missions continued to rule, serving the settlers and the motherland. It resembled other southern African societies, with effectively an apartheid society. When the white administration and management withdrew from power, the relatively weak shell of the state was ready to implode.

A small elite had been groomed for independence, but in a deeply patronising and ineffective way. Higher education had been out of bounds, and only in the mid-1950s was a university education possible for a select few. By 1960, only 16 Congolese had graduated from a university. But then to ensure that no one with a politics, law, economics, or engineering degree graduated pre-independence, education and psychology were the subjects chosen for these students. As a result, no one in the early post-independence leadership knew anything about economics, nor did they have any serious managerial experience.[21] For example, they had to negotiate the ownership of the country's mining assets with Belgian politicians and business leaders, who had top-class advisors.[22] There was no black officer in the Force Publique, nor was there a single black physician. The inexperienced politicians who took over the state were faced with the high expectations of the people, and strong business and church interests. There were railroads and hospitals, and a relatively educated, partly urbanised population. But they had no functioning political or legal institutions, not even a shell, strong enough to fall back on.

What followed is well known. A messy independence transition, lack of unifying political leadership, deep meddling by the US and other foreign powers linked to Cold War politics, a big business-driven attempted secession in Katanga, the brutal execution of Prime Minister Lumumba, the death of a UN general secretary, a quickly collapsing economy, the start of a violent civil war—and all that within two years of independence.[23] The civil war continued and the president, Joseph Kasavubu, did not trust the most popular politician in the country, Moïse Tshombe, who won the 1964 elections. So Joseph-Désiré Mobutu, the 35-year-old former journalist who was by then a general, saw his chance and staged a coup, supported by capital and foreign powers, especially the US. The coup was followed by a period of fragile stability lasting for three decades: Mobutu won every game of chess with his army and his opponents and resorted to violence and plunder when needed. Meanwhile, General Mobutu renamed himself Mobutu Sese Seko, and in 1971 renamed the country Zaire.

Mobutu Sese Seko, the predator-in-chief

The decades that followed were like a tragicomedy, but with no happy ending. Mobutu had a starring role, whether persuading Muhammad Ali to fight in the 'Rumble in the Jungle', attracting his own space programme,[24] or building a massive landing strip near his tiny birthplace, Gbadolite, in the middle of nowhere, suitable for regular visits of the Concorde and for emergency landings of the space shuttle. Even now, the airport strip and his villa are still there, but the opulent murals are fading, and the jungle is reconquering this affront to the natural order.

Mobutu was not just theatrical, but also a shrewd politician. With such limited state foundations and a tiny but divided elite, he had to build his own elite bargain to consolidate his power. First, he needed a monopoly of violence. The army was strengthened, and with the help of brutal white mercenaries the country was brought under control after a few years. Then to sustain power he needed more than just an army. He also needed others across business, politics, and society to support the emergence of a political deal and an economic deal to pay for it. He first nationalised Union Minière, which became Gécamines, thereby allowing the state to capture all the vast copper profits. A small group around him colluded with international business interests to access and control rents from other natural resources as well. He also needed a political base, and the easiest way to get that was to buy it. He built his own elite, a group of nouveau riche, who owed their prosperity to the regime. Beyond this base remained a large group who were relatively well educated and salaried by the end of Belgian colonial times and who were looking for improvement. He became their patron.

Thus was born a state based on patronage and clientelism, with three layers. The first was the military and the top end of the elite, sharing in the natural resource wealth and colluding with more or less shady international businesses. The second was the newly affluent middle class, who managed the state and local business. And third was the white-collar army—mostly given jobs by the state. But Mobutu quickly needed more resources to ensure the loyalty of both his new middle class and the broader groups. Gécamines proved to be insufficient and unreliable, not least because copper prices fluctuated wildly in the 1970s. And so Mobutu needed more than copper and diamonds—not to mention aid, foreign loans, and foreign direct investment to fulfil his promises.[25] There was no long-term horizon, no attempt to drive growth to ensure the rents kept on flowing, as Suharto had done in Indonesia in the mid-1970s[26] and Museveni had done in Uganda in the 1990s. Mobutu chose instead the direct route: steal, on a grand scale, to keep his supporters loyal.

Zairianisation was his next move. In 1973, he kicked out the vast number of foreign small business owners and gave their firms to his cronies. Soon he did the same with many other businesses. A purely predatory state emerged—one that used the wealth generated by natural resources, and also taxed away most profits or expropriated much of the private capital of ordinary people to generate financial resources for those on whose support Mobutu depended. Loyalty was rewarded by access to the state, and the state was organised at all levels to enable it. Loyalty also consolidated power around Mobutu so that no alternative wealth accumulation, offering finance for competition, could emerge. This was hardly a sensible long-term economic strategy. Investment dried up, and a vicious cycle of decline followed—for three decades.

It is reasonable to argue that Mobutu had few other options to consolidate power.[27] The colonial power had fundamentally neglected building up the state, and it left no emerging elite to step in and create formal structures, however imperfect they would have been. The state shell was weak and had to be fortified, quickly. The US, Britain, France, and Belgium signalled disapproval of the extensive plunder combined with occasional violent repression, but they mainly let Mobutu off the hook. Zaire was too important a source of minerals and other military interests. Meanwhile, Mobutu may well have achieved something—a semblance of Zairian or Congolese nationalism, which survives today, especially in urban centres. Zairianisation also involved *recours a l'authenticité* (resume authenticity) in dress, food, and manners. More important, Mobutu ensured some balance between regions and ethnicities in his version of the creation of a state bourgeoisie, ensuring all parts were represented in his patronage network.[28] Together, this approach produced some results, repressing ethnic strife for a long time, and was only disrupted after the Rwandan genocide in 1994. Over these three decades of rule, the patrimonial hippo had turned quickly into a tigerfish, living off eating little fish.

The Kabila era

By the 1990s, as the country became impoverished, the fracturing elite were fighting over the scraps. No amount of printing money, even by Mobutu himself in his villa in Gdabolite,[29] could stave off this collapse, exacerbated now by hyperinflation. The military, the bedrock of Mobutu's regime, had eroded as well. Taking over the state proved to be an easy task for Laurent-Désiré Kabila, even though he was an unlikely guerrilla fighter who had been dismissed as ineffective by the legendary Che Guevara himself in the 1960s.[30] Nevertheless, Kabila captured power in 1997 because of the finance and support provided by the Rwandan military. At first, they were mainly keen to sort out their own fragile northern border and the militia there implicated in the Rwandan genocide three years earlier. But they ended up marching on Kinshasa and, with Ugandan support, were ready to dine for free on the DRC's natural resources, making the armies from Uganda, Angola, Namibia, Zimbabwe, and other countries hungry to join in.

Laurent-Désiré Kabila may have defeated Mobutu, but he was always going to be a weak leader. The Second Congolese War (1998–2003) revealed the extent to which the state had imploded by the end of Mobutu's reign. The war was costly, and more people died than in the wars in Bosnia, Iraq, and Afghanistan combined from violence and war-induced disease and vulnerability. Meanwhile, endless crimes against humanity were committed, with impunity. After he was murdered in 2001, Kabila's son, Joseph, took over, and after a negotiated peace deal, face-saving for all, some semblance of stability emerged. The new 'state' endures today with all the trappings of government (ministers and parliamentarians—overpaid[31] but even at times making policy), but with only the vaguest governance and random implementation, beyond the many lucrative shady deals with extractive firms. Security is maintained by the newly unified army, FARDC. And yet the minimal requirement of a state—to gain a monopoly on violence—has not been achieved. Splits in the army and general ineffectiveness have been the order of the day. Meanwhile, the efforts of the most expensive UN peacekeeping mission in history, at more than $1 billion a year, have been ineffective and just a drop in the bucket because of the size of the country and the complexity of the conflict.

In recent years, everything had to change so all could stay the same. Joseph Kabila surprisingly did not try to further overrule the constitution, and he stepped down in 2018. When his anointed successor performed poorly in the election, another candidate, unlikely to have been the real winner, was declared the victor. Felix Tshisekedi, the son of a frequent ally but mostly opponent of Mobutu, became president, and slowly Kabila's party and cronies have been weakened, at least for now.[32] The state is still predatory, capturing natural resources, as well as making life difficult for anyone trying to build a business or just make a living. Some change may be on the way, but I doubt it, nevertheless.

The predatory economy

The view from Mbandaka across the vast Congo River is breathtaking. Located on the equator, Mbandaka is the capital of the northern province of the DRC, aptly named Equateur. The Congo River is the second-longest river in the world, and thousands of kilometres of it are navigable, especially between Kisangani and Kinshasa. At Mbandaka, transport is possible along the 700-kilometre stretch to Kinshasa. But when I visited in 2014, there were barely any boats on the river—no ferries and no transport ships. There were only a few small ramshackle barges, with little if any protection against the sun. They were carrying people and their produce and goods for petty trade. But these boats have all but disappeared in the last few decades. In most parts of the world, water transport is among the cheapest forms of transport for goods, whether agricultural produce, minerals, or anything else. When I asked my local contact about the lack of boats, he smiled and said that it was almost unaffordable to get a licence. Anyone seeking to transport goods had to receive permission from seventeen different agencies, and it was just not worth it.

As for anyone hoping to sell their Congolese coffee overseas out of Matadi, the main port in the west of the country, apparently they had to collect fifty-seven signatures and seven stamps. And each one would 'cost' something. To sell goods at one of the main markets in Kinshasa, one had to pay seven different taxes or contributions, of dubious provenance, each day.[33] Meanwhile, north of Mbandaka I found the nicely maintained government hospital empty. The register suggested that two to three patients were visiting each day, which was unfathomable in a country with one of the worst health records in the world—until I was given the official price list for services.[34] The doctor showing me around told me he hadn't been paid for five months.

'If you want to steal, steal a little cleverly, in a nice way,' President Mobutu Sese Seko said in 1976, in a speech to civil servants. 'Only if you steal so much as to become rich overnight, you will be caught.'[35] Corruption, whether petty or large-scale, is an existential part of the state that Mobutu built up and that still broadly exists: it is required for the elite bargain to continue to exist. The clientelism involved allows anyone with access to use the state as a means of enriching themselves. The state provides them with the licence to do so, and not necessarily with a salary. Rules, taxes, and regulations force officials to deal with firms and ordinary people, and thus those officials find themselves in the ideal circumstances to expect payments (bribes) for allowing firms and others to avoid the stringent rules or high tax rates.[36] Hence, endless rules, licences, taxes, permissions, and more are hardly designed to create efficient taxation or governance, and, in fact, they lead to negative outcomes for all.[37]

In such a corrupt climate, why would anyone be keen to invest productively? For a country known to be relatively industrialised at the time of independence, much of what is left of value in the national accounts is cigarettes and beer, each mainly involving foreign investors. One of the managers of a beer factory cheerfully mentioned to me that his factory had no problem with attempted extortion. It provided the local army garrison with regular free supplies, and the soldiers made sure no one troubled the factory.

This is organised disorder. Those who must be kept happy so that they leave intact the elite bargain for those at the top are allowed to use the state as a means of enriching themselves, at least a little.[38] This scheme can persist because those with power can afford it, thanks to ample natural resources—including cobalt, diamonds, copper, coltan, lithium, tin, and gold—and reportedly one of the largest overall reserves in the world. The yearly returns are about $15 billion, but if shared across the population, this makes only about $150 per person, which is not so much on which to build growth and development, let alone give all a good life.

Something has, however, changed in recent times. In the late 1990s, all one needed to control a mine in Congo was a gun and a satellite phone. Thus small militias could take over and plunder diamonds and have a buyer flying in. The Kivu region[39] especially in the east has not emerged from this situation, and militias still control smuggling routes. However, the larger, more commercial mines are largely under the control of Laurent Kabila, his family, and his entourage, at least for now.[40] Supply chains are better controlled, and rents are extracted. Meanwhile, the crime economy has become the organised crime economy. Other investments, such as the spread of a functioning mobile phone network, are often cited as the power of the private sector, despite the fragility or failings of the state. It probably helped that, perfectly legally, a company linked to the Kabila family was given a large share in one of the early pioneer investment joint ventures with an international investor.[41]

Other things have changed much less. During Leopold's reign, the Force Publique was decentralised, and violence was condoned. It became a more centralised monopoly of power during colonial times, rather powerful and, as in all colonial regimes, at times brutal. But no serious attempt was made to hand over a functioning military, and the post-independence state proved unable to maintain order and imploded. Mobutu restored some sense of the monopoly of violence, and he partly depended on it to maintain control. There were recurring troubles in this vast country, but relatively few despite the terrible governance in the 1980s. But then the state ran out of things to loot to pay soldiers, and just controlling the central bank's printing press was not a sustainable long-term strategy.[42] In the mid-1990s, the monopoly of violence totally disappeared, and up to now it has not been restored, especially not in the east of the country. Over the last twenty years, the state's inability to control decentralised forces and militias, as well foreign engagement against the state, has been the most fundamental weakness of the DRC. Impunity is fundamental, and only the occasional sacrificial lambs given up after political bargaining have been referred to a national or international justice system to face punishment. Neighbouring countries and various predatory economic interests, such as mining, help sustain the cycle of violence and impunity, especially in the Kivu region and Katanga. But the country is far from achieving a reliable national, controlled army that maintains order with restraint.

What's next?

It would be unfair to say that nothing has improved in the DRC. The state remains weak and often predatory. Still, some local governments are apparently trying to achieve functional services, pay salaries properly, and maintain reasonable health services. The data, impressions, and anecdotes suggest that the DRC is not going further down the drain. The economy has stabilised, and growth has been decent, albeit from extremely low levels. Still, this country is clearly not on the path to development or peace. For that, the change has been far too little.

The peace agreement of 2003 suggested that a technocratic government would lead the country out of the development abyss. However, technocrats were hardly given the power or the incentives to do so. The usual technical fixes offered by the World Bank and IMF—increase the ease of doing business, promote transparent commercial and legal frameworks, reform the labour markets and in general deal with factor market failures, and enact policy changes, such as in the tax structure—are unlikely to work on their own. For example, IMF assistance has been conditional on transparency in natural resource contracts. But seemingly legal contracts hide closed deals that have generated billions for the associates of Kabila.

How did this work? The state would sign a contract with intermediaries linked to the corrupt players in government, who then sold the contract for a much larger sum to another mining company interested in actual mineral extraction. The profits were pocketed while the 'legally procured' contracts were transparently published. A team led by Kofi Annan found, for example, that five contracts were initially underpriced by the government, leading to forgone revenue of up to $3 billion, which was pocketed by the intermediaries with impunity. Meanwhile, the international mining companies involved were aware of the scheme, even if they did not act illegally themselves.[43] The spanking new private jets at Kinshasa airport linked to the mining hub of Lubumbashi tell at least some of this story. With profit margins like these, the resources and incentives of those in power to stick to such a scheme are massive.

A solution requires more than capacity-building. Technical advice in such a setting must take into account politics as well as the predatory incentives. For example, there are good reasons to build state capacity, and increasing tax revenue may be a route.[44] In the process, the state could signal that it intends to build its capacity by organising its tax collection transparently.[45] However, predatory incentives do not just disappear. So the introduction of performance-related pay in the tax authority, which can retain up to 40 per cent to top up salaries, may indeed give collectors incentives to undertake more visits to collect taxes, as they now win twice: either they receive a bribe to avoid payment or they receive a share of the tax receipts. The average level of bribes may rise as well. A proud minister of finance once revealed in a 2013 meeting with foreign representatives, including me, that value added tax (VAT) refunds had been larger than receipts. Hardly a source of pride, for it meant that the tax authorities either had been refunding fake invoices or had 'failed' to collect much of the VAT owed.[46] In any case, the government was incurring a loss on its tax, turning the tax into a subsidy!

Because of the enormous challenges of conflict, the economy, and development, many international partners have re-engaged with the DRC government in recent years. There is no doubt that some in government, and across the state system, are keen to move forward. However, the commitment to development is just too limited; the fragile elite bargain remains uninterested. Even aid money accepted by the government is not being spent: the execution rate, the share of agreed-on programmes that are implemented, is only 17 per cent of funding.

Overall, representatives of aid organisations and others find working in the DRC difficult. For example, one IMF representative, otherwise very engaging and fully understanding of the need to work politically in the DRC, told me, 'This is the worst place I have worked in.' Or as the Chinese economic counsellor exclaimed, '*Ce n'est pas normale,*' while bemoaning how he was unable to complete any of China's grant aid projects.

But this is not how most of Africa works, as is sometimes argued. Throughout this book, I have highlighted many cases of corruption and economic measures seemingly designed to support rent-seeking by those connected to the state in other countries. What appeared during the time of Mobutu in Congo and persists to this day goes much further. It is far more systematic disorder in which the state is organised to support the elite bargain in a way that prevents any growth and development. It is a negative-sum game being played in the economy and society: *débrouillez-vous*,[47] or grab anything that one can, even if the gain is far smaller than the losses suffered by the losers. The result is an extreme informalisation of the economy, with few incentives for investment and a negotiated space between those with some semblance of power or authority and those trying to make a living. This situation is not typical of Africa as a whole— just of the few African countries that have descended into this trap of disorder.[48]

References

Acemoglu, D., T. Verdier, and J. A. Robinson. 2004. 'Kleptocracy and Divide-and-Rule: A Model of Personal Rule'. *Journal of the European Economic Association* 2 (2–3): 162–92.

Africa Confidential. 2013. 'Gertler's Assets Multiply'. 54 (11): 6–7.

———. 2020. '23 Years of Mining Congo for Profit'. 61 (16): 7.

———. 2021. 'Félix Tips the Scale'. 62 (3): 7-8.

Africa Progress Panel. 2013. 'Equity in Extractives: Stewarding Africa's Natural Resources for All'. Annual Report 2013, Geneva.

Bayart, J. F. 2009. *The State in Africa. The Politics of the Belly*, 2nd ed. Cambridge, MA: Polity.

Bergeron, A., G. Tourek, and J. Weigel. 2020. 'The State Capacity Ceiling on Tax Rates: Evidence from Randomized Tax Abatements in the DRC'. Working paper, London School of Economics.

Besley, Timothy, and Torsten Persson. 2009. 'The Origins of State Capacity: Property Rights, Taxation and Politics'. *American Economic Review* 99 (4): 1218–44.

Bevan, D. L., P. Collier, and J. W. Gunning. 1999. *Nigeria and Indonesia: The Political Economy of Poverty, Equity, and Growth*. A World Bank Comparative Study. New York: Oxford University Press.

Booth, A. 2013. 'Variations in Exploitation in Colonial Settings: Dutch and Belgian Policies in Indonesia and the Congo and Their Legacies'. In *Colonial Exploitation and Economic Development: The Belgian Congo and the Netherlands Indies Compared*, edited by E. Frankema and F. Buelens. Abingdon-on-Thames, UK: Routledge.

Burns, S., and O. Owens. 2019. 'Nigeria: No Longer an Oil State?' Oxford Martin School Working Paper, August.

Chabal, P., and J.-P. Daloz. 1998. *Africa Works: The Political Instrumentalization of Disorder*. Woodbridge, UK: James Currey.

Gould, D. J. 1980. 'Patrons and Clients: The Role of the Military in Zaire Politics'. In *The Performance of Soldiers as Governors: African Politics and the African Military*, edited by Isaac Mowoe. Washington, DC: University Press of America.

Hochschild, A. 1999. *King Leopold's Ghost: A Story of Greed, Terror, and Heroism in Colonial Africa*. Boston: Houghton Mifflin Harcourt.

Joseph, R. A. 2014. *Democracy and Prebendal Politics in Nigeria*. Cambridge: Cambridge University Press.

Kohli, A. 2004. *State-Directed Development: Political Power and Industrialization in the Global Periphery*. Cambridge: Cambridge University Press.

Laokri, S., R. Soelaeman, and D. R. Hotchkiss. 2018. 'Assessing Out-of-Pocket Expenditures for Primary Health Care: How Responsive Is the Democratic Republic of Congo Health System to Providing Financial Risk Protection?' *BMC Health Services Research* 18 (1): 1–19.

Lewis, P. 2009. *Growing Apart: Oil, Politics, and Economic Change in Indonesia and Nigeria*. Ann Arbor: University of Michigan Press.

Lhoest, J. J. 1995. 'The Kipushi Mine, Zaire'. *Mineralogical Record* 26 (3): 163–93.

Marivoet, W., and T. de Herdt. 2014. 'Reliable, Challenging or Misleading? A Qualitative Account of the Most Recent National Surveys and Country Statistics in the DRC'. *Canadian Journal of Development Studies / Revue canadienne d'études du développement* 35 (1): 97–119.

Moore, M. 2007. 'How Does Taxation Affect the Quality of Governance?' IDS Working Paper 280.

Ndulu, B. J., J. P. Azam, S. A. O'Connell, R. H. Bates, A. K. Fosu, J. W. Gunning, and D. Nijinkeu, eds. 2008. *The Political Economy of Economic Growth in Africa, 1960–2000*, vol. 2. Cambridge: Cambridge University Press.

Nkuku, A. M., and K. Titeca. 2018. 'Market Governance in Kinshasa: The Competition for Informal Revenue through "Connections" (Branchement)'. Working Paper 2018.3, Institute of Development Policy, University of Antwerp.

Oriakhi, D. E., and I. D. Osaze. 2013. 'Oil Price Volatility and Its Consequences on the Growth of the Nigerian Economy: An Examination (1970–2010)'. *Asian Economic and Financial Review* 3 (5): 683–702.

Robinson, J. 2013. 'Curing the Mal Zaïrois: The Democratic Republic of Congo Edges toward Statehood'. Legatum Institute.

Usman, Z. 2020. 'The Successes and Failures of Economic Reform in Nigeria's Post-military Political Settlement'. *African Affairs* 119 (474): 1–38.

Van Reybrouck, D. 2014. *Congo: The Epic History of a People*. London: Fourth Estate.

Weigel, J. L. 2020. 'The Participation Dividend of Taxation: How Citizens in Congo Engage More with the State When It Tries to Tax Them'. *Quarterly Journal of Economics* 135 (4): 1849–903.

Wiseman, J. 1999. 'Review of: The Criminalization of the State in Africa by J.-F. Bayart, S. Ellis and B. Hibou and Africa Works: Disorder as a Political Instrument by P. Chabal and J.-P. Daloz'. *Journal of Modern African Studies* 37 (3): 507–80.

8

TAMING CLANS OF HYENAS

PEACE AND ECONOMIC DEALS IN SOUTH SUDAN, AFGHANISTAN, NEPAL, LEBANON, AND SOMALILAND

Business leaders from across Afghanistan had congregated at the Kabul Intercontinental to discuss the country's economic opportunities, and I was privileged to be among them. Still grateful for the four British close protection officers who kept an eye on me at all times, I realise now their presence might not have been enough. A few years later, the same hotel was the scene of a vicious attack that killed many dozens of people attending an event like this.

I was in Afghanistan in 2014, not long after Ashraf Ghani became president. He probably won the popular vote in the presidential elections, but the world will never know because not all the votes were counted.[1] The US Embassy had insisted on stopping the vote count, and John Kerry, then US secretary of state, had flown in to force Ghani to strike a deal with his main contender. It was a time for hope: rumour had it that the Taliban were willing to talk, and Ghani, with his widespread Pashtun support, could well be the right person for them, even if it meant sweeping the election results under the rug. Seven years later, all Western troops left, and the Taliban were in power again, just as in 2001.

By 2014, the Western allies in NATO hoped they could step back from a conflict that stemmed from an emotion-driven show of strength to the 9/11 attacks aimed at cutting off the terrorist threat from al-Qaida fighters. In Afghanistan, they were under the protection of the Taliban-led government in Kabul. After NATO drove the Taliban out of Kabul and into the mountains, the NATO campaign quickly came to an end. Or so it seemed. Like the British forces in the nineteenth century and the Russians in the 1980s, NATO forces have since discovered that in Afghanistan conflicts often end in stalemate or defeat.

In 2014, there was relief that the government of Hamid Karzai had come to an end. It had been marred by an inability to build a consensus among the competing groups, a rise in corruption built on patronage, and a general ineptitude in rebuilding the weak, fragmented state, marred by conflict, into a functioning one.[2] Western capitals especially believed Ashraf Ghani was the right person to fix this failed state: surely a former World Bank official and author of the manual *Fixing Failed States* had to be the man for the job.[3] But Afghanistan has not proved to be so fixable.

This chapter is about states in conflict and how they may emerge from it. The economics and political science literature contains much about why civil wars start or persist.[4] I am more interested here in how they end, and how deals bringing peace and stability arise. The framework developed in chapter 2 is helpful. There, it was suggested that a new state arises from a bargain among those with the power to choose peace and stability over conflict. They see it as a better way to gain wealth and power, turning plundering 'roving bandits' into 'stationary bandits', and manipulating the economy to their advantage through their shared control over the state.[5]

Whatever the underlying causes of conflict, or the motivations to seek an end to conflict, my entry point is therefore that peace will succeed only if it has serious economic underpinnings, so that the elite bargain that brings peace can be sustained. Peace will then require a shared commitment to rebuilding an economy of sorts. Because the alternative—remaining in conflict—is so grim, this economic deal may not amount to much. However, even if it serves up redistributive politics so that the gains flow to the parties to the deal, it could offer the beginnings of stability. But even this outcome among parties in conflict often proves hard enough. Trust is low, so commitment needs some form of lock-in. I call this peace a business deal. Not quite peace as John Lennon imagined it, but a start.

In what follows I begin with my experiences with South Sudan and Afghanistan—and they are not stories likely to soon have a happy ending. Peace may not make economic sense for the elites in South Sudan, while peace in Afghanistan may have become economically unsustainable even before the Taliban returned to power. Development assistance is featured in this chapter as well, as it is not neutral. The humanitarian assistance in South Sudan and the large-scale financing of the state in Afghanistan have changed the economic incentives for peace. And when peace deals come, no one should be naive: a benevolent state with a development bargain will not emerge overnight or ever.

Later in this chapter, I turn to Nepal, Lebanon, and Somaliland—countries that give me hope, not because they are spectacular development successes or icons of good governance (they are far from it), but rather because they have found a way of turning the first corner: peace there involves an economic deal among the elite.

The scavenger state of South Sudan

I stepped out of the ramshackle Tupolev helicopter, which was flying with a United Nations roundel. Oil had leaked from the roof throughout our journey, but the Estonian crew had laughed off our concerned looks. We had travelled from South Sudan's capital, Juba, into rebel-held territory to see first-hand the humanitarian relief offered to refugees who had fled to the city, starting with a large food aid warehouse near the runway. This was Ganyiel in 2016.

It struck me that there were no soldiers in sight to check on us. The warehouse was filled with tons of grain, but there were no guards either, even though reportedly thousands of hungry refugees were nearby, and there was an army to feed as well. The tarmac was lined with spacious simple bungalows, each the bustling local headquarters of an NGO. Some had been there for decades. The local commander who had welcomed us, wearing his tight-fitting size XXXL army fatigues, told us later that morning that he was pleased the NGOs looked after the people so he could focus on 'the important matters'.

The hype that followed South Sudan's birth as an independent state in 2011 after many decades of conflict seemed long gone. The state had emerged as part of the Comprehensive Peace Agreement (CPA) in 2005 between the Sudanese government and the rebels of the SPLA/M,[6] who had been waging an armed insurgency since the 1980s. By 2012, a new conflict had broken out between newly minted South Sudan and Sudan, and in 2013 the South Sudanese leaders, President Salva Kiir and his vice president, Riek Machar, fell out violently. Since then, conflict has flared up repeatedly. Even though a peace deal was struck between the main protagonists in 2018, South Sudan remains as fragile as before, and fighting has been reported in many areas in 2021.

Protracted conflict obviously affects people and the economy. The data are incomplete, but estimates suggest that South Sudan's economy as measured by GDP per capita has declined by more than half since independence.[7] The vast majority of people live below the international poverty line of $1.90 per person a day, and one in ten children will not reach age five. In several districts, large numbers of people have faced severe hunger in recent years.[8] Why is peace so hard in South Sudan? Why has independence offered so little to this population?

Peace as an interlude

For the previous forty years, the SPLA had been one of many groups linked to peripheral provincial elites[9] in conflict with the elites controlling politics and the economy from Khartoum, Sudan's capital. After 1989, when President Bashir came to power in Sudan, this control became a balancing act between a military-commercial elite and an Islamist elite. The SPLA's undisputed, charismatic, and highly educated leader, John Garang, was keen to capture power in Khartoum, and at most saw an autonomous South Sudan as a stepping stone to power throughout the country. After his accidental death in 2005 he was succeeded by his deputy, Salva Kiir. With his leadership far more disputed, Kiir focused on an independence deal for his cronies in the provincial elite in South Sudan; he was less interested in Khartoum. Kiir struck a deal with most of the South Sudanese leading groups and factions to support independence, and it was overwhelmingly approved in 2011 in a referendum.

But this is not the story the world heard during this period. A craving to see all conflict as a fight between good and evil, or between plucky rebels and awful oppressors, led to attractive narratives supportive of the SPLA/M leaders. Even Hollywood joined in, painting the conflict as one between poor and excluded Africans and their exploiters—rich, violent Arabs—or as one between devout Christians and the Islamists who had martyred them. The SPLA was cast as the Christian liberators and Kiir as the Joshua who would lead his people to the promised land.[10] Once Khartoum was out of the way, an independent South Sudan would become an enlightened beacon of development, working its way out of poverty and delivering for the South Sudanese people.

Conflict in Sudan has always been about more than ethnicity or religion. However, those vying for more power have tried to use these factors to rally people to their cause. Those in power in Khartoum had little time for the southern province, whether its elite or its people. And yet they did sit up and take notice of a political entrepreneur like John Garang, who in the 1980s began to use the tried and tested technique of resorting to violence to stake southern claims to the rents produced by Sudan's state and economy, in part no doubt with some decent intentions and ideals.[11] In 1999, the stakes vastly increased when oil began to transform the fortunes of the Sudanese state, and oil was exported at scale from the south of Sudan. By 2005, exports from the south rose to about $4 billion, yielding some $3 billion in revenue for the government each year by then and with more expected in the future.

Although oil and the new-found wealth did not cause the conflict, it meant the conflict could not be ignored. And so the door was opened for a peace deal. Khartoum could buy its own supporters, while leaving more than enough for the rebels to get their share of the loot. Rising oil revenue and peaceful exploitation of oil would allow all parties to be better-off.[12] The cost of not settling would make all worse off. The prospect of rent-sharing between northern and southern elites was then on the cards.

The ample oil production made peace possible. The peace deal committed an independent south to paying substantial revenue to the northern remainder of Sudan. Overall, it looked highly sensible. The combined oil production continued to increase, reaching more than 450,000 barrels between 2007 and 2011, 350,000 of which came from what is now South Sudan. At the oil prices of that period, that amount translated into well over $10 billion in export revenue, or $7 billion in potential government rents, half of which would stay in South Sudan. By 2011, oil rents were 55 per cent of the GDP of South Sudan. In theory, this oil wealth should have transformed South Sudan—otherwise essentially a tropical subsistence economy with no obvious other engines of economic progress. In practice, however, the deal gave Kiir and all his rivals for power an opportunity to gain unseen wealth, leaving enough to pay off their supporters and create a stable state, even if built around patronage and clientelism. To be frank, given the state of South Sudan and the endless suffering from conflict and destitution, I would accept this outcome. But the SPLA/M chose neither the route to progress through development nor a cosy life for the elite to live off the rents. It chose the third way: more conflict.

So where did it all go wrong? Peace was based on an explicit economic deal that could support the underlying political deal between the north and the south. The conditions needed to sustain peace seemed to be there. The economic deal was sufficiently lubricated that every warlord and militia leader involved could be paid off, still leaving enough for widespread patronage. But building a state, even one constructed on patronage and clientelism, requires leadership and judgement, but Kiir and other leaders of the SPLA showed they lacked these qualities. Good judgement failed Kiir in 2012 when he raised the stakes by restarting the war with Sudan, trying to get a better oil deal. Little was gained in the end, and the fallout led to a split in 2013 with his deputy, Riek Machar. It also further fractured the loose coalition of provincial elites, all of whom expected more systematic rewards for their support. Meanwhile, state structures, if only to deliver patronage effectively, did not even begin to emerge.[13] All parties played up the ethnic strife and rivalries, with success. In 2016, a young man in Ganyiel told me that he didn't like the leaders' willingness to fight, but if he was called on to defend his people, he, like many of his family members, would do so.

Since then, and unlike in the pre-independence period, oil is of no help in arriving at a peace deal. In 2014, oil prices collapsed, never to recover to the peak around the time of independence. The promised wealth is not there, so no peace deal can offer pay-offs at levels promised before. No leader can easily sell a potential deal in which all will be worse off than before the conflict—a conflict rooted in a quest for higher rents for each group. Kiir and Machar are notoriously bad deal-makers, but no others are in the wings to take these hard decisions. Deals may be signed, but every deal looks temporary—an interlude until the next conflict. It will involve promises of riches for all, again to create an illusion of success. Meanwhile, the country and its leaders are living off the scraps, and even its oil exploration is in tatters. The South Sudanese state and its leaders could have been lions, but they chose to be clans of hyenas fighting over the scraps.

The humanitarian dilemma

With the benefit of hindsight, international aid hasn't helped South Sudan either. Large oil windfalls in 2011, the year of independence, were immediately spent, at levels double the original government budget. The government expenditure rapidly expanded, to $340 per capita, a level much higher than in neighbouring Sudan, Uganda, or Ethiopia. But the overexpenditure did not go to essential services such as education or health care. Instead, virtually all the windfalls were spent on public administration (to pay newly recruited public servants handsomely) and security (to expand and pay off the military). By law, institutional structures were set up, such as an independent central bank, a budget office, and an auditor general, but, in practice, neither budgets nor accountability hardly mattered from day one.

Meanwhile, international aid began to expand, in 2011 to levels similar to that of neighbouring countries such as Uganda and

Ethiopia, but rapidly rising by 2013 to levels per capita three times as high. At this point, the global romcom with South Sudan and its leaders began to turn into a dark reality show with a disreputable cast. At first, ample technical assistance was provided to build the government capacity that this new state clearly lacked but its leaders hardly cared for. Donors stepped in to run social services such as health care and education by means of hundreds of parallel project implementation units (outside government systems).[14] The government was pleased. In fact, in 2016 the president's economic advisor expressed his gratitude to me as a UK official that setting up and funding health care and education in the country 'could be left to the donors'.

With the civil war intensifying, more and more people became dependent on humanitarian support, and some international organisations simply took over all the local health systems, while others provided cash or food, as well as a semblance of safety and protection for displaced populations. Unfortunately, this is not the whole story. The local military authority no longer had to be responsible for the welfare of the local population, and so the rebels could focus on what they wanted—conflict and control and prolonging their stand-off.

Grim times still lie ahead for the impoverished population of South Sudan. Outsiders can make some difference, but less than anyone would ever hope for. Living with conflict has been a normal way of life for many decades, and this is not going to change anytime soon.

Afghanistan: The unaffordable peace

Control of Afghanistan, a crossroads of historical trading routes between East and West and between North and South, has long been contested by tribal clans, including Pashtuns, Tajiks, Uzbeks, and Hazaras. The politics of identity, interwoven with religious ideology, is used as a vehicle for popular support for its competing leaders. Local warlords and strongmen epitomise the notion of a 'stationary bandit', but most have been unable to establish a local or central 'monopoly of violence' for long periods of time.[15] The economics of it all cannot be discounted. For many years, access to resources from fertile valleys, the mining wealth, and trading routes have been at stake as a means to both gain and consolidate power. Even the Taliban, that fusion of Islamic Deobandi fundamentalist ideology and Pashtun tribal values, willingly embraced the benefits of controlling trade routes, taxing trade in the areas they control.

One lesson foreign troops have relearned from their decades in Afghanistan is that entering a conflict in that country is easy, but leaving gracefully is much harder. It is a hornet's nest of shifting local loyalties and distrust. With military campaigns stuck for the last decade, the West just wanted to cut its losses. In 2021, it did so and NATO troops left. Ghani's government collapsed, albeit faster than most expected, and the Taliban were back in charge.

In the years before the return of the Taliban, much commentary on the Afghan peace negotiations of the Taliban with international powers, as well as with the Ghani government, focused on the political deal that may follow: how to achieve power-sharing between groups with deep divides in terms of ideology and identity, bearing in mind the brutal nature of the previous Taliban administration between 1996 and 2001.[16] Here, I focus on the economic dimensions that made an Afghan peace deal quite implausible. Not only have decades of conflict undermined the economic base of the state, but both conflict and the vast military and development aid support from the West had distorted its foundations, creating vested interests that made a deal between the parties hardly possible, let alone affordable. Even though regime change rather than a peace deal has now emerged, this economic reality cannot be ignored even by the Taliban. In the rest of this section, I explore the economics of peace in Afghanistan in more detail.

Not an opium war

With that in mind, during my trip to Afghanistan in 2014 I was keen to understand what economic opportunities emerging after decades of conflict could serve as a basis of renewed stability as part of a new elite bargain. A highlight was venturing out of the Green Zone for conversations over tea in the margins of the event described earlier at

Kabul International. I learned first-hand about the opportunities in the mining and trading of gemstones from well-connected Tajik and Uzbek businessmen, about the dreams of a young Kabuli software entrepreneur, and about the history of Pashtun trading families from Kandahar, who have for more than a century been exporting horticultural products across the region and beyond. That history of Afghanistan tends to be forgotten: the country used to account for 60 per cent of global raisin exports, and it was known as well for selling the best apricots and almonds, grown in the fertile irrigated valleys of Kandahar and Helmand Provinces.[17]

After decades of conflict, the economy is hardly so benign. Most growth opportunities have come from sectors intertwined with the conflict, such as construction and security, on the back of vast foreign spending on military and other aid. And dried fruits have been replaced by that other horticultural export crop, the opium poppy (the basis for heroin), which accounts for even higher shares of the global (illegal) market than raisins in earlier times.

While generating tens of billions for criminal gangs across the world, Afghanistan's profits from the opium poppy are huge as well, but still relatively modest—on average an estimated $3 billion a year, or about 15 per cent of the country's GDP. Of that amount, about $1 billion may end up in the pockets of the farmers,[18] or less than about $90 per capita overall—far less than, say, oil rents per capita in Nigeria (at well over $300 per capita). Of course, many further downstream in the value chain make massive profits from the opium poppy. And the Taliban also used to capture some of this, probably in the range of a few hundred million per year. This amount is nevertheless far less than sometimes suggested.

However, the war with the Taliban never was about control of opium poppy production or trade. It wasn't even financed by it.[19] More important, the end of that conflict is unlikely to end that production and trade: the opium poppy is by far the most lucrative crop in vast areas of the country. For many Afghans with little alternative but subsistence farming, not growing the crop would push them back into poverty.[20] Powerful traders and financiers from all sides of the divide will also not quickly let go. Bans in any case have proved ineffective, and for the last two decades the US has spent about $1.5 million a day on eradication policies in Afghanistan, with no success to show for them.[21] For the opium poppy to lose its attraction, the country will need an economy that offers farmers and traders alike better investment opportunities, unless by some miracle the global heroin demand were to collapse.

The wrong structural transformation

A more immediate problem from decades of foreign meddling is that much of the rest of the economy is directed at the conflict economy, and aid has played a big part in this. The sums involved are extraordinary. The US alone spent at least $45 billion on Afghanistan in 2018 (most of it on military and security objectives), which is more than twice the country's GDP. US military spending has totalled around $1 trillion over the last twenty years.[22] Much of it was spent on its own forces and the private security firms it brought into the country: about 100,000 soldiers in 2010, as well as 94,143 security contractors.[23] Meanwhile, direct US aid to Afghanistan in 2010 was $5.4 billion, of which about two-thirds was spent on the government's military and security sectors. The rest was development aid, as it is usually understood.[24] Overall, international military and other aid spent directly on Afghanistan had actually declined in recent years, having peaked at around $16 billion in 2011, of which again two-thirds was military support.

Even if much of the aid had taken the form of in-kind supplies, including hardware for the Afghan military and other security forces,[25] many billions in security and development aid were still being spent on the ground. No doubt the development part did some good things for people—and I do not in any way want to belittle this. Even if statistics are hard to verify, all point to considerable improvements such as in life expectancy, girls' education, and child mortality statistics. For some, this should be enough: from 1 million children in primary education in 2001, two-thirds of children, or about 6 million, are now in school, of which about 2 million are girls. Vaccination rates went from a quarter of young children to two-thirds.[26] Nevertheless, aid did more than just good things. Conflict settings are difficult places to spend well, not least when a lot needs to be spent, and aid is spent for more than just assisting people (see box 8.1).

Box 8.1 Development aid—hearts and minds

The fact that NATO and especially the US had so many boots on the ground in Afghanistan and were spending massively on the security sector accounted for the extraordinary amounts of development aid directed to that country. The sheer volume says more about the unintended consequences of military campaigns than about aid and its general effectiveness or impact.

There is little doubt that some thought the large volume could help finish the military involvement faster, cement support for the government and a foreign presence, or at least reduce violence by tamping down support for the Taliban— that is, aid would help change the 'hearts and minds' of the local population in support of military objectives.[27] Most evidence suggests that this approach did not work in high-conflict areas, even though expectations there were the highest. Locally, support for or objections to the Taliban rarely revolved around the type of socio-economic issues aid may try to address. More often, it was about the rule of law or local governance, including the role of powerful families and strongmen.

The pressure to spend quickly, with little understanding of local conflict dynamics, hardly improved the chances that good development would take root. Delivery was often dependent on strongmen or officials, too often corrupt, who may have been responsible for some of the alienation of the local population to start with.[28] Aid may then have made the conflict worse locally. There was hardly a systematic change in hearts and minds, and military strategists probably expected far too much from this type of aid. In less conflict-affected areas such as in the north, development efforts operating in parallel to basic security efforts were found to be more conducive to reducing violence.[29]

Aid was not just difficult to spend well on the ground, but it also had wider consequences. In Afghanistan, the astonishing scale of aid spending changed the way the government operated and the structure of and incentives within the economy. Those changes made any peace deal difficult, hard to sustain, and possibly unaffordable. It also meant the Taliban inherited a state that was never sustainable, no matter who was in charge.

Changes in the structure and cost of the public sector

After the fall of the Taliban in 2001, foreign aid had paid for most government spending.[30] But the aid was mostly off-budget—that is, between 2001 and 2010 about 82 per cent of total aid was spent outside the usual government systems of delivery and accountability.[31] At huge expense, the Afghan military had to be built up, boosting troops' wages but also providing them with advanced kits and training.[32] The other large aid flows to support the emergence of a functioning state at speed meant that whole new structures had to be created to manage the state,[33] parallel to the existing state structures and staffed by a 'second civil service'. Members of this service were Afghan, some returning from the diaspora, but benefiting from far better contracts than those of the regular civil service to manage these large aid-funded programmes, supported by a sizeable army of foreign technical assistance consultants.

One can understand the choices made, but they have consequences, and they made a sustainable peace deal harder. After the initial removal of the Taliban, the new government and donors had encountered the remnants of a state with limited accountability, built around patronage and shady informal connections—in short, a hippo state. It was clear that simply rebuilding that state would not suffice, nor could it be easily changed. For the donor countries, this parallel public sector with its second civil service seemed the only way to provide a shortcut to manage security and deliver services to the population, not least when the Taliban began to re-emerge around 2006. The end result is now an Afghan state with many layers and embedded parallel systems that would be unaffordable, whether under Taliban control or not, if aid at the scale of the preceding decade were to be withdrawn.

Changes in the structure of and incentives within the economy

Meanwhile, a whole support structure was built up around the foreign and national military, as well as the development aid effort. Those with entrepreneurial zeal understood that investing in these sectors is how money would be made in the decades to come. The result? A dynamic private sector emerged, providing rapid construction, security, logistics, and other implementation support services, assisted by facilitation services offered by people who could make things happen—in other words, those with a contact list of whoever mattered at home and with a bank account in Dubai. Large-scale corruption and procurement fraud were the name of the game. Compared with this part of the economy, the opium poppy economy became almost benign, productive, and locally impactful.

There's no need to be surprised about the consequences. The same forces that led to a government based on patronage rather than accountability were responsible for the growth of a private sector built on links to those with power and influence with the warlords, clan leaders, and leading families. Large-scale international aid did not cause corruption, but it definitely fuelled it in this patronage-based state, with its fragile balance of fragmented power and influence (see box 8.2). SIGAR, the official US Special Inspector General for Afghanistan Reconstruction,[34] repeatedly issued warnings about the scale of corruption, and in 2020 wrote, in a diplomatic understatement, that SIGAR's 'work has repeatedly identified the impunity of powerful Afghans as an ongoing issue'.[35]

Box 8.2 Corruption in Afghanistan: Some examples

Procurement fraud and embezzlement were the biggest games in town. The amounts involved were in the billions. One case, linked to the Kabul Bank with close connections to President Karzai and other leaders, involved laundering

---

about $1 billion in illicit loot to Dubai.[36] Corruption also occurred in seemingly legal ways. A large number of firms sprang up with links to the Gulf and the US, but they also were connected to various members of the Afghan elite. In the security sector in particular, local firms were subcontractors for international firms providing security and logistics services to NATO or development actors. Their ability to function depended on how they work with those in power across Afghanistan, requiring contacts with local militia and strongmen, and even the Taliban.[37]

At times, the tactics these operations used seem almost amateurish—for example, local strongmen attacking infrastructure projects and then pressing for a security contract to protect the same projects in the future.[38] Other cases were bizarre but common, such as US contractors connected to a former defence minister allegedly paying off the Taliban to allow military equipment to pass through to attack the Taliban.[39] Afghanistan is consistently ranked among the most corrupt countries in the world by Transparency International. To put the country in perspective, most recently it ranked just above the Democratic Republic of Congo.[40]

So what's next?

It is hardly surprising that outside military intervention and vast international cash inflows on the scale observed in Afghanistan over the last two decades have had unintended consequences. Among other things, patronage and clientelism are now even more deeply embedded, undermining the functioning of an emergent state under Taliban control.[41] The economy has been living off public sector procurement—in particular, in the security and construction sectors—but these sectors are hardly the basis for productivity growth.[42] Moreover, many of the existing firms were built on connections to politics and power, and so they are rife with illicit behaviour.[43] Even if the West believed a political deal could be struck, there just is no economic basis for it. It's no wonder endless discussions in Doha never went anywhere: no deal on sharing the rents was going to be credible.

And yet it is not impossible that one day better economic and political deals will emerge, built on the ruins of the unintended economic consequences of massive external support. Afghanistan has mineral wealth, including copper, gold, precious stones, and iron ore. According to the Ministry of Mines, it may have 'up to a trillion dollars in natural resources', perhaps accounting for 20 per cent of GDP in 2030. However, an elite bargain built around natural resources in specific regions in a country of loose alliances and deals with lots of militias and warlords, whether or not brokered through the Taliban, is no basis for sustainability. Fortunately, Afghanistan has more. It has fertile land for horticulture and successful and connected traders. Afghanistan's success in the global opium poppy value chain is a hopeful sign, indicating that poor farmers can grow high-value horticultural crops of the required quality, and smart traders are able to link high-value products into profitable value chains that feed into the ports of Rotterdam and Antwerp, even if at present only illegally. Perhaps some future reconfiguration of power in Afghanistan will open the door for more licit trade links in the region—into Pakistan, India, Iran, or China. Or perhaps Afghanistan's world dominance in raisins and high-quality almonds and apricots may one day resume. Unfortunately, after decades of conflict sustainable peace and development may require not just political wizardry and extensive foreign support, but also an economic miracle.

Peace as a business deal

Magic and miracles happen. Civil wars appear to end, and a future without armed conflict seems possible. In the three countries featured in this section—Nepal, Lebanon, and Somaliland—civil war came to an end in surprising ways that appear to have lasted, and without the spectacle of destructive regime change, as seen in Afghanistan. The descriptions that follow are not a complete analysis of these states and their conflicts, but rather a look at some of the striking features of the peace deals and how they appear to have been self-reinforcing.

Although none of these countries is obviously a success story in terms of development and growth, they are worth considering because the counterfactual—continued conflict on a large scale and with much human suffering—did not materialise. Underlying each story is an elite bargain that was not just an opportunity for peace but also one worth keeping, politically and economically. In Nepal, a changing political landscape allowed leaders to be sensible and step back from the brink. In Lebanon and Somaliland, a way was found to construct an elite bargain appealing to all parties. And in all three countries, the key elite players continued to compete for resources, but without the threat of extreme violence.

In a look at the three countries, two factors stand out. First, one needs enough key players willing to make a deal. They do not have to put aside their fundamental differences, but they do have to be willing to gamble on making progress through stability rather than conflict. Second, the economic deal matters because it shapes the incentives offered to the parties: this is the main point often missed. The examples from Lebanon and Somaliland are in particular instructive.

Royals, Brahmins, and Maoists in Nepal

Our host remarked that all those sitting at the table were Brahmins, and the nine guests smiled. It was an informal dinner held during a visit to Nepal in 2015; a colleague had invited a select group of journalists and academics from across the political divide. We were debating, never heatedly, whether the new constitution would finally be approved and whether it would change much for the population at large. I asked how Nepal had come back from the brink in 2006, after ten years of civil war in which 17,000 people died. I knew that some around the table had supported the violence.

The conflict had pitched Maoists, unhappy with the lack of militancy on the part of the other parties striving for democratic change, against a government supported by the royal family and reluctant to open up. The Maoists had found fertile ground in Nepal because the country continued to suffer from deeply entrenched poverty and a stagnant economy. Even though Nepal is perched between two vying powers, China and India, outside intervention was limited.

In its early stages, the conflict was sporadic, with the rebels and police involved in skirmishes. The stakes were raised in 2001 when a bizarre shooting occurred in the capital, Kathmandu. Crown Prince Dipendra, who reportedly was drunk and high on cocaine, killed the king, the queen, and many of the royal family in a shooting at their residence, the Narayanhiti Palace. His uncle, Prince Gyanendra, who assumed power as the next in line among the survivors, then tried to reintroduce more autocratic rule. A higher level of Maoist activity and a much more violent phase of the conflict followed, with direct army involvement. The new king's actions also led to a unification of the opposition, which demanded his removal. A peace deal in 2006 led to the stripping of the king's powers in 2007 and elections for a constituent assembly, which in 2008 abolished the monarchy. Since then, politics in Nepal have by no means been calm: there have been divisions, infighting, and reunification across the leading blocs. But the process has been broadly peaceful, and few worry about a return to conflict.

One could argue that King Gyanendra made an alternative political deal possible by alienating earlier supporters of royal rule and unifying against a common enemy. Meanwhile, one should not discount the role of those with power across the political divides; they stepped back from the brink and were willing to make deals. In the end, it was no doubt an elite deal. In this highly structured society, the vast majority of leading positions in politics or the economy, across the divide, were held by members of the two upper castes, the Brahmin and Kshatriya—in Nepal called the Bahun and Chhetri.[44] This mattered because locally and nationally they all remained tied together. Even if squabbles continued among them, peace as an elite deal was possible, and when it did come, it could be sustained across the hierarchy of the Maoist rebels, whose underlying structures mirrored society.

In the end, whether by design or by implication, the economic structures did not change fundamentally. What has changed is a stronger focus on development in the poor rural areas in the plains, hills, and mountains, creating not only both more local patronage and corruption, but also a gradual change in living conditions.[45] Poverty and deprivation have declined, according to several indicators: poverty at the international poverty line, the survival chances of children beyond age five, and primary education now reaching levels better than those in India. The economy has picked up as well, with growth of GDP per capita at 4 per cent a year between 2006 and 2019, or double the rate achieved during the conflict decade. In 2021, per capita GDP in current dollars was just about $1,000.[46] As a result, Nepal is clearly on its way to middle-income status.

The economic deal that was chosen retained much of what was there by way of structures and how the elite could enrich themselves, but the distributive agenda was more inclusive. Yes, there were more rents, clientelism, and patronage that had expanded into rural areas, but they were accompanied by a more development orientation.[47] That economic deal bought peace and stability, and with it at least one of the key preconditions for progress in development. Nepal has by no means a development bargain, but what it does have is better than disintegration and conflict and it represents a chance to connect better to the fast growth engines in India and China.

Peace as a Ponzi scheme in Lebanon, or the art of banking

Apparent in Lebanon are the links between peace and stability and the underlying economic deals around the profits from peace. The country has repeatedly been the scene of violence and conflict, most notably during its civil war from 1975 to 1990. Well over 100,000 Lebanese died in that war, which pitched Christian and Druze against Sunni and Shia Muslims in a multi-sectarian conflict. Since the end of the war in 1990, Lebanon has had its ups and downs, not least the conflict with Israel. And yet since 1990, violence in Lebanon has dropped dramatically, allowing people to get on with their lives. Underlying this outcome is an explicit deal on the political architecture and the important offices of state.[48] Central to this is an implicit economic deal offering access to state resources along sectarian lines because both the elite and its clientelist supporters expected a large peace dividend after so much hardship. The familiar features of distributive politics are evident: government jobs, contracts, and licences, and even a 'state' within the state—such as Hezbollah in the south of the country.

How to implement a peace deal in a country with few natural resources and a limited ability to generate high taxation is not obvious. Lebanon needed to attract resources—a task for which it was well suited. Its population numbered only 7 million, but an additional 2 million were scattered across the world, many highly connected in trading, banking, and financial circles. The government sought to attract cash from the wealthy (and the odd shady investor) throughout the region by means of government bonds with exceptionally high rates of return. The funds were to be invested in the state and its patronage.

Such an undertaking required the services of an utterly skilful fund manager, who would be trusted by investors to attract the resources and could be relied on to divide the cash fairly among those participating in the deal. And so Riad Salamé, a Christian Maronite, was chosen to manage the peace deal.[49] He has been in the post of governor of the central bank since 1993, soon after the end of the civil war, acting as the banker in the financing of the messy politics of Lebanon. Salamé is an extraordinarily charming and articulate man, gracefully occupying his large Ottoman office with its stylish French antique furniture. His unassuming style belies his intelligence and his skilful balancing of sincerity and craftiness. Not for nothing is he nicknamed 'the Magician'.

Salamé became a central figure in this way of maintaining peace. He held the macroeconomic balance sheet together for decades through masterful tricks and manipulation of remittance flows, the banking sector, and the issuance of treasury bills. Even officials of the International Monetary Fund praised him for his adroit management of the 2008 financial crisis, suggesting he had a crystal ball.[50]

Meanwhile, all was based on trust—or perhaps illusion. Lebanon's powerful diaspora would invest in dollar-denominated bonds earning remarkably high returns, and this liquidity would be disbursed throughout the sectarian banking system and the state itself. Other investors would follow, bringing in cash to pay off earlier investors. Money would flow in as long as all believed that money would continue to flow in to keep the scheme going.

'It is not a Ponzi scheme,' he told me in 2015, 'it is simply the art of banking.'[51] Many disagreed, but the scheme worked. From their smart villas in the hills, the sectarian elite could see the real estate they had acquired in downtown Beirut through these schemes, so why would they want to take up arms again if this might destroy some of their personal wealth. Peace had become a business deal, and those who were benefiting from it had few incentives to sink it.

Later, however, they found their position in jeopardy when civil unrest and protests erupted against those who have lived off patronage and connections. In March 2020, the financing scheme appeared to have unravelled when there was a debt default on a $1.2 billion bond. Months later, in August 2020, extensive real estate was damaged or destroyed when fertiliser stored in the port in Beirut exploded, as a result of the neglect of a state run only for patronage.

These events left the sectarian elite reluctant to seek conflict. Their lives of wealth and patronage were at stake, making their positions tenuous for the first time in decades. One man remained still firmly in place, however, and was not at all ready to go—Riad Salamé. Whatever one may think of him, he was very likely pleased with himself—he had expertly applied some of the glue that held the peace together, perhaps avoiding decades of conflict. For three decades, this economic deal has sustained a sectarian political deal. It is ugly and corrupt, but still more peaceful than many would have expected and more peaceful than what came before during fifteen years of civil war. The last three decades should have been much better for the population. But they also could have been much worse in this region that seems permanently ablaze. Even if this elite bargain were to unravel now, these three reasonably peaceful decades are worth banking.

Somaliland: Peace in the state that doesn't exist

The ceiling fan only managed to turn slowly, showing its age. I was sitting with about thirty others around a rickety table in the boardroom of the port office in Berbera. This ancient seaport city has long been central to trade routes from present-day Somalia and eastern Ethiopia to the Gulf of Aden. If redeveloped, the port could serve as an alternative to Djibouti, only 300 kilometres farther north-west along the coast, thereby unlocking trade and economic development opportunities for Somaliland and Ethiopia into the Gulf. It was 2015, and I was visiting Somaliland to explore whether these emerging plans could work, as well as whether the tenuous peace in Somaliland might be at risk.

The others in the boardroom were all from Somaliland, senior representatives of the business community at home and of the diaspora. Some had travelled far, from Dubai, Aden, and even London, to ensure their voices were heard at the meeting. Apparently, I was the most senior UK official to visit this former capital of British Somaliland in a long time. Expectations were high, and I know those on hand had expected more from our meeting. Nevertheless, a year later Dubai Port World (DP World) took over the port as part of a half-billion-dollar investment, supported by additional stakes from the governments of Somaliland and Ethiopia. Development funding from Europe and the UK is now contributing to upgrading much of the infrastructure in Berbera and beyond, into Ethiopia as well.

All this was and is remarkable, unprecedented, and, yes, a gamble. Despite having declared independence in 1991, Somaliland is not recognised as a state by any other state in the world and is considered just part of Somalia.[52] Although much of the rest of Somalia had descended further into anarchy in 1991 from which it only slowly re-emerged, in Somaliland the various clans, subclans, and the leading families within them managed to pull back from conflict and bloody fighting between them. They agreed to a formal peace deal a few years later: Somaliland now has been broadly peaceful for almost thirty years.[53]

A lot can be said about why this peace was both possible and has been sustained, not least in comparison with the rest of Somalia. No doubt the fact that Somaliland, with its closely connected clans and subclans, is more homogeneous plays a role.[54] Its apparent ability to avoid having the jihadist group al-Shabaab destabilise its territory, whether as a result of deals or other forms of mutual understanding, helps as well. The society is still based largely on pastoralism and traditional structures, and thus respect for elders remains relatively high.[55] As a result, the elders' role in the reconciliation was meaningful, not least early on when fighting, inside Somaliland as well, intensified after the fall of President Siad Barre in 1991.

Peace in Somaliland involves an elite bargain between leading clans and subclans, building, as noted, on traditional structures.[56] It is not just a political deal among those with power. It also has a noteworthy economic deal, into which those with economic power cleverly lock themselves, making peace worthwhile for all involved.

Peace and business

In Somalia, there are two main types of players in the business community: the more traditional business elite, including those involved in the livestock trade or other commerce, and the elite more closely linked to the diaspora, such as the powerful interests in telecoms and the remittance industry. In most countries, especially those affected by conflict or other factors undermining the rule of law, there is no private sector distinct from the state or politics. This is no different in Somaliland. There, the leading businesses have deep connections to the leading families in the clans and subclans. This structure helps explain the way businesses can emerge and succeed. However, in Somaliland there is more to this story: businesses were central to how peace emerged, and they played a significant role in cementing it.

The livestock trade is big money in Somaliland. Each year live animals, mainly sheep and goats, to the value of about $300 million are shipped to Saudi Arabia and other Middle Eastern markets, mainly in time for the hajj.[57] Raising these animals is the main occupation—indeed, most people still make a living as pastoralists. As for shipping, this is where Berbera comes in. The livestock trade, which is handled through its port, accounts for the most export earnings. Many of the imported consumer goods pass through the port as well. It is then not surprising that much of the conflict in the period leading to independence and the violence that followed centred directly on control of the port.[58] One militia, linked to a local subclan in particular, tried to control the port, and ran it as a racket even after independence, to the violent dismay of all the others.

The port mattered for any chance to achieve economic recovery. It also mattered for the emergent state: it was counting on port fees to be its largest source of revenue. The ongoing conflict drove the business community to act.[59] It sponsored a series of meetings and conferences that brought all leading members of the clans together; a key one in Boroma in 1993 had national reconciliation as its objective. One early win was to make the port a weapons-free zone, thereby allowing trade to flourish.

The business community did more than sponsor conferences: it cemented the local private sector's role in the new state. Any new state needs resources to establish itself, whether to provide services or patronage. The business community stepped in by providing the state with loans to buy off politicians and elders, or by just paying them directly—in simple terms, to buy peace.[60] In return, it expected the peace to be kept, but it also wanted a business environment that suited it, with protection for Somaliland investment and limited regulation and taxation, thereby contributing to booming local businesses. Nevertheless, clan politics still played a role; politicians and elders did not simply look for money and patronage, but made a conscious deal with their own business community as part of cementing the state and the peace.[61] In short, an elite bargain was struck to end conflict, with mutually interdependent political and economic deals.

Peace can be maintained only if it is worthwhile for all involved. Immediately after a conflict, no business has an incentive to invest for the long run because it is not certain that peace will be maintained by the other clans or leading families. At my meeting with business leaders at Berbera's port, they explained they had found the means to overcome this in practice by mostly operating as investment clubs, investing in each other's businesses, even across subclans. Long-term investment could thus proceed, and its possible success was another incentive for maintaining the peace.

The business community went further: it showed trust in the deal by investing and facilitating investments by others. Such investments have been fuelled by remittances from the large diaspora, many of them refugees from the earlier conflict. Estimates suggest that remittances account for about a quarter of Somalia's GDP; in Somaliland, it may well be more.[62] Much of it is handled by Dahabshiil, the Dubai- and London-based remittance company that had its roots in Somaliland, but is now one of the largest across Africa. Competing with several other operators, it has also invested in telecommunications, thereby assisting its mobile banking. Other business families have invested in retail and hotels, in horticulture, and even in a Coca-Cola plant. And all these enterprises are supported by importers with close connections to Dubai and other Gulf ports.

The jewel in the crown is DP World's investment in the port. Development partners from Europe and the UK have complemented this with trade corridor infrastructure investments to connect the port across Somaliland and into Ethiopia. The port will bring new opportunities and much-needed revenue for the government. Still, the investment by DP World may well upset the balance there.[63] The power and reach of the state will increase, making its capture more valuable. And geopolitics are now firmly in the picture, as, more so than before, Somaliland will now be linked to Gulf and Middle Eastern politics.

* * *

Like Lebanon and Nepal, Somaliland does not have a development bargain. And by no means has Somaliland been able to create the accountable state serving the people that some saw emerging a few decades ago[64]—or the democracy that Western donors have been pushing for.[65]

Somaliland still has a desperately poor population, and it has a long way to go.[66] It has demonstrated nevertheless one of the few credible ways in which countries can step back from the brink. Its elite struck a bargain for peace and stability, in which business leaders played a central role. They have delivered a peace that the rest of Somalia envies, with sufficient economic incentives to sustain the deal. Investment has followed, as was essential to cement the deal. The Berbera port and trade corridor investment is risky, but it is a gamble for development.

References

Balthasar, D. 2013. 'Somaliland's Best Kept Secret: Shrewd Politics and War Projects as Means of State-Making'. *Journal of Eastern African Studies* 7 (2): 218–38.

Berman, E., J. Felter, J. Shapiro, and E. Troland. 2013. 'Modest, Secure and Employed: Successful Development in Conflict Zones'. *American Economic Review Papers and Proceedings* 103 (3): 512–17.

Bizhan, N. 2018. 'Aid and State-Building, Part II: Afghanistan and Iraq'. *Third World Quarterly* 39 (5): 1014–31.

Blattman, C., and E. Miguel. 2010. 'Civil War'. *Journal of Economic Literature* 48 (1): 3–57.

Coburn, N., 2015. 'Afghanistan: The 2014 Vote and the Troubled Future of Elections'. *Afghanistan: Opportunity in Crisis Series no. 8. Asia Programme*. London: Chatham House.

Collier, P., and A. Hoeffler. 2007. 'Civil War'. In *Handbook of Defense Economics*, edited by T. Chandler and K. Hartley, vol. 2, 711–39. ScienceDirect. https://www.sciencedirect.com/handbook/handbook-of-defense-economics/vol/2/suppl/C.

De Waal, A. 2015. *The Real Politics of the Horn of Africa: Money, War and the Business of Power*. Chichester, UK: John Wiley and Sons.

Dreazen, Y. 2012. 'The U.S. Spends $14K per Afghan Troop per Year, but Each Earns $1,872'. *Atlantic*, 16 April.

Fearon, J. D., and D. D. Laitin. 2003. 'Ethnicity, Insurgency, and Civil War'. *American Political Science Review* 97 (1): 75–90.

Felbab-Brown, V. 2020. 'Drugs, Security, and Counternarcotics Policies in Afghanistan'. Written evidence (AFG0027), House of Lords Intelligence and Defence Committee's Inquiry into Afghanistan.

Fishstein, P. 2014. 'Despair or Hope: Rural Livelihoods and Opium Poppy Dynamics in Afghanistan'. Afghanistan Research and Evaluation Unit (AREU), August.

———, and A. Wilder. 2012. 'Winning Hearts and Minds? Examining the Relationship between Aid and Security in Afghanistan'. Feinstein International Center, Tufts University, Medford, MA.

Ghani, A., and C. Lockhart. 2009. *Fixing Failed States: A Framework for Rebuilding a Fractured World*. Oxford: Oxford University Press.

Jones, B. 2020. 'The Kabul to Dubai Pipeline: Lessons Learned from the Kabul Bank Scandal'. In *Dubai's Role in Facilitating Corruption and Global Illicit Financial Flows*, edited by M. Page and J. Vittori. Washington, DC: Carnegie Endowment for International Peace.

Kaplan, S. 2008. 'The Remarkable Story of Somaliland'. *Journal of Democracy* 19 (3): 143–57.

Krahmann, E. 2016. 'NATO Contracting in Afghanistan: The Problem of Principal–Agent Networks'. *International Affairs* 92: 1401–26.

Mansfield, D. 2016. *A State Built on Sand: How Opium Undermined Afghanistan*. Oxford: Oxford University Press.

_____. 2017. 'Understanding Control and Influence: What Opium Poppy and Tax Reveal about the Writ of the Afghan State'. Afghanistan Research and Evaluation Unit (AREU).

Musa, A. M., and C. Horst. 2019. 'State Formation and Economic Development in Post-war Somaliland: The Impact of the Private Sector in an Unrecognised State'. *Conflict, Security and Development* 19 (1): 35–53.

North, D., B. Weingast, and J. Wallis. 2009. *Violence and Social Orders: A Conceptual Framework for Interpreting Recorded Human History*. Cambridge: Cambridge University Press.

OECD (Organisation for Economic Co-operation and Development). 2011. *2011 Report on International Engagement in Fragile States: Republic of South Sudan*. Paris: OECD.

Olson, M. 2000. *Power and Prosperity*. New York: Basic Books

Rasoly, M., and H. M. Chandrashekar. 2018. 'Export Performance of Dried Fruits from Afghanistan: A Study in Afghanistan'. *International Journal of Research in Business Studies and Management* 5 (5): 16–22.

Renders, M., and U. Terlinden. 2010. 'Negotiating Statehood in a Hybrid Political Order: The Case of Somaliland'. *Development and Change* 41 (4): 723–46.

Rolandsen, Ø. H. 2015. 'Another Civil War in South Sudan: The Failure of Guerrilla Government?' *Journal of Eastern African Studies* 9 (1): 163–74.

SIGAR (Special Inspector General for Afghanistan Reconstruction). 2020. 'Afghanistan's Anti-corruption Efforts'. SIGAR 21-09-AL.

Stepputat, F., and T. Hagmann. 2019. 'Politics of Circulation: The Makings of the Berbera Corridor in Somali East Africa'. *Environment and Planning D: Society and Space* 37 (5): 794–813.

World Bank. 2019. 'Somali Poverty and Vulnerability Assessment: Findings from Wave 2 of the Somali High Frequency Survey'. Washington, DC: World Bank.

9

BANGLADESH

THE BENGAL TIGER CUB

'Please sit down here,' my minder said with a wide smile but in a commanding voice, pointing to the only chair to be seen. I was about to sit on the concrete floor, thereby joining the five women waiting for me in the small courtyard in front of the tin-roof house. But seated in the chair, I ended up towering awkwardly over the small group.

Early on as a researcher, I had often met with those living in poor rural settings, seeking to learn more about their daily lives, their struggles, and their joys. In more recent times, as a UK development agency official, I found myself meeting those who had been supported by one or other UK development project, and my minders were government officials.

This trip was different, however. On this visit to Bangladesh,[1] I was not the guest of government officials, but of BRAC, the largest nongovernmental organisation (NGO) in the world, almost operating as a shadow civil service across many of the country's poorest communities. I had spent the previous evening with my minders in the simple surroundings of a local training college. They were knowledgeable about the rural community we were visiting, even though they themselves had had more urban upbringings. All men, they were gentle and respectful, even if the next day they still sounded slightly patronising to the women in the courtyard. Meanwhile, it was clear that, as usual, those I would talk to had been carefully screened and would tell me about how much their lives had been changed by the support they received.

But I did not need to be suspicious of the success of the programme up for discussion. I was talking to women who had benefited from BRAC's Ultra-Poor Programme, one of the few successful development programmes to help the extremely poor take the first steps out of poverty. The evidence had been reported in the best scientific journals.[2]

Bangladesh, with 165 million people, is one of largest of the developing countries. It is also one of the most remarkable success stories of the last three decades in the developing world. The country has by no means been perfect in its development trajectory, but the economy and the lives of many millions have improved measurably. At independence in 1971, after a short but bloody secession war with Pakistan, Bangladesh's GDP per capita was only $322, one of the lowest in the world. Over the next seventeen years, until 1989, growth was sluggish—only about 1.3 per cent a year per capita. It then accelerated, doubling to 2.5 per cent on average in the next decade, and from 1995 to 2015 growth was almost 5 per cent per capita a year, raising the country to middle-income status in 2015.[3]

Extreme poverty has declined rapidly over the last three decades: survey estimates suggest levels of 43.7 per cent of people under the international poverty line of $1.90 in 1991, declining to 14.5 per cent in 2016.[4] Other indicators reflect this reduction: one in five children did not survive to age five around independence while the figure now is only one in thirty. Girls score especially well in all types of education statistics. For example, in contrast to neighbouring India or other large Muslim countries, Pakistan and Indonesia, more girls are in secondary education than boys.[5] The fertility rate, a helpful composite sign of female progress driven by a large number of factors from education and nutrition to economic opportunity, dropped from 6.9 children per woman in 1972 to about 2.0 in 2020.[6]

This chapter looks at how this came about: how a state battered by conflict and post-independence famine and turmoil relaunched itself and found its way. The development bargain that emerged is quite different from the others discussed in this book. Some call Bangladesh a tiger cub because it definitely cannot be likened to an adult tiger or other animal. The country is energetic as well as unpredictable, and it is surprising how quickly it has grown in a short period of time. Progress is not at all the result of a grand design. Instead, it is, almost coincidentally, a matter of politics and economics not doing the wrong thing. It seems to have worked in Bangladesh and could serve as an example to others. Next, I discuss what drove the change behind the country's economic and social progress, and then why and how it could happen within the elite bargain.

Drivers of Bangladesh's economic and social progress

In the early years after independence, few had much hope for this country. A senior aide to US Secretary of State Henry Kissinger derisorily called it a basket case. Bangladesh was one of the most densely populated countries in the world, and had a fast population growth rate. It seemed unable to live off the land, but it also had no other sources of earnings and, beyond jute, little to sell to the world. The 1974 famine in which, directly or indirectly, 1.5 million people died prematurely strengthened this pessimistic view of Bangladesh.[7]

Three drivers account for the economic and social progress in Bangladesh. The first driver was the garment industry and its exports, supplemented with remittances. Bangladesh did not pick the garment industry; the garment industry picked Bangladesh. Faced with emerging trade restrictions and cost increases in the Republic of Korea, Daewoo made a deal with a local producer, Desh, to set up a ready-made garment (RMG) factory in 1978.[8] Among other things, the deal brought with it technology, knowledge of global markets, management expertise, and 130 trained key staff from Korea (many of whom later left to set up other garment factories).[9] The sector grew rapidly, weathering changes in the underlying trade constraints by increasing productivity. RMG exports grew from $32 million in 1984 to $34 billion in 2019, or 84 per cent of total exports. Most of the remaining exports were from other light manufacturing such as textiles and shoes.[10]

The economy received a further boost from the inflow of resources—not from foreign direct investment, which is still only about $2 billion a year, but from the remittances from Bangladeshi who found overseas employment, especially in the Gulf. Remittances rose rapidly, from about $2 billion in 2000 to $10 billion in 2010, and they are now around $20 billion.[11] In any case, until the Covid-19 pandemic both garment exports and remittances continued to grow quickly, and GDP per capita growth reached 7 per cent in 2019.

The second driver was the transformation of the structure of the economy, both in composition of GDP and in employment. Exported-oriented manufacturing—that tried-and-tested formula at the core of other Asian success stories—spearheaded this process. The share of manufacturing in GDP grew from 12 per cent in 1991 to over 21 per cent in 2017.[12] Agriculture now accounts for only about 13 per cent, its share having more than halved since 1991. In terms of employment, the figures are equally striking: Bangladesh is now far less agricultural and far more urban.[13] The RMG sector employs an estimated 4–5 million workers out of the 100 million or so of working age. The majority are women, but many more are working in the sectors servicing the garment industry.[14] Meanwhile, many other workers, mainly men, ended up leaving the country to work abroad. Estimates are hard to come by, but at least 5 million Bangladeshi are living and working outside their own country, large numbers of them in the Middle East.[15]

For some observers, what is playing out in Bangladesh is the ultimate form of global capitalist exploitation: millions of people, not least young women, are forced to move off the land into poorly paid jobs in awful conditions in cities to make garments for rich Western consumers, while young men leave the country to work at construction sites in the Gulf states because the economy does not deliver opportunities. The situation has echoes of how Karl Marx wrote disparagingly about the poor, saying they had nothing but their labour to sell.[16] Still, it is worth remembering the words of another Marxist economist, Joan Robinson, written a century later: 'The misery of being exploited by capitalists is nothing compared to the misery of not being exploited at all.'[17]

Bangladesh found a way to exploit the only resource it had: labour. And in the process, the workers, men and women, saw their earnings increase: industrial wages, adjusted for hikes in the cost of living, rose by 37 per cent between 1995 and 2014. What is even more striking, the higher demand for urban labour, along with increases in agricultural yields, boosted rural incomes: casual agricultural wage labour rates more than doubled during the same period.[18] It is this increase in rural earnings, consistent with classic theories of structural transformation, that delivered the scale of income poverty reduction observed.[19]

The third driver was social action, largely the work of NGOs. The scale of poverty, the improved health and education outcomes, especially for women, and the growth of rural incomes, outside agriculture as well, stemmed from deliberate social action. Success in delivering effective health services stands out. Although the government expanded services, the most dynamism at scale was offered by NGOs. The role of BRAC (originally the Bangladesh Rural Advancement Committee) was pivotal. In 1990, it developed a model of community health workers, some paid but many volunteers, who offered advice but were equipped with basic health and sanitary products they were allowed to sell. By 2005, BRAC workers were outnumbering government community health workers.[20] With other NGOs following suit, more than three-quarters of health workers are now supplied by NGOs. BRAC alone reached up to 110 million people with health information and basic services, such as detecting the vast majority of malaria and tuberculosis cases in the country.[21]

Besides health, education also expanded considerably, along with welfare programmes and targeted credit programmes. What makes Bangladesh unique is that this expansion was driven not by government, but largely by local NGOs—thousands of them, some globally known (see box 9.1). In no other developing countries have indigenous development organisations, set up explicitly to support poor populations, had such an impact.[22]

Box 9.1 Grameen and BRAC: NGOs on the march in Bangladesh

Local NGOs have played a central role in providing protection against disasters as well as support programmes to help the rural population escape from poverty. Grameen Bank and its founder, Mohammad Yunus, a pioneer in microcredit, have over the last decades received the most attention. Since 1976, Grameen Bank has offered small loans to millions of poor women, without expecting collateral, to (in principle) allow them to invest in micro-enterprises. Despite receiving the Nobel Peace Prize in 2006, the bank finds its effectiveness still being disputed, and it is hardly the magic wand that will fight deep poverty, despite the promotion of microcredit by aid entrepreneurs around the world.[23] Nevertheless, the many microcredit institutions remain attractive because there are few other affordable alternatives to obtain credit, and they are helping millions to manage their finances.[24]

After Grameen, BRAC is the second-largest microcredit provider. With famine looming, it was founded in 1972 by Sir Fazle Hasan Abed in the aftermath of the independence war. It is now the largest NGO in the world, and it is active well beyond Bangladesh. Unlike Grameen, it is far more than a microcredit institution. In Bangladesh and in other countries too, it provides a diversified portfolio of programmes to support livelihoods, arguably with more proven success than Grameen. Its Ultra-Poor Programme offers the poorest free asset transfers, as well as intensive coaching and information in areas such as health, recognising that microdebt is risky for the most vulnerable. Unlike microcredit for the poorest, this model has achieved strong support by undergoing rigorous evaluations and has been shown to work in various local settings.[25]

The role of large NGOs such as Grameen and BRAC in Bangladeshi society and its economy should not be underestimated. They are not quite the glitzy or techy social enterprises so favoured by Western philanthropists in which middle-class Westerners and diaspora mostly try to solve the middle-class problems of the developing world with silver bullets. Instead, they are classic enterprises with large local markets, founded and run with social impacts in mind, Bangladeshi-style. For example, Grameenphone is Bangladesh's largest mobile communications provider, and both BRAC and Grameen have ventures in manufacturing and agroprocessing. These businesses provide jobs, goods, and services, as well as profits, allowing them to partially self-finance their own development activities.

A development bargain like no other

In many ways, Bangladesh's experience over the last three decades was textbook development, based on strong, outward-oriented economic growth (garments and remittances). Macroeconomic management avoided the risk of derailment. By its very nature, development delivered many new jobs and opportunities for men and women, better than what was on offer in the rural economy. This labour-intensive growth was made even more inclusive through health, education, and welfare programmes.

Despite being a country highly vulnerable to extreme weather events and flooding, Bangladesh has managed to grow quickly and with less variability than almost any other developing country. It also has ensured it has played the foreign assistance game well, maintaining good relations with organisations such as the World Bank and the International Monetary Fund, as well as international aid agencies from the UK, US, and Australia. Bangladesh has received $68 billion in foreign aid since 1971.[26] Even if the job is by no means finished, Bangladesh is not just a development success; it is also a model of development cooperation. For some, this may seem all that needs to be said. And yet the country's success is a surprise, and not just because Bangladesh was considered a basket case in the 1970s. Throughout this period, the state was weak, dysfunctional, and often unstable and violent.

Indeed, since their inception Bangladesh has appeared on the lists of states categorised as fragile.[27] Its inclusion on these lists stems first and foremost from its political instability. After it emerged from a violent secession war with Pakistan (then West Pakistan) in 1971, two heads of state were murdered in the first decade, independence leader Sheikh Mujibur Rahman in 1975 and army officer turned elected leader Zia Rahman in 1981. After Zia Rahman's death, military rule ensued until 1990. An increasingly fractured democracy then emerged, with power moving back and forth between the Awani League and the Bangladesh National Party, led, respectively, by Sheikh Hasina and Khaleda Zia, the daughters of the two murdered heads of state. Since 2009, it is Sheikh Hasina who has consolidated her power. The two parties nevertheless continue to battle in the political arena and on the streets, although the differences in their actual policies are few. Meanwhile, the country has a clientelist regime, requiring the distribution of favours and patronage to supporters across all echelons of power.[28] Petty corruption is widespread, and there is organised fraud, whether in elections or public procurement, as well as organised political violence and extortion.[29]

The political and economic deals

Nevertheless, Bangladesh has in practice a development bargain: a shared commitment among those with power that growth and development ought to be pursued. It was forged in the chaotic period following the independence war, the famine years, and the assassination of Sheikh Mujibur Rahman. At first, the elite bargain was only an implicit political deal because it had no clear-cut economic agenda, but rather a commitment to avoiding the populism in politics and the short-term resource grabs by leading groups that had led to the breakdown of stability and political order during this period.[30] An elite bargain followed that has held, first during authoritarian military rule up to 1990 and then during the period of democracy, however fractured and possibly increasingly fragile.

The politics of the elite bargain are sustained by an economic deal broadly seen as essential to keeping the political deal going— not just in generating rents for the elite, but also in delivering growth and development. By the late 1970s, a commitment to reasonable macroeconomic policies as well as openness to global markets and foreign investment had emerged, overcoming the failed economic experimentation that contributed to the instability in the post-conflict years. There was no specific grand design to build a globally competitive economy, but, with the benefit of hindsight, these macroeconomic policies proved to be useful in preventing the state from turning predatory by pursuing excessive rent-seeking. Likewise, in the emergence of the garment industry in the early 1970s there was no grand investment plan to build up this sector. At the same time, there was hardly an attempt to halt or impede its emergence through quick capture of its profits as rents. Instead, the government was responsive and assisted with specific industrial policy innovations, such as bonded warehouses for essential inputs, that allowed the sector to grow without much impediment.[31]

'Bangladesh is the true country of laissez-faire,' a senior advisor to the Bangladesh Bank, the central bank, had told me when I visited in 2014. But laissez-faire is not the textbook version of a perfect market. The government of Bangladesh is not just an enabler or provider of public goods; it also relies on growth to deliver rents for this clientelist state. Even the RMG firms, its most successful sector, are not exempt: firms on average have reported paying tens of thousands of dollars in bribes in recent years.[32] And yet the economic deal, with generally pro-business policies, will ensure that the growth of this sector is not hindered, so long as one knows how to manoeuvre in this space.

Indeed, over time incentives and institutional structures have evolved to ensure the garment industry will continue to grow.[33] In the early growth period, garment industrialists were not particularly connected to the state and politics,[34] and thus required the patronage of influential politicians. Eventually, however, they safeguarded their positions by gradually assuming more control of politics themselves. In fact, many factory owners are now themselves members of parliament.[35] As indicators show, Bangladesh is not an easy place to do business without connections, and, not surprisingly, it is not a favoured destination for foreign direct investment in Asia.[36]

In summary, this pro-business and pro-growth economic deal emerged as an elite bargain for stability—very much in line with the analysis in chapter 2 of *why* such deals emerge (to keep the peace, or as a better route for rents, or for returns for the elite), as well as *how* they emerge (often out of conflict and chaos). But the deal involved more than just 'trickle-down' growth through better jobs and opportunities from garments; that would not explain the early focus on broader development outcomes such as health. Was the deal driven simply by the quest for legitimacy and even political survival of the elite, or was it a genuine and enlightened commitment to the Bangladeshi population who had suffered so much in the early part of the 1970s, not least during the famine of 1972–3?[37] In any case, a national and even global elite perception emerged that concerted action was needed in areas such as health, fertility, and education for the country's survival.[38]

The laissez-faire developmental state

An elite commitment to growth and development is not enough to make this development bargain successful—and, indeed, sustain it. A developmental state—a powerful state in which all effort is directed at delivering growth and economic progress—does not necessarily have to be in place, as illustrated by Indonesia (chapter 4)—even if it had been highly effective in Korea and China.[39] In fact, much can be accomplished without active intervention. Despite (or maybe because of) Bangladesh's weak state capability and governance challenges, its own recipe for success—macroeconomic stability and doing just enough to favour growth and business—appears to have worked.

The problem is that such an approach doesn't work in achieving broader access to health care and education, let alone in devising programmes that specifically target the poor. This part of the development bargain cannot be resolved by the 'private sector' or the 'market'. It needs proactive public action, such as shown in China, Indonesia, and India (chapter 4). Strikingly, as part of its development bargain, Bangladesh appears to have found a way around public action that worked, despite the fundamentally weak and ineffective state. Organisations such as Grameen and BRAC emerged from this turbulent period in the 1970s (see box 9.1), as well as thousands of smaller grassroots organisations. Soon, they were growing quickly, some by means of extensive foreign financial support. In many developing countries, the role and influence of such organisations have been curtailed,[40] but in Bangladesh they have been condoned, as long as they stayed away from high-level politics.[41] If anything, the state even encourages them, conscious of its own failings or other preoccupations, such as delivering patronage.[42]

This arrangement is, in fact, a form of laissez-faire in which organisations fill the gaps left by the state.[43] By contrast, some states in other settings are incapable of delivering for their people, but actively set out to hinder anyone else trying to do so by extracting excessive rents or by just obstruction. Bangladesh also serves as a useful counter to the claim that only a well-developed state that leads with a strong hand can make progress. In this respect, Bangladesh is indeed a study in hope: a fragile, dysfunctional state can deliver for development too.

The aid bargain

This laissez-faire aspect is particularly pertinent in respect of the way foreign donors, and the organisations they chose to cooperate with and the experts they brought with them, were able to work in this country. This is not a story of exceptional quantities of aid: since 1975, Bangladesh has received on average $10 per capita in aid a year, whereas similarly poor or even better-off countries such as Nepal, Uganda, Kenya, and Ghana (see chapters 6 and 8) received two to four times as much. Even in the deep crisis of the early 1970s, aid never made up more than 7 per cent of Bangladesh's gross national income.[44] If aid played a role, as most researchers suggest, then it has to be about the effectiveness with which aid was used.[45]

It clearly helped that after 1975 and a period of post-independence chaos that saw an attempt at ideologically driven governance, policy-making became pragmatic, devoid of dogma or religion. The few essential parts of the state that required careful handling, such as the central bank, were given enough independence for its experts to maintain stability, working with international institutions. From early on, aid was also used to support learning from doing, allowing the kind of experimentation and course correction that was needed to use resources well and that in various forms had played a role in other successful countries. Some of this learning was carried out within the state with extensive assistance.[46] One example was an early investment in a statistics capability so that progress was measured and learning from success and failure was possible. In no other country in which I have worked is the emphasis on measurement of progress so noticeable, and by now it is second nature in the organisations involved in development rather than a requirement imposed by funders. To be effective on the ground, Bangladesh also needed organisations that had sufficient humility to systematically learn and improve, as well as with a real commitment to scale. BRAC is a good example, investing as it does in experimentation and vast monitoring and evaluation systems. It has also opened its programmes in both health and social advancement to outside research evaluation.[47]

Will the tiger cub grow up?

Bangladesh is now a middle-income country. It is no doubt one of the biggest success stories in development and the use of aid in recent decades, despite its fragile political deal and a dysfunctional state. It did some things right—such as committing to sensible macroeconomic policies, maintaining stability, and encouraging an outward orientation when the opportunities arose in its garment industry and as a result of migration. It delivered much progress in health, education, and social protection, not least for women. Having achieved this within a weak state and fragile political set-up, Bangladesh offers a valuable alternative to the usual East Asian examples of how to achieve development progress.

What's next for Bangladesh? Few believe it can continue to improve its development indicators without strengthening the capability of the state. And only with improved political governance can it seriously reduce corruption and clientelism to levels less damaging to an evolving economy and society. And only with a serious redirection of economic incentives will the required economic diversification—away from RMG as by far the only export industry—happen. Otherwise, isn't growth bound to stall? There are thus serious questions about the current model. And yet similar questions have been posed about the country's future for at least the last fifteen years. Maybe Bangladesh will continue to surprise us.

References

Alamgir, M. 1980. *Famine in South Asia: Political Economy of Mass Starvation*. Cambridge, MA: Oelgeschlager, Gunn and Hain Publishers.

Amsden, A. H. 1989. *Asia's Next Giant: South Korea and Late Industrialization*. Oxford: Oxford University Press on Demand.

Asadullah, M. N., and N. T. Chakravorty. 2019. 'Growth, Governance and Corruption in Bangladesh: A Re-assessment'. *Third World Quarterly* 40 (5): 947–65.

Bandiera, O., R. Burgess, N. Das, S. Gulesci, I. Rasul, and M. Sulaiman. 2017. 'Labor Markets and Poverty in Village Economies'. *Quarterly Journal of Economics* 132 (2): 811–70.

Banerjee, A., E. Duflo, N. Goldberg, D. Karlan, R. Osei, W. Parienté, J. Shapiro, B. Thuysbaert, and C. Udry. 2015. 'A Multifaceted Program Causes Lasting Progress for the Very Poor: Evidence from Six Countries'. *Science* 348 (6236).

Banerjee, A., D. Karlan, and J. Zinman. 2015. 'Six Randomized Evaluations of Microcredit: Introduction and Further Steps'. *American Economic Journal: Applied Economics* 7 (1): 1–21.

Bora, J., N. Saikia, and W. Lutz. 2019. 'Revisiting the Causes of Fertility Decline in Bangladesh: Family Planning Program or Female Education?' IIASA Working Paper WP-19-01, International Institute for Applied Systems Analysis, Laxenburg, Austria.

BRAC (Bangladesh Rural Advancement Committee). 2019. *BRAC Bangladesh Annual Report 2019*. Dhaka.

Christensen, D., and J. M. Weinstein. 2013. 'Defunding Dissent: Restrictions on Aid to NGOs'. *Journal of Democracy* 24 (2): 77 -91.

Collins, D., J. Morduch, S. Rutherford, and O. Ruthven. 2009. *Portfolios of the Poor: How the World's Poor Live on $2 a Day*. Princeton, NJ: Princeton University Press.

El Arifeen, S., A. Christou, L. Reichenbach, F. A. Osman, K. Fazad, K. S. Islam, F. Ahmed, H. B. Perry, and D. H. Peters. 2013. 'Community-Based Approaches and Partnerships: Innovations in Health-Service Delivery in Bangladesh'. *Lancet* 382 (9909): 2012–26.

Hassan, Mirza. 2013. 'Political Settlement Dynamics in a Limited-Access Order: The Case of Bangladesh'. ESID Working Paper, Effective States and Inclusive Development Research Centre, Manchester.

———, and L. Kornher. 2019. 'Farm Wage and Rice Price Dynamics in Bangladesh'. *ZEF Discussion Papers on Development Policy* (273).

———, and S. Raihan. 2017. 'Navigating the Deals World: The Politics of Economic Growth in Bangladesh'. In *Deals and Development: The Political Dynamics of Growth Episodes,* edited by L. Pritchett, K. Sen, and E. Werker, 96–128. Oxford: Oxford University Press.

Hossain, N. 2017. *The Aid Lab: Understanding Bangladesh's Unexpected Success.* Oxford: Oxford University Press.

IOM (International Organization for Migration). 2019. *World Migration Report 2020.* Geneva: IOM.

Jahan, R. 2015. 'The Parliament of Bangladesh: Representation and Accountability'. *Journal of Legislative Studies* 21 (2): 250–69.

Johnson, C. 1982. *MITI and the Japanese Miracle: The Growth of Industrial Policy, 1925–1975.* Stanford, CA: Stanford University Press.

Kabeer, N., L. Huq, and M. Sulaiman. 2020. 'Paradigm Shift or Business as Usual? Workers' Views on Multi-stakeholder Initiatives in Bangladesh'. *Development and Change* 51 (5): 1360–98.

Khan, M. H. 2017. 'Anti-Corruption in Bangladesh: A Political Settlements Analysis'. ACE Working Paper 003, SOAS, University of London.

———. 2013. 'The Political Settlement, Growth and Technical Progress in Bangladesh'. DIIS Working Paper no. 2013: 01, Danish Institute for International Studies, Copenhagen.

Lewis, W. A. 1954. 'Economic Development with Unlimited Supplies of Labour'. *The Manchester School* 22 (2): 139–91.

Mahmood, S. A. I. 2010. 'Public Procurement and Corruption in Bangladesh Confronting the Challenges and Opportunities'. *Journal of Public Administration and Policy Research* 2 (6): 103–11.

Marx, K. 1990. *Das Kapital: A Critique of Political Economy*, vol. 1. London: Penguin Classics.

Mcloughlin, C. 2009. 'Fragile States'. Governance and Social Development Resource Centre.

Mostafa, R., and S. Klepper. 2018. 'Industrial Development through Tacit Knowledge Seeding: Evidence from the Bangladesh Garment Industry'. *Management Science* 64 (2): 613–32.

OECD (Organisation for Economic Co-operation and Development). 2020. *States of Fragility 2020.* Paris: OECD Publishing.

Raihan, S., and S. S. Khan. 2020. 'Structural Transformation, Inequality

Dynamics, and Inclusive Growth in Bangladesh'. WIDER Working Paper 2020/44, UNU-WIDER, Helsinki.

Rhee, Y. W. 1990. 'The Catalyst Model of Development: Lessons from Bangladesh's Success with Garment Exports'. *World Development* 18 (2): 333–46.

Robinson, J. 1962. *Economic Philosophy.* Piscataway, NJ: Transaction Publishers.

Roodman, D. 2012. *Due Diligence: An Impertinent Inquiry into Microfinance.* Washington, DC: CGD Books.

Yunus, M. 2009. *Creating a World without Poverty: Social Business and the Future of Capitalism.* New York: PublicAffairs.

Zafarullah, H., and N. A. Siddiquee. 2001. 'Dissecting Public Sector Corruption in Bangladesh: Issues and Problems of Control'. *Public Organization Review* 1 (4): 465–86.

Zhang, X., S. Rashid, K. Ahmad, and A. Ahmed. 2014. 'Escalation of Real Wages in Bangladesh: Is It the Beginning of Structural Transformation?' *World Development* 64: 273–85.

10

ETHIOPIA AND RWANDA

AFRICAN LIONS?

The woman was keen to tell her story, even though she looked distressed. 'I had five cows, but I had to sell one a month ago to buy food. And I fear that I will lose the others too before I can plant seed again.' It was November 2015, and we were talking in front of her small hut. Around it, the soil was hardened by the sun—this part of southern Ethiopia was in the grip of a drought. The last time the drought had been this bad was in 2002, when reportedly more than 13 million people were at risk of starvation.[1] Hunger in Ethiopia is an image of Africa that persists, shaped by the most dreadful crisis in living memory, the famine of 1984–5, when up to a million people perished. For the survivors, its consequences were still evident decades later.[2]

Despite the press reports during my visit playing up the connection between the two droughts, I was confident the current drought would not turn into a crisis of the magnitude experienced in 2002. Much had been learned since 2002, but, even then, support had been mobilised and, although people suffered, large-scale starvation and mortality were in the end avoided.[3] This time it would be better. This Ethiopia was far better organised. About 8 million households were connected through the Productive Safety Net Programme—the largest well-targeted safety net programme in Africa.[4] Increasingly better collaboration with international agencies was in place in the more remote pastoral areas of the east and south, delivering water and basic support on an unprecedented scale. And the rural economy had become stronger and better connected. Even though the official United Nations and other assessments stated that about 10 million people were at risk of starvation, studies have since shown that mortality did not increase, and even no systematic increases in child undernutrition were detected.[5]

Overall, Ethiopia had come a long way. In 2004, it launched an ambitious phase of development, boosting agriculture and later on targeting industrialisation, fortified by an East Asia-inspired big push through public infrastructure investment. Growth had picked up, and by the end of 2019 the International Monetary Fund (IMF) would declare Ethiopia the fastest-growing country in the world of the previous decade. It still meant that during the 2015 drought this woman was bound to have lost some of her cows—and with that some of her hopes for a better future would be dashed. I asked her whether 2002 had been as bad. She looked bemused and said, 'It was much worse, of course. I did not have any cows to start with.' It is still a life of hardship and regular suffering, but at least many have some buffer for bad years, and so she is not at risk of dying from starvation and illness. For the poorest in Ethiopia, that is considerable progress.

In this chapter, I explore what lies behind Ethiopia's success. I have been a privileged witness of Ethiopia's progress ever since my first academic post, teaching and researching at Addis Ababa University from 1992. I have been back every year, feeling every time I have reached home when smelling the charcoal-filled mountain air after arrival at Bole Airport. I have observed first-hand how the Ethiopian leadership has gambled on development. And for a long time it looked as though that gamble would pay off. Because it tends to be poorly understood, I will in this chapter go into more detail on Ethiopia's gamble on development in recent decades, but also how and why it is now at risk.

This chapter also features another country that is a surprising success in Africa—Rwanda. That country is tiny compared with Ethiopia: it is home to 13 million people, whereas Ethiopia's population is almost ten times as large. Still, there are similarities in how they have gone about making progress. Rwanda has also emerged from deep violence—the genocidal killings in 1994—to become a haven of stability. The state is playing an obvious role in its gradual developmental progress, which is driven by a strong political commitment to growth and development.

But neither country has made its progress a beacon of political openness and liberal values. Whether the way politics were conducted was essential to boosting development efforts can and should be debated. In any case, in both countries there is a strong elite bargain on pursuing development and growth, but it is among those 'in power'. They stand out in terms of their visionary commitment to development and the use of the state with all its force to try to make it happen—and they are not letting anyone stand in the way. For most of at least two decades, these states have had governments 'for the people' but not quite 'by the people'.[6]

In Ethiopia, the elite bargain has now become unstuck. As I write this, violence and conflict—the scourges that have defined Ethiopia for centuries—are surging across the country, especially in the northern regions. The political part of the elite bargain has broken down, and political and military leaders who had been part of the coalition of interests ruling the country since 1991 have fallen out with each other. It is too early to say whether the leading figures in the elite on both sides will be able to step back from long-lasting conflict and human disaster and keep the country's progress on track.

Half a miracle in Ethiopia

The year 1991 was a turning point for this Ethiopia. The Marxist-Leninist military regime that had deposed Emperor Haile Selassie in 1974 was defeated by a coalition of armed groups, led by the Tigrayan People's Liberation Front (TPLF). Its leader, Meles Zenawi, assumed power of the coalition, which had morphed into the Ethiopian People's Revolutionary Democratic Front (EPRDF). The preceding seventeen years had seen brutal state-led terror, on the streets of the capital, Addis Ababa, and in other cities as well. The state also had used systematic starvation of areas of Tigray as part of its fight with the TPLF, and that effort had led to the 1984–5 famine.[7]

In 1991, after the military regime was defeated, the country became largely stable and peaceful, at least for some years. In the first decade of the new government, many rural areas saw recovery, but ever so slowly. The data, and a comparison with what was to come, reveal the modesty of this recovery: from its lowest point in 1992, growth until 2003 was 1.6 per cent per capita a year, reaching levels of GDP per capita still below $200. Ethiopia thus remained among the poorest countries in the world.[8] Some good things were happening, nevertheless. During this period, the survival odds for children improved considerably, by a third, even if one in eight children would not live beyond age five by 2003. And more and more children began to go to school: from only a quarter by 1992 to two-thirds by 2003.[9]

In the fifteen years that followed, this progress in development outcomes continued steadily. For the economy, the change after 2003 was far more dramatic. Growth accelerated, and was never below 7 per cent over the next fifteen years (or more than 4 per cent in per capita terms). GDP per capita rose from $195 in 2003 to $603 in 2019, or per capita growth of 7.3 per cent over that period.[10] At this rate, Ethiopia will easily reach middle-income status before 2030. However, extreme poverty remains high: by 2015, around 30 per cent of the population continued to live below the international poverty line, but there has been a declining trend because since 1999 this share has halved.[11]

Ethiopia achieved in the fifteen years after 2003 something no other African state had done: persistent growth at levels of over 7 per cent. As discussed in chapter 2, the Growth Commission suggested that any country labelled a 'growth miracle' had to maintain such a level of growth every year for twenty-five years. So Ethiopia was on the right path. Still, as one of the few international economists to spend much time in this country since 1991, I have to say this growth surprised me: Ethiopia was over halfway towards finding itself a growth miracle, but still it was a half-miracle that the country had moved so far.

How did Ethiopia do it? No doubt by means of a gamble on the economy, but that gamble was driven by an elite bargain on growth and development—a development bargain. The rest of this section describes the features of this success: the actions and policies that grew out of this underlying shared elite commitment, how the state was used to achieve these outcomes, and how much learning and correction took place. I then dig deeper. In the section that follows, I assess some of the underlying factors central to understanding this period and the development bargain: the political and economic deal, the development bargain's historical roots, and the question of its sustainability, especially in view of recent conflict and violence.

The ingredients of the half-miracle

Ethiopia's choices of areas in which to push growth were utterly sensible. In the first few years after 2004, it directed its efforts towards reversing the sluggish performance of agriculture, especially its staples such as teff, maize, wheat, and sorghum. These were clearly low-hanging fruit because better seeds and practices were available although just not widespread. By 2015, cereal yields had doubled, and output had tripled over that for 1995.[12] Rural incomes of the poor in less agriculturally favourable and food-insecure areas were stabilised through the large-scale Productive Safety Net Programme, providing transfers in return for work on local infrastructure. Health care and education continued to be expanded by reaching ever deeper—for example, by 2019 more than four out of five girls and boys of primary school age were attending school, or four times more than in the early 1990s, while the chances of a child surviving past age five are now four times higher than they were then.[13]

Over time, the role of infrastructure investment increased. From about 2011, it reached 37 per cent as a share of GDP on average, or almost double that typically observed in sub-Saharan Africa, which was up from less than 15 per cent in the 1990s and 22 per cent in the 2000s. Much of this investment was either public or based on directed lending through state-linked enterprises. The road network was vastly expanded, in rural areas as well. And several large hydroelectric projects were launched, the largest being the

Grand Ethiopian Renaissance Dam (GERD) on the Nile, boosting substantially the country's electricity capacity. Meanwhile, Ethiopian Airlines, a state-owned company set up in 1945, expanded and evolved to become Africa's most successful airline, and it remained highly profitable. Its cargo operations allowed the emergence of a relatively small but rapidly expanding horticultural industry, which enticed early Dutch investors to leave Kenya for flower production in Ethiopia.

Those investments only whetted Ethiopia's appetite for more. By 2014, industrial parks had emerged, first one near Addis Ababa and then the flagship industrial park devoted to garments on the outskirts of Hawassa, 300 kilometres south of Addis Ababa. The US anchor investor, PVH, then enticed other firms, largely from Asia, in its own supply chain to join it. A railway from Addis Ababa to Djibouti and urban infrastructure, including a light railway, emerged, while the 50 kilometres between Bishoftu and Addis Ababa began to be dotted with new housing developments and industrial zones, including a Chinese industrial park. Other parks sprang up in cities such as Mekelle, Kombolcha, and Dire Dawa.

In the meantime, the rest of the world began to sit up and take notice of a determined, fiercely independent Ethiopia. What impressed was not just that it was the fastest-growing African economy since 2010, but also how it went about achieving that, for example by making a bid to attract the manufacturing investment from Asia that others had only dreamt about. That said, its success in manufacturing is still in its early days—manufacturing as a share of the country's GDP was by 2019 still only about 6 per cent, or one-third of Bangladesh's but also lower than that of Kenya, Uganda, Tanzania, or Ghana.

The developmental state and its plans

Growth accelerated steeply from 2004, but it is easily forgotten that this occurred under the same leadership in power since 1991. As with all successful cases described in this book, finding one's way and correcting course when required are important. At the time the TPLF under Meles Zenawi took power, it was not just a Marxist-

Leninist movement. Meles looked to Albanian socialism as practised by President Enver Hoxha as inspiration for his economic policies. Suffice it to say, few books or articles have been written about the economic and development success of Albania.

The pragmatism of Meles and his closest advisors quickly became clear.[14] At the time they took power, inflation was raging, and the black market exchange rate premium had reached 150 per cent. They then realised they needed support from the IMF to stabilise the economy—although the IMF was hardly an organisation committed to Marxism. But the Ethiopian leadership did not just accept the IMF's terms and conditions; even in that age of structural adjustment they wanted a choice. Aware of the standard package the IMF would expect in exchange for financial support—such as liberalisation, privatisation, and government spending cuts—the Ethiopian team commissioned a report on the likely social consequences of such a package. When the IMF team arrived in 1992 and explained their standard expectations, the Ethiopians shared their analysis. The scene was set. Ethiopia would work with the outside world, but it would not simply do what it was told; it would own its destiny.

As it happened, with IMF support the economy was quickly stabilised, and gradually some liberalisation was undertaken with the help of the World Bank. But it did not go well at first. Over the previous few decades, fertiliser had become an essential input for much of the cereal production, and by the early 1990s more than a quarter of cereal farmers were using it. Fertiliser imports, distribution, and finance were handled by state-owned enterprises, but, with World Bank support, privatisation and liberalisation were attempted in the mid-1990s. In response, the market almost collapsed, and distribution was disrupted. The Ethiopian government learned quickly: in the future, it had to plot its own way.

Engaged in a war with Eritrea between 1998 and 2000, Ethiopia made little progress, and resources became tight. It had barely managed to stabilise the economy again afterwards, when the 2002–3 drought hit, prompting the huge international relief response described at the beginning of this chapter. This crisis had a big impact on Meles and his team, and they became determined to change course in a more dramatic way.

It's not that they changed their views on how they thought the country would develop. Strongly committed to the peasantry, they had focused on agriculture since adopting the Agricultural Development Led Industrialisation (ADLI) strategy. It called for building an industrial sector from the surplus created in the rural economy in the form of industrial inputs from agriculture. The first formal document, drafted in 1993, was written in rather dated economic language, with echoes of both Marxist theories, and early economic models of structural transformation. But they were not unreasonably articulated, not least in an age in which national strategies for African development were rare and unsatisfactory.[15]

Until 2002, these ideas appear to have mainly gathered dust. From then onwards, they became the backbone of a set of plans with unappealing acronyms: SDPRP (2002–5), PASDEP (2005–10), GTP1 (2010–15), and GTP2 (2015–20).[16] In content, these important plans were broad, but at the core of the SDPRP and PASDEP plans especially was growth through cereal agriculture, with expectations that it would seed or feed industrialisation. The agricultural side, starting from a low base in productivity, delivered fantastic growth. Even though the results may have been somewhat overstated, there is no doubt that the sector was a big success. The structural transformation of other sectors did not quite happen. But GTP1 and GTP2 produced a stronger focus on industrialisation in sectors with agricultural linkages such as textiles and garments, as well as leather. Meanwhile, the industrial parks took shape, accompanied by ever more ambitious infrastructure programmes.

These plans were not based on documents produced in Washington or by the local World Bank office in return for finance, as happens so often with African countries. They were Ethiopia's plans, often tightly held away from donors until late in the day, even if the consulting firm McKinsey from early on helped with what its consultants do best: making the plans more coherent and costed in spreadsheets, with stretching but achievable milestones—all delivered in a slick slide pack.

The most striking thing about these plans was that they were essentially carried out and produced results, unlike the plans that too many developing countries draft and then ignore. All political and administrative levels of the entire state apparatus were committed to achieving them. In effect, then, Ethiopia was an emerging developmental state—a state that used all its levers, including extensive rules and regulation, and that staked its legitimacy on delivering on its plans.[17]

It's no wonder that outside development agencies took note. International support was widely welcomed, wherever it came from, East or West, so long as it was aimed at delivering on the government's plans. Large US and EU support followed, and the UK's DFID programme in Ethiopia became the largest in any country in which it worked. Over time, Chinese involvement increased as well. China became constructor and financier of choice for a large part of the infrastructure development. Aid from Western countries rose from about $690 million in 2000 to some $5 billion in 2018, although only in the most recent years did it achieve levels comparable to those for Uganda, Ghana, or Tanzania once population is taken into account.[18] How the Ethiopian state managed to pull this all off was far from orthodox. It expressed a deep commitment to the underlying ideas but enlisted much pragmatism and even improvisation to get it all done. That is the subject of the next section.

Tinkering technocrats

Meles Zenawi, the country's leader from 1991 until his early death from illness in 2012 at the age of 57, definitely made an impression. 'He is one of the smartest people I have ever met,' a former World Bank chief economist told me a decade ago. I heard similar statements from Nobel Prize winners, leading academics, and former top Western politicians. And based on my own experience, I can only agree. Meles ruled the country as a 'philosopher-king'. But make no mistake; he was utterly ruthless, too.

Meles embodied the underlying development bargain among those with power, but he also understood the finer details of it. When he first took power, he instructed his leading team and cabinet to pursue a master's in business administration from the UK's Open University—and he was the top student in the group. As prime minister, he took a master's degree in economics in the Netherlands and wrote a thesis on the developmental state, drawing inspiration from East Asian examples such as the Republic of Korea and Taiwan.[19]

Although Meles was a micromanager, he needed a group of trusted technocrats to develop the details of the development bargain and ensure it was all put into practice. One inspirational figure was Newai Gebre-Ab, the main economic advisor to Meles from 1991 until Meles's death. Utterly charming and deeply erudite, he was the early architect of the ADLI strategy. As the main lead on macroeconomic issues as well, he was behind the sensible macroeconomic management during the turbulence of conflict and occasional fallout with international funders. He also embodied the essence of economic management as the ultimate tinkering technocrat. 'We are sowing the seeds of capitalism', he told me when I asked him in 2010 to sum up the essence of the GTP1 plan. Inspired and emboldened by thinkers such as Joseph Stiglitz, he said a market economy was the ultimate aim, but that the markets were fundamentally failing. The government had to step in to ensure the markets were working, nudging or forcing them to fuel the growth of the economy, led by agriculture and subsequently towards an industrialised economy.

There were others such as Tedros Adhanom, now director general of the World Health Organization. He trained in public health up to PhD level in the UK, and then drove progress in health from 2001, first in Tigray and then nationally as minister of health until 2012. Then there was the succession of able ministers and deputy ministers in the Ministry of Finance and Economic Development such as Sufian Ahmed and Abraham Tekeste. Arkebe Oqubay was the architect and key implementer of the industrial park strategy, embodying the ambition and drive to attract foreign direct investment. He pulled off the deal with clothing giant PVH for the Hawassa industrial park, and many others.[20] Why these technocrats got so far had more to do with their willingness to learn, both from the data and from their failures, and to solve problems, often not in the most conventional ways and by no means perfectly or permanently, but more or less successfully.

Getting markets to work in ways that would serve Ethiopia's growth and development plans in particular involved endless improvisation. New ideas were tried, and plenty of errors were made, but the leading technocrats learned and typically found solutions. For example, the 2002 SDPRP plan called for enhancing the role of technological change in agricultural growth, but that meant fertiliser uptake had to increase. In response, the government vastly expanded the fertiliser credit so that farmers had to repay only after the harvest. This change involved a huge rural credit provision, but because the state-owned Commercial Bank of Ethiopia could not put its entire portfolio at risk, regional governments were told their budgets would become the collateral for these loans. Regional government officials were then forced to halt all activity for weeks so they could collect the monies owed or their salaries could not be paid.[21] This arrangement, however, became quickly untenable. Lessons were learned, and buying fertiliser on credit at scale was abolished. Instead, supported by the expansion of extension services, favourable prices, and market penetration through better roads, the use of modern inputs nevertheless increased considerably, and yields improved.[22]

Capable technocrats were also an Achilles heel of this period. As the economy became more complex and ambition grew on all fronts, dependence on a few dozen high-quality technocrats meant they were overstretched. I recall asking the manager of a Dutch flower investor in 2012 how he dealt with likely difficulties, such as delays at the airport, power cuts, or transport problems. 'I have the phone numbers of all ministers and the PM on my mobile phone,' he said, 'so any problems are quickly resolved.' An investment climate based on calls to the top people is hardly sustainable as the number of investors grows. In fact, the manager of a Chinese shoe factory told me a few years later that she too had been given these numbers. But after a pause she added, 'Unfortunately, most of these telephone numbers are always engaged.'

So a rather small cadre of technically able people were driving both the ideas and their implementation, but tinkering alone cannot overcome more fundamental imbalances. For example, by the time GTP2 was being prepared in 2014, the pressure was beginning to tell. The expansion of exports slowed, and thus, with high GDP growth, exports as a share of GDP fell from over 10 per cent in 2010 to about 8 per cent since 2016. Meanwhile, foreign exchange was becoming scarce for those firms not connected to the government, and increasingly for some of the foreign investors as well.

Nevertheless, overall the fifteen years between 2004 and 2019 were a remarkable period of growth and considerable progress. What marks out the period is a number of features that make for a successful development bargain—a shared commitment to growth and development by those in power, a state that does all it can to deliver on its commitment, and support by committed technocrats willing to experiment and learn. How was this pulled off in Ethiopia? Before anyone assumes, on the basis of this narrative, that the Ethiopian model is easily transferable, it is important to dig deeper into this development bargain, which is the subject of the next section.

The development bargain unpacked

History determines the nature of a state, and use of the state is determined by those who control it at any one time. The boundaries of today's Ethiopia were largely set down in the nineteenth century. When Europe colonised most of Africa, Ethiopia resisted: Italian forces attempting to conquer it from Italian-held Eritrea were defeated in 1896 under Emperor Menelik II, the Amhara king and Ethiopian emperor.

Ethiopia is well described as a non-colonial state,[23] even though the Ethiopian state was every bit as expansive—dare I say colonial. Menelik and his Tigrayan predecessor, Emperor Yohannes, conquered land to the west, south, and east, and built an empire centred around the historical northern Orthodox Christian highland kingdoms covering the Amhara and Tigray. Peripheral areas with large populations in both the highlands and lowlands were incorporated: the Oromo, the Somali, and many smaller groups and nations in the south, such as the Gurage and Sidama. Power was consolidated by making deals with local rulers and by offering conquering army officers and soldiers the chance to settle with substantial landholdings. The state that resulted was reminiscent of a medieval feudal state. Eventually, this state was further stabilised and turned into an internationally recognised country under Empress Zewditu and then Emperor Haile Selassie, who ruled from 1930 until his overthrow in 1974.

The state that emerged at this stage was centralised within a strictly hierarchal society. It consisted of a court, aristocratic landowners, an organised but often brutal military, and a mostly Amharan bureaucratic class, all with roots in the northern highlands. Being Ethiopian primarily meant being Amharised and an Orthodox Christian. In fact, this became an identity one could acquire, not simply be born into.[24] Outside most urban areas, peasants lived within hierarchical structures in which they were at the bottom and knew their place.

This was the state anyone in power had to handle, and three characteristics set the scene for the political and economic deals of recent decades: a centralised state, a population composed of a large number of central and peripheral ethnicities and identities, and a hierarchical, largely agrarian society. The first characteristic—the presence of a historically centralised state, with an administrative system built over more than a century—was no doubt an opportunity. This bureaucracy did not emerge 'to serve itself' as in so many other countries in which being part of the state is to be part of a clientelist system that offers jobs as rewards for support. Instead, in Ethiopia the bureaucracy emerged to deliver for whoever pulled the strings at the top.[25] The second characteristic is a key challenge—Ethiopia's 'national question'.[26] It is a country struggling with national versus ethnic identity. The largest group, the Oromo (by 2007, 34 per cent of the population), and many of the groups from the south of the country feel disenfranchised by the northern highland groups, historically the Amharas (27 per cent of the population) or in more recent years the Tigrayans (6 per cent of the population).[27] The third characteristic is a country with few natural resources and a huge impoverished rural population, who live in a fragile environment and make a living mainly from rain-fed crop agriculture. Even by 2000 only 15 per cent of the population was urbanised.[28]

The roots of the political and economic deals

During Haile Selassie's rule, a traditional military and aristocratic elite held power, supported by the Ethiopian Orthodox Church and served by an emerging urban, educated bureaucratic class. It was an elite bargain intended to keep the traditional imperial structures from the northern highlands in place, with legitimacy supposedly derived from divine right. But despite its centralised power structures, it proved to be a regime ill-suited to handle the pressures for change in the 1950s and 1960s. Development and economic change were slow, and many rural areas remained deeply impoverished, drought and other crises being poorly handled. Meanwhile, the regime failed to bow to pressure to accommodate the emerging educated groups or representatives of the different ethnic groups.

Protests and tensions allowed the military to take power in 1974, imprisoning and later killing the emperor. After considerable turmoil and murderous infighting, Mengistu Hailemariam took charge of a military council that became known as the Derg. It was more than a military regime; it was a violent revolution, uprooting the previous power structures, but using the centralised state structures to maintain control of the regime. Steps taken by the state included embarking on land reform whereby the state became owner of all land, and farmers were given user rights to land held previously by landowners or the church. The state also nationalised much of the economy.

With its relatively strong state structures, Ethiopia had an opportunity to use them for growth and development. But the Derg did not take a sensible route. The economy that emerged was inspired by ideology and enthusiastically supported by advisors from Eastern Europe, Ethiopia's new best friend in this late-Cold War period. But it was a dead end, and stagnation followed: GDP per capita shrank each year by about 1 per cent in the 1980s, to end barely above $200 per capita in 1990 on the eve of the Derg's collapse.[29] Ethiopia became identified with state failure, stark poverty, and the desperation of its population.

That other feature of the centralised Ethiopian state that predominated during this period was the use of military might and violence to maintain power and control. Violence is a central part of Ethiopia's history, even today, and the Derg perfected its use. This was a regime preoccupied with crushing any opposition at all cost, whether among the urban educated groups or across the regions. The military leadership believed in centralised Ethiopian nationalism and had no time for the growing struggles for greater self-determination by other peoples and nationalities, not least in Eritrea (which after World War II was incorporated into Ethiopia), as well as in Tigray, where the TPLF emerged as the main challenger.

After the EPRDF coalition led by the TPLF finally defeated the remnants of the Derg regime in 1991, it revealed it had learned from history. The coalition embraced the power of the centralised state: it initially left the bureaucratic class mainly intact, but put the class under its political control, while it replaced the military with its own by now powerful centralised army under Tigrayan control. At the same time, its political deal had to recognise the diversity of its coalition of power, made up as it was of various ethnicities and nationalities, and a new constitution in 1995 gave the regions extensive powers of policy and implementation, as well as rights to self-determination in what could be interpreted as an insurance policy for the TPLF in Tigray.[30]

The most fascinating part of these recent times is how the economic deal was conceived: as a source of political legitimacy. The Agricultural Development Led Industrialisation strategy was as much a political agenda as an economic blueprint. Improving rural areas was not just an economic policy choice but also a political necessity for continuing support.[31] Indeed, there were pragmatic political reasons why this emphasis on development emerged a decade after the EPRDF coalition, led by the TPLF, assumed power. In May 1998 a border dispute led to a two-year-long war with Eritrea.[32] The fallout from that war led to a split in the TPLF that Meles only narrowly survived. He not only had to seek more support from his other coalition partners, previously often marginalised, but also had to deal with the drought of 2002–3, which made it politically imperative to overcome the country's ongoing food insecurity. The urgency of the need for legitimacy became clear in 2005 when overconfidence in its own popularity led the governing coalition to hold broadly free and fair elections. Although most rural areas supported Meles, it quickly became clear during the vote count that urban areas, not least Addis Ababa, had not supported Meles and his party. The count was then halted, and eventually the ruling coalition received a clear majority after all.

This outcome accelerated the determination to put into action what by then had already become a conviction: to use all the might of the state, with its historically centralised structures, to push for development. Whereas the imperial government had used the strong state only to maintain the status quo, and the Derg had used it for ideological blueprints and especially military control, a developmental state had now emerged in which carrying out the developmental goals of its plans became central. Although Meles later wrote, with familiar Marxist-Leninist conviction, that it is universally the historical role of the state to be developmental as part of Africa's 'renaissance',[33] it cannot be emphasised enough that the Ethiopian state was able to play this role because it was relatively capable to start with.

The elite bargain of this period can thus be called a development bargain. Political and economic deals ensured that growth and development became a shared commitment among those with power, and the state was used in line with its capabilities and pragmatically enough to overcome challenges. Meanwhile, the functioning, centralised state was put to good use in dealing with the fundamental challenge of improving the lives of an impoverished, largely agrarian society. Along the way, Meles and his core team believed that this would overcome the 'national question'—that other key challenge of the Ethiopian state—and achieve peaceful coexistence among the country's many ethnicities and identities. In any case, Meles was not going to let aspirations from any of these groups derail his political direction.

Contested power

The new prime minister, Hailemariam Dessalegn, continued down this path after Meles's death in 2012. He did so with less ideology and more pragmatism and tinkering, but with no less of a quest for political legitimacy through development. In the end, this was a regime that had come to power through violence, and even though many of those holding key positions over time had been non-Tigrayan, most power, not least in the military, remained biased in favour of the TPLF. Legitimacy was sought by winning hearts and minds through progress in growth and development.

Meles had pursued this goal impatiently, especially when dealing with dissent internally as well as on the streets. The ruthlessness of this former insurgent leader was abundantly clear in the way he violently suppressed protests after the election results of 2005 were revisited. 'We did not fight for years in the trenches [against the Derg] to give power to these people through some election,' he told UK prime minister Tony Blair in 2005 when challenged, or at least that is what Meles told me and a few others a few years later.[34] Deeply self-righteous, he was going to pursue growth and development his way. But he recognised that these electoral challenges had shown that the blind pursuit of these objectives did not satisfy Ethiopia's huge youth population. For them, the growth figures did not translate into rapid improvements in their opportunities.

Technically, one of the best urban development plans Africa has seen, the Addis Ababa Master Plan (AAMP), triggered the political undoing of the EPRDF regime by means of widespread violence; the emergence of a reformist prime minister, Abiy Ahmed; and ultimately the ongoing conflict between the Addis Ababa government and the remainder of the TPLF in Tigray. Addis Ababa, governed as a separate region, lies within the largest region, Oromiya, and it had been growing rapidly because of its booming economy. In line with the best thinking in economic geography, the AAMP correctly recognised that careful urban planning aimed at systematic housing, industrial, and commercial development was the rational way to boost economic growth in the capital instead of the current, mostly organic growth. However, the planners overlooked a possibly emotive issue for Oromo nationalist supporters: the plan called for moving Oromo farmers off their land to make room for expanding the capital into foreign-owned industrial zones and building housing developments for the nouveau riche urban elite, many of them Tigrayans and Amharas, or at least 'Amharised' Oromos and other groups.

In 2014, protests against the AAMP ignited a series of large-scale protests that began largely in the Oromiya region, but later spread to the Amhara region. The protests were often violently repressed, leading to the further limiting of political opposition, not least by the imposition of a state of emergency in 2016. Increasingly, these protests were directed at the lack of freedom. Oromo and Amhara groups also protested against the power of the TPLF and Tigrayans in general in the state. When leaders of two of the four coalition partners in the EPRDF—the Amhara National Democratic Movement (ANDM) and the Oromo People's Democratic Organization (OPDO)—revealed their sympathy for the protestors' demands, change was on the cards. In 2018, Dessalegn Hailemariam resigned, and Abiy Ahmed, the deputy leader of the OPDO, was chosen as prime minister, even though he was opposed by the TPLF.

What's next?

By early 2021, the breakdown among the old comrades in the EPRDF was complete. Abiy had released or welcomed back large numbers of political opponents targeted by the EPRDF under Meles. The TPLF leadership had retreated to Tigray's capital, Mekelle, and tensions had risen further, seemingly around constitutional interpretations, and also because Abiy had restored relations with Isayas Afwerki, the leader of Eritrea, enemy number one of the TPLF. Violent conflict broke out after TPLF forces attacked the Northern Command in Mekelle. The Ethiopian army then moved on Tigray, supported by Amhara militias and by Eritrean soldiers coming from the north. Widespread atrocities followed, especially at the hands of Eritrean forces. By July 2021, government forces retreated, with the prospect of man-made famine likely, more conflict and further state disintegration.

As I write this book, no end is in sight, and several decades of development are at serious risk. The gamble on development may prove a failure. Still, Ethiopia is not simply about Tigray versus Addis Ababa. Although Abiy, contesting as the Prosperity Party, could claim legitimacy after elections in the rest of the country,[35] deep ethnic and political tensions remain. Abiy started quite a few fires after coming into power, and it is not clear how he can put them out.[36]

What is the future of the development bargain in Ethiopia? The underlying political deal was an elite bargain among those with power in the military, political, and economic arenas, but it was highly selective, with little attempt to accommodate other influential groups. Meles and his core political companions had little time for even considering alternative voices, both those in politics and those in the economy, calling them all 'rent-seekers' who would deflect the economy from its long-term path for quick personal gain.[37] In some sense, he was right because many of the voices on the street called for a piece of the cake immediately, and not just investments in long-term development. Nevertheless, rent distribution must be part of any stable elite bargain, especially in such a politically, historically, and ethnically divided country. Abiy's imperfect opening up to political contestation is bound to lead to this, even if it may come at some cost to growth. After all, the 'national question' cannot be ignored.

Provided some national reconciliation can be achieved, it is premature to declare Ethiopia's economic and development success at an end. Nevertheless, the Ethiopian state's ability to lead development is reaching its limit. Tinkering with the economy has led to distortions. The practice of directing all resources, whether credit or ever-scarcer foreign exchange, to vast public investment has stifled the nascent, more dynamic domestic private sector. Ethiopia's development state may have overreached itself. It's not necessarily that its debt is becoming too high—while high, it is not exceptionally so for sub-Saharan Africa.[38] Rather, it is because the complementary private investment has simply not materialised to deliver the return to the vast infrastructure built in recent years, for instance through faster-growing exports. Ethiopia will need some more laissez-faire to harvest the fruits of the capitalist seeds of recent development plans.

Abiy has committed himself to some liberalisation of the economy through a 'home-grown economic agenda' that is a mix of the developmental state and a more liberal economy. But because this is

Ethiopia, where the centre is hardly keen to give up control, some time must pass and courage gathered before the regime is willing to gamble seriously on these reforms. If a political deal can be reached, the first step will be to stabilise the macroeconomy. The momentum may return, and the vast infrastructure investments may pay off. Will the half-miracle become a full miracle? Can widening conflict and state disintegration be avoided? Can Ethiopia reinvigorate its development bargain? Time will tell.

Rwanda, the clawing lion

Officials of rank visiting this country routinely first pay their respects at the Genocide Memorial. I was no exception when I visited Rwanda in 2015. Walking around the mass graves and touring the museum make for a moving experience, even if it is hard to imagine what happened. When the past is interpreted, as it is in the museum, it seems obvious that the world could have avoided the genocide.

I was in Rwanda three years before the genocide, in 1991. My notes from that time refer not only to the sluggish economy and often indiscriminate killings, but also to hopes for a multiparty democracy. I did not mention that a genocide was likely.[39] But it happened in 1994, organised by extreme elements of the state and government. In about a hundred days, 800,000 Rwandans were slaughtered (the population totalled only about 7 million in 1990). Most were Tutsis, a minority group that constituted about 14 per cent of the population before the genocide. At the end, the Rwandan Patriotic Front (RPF), a mainly Tutsi rebel army led by Paul Kagame, took power. Kagame has been the de facto leader ever since, first as vice president and then since 2000 as president.

Much has changed since 1994, when the economy took a massive hit. It did not regain the levels of GDP per capita before the genocide until 2000. From 2003 to 2019, growth was steady at 5 per cent per capita on average, making Rwanda, along with Ethiopia, one of Africa's fastest- and steadiest-growing economies in this period.[40] Its health and education indicators were improving as well, typically performing far better than those of most African countries, even though many of them have higher GDP per capita. For example,

Rwanda now has the lowest child mortality rate in mainland sub-Saharan Africa, a vast improvement since 2000.[41] Poverty remains nevertheless high, even though it probably has declined.[42]

The scale of progress and the way in which Rwanda has gone about it suggest the presence of a development bargain. There are some striking similarities between Ethiopia and Rwanda in how change has come about. Are the two countries examples of 'illiberal statebuilders', as some have claimed?[43] In any case, if Ethiopia is a lion, then Rwanda is one, too. The rest of this chapter looks more closely at Rwanda's development bargain and both the similarities and the differences with Ethiopia.

A different lion

The commonalities are manifold. Both the Ethiopian and Rwandan governments initially emerged from conflict, replacing those previously in power. In both countries, the removal of the previous elite was complete. The new leaders were committed to transforming their country's economy, with growth and development at the core of their plans. At the same time, when they came to power, the new governments were dominated by one minority group, the Tigrayans in Ethiopia and the Tutsi in Rwanda. Rather than seeking early legitimacy through the ballot box, in both countries development became a way to seek legitimacy. An elite commitment was definitely present, and, as in Ethiopia, one individual in Rwanda embodied it. Paul Kagame, the former military brain of the RPF, became the strategic policy thinker, pulling all the strings.

In other similarities, the Rwandan state sought to deliver progress in growth and development, and both countries had a reasonable state capability, even though Rwanda had had colonial rulers, first German and then Belgian until independence. The origins of this capability lay in the pre-colonial kingdom, located within the current borders and exhibiting well-documented central political and administrative structures.[44] In Rwanda, then just as now, respect for hierarchy and obedience to a central authority were deeply embedded.[45] The state could be used to play, at least in principle, a defining role, delivering on development, provided it was directed towards it.

And directed it was. Nothing would stop the Rwandan leadership from ensuring that state structures, previously used for patronage and corruption and exploited during the genocide, would be redirected so as to function for its purposes. However, more than in Ethiopia, Rwanda perfected the use of the state, not just as a matter of ideology but also in practice. For example, World Bank indicators of perceived government effectiveness over the last twenty years reveal a vast improvement for Rwanda, reaching levels typically seen only in far better-off countries such as South Africa, India, and Indonesia.[46] Petty corruption and procurement fraud disappeared over time, and eventually Rwanda was perceived to be one of the least corrupt developing countries, only below Botswana in sub-Saharan Africa and at the levels of a European country such as the Czech Republic, and well ahead of countries such as India, Indonesia, Ghana, and Ethiopia.[47]

Yet not all is so rosy; there is a dark side as well. Like Meles in Ethiopia, Kagame and his team would not allow anything or anyone to divert them from their path, not least a serious political challenge. The opportunity for any form of democratic accountability has been limited. Whereas in Ethiopia this limitation took the form of violent repression of street protests and defined opposition at home and abroad, the Rwandan government appears to have been far more effective at quashing it. Government effectiveness also appears to extend to its intelligence services, targeting opposition wherever it is found and leaving a bloody trail, while imprisoning internal opposition within the RPF.[48] At first, this crackdown was justified by the external threats presented by the large numbers of Hutu refugees in the eastern Democratic Republic of Congo (DRC), including genocidaires (those who committed the genocide but escaped). Over time, it was hardly clear, not least to the outside world, why it was necessary to take such an approach to opposition. President Kagame is undoubtedly highly popular throughout the country, even if some argue that his popularity is more linked to the historical trait of obedience to whoever has central authority in Rwanda. In any case, with no space for serious opposition, he was re-elected in 2017 with more than 98 per cent of the vote.

Perhaps more a leopard than a lion

It is hard not to admire how the Rwandan government pursued development. A strong emphasis on water, sanitation, and health, as well as education, was a key part of the government's plans. Improvement of state capability and low corruption created conditions for ever closer cooperation between the government and international aid agencies. By 2010, international aid per person had climbed to over $100, or more than double the levels in Ethiopia.[49] Meanwhile, senior Rwandan officials up to President Kagame were always willing to listen to technical advice and support, but they expected outsiders to act on their terms. For me, this is the way it should be, even if in practice development agencies are not accustomed to such an attitude.

Boosting the economy was always going to be a harder task, but it had a lot in its favour: peace and stability; a macroeconomy with broad stability, low indebtedness, and prudent management; and a well-functioning state with low corruption. Rwanda was the highest-ranked mainland African economy according to the Ease of Doing Business indicators in 2020; it was ranked 38th, just below Switzerland and higher than Belgium and the Netherlands.[50] It's no wonder, then, that Rwanda tends to receive glowing reports from the IMF, the World Bank, and other donors. But such reviews do not automatically lead to great interest from investors. As noted, Rwanda is tiny, home to only about one-tenth of Ethiopia's population, but with a population density five times as high. The nearest ports, Dar es Salaam in Tanzania and Mombasa in Kenya, are each about 1,500 kilometres away. The regional geopolitics are complicated, not least because of Rwanda's own doing, limiting the potential markets in all directions. Rwanda's repeated conflicts with the DRC and ongoing support for some violent groups in the eastern DRC have limited access to its nearest large market.

For some firms, though, Rwanda has become a very attractive business destination. In the perfectly maintained business park just outside Kigali, the owner of a small Lebanese food-processing factory extolled its virtues: 'This is the best place in the world to do business,' he said, having moved his factory from Uganda. However, just getting such small investors is taking a gamble. Being landlocked, Rwanda is gambling on the emergence of a new economy built around high value-added goods and especially services. Thus investments are geared towards making Rwanda a high-value conference and tourism destination, centred around excellent telecommunications, highly efficient venues, and visits to see the mountain gorillas near the DRC border. And a new passenger airline, RwandAir, has been heavily promoted, even tempting those visiting Rwanda with Arsenal football shirts. Moreover, there have been investments such as a joint venture with the Brazilian computer producer Positivo to assemble notebooks, for use in Rwandan schools as well, and a smartphone factory with Mara Group, all sporting the motto 'Made in Rwanda'.

Rwanda is still, though, a model heavily dependent on the public sector, with hand-picked firms and sectors and lavish support. It is attracting investors' interest, but it is still not a country doing dramatically better in this than, say, neighbouring Uganda, which is ranked far lower in any indicators, whether related to corruption or ease of doing business. It is also a model that tries to run before it can walk, seeking to deliver high-quality goods when the industrial capabilities for delivering simpler goods and services have not been established.[51] Time will tell whether this gamble will succeed.

This point, however, touches on one other issue: how Rwanda goes about implementing every aspect of its development bargain. It does so in the only way it knows: command and control—the military system in which all problems are addressed using strict hierarchical structures, all the way to the top. In areas such as basic health care and sanitation, the underlying technical knowledge is well established, so delivery through command and control can work—and it has done so in Rwanda. Bureaucratic processes and bottlenecks can similarly be solved through this process. But does it work in building a new economy, focusing on exporting services?

Command and control models can evolve into more effective systems for complex problem-solving, but they need space for autonomy and initiative. Some observers are sceptical about whether the way Rwanda is going about changing its economy will succeed. For example, the former Chinese ambassador to Ethiopia and to Rwanda thought Ethiopia would succeed but not Rwanda because Rwanda was a military state. Ethiopia depended more on its party and civil service processes, which were, according to him, the only way to try to put in place a development strategy, as there is more scope for autonomy, learning, and correcting. Is he right about Rwanda? Will Rwanda succeed in being a lion? Or has the RPF which controls it shaped the state in the only way it knows: secretive, even dangerous, rather like a leopard, an animal that can't change its spots.

Does it have to be like this?

The cases of Ethiopia and Rwanda pose a dilemma for anyone keen to support better living conditions for poor populations. The two countries emerged from conflict with an elite bargain that elevated growth and development to central importance. The bargain was nevertheless highly selective in who was included in power, and little space was left for competing voices. Because Ethiopia could not settle its 'national question', violence replaced peace and stability. Rwanda's leadership used an iron fist to control dissent, resorting to command and control in everything it did. At the same time, its progress in economic growth, health, education, and living conditions is undeniable, whatever some try to claim.

In the long run, though, this is a false dilemma, as Western societies have shown. What about the first steps? The path towards progress is less clearly charted. As Ethiopia has illustrated, it is easy to praise grand gestures such as peace deals with Eritrea or releasing and welcoming all political opponents into the fold. A Nobel Peace Prize for Prime Minister Abiy Ahmed appeared to be an apt reward. Indeed, Ethiopia's politics have now opened up, but the result has proved to be a Pandora's box. Some of the same people welcomed back speak of ethnic hatred, and conflict is raging with no end in sight. Both Ethiopia and Rwanda delivered progress within highly imperfect politics, with limited openness, voice, and local accountability.

But no country featured in this book can claim to have made progress in development with an unblemished record. It's easy to design blueprints for development delivered by a perfect, open society. But delivering economic progress is not so easy. It has to take place within countries and societies facing today's politics. It remains a dilemma for those who, like me, are impatient to see those countries staying behind develop and keen to ask what one can do. This is the subject of the final part of this book.

References

Abay, K. A., G. Berhane, J. Hoddinott, and K. Tafere. 2020. 'Covid-19 and Food Security in Ethiopia: Do Social Protection Programs Protect?' Policy Research Working Paper 9475. World Bank, Washington, DC.

Africa Confidential. 2021. 'Western Pressure Grows on Kagame Human Rights Abuses'. 62 (3).

Africa Watch. 1993. 'Beyond the Rhetoric: Continuing Human Rights Abuses in Rwanda'. Human Rights Watch.

Amsden, A. H. 1989. *Asia's Next Giant: South Korea and Late Industrialization*. Oxford: Oxford University Press on Demand.

Bachewe, F. N., G. Berhane, B. Minten, and A. S. Taffesse. 2018. 'Agricultural Transformation in Africa? Assessing the Evidence in Ethiopia'. *World Development* 105: 286–98.

Central Statistical Agency. 2010. 'Population and Housing Census 2007 Report'. National Report, Federal Government of Ethiopia, Addis Ababa.

Clapham, C. 2017. *The Horn of Africa: State Formation and Decay*. Oxford: Oxford University Press.

De Waal, A. 2013. 'The Theory and Practice of Meles Zenawi'. *African Affairs* 112 (446): 148–55.

———, A. S. Taffesse, and L. Carruth. 2006. 'Child Survival during the 2002–2003 Drought in Ethiopia'. *Global Public Health* 1 (2): 125–32.

Dercon, S., and D. Gollin. 2019. 'Agriculture's Changing Role in Ethiopia's Economic Transformation'. In *The Oxford Handbook of the Ethiopian Economy*, edited by F. Cheru, C. Cramer, and A. Oqubay. Oxford: Oxford University Press.

Dercon, S., R. V. Hill, and A. Zeitin. 2009. 'In Search of a Strategy: Rethinking Agriculture-Led Growth in Ethiopia'. Synthesis paper prepared as part of a study on Agriculture and Growth in Ethiopia, University of Oxford.

Dercon, S., and C. Porter, 2014. 'Live Aid Revisited: Long-Term Impacts of the 1984 Ethiopian Famine on Children'. *Journal of the European Economic Association* 12 (4): 927–48.

Dorn, A., and J. Matloff. 2000. 'Preventing the Bloodbath: Could the UN Have Predicted and Prevented the Rwandan Genocide?' *Journal of Conflict Studies* 20 (1): 9–52.

Federal Democratic Republic of Ethiopia. 2002. *Foreign Affairs and National Security Policy and Strategy*. Addis Ababa: Ministry of Information.

Heldring, L. 2021. 'The Origins of Violence in Rwanda'. *Review of Economic Studies* 88 (2): 730–63.

Hirvonen, K., T. P. Sohnesen, and T. Bundervoet. 2020. 'Impact of Ethiopia's 2015 Drought on Child Undernutrition'. *World Development* 131: 1049–64.

Johnson, C. 1982. *MITI and the Japanese Miracle: The Growth of Industrial Policy, 1925–1975*. Stanford, CA: Stanford University Press.

Jones, W., R. S. de Oliveira, and H. Verhoeven. 2012. *Africa's Illiberal State-Builders*. Refugee Studies Centre, Department of International Development, Oxford University.

Keller, E. J. 1981. 'The Revolutionary Transformation of Ethiopia's Twentieth-Century Bureaucratic Empire'. *Journal of Modern African Studies* 19 (2): 307–35.

Krishnan, P. 1996. 'Family Background, Education and Employment in Urban Ethiopia'. *Oxford Bulletin of Economics and Statistics* 58 (1): 167–83.

Lata, L. 2003. 'The Ethiopia–Eritrea War'. In *Dealing with Conflict in Africa: The United Nations and Regional Organizations*, edited by J. Boulden. New York: Palgrave Macmillan.

Lefort, R. 2013. 'The Theory and Practice of Meles Zenawi: A Response to Alex de Waal'. *African Affairs* 112 (448): 460–70.

Lemarchand, R. 1970. *Rwanda and Burundi*. London: Pall Mall Press.

Levine, D. N. 1965. *Wax and Gold: Tradition and Innovation in Ethiopian Culture*. Chicago: University of Chicago Press.

Marcus, H. G. 2002. *A History of Ethiopia*. Berkeley, CA: University of California Press.

Ministry of Planning and Economic Development. 1993. 'An Economic Development Strategy for Ethiopia: A Comprehensive Guidance and Development Strategy for the Future'. Addis Ababa, September.

NDRMC (National Disaster Risk Management Commission). 2016. 'Ethiopia: Humanitarian Requirements Document 2016'. Joint Government and Humanitarian Partners' Document, NDRMC, Addis Ababa.

Oqubay, A. 2015. *Made in Africa: Industrial Policy in Ethiopia*. Oxford: Oxford University Press.

Ottaway, M., and D. Ottaway. 1978. *Ethiopia: Empire in Revolution*. New York: Holmes and Meier Publishers.

Prunier, G. 1995. *The Rwanda Crisis: History of a Genocide*. New York: Columbia University Press.

Sabates-Wheeler, R. J. Lind, J. Hoddinott, and T. M. Tefera. 2020. 'Graduation after 10 Years of Ethiopia's Productive Safety Net Programme: Surviving but Still Not Thriving'. *Development Policy Review* 2020: 1–21.

Sutton, J. 2012. *Competing in Capabilities: The Globalization Process*. Oxford: Oxford University Press.

Vansina, J. 2004. *Antecedents to Modern Rwanda: The Nyiginya Kingdom*. Madison: University of Wisconsin Press.

Zenawi, Meles. 2009. 'African Development: Dead Ends and New Beginnings'. http://www.ethiopiantreasures.co.uk/meleszenawi/pdf/zenawi_dead_ends_and_new_beginnings.pdf.

PART III

CHASING CHANGE

A BRIEF GUIDE TO PART III

'We will only spend our money on what works,' the secretary of state for international development said in her speech in 2017. The bold promise was made to deflect persistent criticism from within her own party that the UK's aid was poorly spent. It wasn't that before her speech anyone at DFID consciously tried to spend on programmes that didn't work. For her officials, it was code for saying that evidence would be more rigorously used to identify 'what works' in development. As a savvy political operator, she was trying to imply more: that only programmes would be supported that carried no risk of failure for the taxpayer. That is a remarkable statement for any public spending, let alone spending outside the UK in the contexts described in this book. It hardly is a commitment to gamble on development.

This final part of the book discusses how change in a country's development path could come about. In particular, it looks at how those inside and outside these countries—citizens, firms, organisations, and governments—some powerful and some not so much, can contribute to the pursuit of beneficial change. It has a focus on aid—not because I believe it is the main route to change but because it is a mechanism I know well.

That I feature a role for development assistance in change, and therefore for those *outside* a country, may be surprising. Throughout this book, I have argued that progress in development and growth can come about only if there is an elite bargain among those with power *within* a country, and only if they make a credible commitment to these objectives. Thus, fundamentally, what happens inside countries is crucial. And yet chapter 11 takes up the subject of outside help by exploring some of the standard models pursued by international aid agencies, as well as governmental and nongovernmental development organisations.

One is the current UN-led framework, the Sustainable Development Goals (SDGs). They are promoted with much fanfare, but are they a force for change? I question whether the answer is yes, not least because they tend to put the spotlight too much on finance. I also discuss the weaknesses of other traditional models that drive development assistance and its finance, whether coming out of Washington or Beijing. All these models could be successful or failures, depending on the underlying elite bargain. In fact, the circumstances under which aid and other finance-led models tend to work are somewhat like dancing the tango: both parties must be seriously committed and remain in step. If so, the tango goes smoothly. If not, there could easily be a few trip-ups along the way.

Criticising standard models of assistance is easy. Chapter 12 takes up the challenge of how the international community could nevertheless help, empowering citizens of these countries while nudging elite bargains towards development and growth. The best way to help nascent development bargains is to increase the upside of the gambles by the elite that favour growth and development and to reduce the risks of failure. How to do this both locally and internationally is the subject of chapter 12.

Chapter 13 acknowledges that waiting for elite bargains that favour growth and development may leave large populations living in abject poverty. Part II cited many examples. The moral imperative to try to assist is strong. Likewise, the imperative to avoid making things worse by providing elites with excuses not to act is also crucial. In this final chapter, I delve into how to find a balance between these pressures and ways to support poor populations, identifying those that are the most effective and do the least to undermine the required genuine change in the elite bargain.

The starting point for these final two chapters is an acknowledgement that outsiders, whether governments, aid agencies, NGOs, or development funders, cannot simply engineer change and development, whether through aid or other means. They should strongly support those local elite bargains choosing to gamble on growth and development. Rewarding those elites that don't make this choice is wrong, while simply punishing them is unlikely to change much. Finding ways to make gambling on development more attractive, and empowering those that can nudge the elite bargain in that direction, is the right approach.

11

THE SWEDISH AND OTHER MODELS

Never before had so many world leaders posed together for a photograph. The date was 8 September 2000, and the occasion was the Millennium Summit in New York City, organised by the United Nations. The photograph, capturing 149 heads of state and other very high-ranking officials, was symbolic of the unity of the 189 leaders who had signed the Millennium Declaration. Its architect, the United Nations secretary general Kofi Annan, was standing front and centre.[1]

The Declaration was a grandiose statement of intent, adopting some 60 goals aimed at delivering peace, development, and protection of the environment, human rights, and the poor and vulnerable. It led a few months later to the Millennium Development Goals (MDGs), a set of eight goals to be met by 2015 on extreme poverty, education, gender equality, health, the environment, and global development cooperation.[2] Some good but imperfect progress was reported by 2015, when they were replaced by the Sustainable Development Goals (SDGs), a far expanded list of 17 goals, covering a broader and more universal vision of development.[3]

The photograph is as close as one can get to a glimpse of the global political elite. It also clearly indicates who carried the most weight. The United States' Bill Clinton, France's Jacques Chirac, and the UK's Tony Blair are standing next to Secretary General Annan on one side, with China's Jiang Zemin and Russia's Vladimir Putin on the other. Leaders from Germany, Italy, Japan, Nigeria, and Indonesia are also positioned prominently. The deal they struck looked like a genuine global development bargain: a set of shared commitments to development. By turning them into goals, first in 2000 and then again in 2015, these leaders in 2000 and those who followed them in 2015 appear to have enshrined their commitments in an explicit international contract with clear performance indicators. From it, a renewed focus and rhetoric emerged on aid and international finance, confirmed in large conferences such as those in Monterrey in 2002 and Addis Ababa in 2015. That said, some readers may expect this chapter to be a short one. After all, the SDGs appear to offer an international development bargain—the deal on development that ensures no longer will anyone be left behind.

Unfortunately, it's not so simple. This chapter delves into why simple models of global aid and cooperation approaches in this spirit are unlikely to make much difference in themselves. The leap from objectives to a focus on aid and finance, without much concern about how states or organisations function in practice, is a serious shortcoming of this simple model of financing the SDGs. Even some of the current more sophisticated models of development assistance, whether peddled from Washington, Beijing, or other capitals, are no guarantee of success, despite the firmer ideas behind them of how change will happen. In the spirit of chapters 1 and 2, they may offer one of many possible recipes, but their focus on finance is again distracting and probably counterproductive.

Dreaming of Sweden

I have always found Sweden an outstanding example of what equitable progress in a society looks like. Sweden has a rich, growing, dynamic economy within its well-funded and effective welfare state with its broad access to health, education, and social transfers. It attends to the needs of the poor and vulnerable, as well as continues its early persistent focus on environmental issues.[4] Many decades passed before I realised that this 'Swedish model' wasn't totally perfect or that the history of Sweden's progress hadn't been smooth or achieved quickly.[5] But that didn't matter: the *idea* of Sweden was rather attractive.[6]

When much later I became immersed in the world of international development, I recognised the idea of Sweden in what I heard and read: not so much the quest for a tolerant, open society or a dynamic economy, but its moral high ground with an emphasis on the poorest, on fighting inequality, on gender rights, and on building a fair society with high spending on social sectors. The activists' drumbeat of 'Let's build Sweden across the world!' would be stuck in my head.

***

The MDGs, and even more so the SDGs, encapsulate the Swedish model as well, with targets such as ending poverty and hunger, boosting education for all, fighting against inequality and for women's rights, and taking climate action. It's as though the development community launched a global rallying cry, but now with a target date: 'Let's build Sweden by 2030!' It still surprises me, nevertheless, to hear politicians from rich and poor countries alike repeating these commitments in public, especially those who today stand for domestic policy advocacy hardly consistent with many of the SDGs.

Don't get me wrong; I still rather like Sweden, just as I like the SDGs. Progress in development could well be seen in these terms. But for three reasons, the Millennium Declaration or similar appeals and processes should not be exempt from criticism. First, the SDGs tend to be irrelevant as a mechanism to achieve progress in the countries that most urgently need to make progress. Second, these UN processes may have been more useful for development financiers and agencies than impoverished countries. Third, and most important, first the MDGs and then the SDGs risk conveying a misconception about how development will come about.

Goals and targets have not led to development

I cannot think of a single country that, because it signed the Millennium Declaration and stated its commitment first to the MDGs and then to the SDGs, fundamentally shifted from political and economic deals favouring a narrow set of groups to long-term investment in development. In fact, throughout history there is no evidence that prioritising these or similar goals that targeted extreme poverty was the way in which any country succeeded in developing. Clearly, the world's richest economies didn't achieve progress in poverty reduction and inclusion in development overnight.[7] Instead, it was a process of both gradual and disruptive change, often first with conflict rather than consensus. And even then, across Europe and the US much unfinished business remains. No one builds a Sweden overnight; indeed, few rich countries really try. The others that have tried are mostly its neighbours.

The main lesson from Sweden is not where it has ended up, but how it got there. Sweden was already a high-income country by the time the Swedish model and the *idea* of Sweden emerged.[8] What defined this and other Nordic countries is that early on an elite had put in place a development bargain. They found it in their interest to work with leaders across business, religion, social movements, and politics to forge a broad consensus on the nature of the political and economic deal, with regular course corrections. This shared commitment was no doubt facilitated by high levels of religious, language, ethnic, and cultural homogeneity, and Sweden's ability to remain above the fray of conflict over the last two centuries. For example, even the Swedish version of the hunger riots of 1917, which were violent, disruptive, and even revolutionary in many parts of Europe, were described by a historian as a 'Swedish revolution, a revolution granted permission by the police chief', with mutual understanding and respect between workers and authorities.[9] What made Sweden stand out is not simply *what* was pursued, but *how*.

As for the MDGs and SDGs, just setting some goals and targets and telling everyone to get on with them will hardly do the trick. In any case, just look at who signed the Millennium Declaration. Several in the photograph were the political leaders of elite bargains who had little intention of promoting longer-term growth or inclusive development. In fact, many of them were rather greedy, power-thirsty, or just incompetent politicians. What happened in the Democratic Republic of Congo (DRC), Sudan, Sierra Leone, Nigeria, Malawi, Somalia, and many more countries in the two decades since 2000 confirms this observation. Economies and societies were disintegrating in some, while in others they were facing prolonged stagnation. In fact, several of the signatories were the architects of this decline.

Are these signatures then worthless? Not necessarily, but none of the goals is a binding commitment—that is, they are not legally or otherwise enforceable. The commitments, then, are simply not credible, not least in locations where they would make the most difference. Those that will make progress anyway by engaging in an elite bargain with a shared commitment to development and growth may be helped somewhat because it allows them to prove their progress, but it is unlikely in practice to change much in the speed and character of development. The MDGs and SDGs are thus at best a way to remind those interested of what progress is being made and about the persistent gaps across countries—useful, yes, but not quite matching the rhetoric.[10]

Resetting the development aid narrative for donors

And yet the MDGs and SDGs have played their role in resetting the narrative around foreign aid at least for some time (see box 11.1). The renewed focus on specific, identifiable goals has helped introduce a new sense of accountability and boosted the political acceptance in richer economies of spending in poorer countries. Aid would not just be spent—or wasted—but spent on achieving particular outcomes or results, such as the MDGs or SDGs. It would be used to meet specific targets such as 'to end extreme poverty' and 'to lower child mortality to at most 25 per 1,000, both by 2030'.

Box 11.1 Official development assistance data

One may be forgiven for getting confused by aid and development finance statistics. Countries may give grants and loans directly to developing countries (bilateral aid) or to multilateral organisations, such as UNICEF or the World Health Organization (WHO), for them to use in

---

developing countries. Donors also give capital and grants to multilateral banks, such as the World Bank or the Asian Development Bank, which they then provide to countries as loans. Loans by countries or by development banks are offered either at terms just above the cost to these banks (non-concessional) or with terms and conditions that make them better than that (concessional), so that in fact they have a grant element. Some of this finance is tied to specific sets of countries, themes, sectors, and programmes. And some is spent by the receiving governments, as well as by delivery systems with less control or even outside the control of the receiving government, such as through private local or international firms or NGOs.[11]

The OECD Development Assistance Committee (DAC) defines aid as resource flows to countries and territories on the DAC list of official development assistance (ODA) recipients (essentially low- and middle-income countries) and to multilateral development organisations and agencies. These flows count as ODA when they are provided by the public sectors of donor countries to promote the economic development and welfare of receiving countries as their main objective. In their aid statistics, the DAC assesses the 'grant equivalent' of all this finance to define its concept of ODA or, essentially, what I call foreign or development aid throughout this book. For grants, this is easy: the total grant is counted. For loans, the extent of the concessionality of each loan offered is counted in its definition, not the total loan, thereby helping comparability and transparency. This makes it about aid and not about just any financial flows into developing countries provided on non-concessional or market terms.[12] Some countries, such as China, do not follow these conventions, and so numbers quoted for that country are not easily comparable with those of the DAC members.

Between 1980 and 2000, development aid did not change in real terms, despite the fact that the overall GDP of high-income countries almost doubled.[13] This changed around 2000, however. Between 2000 and 2016, aid in real terms doubled, reaching about $150 billion a year, even though the GDP in high-income countries had only increased by about a quarter over this entire period. Since then, development aid has barely changed in real terms, reaching $161 billion in nominal dollars in 2020.[14]

This boost in aid since 2000 is likely to have been assisted by the MDGs. Increasingly sceptical taxpayers were offered more clarity on how their money would be used—that is, it would go towards promoting the MDGs, a set of indicators consistent with simple ideas of deprivation and progress in development. Overall, the MDGs and the SDGs have helped foster a larger yet still modest commitment by richer countries to financing development. They have done so by offering taxpayers a sense of accountability: aid will be used to reach these quantifiable targets.[15]

The cost of development

It is worrisome that the question of how to achieve these goals and targets has too often been reduced to how much it will cost.[16] The UN itself often quotes a figure of $5–$7 trillion a year as the cost of achieving the SDGs by 2030.[17] These figures feed the rallying cry for more aid by other rich economies and a new push for more development finance. Meanwhile, in 2014 while I was chief economist at DFID, I ignored an order from my boss to calculate how much it would cost to achieve the SDGs. It felt wrong, nested in a troubling idea about how development comes about. I am still glad I ignored it.[18]

To be clear, alleviating poverty, improving health and education systems, and building better infrastructure will obviously cost huge amounts of money, just as the recovery from Covid-19 will require vast sums. However, as ample examples in this book have shown, the remaining poor countries have failed to take off not because they have lacked financial resources. Reducing development simply to a finance problem across *all* developing countries is an affront to those countries and to some of their political and other elites who are genuinely trying to steer their countries towards take-off. It is also a perfect excuse for those countries whose elites have continued to pursue rents and profits without regard to development.

Should I blame the MDGs or SDGs for all this? Of course not. These are worthwhile goals, and anything that steers spending of resources towards outcomes rather than wastage has to be applauded. However, making these goals the focus of all rhetoric on development, with its implicit and recurring emphasis on the total volume of aid and finance needed 'to achieve the goals', has not been particularly helpful, steering discussions away from crucial debates about how development comes about. All this does not mean that aid and other development finance do not matter, but that how they are used is more important.

Aid models and modalities

Why do some countries give aid to other countries? Plenty of studies show rather convincingly that aid flows are correlated with the needs and poverty of the recipient countries. Nevertheless, other factors matter such as historical or colonial links, as well as more transactional political factors such as political alignment, support in the UN Security Council, or commercial interests.[19] In the end, whether a donor country wants to burnish its image as a do-gooder in the world or wants to pursue its own national objectives, foreign aid is always an explicit foreign policy decision.

That political motives matter does not mean aid will be spent poorly with no regard for impact.[20] The cartoonish view espoused by critics of aid, that foreign assistance is simply passed on to corrupt politicians or incompetent governments with little concern for what it is spent on, is indeed far from the truth. Calling all aid wasted is unfair—there is much sophistication in the way aid is spent. Nevertheless, critics are right that the overall record is typically not so impressive when assessing the overall impact on growth and development of aid spending in the last five decades across all developing countries. For example, the impact of foreign aid on the economic growth of recipient countries has at best been relatively modest *on average*.[21] How can I square this evidence with my view that aid can be spent in ways that stimulate growth and development?

It helps to recognise that aid spending is a form of public spending, and anywhere in the world, in rich countries as well, the public sector sometimes spends productively, whereas at other times its programmes have only limited impact on longer-term growth and development. Obviously, it matters on what it actually spends. There is no point in spending public resources including aid on supporting a failing economic sector, on ineffective health treatments or excessive salaries. When wasteful spending happens at scale, there is likely to be more to it than just ignorance.

As this book has argued, the elite bargain is central to understanding the trajectory towards growth and development. The political and economic deals, and what they mean for how well the state functions, will influence the productivity of public spending— and, by implication, the effectiveness of aid. Making better use of aid is then not a matter of more technical advice or capacity-building; it is fundamentally linked with the nature of the elite bargain and the way it encourages the state to improve its performance.

The questions when and how aid may be productive are addressed in the rest of this chapter, along with whether current aid and finance models, specifically those favoured by China and Western countries as well as multilateral finance institutions, are likely to be effective.

Aid as dancing the tango

In countries with a development bargain and thus a commitment by those with the power to pursue growth and development, aid may well be used effectively over time, so long as it is provided in ways consistent with the country's own plans and elite deals. As I have said before, it is like dancing the tango: a strong, passionate commitment is needed from both the giving and receiving parties, as well as a shared direction. Still, one party has to lead—and in the foreign aid world it should be the receiving country. It then becomes a gamble by the donor, and all will depend on the strength of the shared commitment to growth and development, and especially on the country's ability to correct course if progress is derailed.

As described in part II, Ghana, Bangladesh, Ethiopia, Rwanda, Vietnam, and even Uganda have in recent times made considerable progress in development outcomes, as well as in growth, whatever their other imperfections. Although it is hard to prove quantitatively, in all of them aid has played a helpful role in their progress.[22] It has been in general consistent with the direction in which the countries' political and economic elites have been heading, across very different systems and state capabilities.

It should not come as a surprise that aid 'works' in such settings, even if not perfectly. A development bargain offers a low-cost route to aid effectiveness. There is no need for donors to impose endless conditions on how resources are used—aid is simply a way to enshrine a joint commitment to implementing an agreed-on plan, totally consistent with the country's own vision. Aid then becomes a simple means of extending the public sector's budget. In fact, offering aid as budget support, directly topping up the government's budget, is likely to be a very effective way of achieving the shared objectives.[23]

Contrast this with countries such as the DRC, Malawi, Nigeria, and South Sudan. As chapter 3 and part II described, such countries have dreadful records of development outcomes. The needs of some may justify their receiving large volumes of aid. Indeed, few donors would suggest that those needs be ignored. Still, spending aid productively is not easy when the elite bargain has other uses in mind for it—as a source of funding for self-enrichment in Malawi (chapter 5), or for patronage or clientelism in Kenya or Uganda (chapter 6), or as just another source of cash to steal in the DRC (chapter 7), or as a welcome source of funding to allow a conflict to be sustained in South Sudan (chapter 8).

All this leads to a stark conclusion—and a highly selective model of foreign aid. Aid could be highly effective in countries moving towards a development bargain. Because they have a commitment to development, these countries tend to be open to using, when offered, evidence, best practice, and expertise, thereby accelerating their development—that is, the givers and receivers of aid are dancing in sync. Here, outsiders could have a huge impact, not just in improving some specific outcomes, but also supporting countries on their path to development.[24] Meanwhile, in practice, spending foreign aid remains hard work, even in such countries. A development bargain must be continually tested. All these countries still struggle with corruption, rent-seeking, lapses in the rule of law, and at times poor policy-making and deeper political challenges. Still, they are nevertheless a low-risk gamble for those keen to spend aid well. Patience by aid givers is required, and they should not jump in alarm at every misuse or misstep but give time for a development bargain to become stable and persistent.

If a development bargain is not present, aid can be far less ambitious. In such countries, foreign aid may help improve some outcomes, but it would not lead to transformation and change. It may even make the elite bargain worse. Aid risks enshrining the status quo, blocking development and progress, and ending political change. Indeed, it could lead back to the gloom and doom some authors see in the whole aid endeavour, as discussed in chapter 1.[25]

The next two chapters discuss how to provide aid in settings with a development bargain and in settings with none. They ask what outsiders can do to help a better elite bargain emerge or make it stronger, through foreign aid as well. In fact, outsiders, both in and outside the country, could, through development-focused international policy-making and careful use of foreign aid, persuade the elites to gamble on a better bargain. And a key decision for outsiders is whether to be willing to gamble with substantial support on those elite bargains that seem to turn into nascent development bargains. The final chapter also turns to those countries that risk staying behind but where the needs remain extremely high. There, a well-informed humanitarian and broader development agenda is still possible, based on a thorough understanding of local political contexts.

But first it is worth reflecting on whether the current dominant standard finance models for development can overcome the challenge of spending aid effectively in countries without a development bargain. For that, a look at both the Chinese model of development finance and the standard model used by Western countries and multilateral development banks would be helpful.

Development finance the Chinese way

'Trust me, we will never have to pay it back', Abba Kyari, the powerful chief of staff to Nigeria's President Muhammadu Buhari, told me about six years ago. We were discussing my belief that without further economic reforms and moving exports away from oil, Nigeria would struggle to receive international finance. 'If you don't give us more, then we just ask our Chinese friends—they are offering $10 billion dollars,' he argued. 'You still have to pay it back,' I countered. His view—that the Chinese never had to be paid back—was all too common in the countries seeking its finance at that time. I heard it in Ghana, Zambia, and the DRC as well. China's biggest lenders in Africa, China EXIM Bank and China Development Bank, definitely never intended to be handing out gifts, even if they are fully state-owned, so-called policy banks that were instructed by the leadership to support Chinese investments across the world. More recently, Covid-19's punishment of African economies and rising debts left China taking a big reputational hit, and it continues to struggle to be viewed as constructive in debt-restructuring discussions.

In many ways, China created this misperception itself—easy finance has undermined what otherwise would have been a decent proposition for development: building stronger economic links between lower-income countries and China, using investment as the mechanism. If not for shifting geopolitics and its carelessness, China's missteps would hardly have been a reasonable target for criticism by Western rivals.

Three things went wrong. First, China loves telling its own polished narrative of how it developed, with the state taking the lead and then building up infrastructure, as described in chapter 4. When extending its efforts overseas, China simply promised to finance what governments wanted in infrastructure, deliver it through its own construction firms, and otherwise not interfere. The leaders with whom Chinese delegations met, whether in Asia or Africa, loved the simplicity of the arrangement and the way it would be delivered. After all, it put the country's leaders in charge of large flagship infrastructure projects, and no one would be telling them what to do. Yet China's progress was a bit more complicated, involving serious reforms of how the state functioned and a deep commitment to making it work. That final central aspect of China's progress was left out of its glossy sales brochure.

Second, China failed to explain what it really thought about finance, feeding the illusions of developing country leaders that their debts to China were not quite real. China focused instead on announcing ever-larger cumulative funding streams during conferences such as its Forum on China–Africa Cooperation (FOCAC), which has been held every three years since 2000. It is hard for observers to get a handle on these numbers because China's reporting on this finance differs from that of Western countries.[26] If one goes by a definition of foreign aid similar to that used by the OECD Development Assistance Committee, Chinese aid is still relatively small—about $6.4 billion a year, or well below that of the US, the UK, Germany, France, or Japan.[27] This figure contrasts with the vast numbers one hears for China's development finance, and even reliable sources suggest China is currently sending about $10 billion a year to Africa.[28] This number is, however, bulked out by non-aid flows such as export credits or loans without some grant element, and not foreign aid in the conventional sense.[29] Still, these are the numbers largely cited for infrastructure projects—such as railways in Kenya or Ethiopia—and often reported in the press.

Chinese banks have never considered these loans to be 'concessional' in the sense of aid (loans with a grant element), even though the terms are usually very competitive and at interest rates lower than those of multilateral development banks.[30] In fact, Chinese banks even object to having these loans classified as official flows.[31] At numerous events in Beijing, I was told that China and its banks were putting in practice a new finance model, a private–public partnership. China's 'private' banks would provide finance so governments in other developing countries could 'buy' infrastructure from Chinese 'private' contractors. The few details known about the underlying contracts from these banks suggest they tried hard to make them resemble strict private loan contracts, with specified assets as collateral. For example, the port of Mombasa is the collateral that may fall under Chinese control if the $3.2-billion loan from EXIM Bank for the railway to Nairobi is not repaid.[32] This helps explain why, with debts and macroeconomic crises amongst creditors mounting, the Chinese banks involved are now balking at having to reschedule or cancel these loans.[33] Even while these banks ended up writing contracts that looked more like a Credit Suisse or a JPMorgan loan than a World Bank or a European government loan, the ease with which finance and attractive interest rates were offered fuelled expectations that these loans were closer to grants and definitely not commercial loans. In short, China fed the expectations of recipient governments that the loans were special ones whose repayment could be easily renegotiated or ignored.

Finally, China is learning that countries will not always use resources as carefully as the Chinese themselves. It has assumed that the political elites with whom it works wants these projects to be successful instead of just seeing an opportunity for a quick political gain or personal profit for cronies. But corruption is not the only problem: many of these projects are not economically viable, creating a headache even beyond debt. The viability has much to do with limited economic progress and lack of growth relative to what the banks expect—not that these are bad projects per se. Simply expecting countries to be deeply committed to growing their economies is clearly a mistake. Too many in China's policy banks and government have assumed that a development bargain as strong and strict as China's is in place everywhere it goes. China may have vowed to continue with its own cherished principle of 'non-interference' in the economy or the politics of the countries with which it deals, but once easy finance is offered, one had better know with whom one is dealing.

Classic development finance

The approaches to financial aid used by multilateral development banks—the World Bank as well as the regional development banks—differ from China's. I focus here on concessional loans, the low-cost loans offered by, for instance, the International Development Association (IDA) of the World Bank. IDA is the main source of aid for the countries with high levels of poverty featured in this book.

In 2019 IDA disbursed $14.2 billion to 74 countries, home to about half a billion of the extreme poor. It is the largest single source of development finance.

The World Bank likens itself to a cooperative bank, a mutual aid society, because its members are its owners.[34] All members that satisfy some criteria in respect of low income and creditworthiness receive access to the lowest-cost financial product, IDA loans. These may be offered well below market terms, thereby making half of the loan essentially a grant. How much a country could receive is qualified by further criteria, of which the Country Policy and Institutional Assessment (CPIA) is a central one. It is a (subjective) assessment by World Bank staff of how well a country scores on its economic and social policies and its quality of public administration. In the end, it typically only determines how much a country gets, not whether loans are disbursed. So among IDA's top five borrowers in 2020 were countries such as Nigeria and the DRC, hardly beacons of enlightened development, as well as the more ambitious Ethiopia and Bangladesh. In the end, it is in the interests of the World Bank that countries receive these loans, and so they are rarely not given.

That said, countries are not let off lightly. Over the years, IDA has avoided creating the impression that it is a pushover, or that its terms and conditions should not be taken seriously, unlike the way some recipients of loans from China view their lender. Recipient countries find dealing with the IDA and the World Bank cumbersome, involving long design phases and endless assessments of likely impacts. For example, arranging finance from the World Bank's Crisis Response Window, a special low-cost IDA loan in response to a crisis, tends to take on average 398 days from crisis to disbursement.[35] Lending is accompanied by a range of conditions, often extending beyond the narrow confines of the programme.

Frequently, lending is sequenced with the International Monetary Fund (IMF) when countries also need emergency finance to deal with macroeconomic pressures. In such circumstances, the loans offered often take the form of development policy loans, which are disbursed as general budget support rather than finance for one particular project. These loans tend to include conditions relating to economic policies, including the IMF seal of approval of the country's macroeconomic policies, or to more 'structural' issues, often related to improvements in the investment climate. They may complement the IMF programme, aiming to steer the country back to the straight and narrow in fiscal and monetary policies, as well as to sustain economic growth.

Other support by Western bilateral donors tends to track IMF and World Bank support, at least when it comes to supporting government at scale. There is no doubt that both institutions have moved a long way since the type of one-size-fits-all conditions of the 1990s that were criticised as the 'Washington Consensus'. But the conditions for economic reforms have remained, even if they are now often more negotiated than imposed.[36]

Plenty of examples from past and present suggest that conditionality as an enforcement mechanism does not work.[37] In the 1990s, one-third of World Bank policy-focused programmes clearly failed to produce the required reforms, even though the finance was fully disbursed.[38] More recently, in 2019 Pakistan entered its 22nd IMF bailout programme since 1950, and the 13th in the last thirty years, having 'completed' (with full disbursement) the previous one only in 2016. In 2020, it received the fourth-largest IDA loan, just after that given to the DRC. Current conditions, linked to raising taxes, abolishing energy subsidies, and privatisation, are remarkably similar to those in the previous IMF programme. Maybe the 22nd time will be lucky, but Pakistan's record suggests that this is hardly a country on track for stable growth and transformation. It is not at all obvious that the vast resources flowing to Pakistan over the years have contributed much to setting it on this path.

Nevertheless, in theory the conditions linked to the finance offer will contribute to ensuring that the recipient undertakes the required reforms. On the one hand, if the recipient is committed to these reforms, then surely no conditions would be needed. But then they come at no extra cost to anyone, so long as the reforms and conditions are genuinely locally owned in ways consistent with the underlying political and economic deals. But that is just the theory. In practice, the development bargain is not always resistant to pressures, and, as the examples in part II suggested about Indonesia or Uganda, the conditions can help the technocrats who need to keep economic stability and growth on track. In short, here the model makes sense.

On the other hand, if countries are not genuinely committed to reforms, then the conditions can at least make them undertake the reforms and set the country on a better growth trajectory—so the theory goes. Herein lies the problem: if there is no development bargain, but rather political and economic deals focused on other objectives, then conditions are unlikely to make much difference. Lenders may impose certain policies, but the elite players in politics or the economy will no doubt look for ways to water them down or circumvent them. Conditions may seem satisfied and loans and other aid may be disbursed, but they are hardly putting the country on the path of transformation through growth and development.[39]

* * *

Despite hugely contrasting modalities, many of the models underlying both Chinese and Western development programmes, such as those financed by multilateral development banks, often do not offer the scale of success they promise. This finance-led model is too strongly supply-driven, and it overestimates the extent to which recipient governments really care about whether these programmes will succeed. Ample development finance should be a no-brainer for countries seriously committed to growth and development (chapter 12). What to do in those countries without a development bargain is the subject of chapter 13.

References

Africa Confidential. 2020. 'Freight Storm Hits the Port'. 61 (8): 6.

Alesina, A., and D. Dollar. 2000. 'Who Gives Foreign Aid to Whom and Why?' *Journal of Economic Growth* 5 (1): 33–63.

Banerjee, A. V., and E. Duflo. 2011. *Poor Economics: A Radical Rethinking of the Way to Fight Global Poverty*. New York: PublicAffairs.

Clemens, M. A., C. J. Kenny, and T. J. Moss. 2007. 'The Trouble with the MDGs: Confronting Expectations of Aid and Development Success'. *World Development* 35 (5): 735–51.

Clemens, M. A., and T. J. Moss. 2007. 'The Ghost of 0.7 Per Cent: Origins and Relevance of the International Aid Target'. *International Journal of Development Issues* 6 (1): 3–25.

Clemens, M.A., S. Radelet, R. R. Bhavnani, and S. Bazzi. 2012. 'Counting Chickens When They Hatch: Timing and the Effects of Aid on Growth'. *Economic Journal* 122 (561): 590–617.

Collier, P., and S. Dercon. 2006. 'The Complementarities of Poverty Reduction, Equity, and Growth: A Perspective on the *World Development Report 2006*'. *Economic Development and Cultural Change* 55 (1): 223–36.

Collier, P., P. Guillaumont, S. Guillaumont, and J. W. Gunning. 1997. 'Redesigning Conditionality'. *World Development* 25 (9): 1399–407.

Cormier, B., and M. S. Manger. 2020. 'The Evolution of World Bank Conditionality: A Quantitative Text Analysis'. Paper prepared for the 13th annual conference on 'The Political Economy of International Organization', Vancouver.

Devarajan, S., M. J. Miller, and E. V. Swanson. 2002. *Goals for Development: History, Prospects, and Costs*. Washington, DC: World Bank.

Dollar, D., and J. Svensson. 2000. 'What Explains the Success or Failure of Structural Adjustment Programmes?' *Economic Journal* 110 (466): 894–917.

Edvinsson, R. 2013. 'New Annual Estimates of Swedish GDP, 1800–2010'. *Economic History Review* 66 (4): 1101–26.

Kitano, N., and Y. Harada. 2016. 'Estimating China's Foreign Aid 2001–2013'. *Journal of International Development* 28 (7): 1050–74.

Morris, S., B. Parks, and A. Gardner. 2020. *Chinese and World Bank Lending Terms: A Systematic Comparison across 157 Countries and 15 Years*. Center for Global Development.

OECD (Organisation for Economic Co-operation and Development). 2020. *Multilateral Development Finance 2020*. Paris: OECD Publishing.,

Sachs, J. D. 2019. *UN Millennium Development Library: Investing in Development; A Practical Plan to Achieve the Millennium Development Goals*. New York: Routledge.

Salonen, T. 2009. 'Sweden: Between Model and Reality'. Chapter 7 in *International Social Policy: Welfare Regimes in the Developed* World, edited by P. Alcock and G. Craig. New York: Red Globe Press.

Spearing, M. 2019. 'The IDA Crisis Response Window: Lessons and Recommendations to Increase Impact'. Working paper, Centre for Disaster Protection, London.

Strange, A.M., A. Dreher, A. Fuchs, B. Parks, and M. J. Tierney. 2017. 'Tracking Underreported Financial Flows: China's Development Finance and the Aid–Conflict Nexus Revisited'. *Journal of Conflict Resolution* 61 (5): 935–63.

Sturfelt, L. 2019. 'Wartime and Post-war Societies (Sweden)'. In *The International Encyclopedia of the First World War, 1914–1918 online*, edited by U. Daniel, P. Gatrell, O. Oliver, H. Jones, J. Keene, A. Kramer, and B. Nasson. Berlin: Freie Universität Berlin.

UNCTAD (United Nations Conference on Trade and Development). 2014. *World Investment Report 2014: Investing in the SDGs; An Action Plan*. New York: United Nations.

Zedillo, E. 2001. *Report of the High-Level Panel on Financing for Development: United Nations General Assembly*. A/55/1000. New York: United Nations.

12

ABOUT WARREN BUFFETT AND
THE OBVIOUS USES OF AID

Warren Buffett is not just one of the ten richest people in the world. He's also often heralded as the world's most successful investor. Buffett believes in 'value investing'—that is, investing in stocks that underperform and likely will perform much better in the long term. But this is not blind investing. Before making an investment, his company, Berkshire Hathaway, conducts intensive research, carefully assessing the management of the firms it invests in. It then trusts them to bring value to the investments made. So Berkshire Hathaway is a patient investor for the long term—it's not just looking for a quick return. As Buffett himself reportedly said, 'Someone's sitting in the shade today because someone planted a tree a long time ago.'

Those engaging in development aid would do well to learn from Warren Buffett's investing method. Just spending to meet a need is not a recipe for success, even if it is clear that the needy country ought to do better. At the same time, aid investors should take a long-term view. There must be a decent chance of lasting benefits. The quality of a country's management—the elite with power and influence and how they run the country—matters. In the end, though, donors, just like Buffett, have to let the managers of the recipient countries get on with it, trusting them to drive success in their own way.

These final two chapters describe how to construct a portfolio of development programmes, like a value investor in development. Buffett's approach to building a portfolio offers some practical principles for investing in aid programmes—and for what not to do. First, invest where there is an upside: spend aid not just because there is need but because there is a window of opportunity for impact and change. Second, who and how matters: do not be concerned just about what sector or intervention to invest in. Instead, pay attention to whom one invests in and how investments will be run, ensuring that those in charge are themselves aiming for success. Third, and most important, focus on the long-term outcomes in growth, development, and even the political and economic deals of countries—not just on quick results.[1] For those providing aid, it is a risky proposition, but donors from rich countries can afford this gamble on development.

All this is a tall order, and the risk of deluding oneself about the likely impact is real. Foreign aid (defined as official development assistance—see box 11.1 in chapter 11) rose only from about $150 billion to $161 billion in nominal US dollars between 2016 and 2020. Overall, across all low- and middle-income countries that are eligible, this is about 0.5 per cent in 2019 of their gross national income (GNI).[2] In poorer countries, it is higher, but still only 9 per cent of their GNI, whereas for sub-Saharan Africa it is only about 3 per cent on average. Aid is therefore a very scarce resource.

The easy part: Directing aid to countries with development bargains

A decade ago, I asked one of my predecessors as chief economist of DFID where he thought UK development aid had been spent most effectively in recent decades. Without hesitation, he said 'western China'. If today I put the same question to experienced development practitioners who have worked with large aid budgets, their list is bound to include parts of India, Indonesia, Vietnam, and in more recent times Bangladesh, Rwanda, Ghana, and Ethiopia. In short, these are all countries that I have suggested have had a development bargain—some more established and some more fragile, within otherwise very different political systems. This practitioners' list should not come as a surprise: when the donor and recipient are in close agreement on what they want to achieve and the receiving country is committed to success, at least in development terms, and not just hell-bent on spending on patronage or corruption, aid spending is just an extension of their own fiscal resources, an extension of a public sector keen to solve the basic challenges of development, learning to implement better and holding itself to account along the way. This can still go wrong, of course. Politicians and civil servants may pursue pet projects. Some may be corrupt, or just incompetent, as in any public sector across the world. How can aid be used most effectively in such countries to sustain a development bargain and support growth and development?

Aid for institutional development

One characteristic of a self-sustaining development bargain is a mature, effective state that acts when it should but does not try to take on more than it can. With accelerating growth and development, more demands will be made on the state to adapt and evolve.

What are the demands put on a state so it will effectively support growth and development? First is a functioning tax system that raises resources from citizens and firms to finance the country's development, such as through the provision of public services.[3] Although taxation in itself does not drive accountability, when combined with an underlying elite commitment to growth and development, the conditions are in place for a 'fiscal social contract' of more taxation in return for accountability and the provision of services.[4] Second, the state will need to improve in both efficiency and predictability as its economy and society evolve. Development bargains are often fragile in the early stages, when the political and economic deals are not quite settled. Third, the state must be able to continually upgrade its investment regime—the underlying legal frameworks as well as their enforcement such as of property rights, investment law, and taxation—to ensure confidence in a trajectory of sustained growth.[5] Such growth will require investment for the long term by trusting investors, both local and international.

The fiscal social contract, state capability, and the investment climate are key aspects of institutional development. As successful development bargains have shown, no country that has experienced fast growth in recent decades began its transformation with good institutions in place. For example, no perfect or even strong institutions were evident in China, Indonesia, and India when their development bargain emerged. As chapter 4 recounted, China began its journey after a period of deep turmoil, and only after the 1980s and beyond was it able to establish the economic institutions and overall governance that could complement the fast growth on which it was embarking.[6] Meanwhile, Rwanda, Bangladesh, and Ghana are clearly works in progress, and Ethiopia's current troubles reveal the fragility that results from failing to adjust an elite bargain to be more responsive to deep-rooted tensions between regional elites.

To be clear, outsiders can do relatively little to engineer such institutional changes. Chapter 13 suggests a few ways, but they have a whiff of hope over experience. That said, when a self-sustaining development bargain is solidly supported by the elite in the state and politics, the technical assistance provided by institutions such as the World Bank or International Monetary Fund (IMF) can be instrumental in achieving progress, especially when targeting well-chosen potential pockets of excellence in the state. Such governments may also be highly receptive to incorporating research into their development efforts and to emphasising effectiveness of spending over patronage and clientelism. These settings are also excellent places to try out the recipes in Banerjee and Duflo's *Poor Economics*[7] as well as those arising from other intervention-based research. The idea is not necessarily to adopt research findings blindly, but to use them to experiment and build stronger evidence-based policy-making cultures in organisations and drive better service provision. Aid can also be used to help those seeking to improve the elite bargain and the functioning of the state, such as by supporting civil society organisations and local nongovernmental organisations (NGOs), if the conditions are present.[8]

Institutional change will not occur quickly. The elite bargain that sustain development and growth is typically quite imperfect, and corruption may be part of that bargain—a means of ongoing access to rents for some, despite an overall commitment to growth and development. Without a serious shared commitment to change among the key elite players, anti-corruption efforts will hardly be successful.[9] And even if those players are committed, disentangling corruption from the political and economic deals is still not easy.[10]

Using aid in the early days to bet on development

Using foreign aid (grants) to directly fulfil all the financing needs of countries with a development bargain is not the best idea, even if it may seem that the returns are high and low-risk, such as with large-scale spending on infrastructure or on health or education systems. Growing economies like these tend to have access to global capital markets. Even better, multilateral development banks, such as the International Bank for Reconstruction and Development and its regional equivalents, are especially well suited to finance investments for growth and development in such settings—leveraging capital from their members and offering loans at better-than-commercial rates in capital markets, even if most of these loans are then not aid in the sense of official development assistance (ODA).[11]

Larger-scale ODA finance can be justified in certain situations, however. In the early days of a development bargain, such finance is a bet with a huge potential upside. A value investor in development should try to spot these opportunities, researching a country's political and economic deals and the seriousness of its commitment to growth and development. It appears, though, that the opportunities are quite often missed. Take Vietnam, which is clearly an important success story, in the use of aid as well.[12] By 2000, when it became obvious how well aid was used, Vietnam was receiving about $19 per person in ODA, or less than half of what Malawi, which was going nowhere, was enjoying.[13] Bangladesh, a messy state but one with the necessary structures in and outside government to spend well and to benefit from aid, received only about $10 per capita a year between 2000 and 2010. By 2010, Nigeria was receiving more, despite having a GDP per capita twice that of Bangladesh, despite being hardly better equipped to spend transparently or effectively, and despite increasingly going nowhere.

These figures reflect biases on the part of ODA donors, who ignore some development investment opportunities with substantial upsides, while continuing to spend extensively in countries with limited change. Contrast, for example, Kenya and Ethiopia in 2010, when it was becoming clear that Ethiopia's leading elite were trying to accelerate growth and development, unlike Kenya's, which were still looking for resolution after the electoral challenges in 2007–8. Then, Kenya had a GDP per capita three times that of Ethiopia, but aid levels were similar at around $40 per capita. Although Ethiopia set off on a course of faster growth, albeit in its own way, aid per capita did not increase over the next decade, whereas Kenya's reached more than $60 per capita by 2019. Unlike Ethiopia's, Rwanda's aid increased substantially when its commitment to development became clear in recent decades, reaching a peak of more than $100 per capita in 2010. Meanwhile, Malawi continued to receive high aid levels as well, peaking at $86 per capita, or still double Ethiopia's, despite few signs of emerging conditions for growth and development.

There is a case to boost finance for development, targeting countries with emerging development bargains. But as these examples suggest, such selectivity is not easy. It is about looking for potential winners and adopting a long investment horizon, while being willing to take early bets, at scale. Identifying countries with such a substantial upside is typically not straightforward when using existing aid models, such as the World Bank's development finance, as was discussed in the previous chapter. Better selectivity will involve making long-term bets on countries, based on a careful assessment using tools from political economy analysis, to understand the prevailing political and economic deals.[14]

The special case of climate finance

Another challenge in countries with an emerging or consolidated development bargain is that one can simply no longer take for granted that the conventional growth paths will work in the future because of their effects on global climate change. As discussed in chapter 3, the economic growth of richer economies has led to cumulative levels of CO_2 emissions. Thus the additional emissions produced by developing countries could further stress the planet. Fortunately it is increasingly possible to transition to cleaner energy and to build infrastructure in more sustainable ways. However, this switch to more sustainable growth will require more finance. Here the case is strong for richer economies to provide growing economies that have a development bargain with more development finance, thereby allowing them to adapt to this new reality and mitigate their impacts on the planet.

Given the scale of finance required, foreign aid as grants is unlikely to be sufficient. Although these growing economies have big needs, they should concentrate on self-financing their development. A better use of scarce foreign aid would be to boost substantially the capital base of multilateral development banks, so they can offer these countries much more climate finance. Even if loans are provided at non-concessional rates, they are attractive relative to those of commercial lenders. And when multilateral development banks work at their best, they tend to provide sensible advice as well, encouraging committed technocrats and politicians in receiving countries to move to greener growth paths.

The obvious part: International policy-making to support development bargains

Recognising development bargains when they are successful is straightforward: check the data. That's where the commitment to growth and development is bound to shine through.[15] Doing so when such elite bargains are nascent is harder, but this is just when such countries need encouragement. Although selecting countries for substantial finance and other support on this basis is a worthwhile approach on the part of donors, it is a gamble nevertheless. There are, however, other steps that rich nations could take to boost the chances of such countries and make the emergence and success of elite bargains in favour of growth and development more likely. In this section, I discuss some areas of international policy-making that, when done well, can present those countries committed to growth and development with opportunities, while upping the cost of political and economic deals aimed mainly at rent-seeking and profit-sharing among the elite. I consider three areas: trade policy, illicit finance flows, and the promotion of global public goods—that special type of goods often talked about but not always well understood.

Trade policy and development bargains

Anyone looking at the development indicators for Vietnam or Bangladesh would find it hard not to be impressed by the development turnarounds of these countries, both emerging from violent conflict in the 1970s. In Vietnam, it was the state that took a leading role in turning to exports, a path different from but still inspired by China's model. In Bangladesh, the state, as dysfunctional as it was, left space for other actors, such as businesses in their pursuit of global trade, and NGOs. Development agencies and their finance also played their role.[16] More was, however, essential for their success: they faced benign global trade conditions in pursuing economic growth through exports. It was not simply a matter of luck that these extremely poor countries faced these conditions when they emerged and started their take-off. Other countries faced them, too, but they did not take advantage of them.

For those looking on from the West, it's been easy to vilify globalisation. Asia's and especially China's rise as the workshops of the world in recent decades coincided with the slow and uneven recovery of Western economies from the 2007 financial crisis. Meanwhile, even before the pandemic a dark view of the globalisation of trade was on the increase in the West. Although the evidence was subtle, globalisation was increasingly cited as the cause of stagnation in job opportunities and in the standard of living for blue- and lower-end white-collar workers in Western economies.[17] During the pandemic, with its disruption of the complex global supply chains, globalisation became a symbol of the kind of vulnerability and interdependence to which no proud nation should succumb. Political anti-China sentiment fuelled this unhappiness with globalisation even further. Still, trade remains one of the key mechanisms for providing poor developing countries seeking economic development with higher returns. It was an essential part of the progress made in recent times in countries such as Indonesia, Vietnam, and Bangladesh, offering high returns for and lowering the risks of growth-oriented policies. As chapter 9 highlighted, the success of Bangladesh's export industries provided growth and rewards that helped support and sustain the elite bargain.

The logic is simple. Exporting raw materials, such as diamonds or offshore oil, isn't very hard, even in the most unstable or poorly run economies. Some local stability and some investment are required, but a deal with a foreign mining company and a local powerful elite player is all that's really needed.[18] Successfully growing flowers or vegetables for export, selling garments to the world, or returning a group of tourist resorts to profitability requires a bigger investment. Because such investments usually take several years to turn a profit, they need a stable, long-term investment horizon. Supply chains are more complicated, and they are highly time-sensitive. In fact, they can't afford much to go wrong. For example, shipping hubs have to function smoothly without delays or tax processing, and all costs have to be predictable. Such predictability will limit opportunities for rent-seeking and other ways of making quick profits for those controlling the state, unlike the shenanigans affecting natural resource exports.[19]

It is not surprising, then, that success at exporting goods and services beyond natural resources is strongly correlated with successful growth in the long term and is a sign of the presence and continuation of a reasonable elite bargain, even if imperfect. By encouraging and contributing to more profitable export trade, outsiders can help nudge elite bargains towards a development bargain. Providing preferential access to markets in particular is a powerful tool.

A quick look back at Asia's success in garment manufacturing is helpful. By design and by coincidence, a favourable trade environment had begun to emerge in the 1960s, and economies such as Taiwan and the Republic of Korea began to break into the garment sector, aided by dramatic declines in the global costs of trading, especially for shipping. Between 1930 and 1990, these costs fell by three-quarters.[20]

It helped tremendously that, at first, Western countries did not try to stop these garment imports through targeted protectionism. However, especially during the economic crisis of the 1970s, they pushed for more restrictions to protect their own garment industries. Among them, the Multifibre Agreement (MFA) placed quota restrictions on developing countries' exports, including garments. Interestingly, it gave a break to budding newcomers, and so manufacturers began to move to countries producing well beneath their quotas, such as Vietnam, and, as described in chapter 9, Bangladesh. Those countries' relative advantage gave them an extra impetus to attract investment.

Today, Asian and other garment manufacturers acknowledge that the expectation of stricter trade barriers on Asian goods is one reason there is renewed interest in countries such as Ethiopia, Kenya, and Tanzania, in the expectation that they will continue to benefit from targeted trade preferences by the US and EU. Various programmes governed by the World Trade Organization's Generalized System of Preferences rules are offering a large number of developing countries tariff reductions. Other programmes offering further tariff reductions are the EU's Everything But Arms (EBA) programme aimed at developing countries, and the US's African Growth and Opportunity Act (AGOA).

Existing agreements, including AGOA and EBA are good, but they could go much further. Anyone implying that the poorest developing countries have tariff-free access to rich economies' markets ignores the fine print in these agreements. There are always many exceptions—often with some restrictions on products that really matter, such as agricultural products or garments and textiles. There are also rules that could be made far more favourable to new exporting countries, such as more generous rules of origin that limit the shares of imported inputs that can be used, which are often well below what is now common in global value chains. In the end, then, products such as natural resources are more favourably treated than the kinds of goods and services that provide engines of growth and that require a real local commitment to attract investment.

Trade policy targeting the emergence or strengthening of development bargains has to be favourable to goods and services that require more complex supply chains and production processes, that require and are attractive for long-term investment, and whose more generous rules of origin are sensitive to the difficulty of adding value. In short, it would involve sharply upping the returns to engage in the kind of economic activity that needs a shared commitment to thrive.

Globalisation with integrity

The last half-century has seen the vast deregulation and internationalisation of financial markets, thereby giving rise to tax havens and other places to hide illicit money. Today, both companies and the wealthy can stash their money in secret 'offshore' accounts with ease. For example, recent estimates suggest that about 8 per cent of global financial wealth is hidden in such spots. This includes about 30 per cent of Africa's financial wealth (some $500 billion) sent abroad by corporations and wealthy individuals. Bermuda, the Cayman Islands, and Switzerland are well-known locations for such accounts, as well as, increasingly, Singapore, Hong Kong, and the United Arab Emirates. And then there are the perfectly legal 'onshore' centres in the US, UK, and Europe, using virtual 'offshore' constructs.

Some estimates suggest that about $89 billion in capital leaves Africa each year (or about 3.6 per cent of Africa's total GDP, but more than the total net foreign direct investment it receives).[21] To be clear, the fact that this wealth is stashed outside Africa is regrettable. The lost government resources from unpaid taxes are a missed opportunity as well.[22] But my main concern is where these funds come from and how they are kept from view—that is, the ease by which ill-gotten gains can be obtained, spirited away, or laundered to re-emerge as legitimate wealth. Such offshore centres add to the incentives for sustaining dodgy elite bargains, making the move to a development bargain so much harder.

The examples that see the light of day are outrageous. The Luanda Leaks exposed how much of the web of interests held by Isabel dos Santos, the daughter of Angola's former president, and her associates was illicit.[23] She allegedly used state funds to finance shell companies under her control, which, in turn, set up investment companies in the Netherlands, Portugal, and Angola to launder funds into a high-profile legal business empire that made her Africa's richest woman. The interests overseas of the family of President Teodoro Obiang, who has ruled oil-rich Equatorial Guinea for more than forty years, have long been on the radar of law enforcement agencies in the US, Switzerland, and France, with some limited effect. As much of the looted wealth is closely connected to the Obiang family, not only is Equatorial Guinea ranked the sixth most corrupt state in the world (close to South Sudan, Somalia, the DRC, and Afghanistan), but President Obiang is probably the most corrupt head of state in the world.[24] He likely wasn't always in that top position: General Abacha, Nigeria's leader from 1993 until his death in 1998, may have amassed illicitly and stashed offshore about $3–$5 billion.[25]

As noted, my main concern is not about the money per se, but about the impacts that offshore financial centres have on the incentives for elite bargains. The ability to engage in illicit financial dealings dramatically boosts the returns to elite bargains that are built around predatory behaviour, or that are built around clientelism and patronage. Such dealings provide the additional finance that allows the holders of the wealth to buy elections or to avoid having to hold them, and they are a means of easy finance to control the state and avoid changing the way it works, even if such misbehaviour puts a halt to growth and development.

What can be done? Three areas of international action could contribute here. In each area, some progress has been made, mainly on the back of cooperation through the Organisation for Economic Co-operation and Development (OECD) and work by the Financial Action Task Force (FAFT), but by no means is it going far or fast enough—a reflection of limited commitment in the end by rich countries.[26]

First, a further push to obtain global transparency about who owns and controls wealth is essential. Best known is the challenge of bank secrecy, whereby banks are allowed to agree with their clients to keep all dealings confidential, even excluding national authorities and not just other jurisdictions. This fundamental feature of offshore banking is still a factor in Switzerland, Luxembourg, Hong Kong,

Singapore, and many more offshore havens. Who controls assets, such as companies or real estate, is also shrouded in secrecy worldwide. This feature is usually referred to as beneficial ownership—that is, the identity of the individuals who in the end benefit from owning specific assets is hidden. The solution is in principle simple: make registers of assets of all kinds, and the owners who benefit from controlling them, accessible across borders. Among the twenty largest economies (the G20), half have made progress in tightening national beneficial ownership legislation, but by no means sufficiently. Not only China and other emerging economies lag behind, but Canada and the US as well.[27] If even the leading economies have not taken sufficient action, what hope is there of changing the behaviour of the authorities in the most important offshore financial centres themselves?

Second, what will help is internationally much stronger and broader rules and enforcement to counter the corrupt and illicit behaviour of international corporations active in developing countries. For politicians and public officials to fall prey to corruption, someone must be willing to pay them. Petty corruption never makes anyone filthy rich. It needs big players (businesses) that find it profitable to pay the serious bribes, or those that for a generous commission are able to fix the deals that are mutually profitable. Because limited private sector capabilities are available in many hippo or tigerfish economies, experienced foreign contractors have to bribe state workers so they can implement their lucrative contracts. These private sector companies and their beneficial owners are thus the facilitators of the elite bargains that halt growth and development.

One step towards hindering this type of corruption is the 1997 OECD Convention on Combating Bribery of Foreign Officials in International Business Transactions. Its current 44 signatories, including 7 non-OECD countries, together represent 65–70 per cent of both world exports and foreign direct investment.[28] When reflected in domestic law, the convention criminalises bribery in international business transactions. In those countries where it is enforced, such as the UK and the US, the convention definitely makes firms more cautious. But it has its weaknesses and limitations.

First, offshore financial centres and the use of shell companies limit detection. Second, about a third of global trade and FDI is not covered by these laws: this includes firms from China, Hong Kong, Singapore, India, and the United Arab Emirates. China has its own anti-bribery laws, but there is little evidence they are ever enforced. Third, even among signatories, including OECD members, enforcement is weak or lacking in countries representing more than a third of global trade, including France, Belgium, the Netherlands, Luxembourg, Canada, Japan, Korea, and Turkey, at least according to data from Transparency International.[29] Much more of an effort is needed to expand the number of countries introducing and enforcing such legislation.

A final area of action is to target those who serve the corrupt, even if what they do is currently entirely legal. None of these offshore financial centres could flourish in the ways they do, nor would many of the dodgy contracts in problematic countries emerge, if it were not for the financial, tax, and legal advice and facilitation that these corporations and the political elite receive from entities operating legally from London, New York, and Paris. Many of those advising corrupt politicians and others work for well-known established and respectable advisory, audit, and other professional services firms.[30] Furthermore, the banks and other entities operating in tax havens and the broader non-regulated financial markets are the same as those operating in the far more tightly regulated jurisdictions. Some are occasionally named and shamed, such as Bell Pottinger, the public relations company that fought the cause of the corrupt Gupta brothers in South Africa, or PwC, the audit firm with links to Isabel dos Santos in Angola and Dan Gertler in the DRC. But this gesture has a limited effect, and other audit firms were no doubt available to do the same job.[31] In fact, rarely are there consequences for the companies or individuals involved. Tighter regulation of these professional services firms could do a world of good.

Global public goods

Trade preferences are an example of how to boost growth and nudge elites towards embracing longer-term economic activity, whereas financial integrity policies reduce the returns and increase the risks of predatory elite bargains. Meanwhile, countries embarking on a development bargain may also find that certain global public goods are particularly beneficial. Public goods are free goods, and even if someone is using them, others can benefit from them as well.[32] These goods do not tend to be provided by the private sector because producing them is not cost-free and because users have no incentive to pay for them. So they invite free-riding. Adding the term 'global' to these goods suggests that their benefits can accrue to all countries and populations.

As for the term 'global public goods' itself, it can be misleading or confusing. Examples help. Success in limiting global warming to only 1.5 degrees by 2050 is a global public good: if it is achieved, no one can be stopped from benefiting from it. A vaccine is obviously something good, but it is not a global public good because it is easy to prevent access to it by not selling it to certain countries and restricting who can produce it by, for example, enforcing rules on international property rights. But a high global vaccination rate is a global public good because it will stop the spread of disease. Although the United Nations and the multilateral system are not global public goods, if the United Nations Security Council could guarantee world peace, then it would have produced an amazing global public good!

Some global public goods are particularly beneficial to developing country populations, and if rich countries contribute to their production, they help create conditions for development in ways other than through aid transfers to poorer countries. Producing these global public goods does not directly translate into better outcomes, but it gives elites incentives to focus more on growth and development. Three areas are of particular value: mitigating climate change, conflict resolution and security, and knowledge and research to solve specific problems faced by poorer countries.

Slowing or even reversing global warming is clearly important. But as befits a public good, it is quite hard to achieve because all countries want to limit how much they have to contribute to such an effort, and they want to free-ride as much possible on others' efforts. As highlighted in chapter 3, most of the arguments are between the high-income economies that contributed most to the stock of CO_2 emissions but are beginning to contain the flows, and the fast-growing middle-income countries, who contributed less to the global stock but whose yearly emissions are rising quickly. China and the US are at the centre of the need to come to an agreement; it is their behaviour that will be central to producing this public good.

The poorer countries discussed in this book—both those with an emerging development bargain and others stuck in elite bargains undermining development—will all gain from limiting global warming because their poverty means that their ability to cope with the increasingly destructive nature of extreme events and other climate impacts is constrained. It is too easy, though, to suggest that delivering progress on this global public good presents no challenges. In particular, there are risks that climate change agreements will make the move towards a development bargain harder by driving up the cost of the substantial economic growth needed by developing countries. Fortunately, it does not have to play out this way at all. For example, the cost of low-carbon energy has declined dramatically, and it is now far cheaper to build a plant running on photovoltaic solar or onshore wind than coal. Meanwhile, hydropower remains underexploited in many of the countries featured in this book.[33] Echoing the earlier discussion in this chapter, simply providing large-scale climate finance to all developing countries is by no means sufficient or without risk. Countries trying to move to more sustained growth and development will need additional support in selective ways, or else worse elite bargains risk becoming more attractive.

This dilemma is less of a factor in the next global public good, security. No country can gamble on development without security and stability. Anything that global actors can do to limit violent conflict is likely to help sustain a development bargain and increase its odds of success.[34] They can, among other things, try to reduce weapon imports or conflict finance and promote conflict mediation, regional cooperation, targeted sanctions, and more.[35] As chapter 8 highlighted, it is not easy for outsiders to foster peace, and unintended consequences are likely. In the end, peace has to be consistent with the local political and economic deals rather than simply imposed.

What to do and how to do it will depend on each conflict setting, but peace remains one of these essential public goods.

Knowledge, such as how to set up health systems, to boost agricultural yields, or to manage an economy better, can be provided as a global public good, passed to anyone keen to use it and with no limits. Research aimed at the issues of poor developing countries is underprovided by the private sector as well as rich countries' funding models of their own researchers and of those based in developing countries. For example, patents for treatments for diseases typically prevalent in poorer countries are less profitable there because neither governments nor patients can afford much. A careful, well-directed research effort by private and public research funders may thus be hugely beneficial for a country eager to embark on development and growth, providing ideas and solutions to development challenges.[36]

Even if research findings are later provided as a global public good, it is not necessarily an appropriate use of development finance. As I have argued throughout this book, many of the countries that stay behind are not desperately poor and badly run because of some general ignorance by their governments. Instead, their elite bargains simply don't give importance to growth and development. This helps explain why so many sensible health or education interventions, or improved seeds and agricultural practices, or other innovations are still not widely disseminated in some countries. The problem often is not linked to knowledge but to poorly functioning government systems or private markets captured by vested interests, which in turn are linked to the nature of the elite bargain, and the incentives for patronage or clientelism, rather than a deep commitment to deliver better.

Nevertheless, creating knowledge and innovations through research could be a sensible development investment, welcomed by countries with a development bargain, even if largely ignored by other elite bargains. Still, one should not assume that all research is worthwhile. Too often ideas and solutions to challenges are unlikely ever to be delivered at reasonable cost or scale, or they show poor understanding of the context of these countries. For example, a new crop variety that performs well on an experimental farm has limited value unless it could be adopted by local farmers at scale, or a new complicated treatment for a tropical disease may end up only serving the richest populations of developing countries unless designed to be delivered within health systems with limited funding.[37]

Research and innovations that can be brought to fruition at low cost and at scale result in the most valuable global public goods. They can then bring down the cost of development and improve the incentives to shift towards a development bargain. That said, they have to be adopted and used widely for them to make a real difference, and that is hard work. Countries with elite bargains that show no enthusiasm for such hard work are hardly going to put in the effort to make a difference. That is the subject of the next chapter: what to do in those countries that stay behind, and the challenges of using aid to try to move their elite bargains.

References

Africa Confidential. 2020. 'The Fight over Missing Millions Goes Global'. 61 (3): 8.

————. 2021. 'Bank Officials "Expose Money Laundering Network"'. 62 (5).

Ang, Y. Y. 2016. *How China Escaped the Poverty Trap.* Ithaca, NY: Cornell University Press.

Banerjee, A. V., and E. Duflo. 2011. *Poor Economics: A Radical Rethinking of the Way to Fight Global Poverty.* New York: PublicAffairs.

Besley, T., and T. Persson. 2009. 'The Origins of State Capacity: Property Rights, Taxation, and Politics'. *American Economic Review* 99 (4): 1218–44.

Jones, C., Y. Temouri, and A. Cobham. 2018. 'Tax Haven Networks and the Role of the Big 4 Accountancy Firms'. *Journal of World Business* 53 (2): 177–93.

Marquette, H., and C. Peiffer. 2015. 'Corruption and Collective Action'. DLP Research Paper 32, University of Birmingham, UK.

Milanovic, B. 2016. *Global Inequality: A New Approach for the Age of Globalization.* Cambridge, MA: Harvard University Press.

Persson, A., B. Rothstein, and B. Teorell. 2013. 'Why Anticorruption Reforms Fail: Systemic Corruption as a Collective Action Problem'. *Governance: An International Journal of Policy, Administration and Institutions* 26 (1): 449–71.

Prichard, W. 2015. *Taxation, Responsiveness and Accountability in Sub-*

Saharan Africa: The Dynamics of Tax Bargaining. Cambridge: Cambridge University Press.

Ravallion, M. 2018. 'Inequality and Globalization: A Review Essay'. *Journal of Economic Literature* 56 (2): 620–42.

Transparency International. 2018a. *Exporting Corruption—Progress Report 2018: Assessing Enforcement of the OECD Anti-bribery Convention.* Berlin.

———. 2018b. *G20 Leaders or Laggards? Reviewing G20 Promises on Ending Anonymous Companies.* Berlin.

UNCTAD (United Nations Conference on Trade and Development). 2020. *Tackling Illicit Financial Flows for Sustainable Development in Africa: Economic Development in Africa Report 2020*. Geneva: United Nations.

Zucman, G. 2015. *The Hidden Wealth of Nations: The Scourge of Tax Havens.* Chicago: University of Chicago Press.

13

AID IN MESSY PLACES

'We just make sure we hire all the best accountants and lawyers we can find in Mozambique,' said the director of the mobile phone operator, looking pleased with his answer. It was 2013, and I was in the capital, Maputo, convening a meeting with some of Mozambique's largest investors to discuss the troublesome investment climate. At the meeting, some of the usual complaints had emerged, such as bureaucratic intransigence and predatory tax officials. Stories similar to those recounted in chapter 7 about Nigeria and the Democratic Republic of Congo (DRC) were also heard here—mainly complaints about complex tax laws and faux tax demands, presumably as invitations to bribe the tax collectors or their bosses for demands to disappear.

At the Maputo meeting, the operator's boss explained further that his firm spends twice as much on accountancy and legal fees as it would in Europe. 'Our best way to avoid having to pay tax bribes is to never make an error in the books and to never settle a court case. In the end, those asking bribes give up.' It is expensive, but it works. This multinational avoids breaking international anti-bribery laws, while it finds a way to cope with predatory tax authorities in-country. He said his firm does the same in other countries, but it doesn't always work everywhere. 'In the DRC, we solved the problem by forming a joint venture.' Later, I learned that one local partner was President Joseph Kabila's twin sister, which seems quite an effective strategy to avoid predatory behaviour by tax officials.

Much can be learned about how firms manoeuvre in these messy places. They are opportunistic, looking for places and investments that can make them money. In the end, though, they know that all investments are risky, and they must weigh the risks and returns.

They also know that they can change the odds of success, such as by investing in the best lawyers in Mozambique or in Joseph Kabila's sister.

When giving aid, donors, unlike private investors, are not interested in making money. Instead, they seek returns in terms of development. However, like private investors, they find being opportunistic is worthwhile. Any spending is risky, and risks and returns have to be weighed. The most important consideration, though, is how to adapt investments to local circumstances and invest in ways that change the odds of success.

In this chapter, the value-investing approach to aid is extended to settings where the elite bargain is not aimed at development and growth. Although such lack of interest stymies the effectiveness of aid, donors will find it helpful to follow the value-investing principles: don't simply focus on need, but also on actual impact and outcomes; eye long-term change, including shifting the odds towards a better elite bargain; and, in doing so, pay attention to how and in whom one is investing. Still, at times the need is so great and urgent that the human instinct to help now may dominate. Nevertheless, even humanitarian aid is better offered with the long term in mind. How that is done is discussed at the end of this chapter.

The challenging part: Using aid to shift the politics and economics of the elite bargain

Although outsiders such as development agencies and local and international nongovernmental organisations (NGOs) committed to development may try to use aid to shift the odds of a development bargain, developmental change will never come simply from outside. With that in mind, I propose asking a simple question to assess aid spending in a country: beyond any development outcomes achieved directly, how much more likely will it be that a development bargain emerges or will be strengthened? Answering this question requires a thorough understanding of the nature of the elite bargain in place and the current political and economic deals.[1]

Some may argue that this strategy is not the purpose of aid—in fact, it turns aid into a political act. However, aid is always political. For example, when a multilateral development bank gives a government resources, that is a political act. It will strengthen the positions of those controlling the state at that moment. Changing aid modalities or imposing conditions, however technical they may seem, is a political act as well. It will influence the incentives and actions of those with power, either inducing them to change or helping them consolidate their power. It is a political act when a European donor makes aid decisions taking into account how elections have been run. It is also a political choice when a Chinese state-owned bank intentionally does not apply governance conditions to a large infrastructure project in keeping with official non-interference policies.

The aid challenge

Putting aside conditions or modalities, how does one design an aid programme explicitly with the underlying elite bargain in mind? What incentives follow from the way aid is offered for the existing elite bargain, and what incentives may even change it? Or will aid programmes, even though addressing need, risk further embedding an unhealthy status quo?

A closer look at health outcomes and aid in Nigeria will help explain the challenge faced. Nigeria has an elite bargain that is not aligned with development (see chapter 7). It is often compared with Ghana, where the elite bargain, even if not perfect, has moved in the last few decades towards a commitment to development and growth (as discussed in chapter 6). Both countries are roughly at the same level in terms of GDP per capita, which is also about the average across all low- and middle-income countries (LMICs).[2] The total health expenditure, adding up government, private, and foreign aid spending, is also similar in the two countries and is average for

LMICs, at about $80 per person. Foreign aid directed at health care is similar as well—about $7–$9 per capita for each country. Despite similar total spending and aid received for health, there is, however, a clear difference in health outcomes. For example, in Ghana the under-five mortality rate is below 50 deaths per 1,000 live births, which is about the average for all LMICs, whereas in Nigeria it is far worse at 120 deaths per 1,000 live births. Other health outcomes show similar patterns.[3] Another indicator is staff inputs: in Ghana, twice the share of births is attended by skilled staff as in Nigeria.[4] Such massive difference in outcomes for comparable health spending must mean health systems are inequitable and ineffective in Nigeria, which in this and other respects lags behind most other middle-income countries.

One likely explanation is a clear failure of the Nigerian state's commitment to health care, unlike in Ghana. In Ghana and on average across the LMICs, governments spend $28 per person a year on health care. In Nigeria, nearly three-quarters of spending on health care is out-of-pocket spending by patients because the government expenditure on health care is only $12 per person a year. The Nigerian state, as discussed in chapter 7, despite the fact that its oil revenue generates about $240 per capita a year for the government, barely spends on health.

In view of Nigeria's weak indicators and high needs, and the government's low commitment to spending more and better on health care, the temptation to step in and provide more aid to boost health care in Nigeria is strong. In fact, there are ways to spend aid that would lead to some improvement in health outcomes, although likely with lower cost effectiveness than in Ghana and many other lower- and middle-income countries.[5]

My concern is that in Nigeria, because of the nature of the elite bargain and the limited commitment to development that permeates politics and the functioning of the state, aid may alleviate some suffering today, but it will hardly transform the country's health care or have persistent impacts in the future. In fact, just as oil creates few incentives to make the economy more productive (rents are still too easily generated, at least for the few), foreign aid offers few incentives—or just excuses—to build up better-functioning health care services.[6]

That said, simply disengaging and withdrawing aid will not do much to shift the elite bargain in Nigeria or similar countries. And the needs are high. So how can aid deliver better outcomes, be an agent of change for the long term, and avoid locking in the status quo? At a minimum, this requires understanding the nature of the elite bargain and consciously looking for ways to encourage change.

The remainder of this section describes three ways in which to use aid with this in mind: (1) shift incentives in the economy to serve as the foundation of the political and economic deals underlying the elite bargain; (2) improve the accountability and functioning of the state; and (3) on a more practical, daily level, enhance the delivery of programmes targeting people, such as those aimed at improving health care, but bearing in mind the economic and political incentives of the existing elite bargain and the way the state functions.[7]

Aid and the political and economic deals

It is not too hard to describe what better political and economic deals would look like in Nigeria or elsewhere: more accountability, better economic policy-making, and less destructive forms of clientelism, patronage, and corruption. It may then be tempting to conclude that outsiders should use aid to build the state, and to set up and support the kinds of organisations that in successful countries ensure accountability, such as independent election or anti-corruption commissions, or to build the capacity of tax authorities, government audit offices, or independent central banks. But here is the problem. These organisations are already in place everywhere, with extensive legal frameworks approved by legislative bodies and upheld through due process and, if required, the courts. All of these are therefore largely controlled by those in power and so serve the elite bargain, ensuring there is little incentive to make these bodies function better. Just spending resources to set up organisations or legal frameworks in low-income countries that mimic those in successful countries will hardly be productive unless elites are clearly committed to their success.[8]

311

So what could be done to nudge these state institutions, and the underlying political and economic deals, down the path to growth and development? The key is in the economy. Although deal-making is all about politics, the underlying elite bargain requires an economic deal that serves those in the elite with power. The ingredients of a growing, vibrant economy were described in chapter 2: sensible macroeconomic policies, investment in infrastructure, a market orientation preferably towards the export sector, and an investment climate that will attract private sector investors, thereby making growth self-sustaining. Reforms to make economies look more like this are not a simple technical matter. Their success will depend on whether they fit with the elite bargain present.

Take, for example, this oft-heard advice long at the heart of many International Monetary Fund (IMF) programmes: push for privatisation and liberalisation of the economy. The underlying rationale is strong. After all, basing economies on 'capitalism', whereby 'industry and trade are controlled by private owners for profit and not by the state',[9] has led to considerable long-term growth in Western economies and, in recent decades, well beyond them. Privatisation and liberalisation, the reasoning goes, will bring a country closer to these capitalist principles. This definition of capitalism has one key implicit assumption: there is a clear separation between the private sector, on the one hand, and the state, on the other.

By contrast, in the kinds of economies of interest here, not just industry or trade, but also the state, is controlled by private owners for profit and without the boundaries just described. This is a feature of the hippo and tigerfish states described in part II. The result is a cosy, connected business sector, hardly private and separate from the state and the public sector. Actions taken by the state thus typically profit the same connected people who are using the state as an instrument for capturing wealth. Therefore, privatisation often just rearranges the way power is held, with the result that firms and individuals connected to the incumbent elite acquire public assets and liberalisation often does not materialise. Perhaps it isn't surprising that Nigeria offers some of the best stories, such as in 2012 when the minister in charge of privatisation of electricity distribution was himself involved in several of the bids.[10]

So what specific steps should development agencies take to use aid to move the economic deal more towards growth and development?

First, identify and invest in respected, influential government advisors who can help shape the economic deal. Many will be technocrats—but they have to be imbued with a deep understanding of the politics of their own country and fundamentally committed to better economic outcomes, even if politics hold them back.[11] As described in part II, in China, Indonesia, and India such advisors played important roles in finding ways to shift their countries towards a development bargain, and in Ghana, Uganda, Bangladesh, and Ethiopia they were the drivers and implementers of change. Such advisors often work in the president's office or run the ministry of finance or the central bank. Empowering them within their own state system rather than simply, as often is the case, poaching them to work for international and other development agencies is the right approach. Then, they often end up being the skilful negotiators with these outside agencies, while providing a bridge to their own country's leadership and nudging it along to more growth and development-oriented policies.

Second, strengthening the capabilities of specific units within ministries performing the tasks could lay the foundation for a better economic deal within the elite. A competent central bank, a better-functioning agency managing natural resource contracts, a regulatory authority that follows the letter of the law, and a tax authority that sets higher standards for its staff can respond more appropriately when political leaders and their key advisors are able to move the elite bargain along, bit by bit. Such progress often requires working along the grain, making gradual progress in a targeted way.[12] Problems may arise if progress is stifled by political interests or captured by patronage and corruption, but, when executed well, such an approach can help change the returns to existing and alternative elite bargains and reduce the risks of moving to a more ambitious development bargain. Aid has no doubt contributed to building state organisations supporting macroeconomic stability through capable central banks such as in East Africa and Bangladesh.

Third, rather than focusing on how the economy is governed, development funders could shift the risks and returns in the economy by working directly

313

with firms. This is not a question of just working with the private sector. Many of the crucial incumbent firms in these settings are too closely connected to the patronage system to be helpful. Alternatively, just focusing on very small firms is no doubt good for the people involved, but it is hardly going to change the elite bargain. A better approach would be to find ways of working with the kinds of domestic private sector firms that could be influential and would flourish if the economy were to shift towards self-sustaining growth. The garment industry in Bangladesh and light manufacturing in Indonesia and Vietnam have thrived on connections with government since the beginning. However, they took up the challenge to compete globally rather than persistently live off protectionism and procurement in return for clientelist payments.

So what could be done to boost these domestic private sector firms? Beyond targeted trade preferences or genuinely strengthening those inside government, who can improve the business climate for such firms? Should firms in this sector be supported directly? Perhaps, but support should not shift incentives and so give rise to complacency within these firms themselves. There may be room for some technical assistance or information on market opportunities, but generous aid may also weaken their drive to be competitive.

One mechanism suitable for support by aid agencies is worth dwelling on. Outside agencies could encourage investors to bring international capital into domestic firms because foreign direct investment often goes hand in hand with expertise and access to markets with economy-wide benefits. [13] Such efforts tend to build up domestic capabilities, thereby increasing returns and reducing risks for future investment—which is exactly what is needed to create incentives to shift the elite bargain towards promoting such sectors. [14] International anti-bribery laws can help ensure that domestic firms conduct business with integrity as well.

For any investor, this is a highly risky proposition to start with, and so it is hard to persuade foreign direct investors to gamble on the domestic private sector in these more difficult countries. Development finance institutions (DFIs)—the private sector investment vehicles such the International Finance Corporation (IFC) of the World Bank Group and the CDC Group in the UK—

perform such a role. They invest in private sector opportunities across the developing world, including the kinds of countries featured here. No doubt these institutions could do much better by further increasing their expertise and investments in these more difficult settings.[15] A deeper understanding of how politics and the economy interact locally should help them as well as they target investments, not just for due diligence but as part of pushing for change. For example, although an investment in a bank, commercial real estate, or a shopping centre for the elite may offer good returns to such a DFI, even if it is located in Abuja, Kinshasa, or Lilongwe, it is not clear that such an investment will shift any of the incentives for risky investments in non-connected businesses. Ensuring that investors focus more on firms and investments that might genuinely change the incentives within the elite and their connected businesses could step up the role of these institutions in developmental change.

Aid, accountability, and the state

Helping to steer the risks and returns in an economy towards growth instead of the profits of the political class that controls it is one step for a value investor in development. How can aid be used to encourage states engaging in patronage and clientelism—even large-scale theft and corruption—to pursue a credible commitment to collecting tax revenues fairly and spending resources more productively on growth and development?

Chapter 12 noted the importance of a fair tax system for the emergence of a stronger, healthier state. A core argument in favour of taxes is that if citizens and firms have to pay taxes, they are more likely to force the state to be accountable for how those resources are used.[16] Many aid programmes therefore seek to increase tax collection. Although there are good reasons that increasing tax will contribute to building an accountable, trustworthy state in countries with a development bargain, with the kind of elite bargains considered in this chapter it is not self-evident. Research projects have been able to identify specific ways in which revenue collection could be increased, in unstable countries such as Pakistan and the DRC as well, but a World Bank review of its own large-scale programmes concluded that benefits require serious political commitments in order to target connected firms, high net worth individuals, or the state's patron–client networks.[17] As a result, it found that many of the Bank's and other tax programmes have had a limited impact. Moreover, the evidence is not at all clear that citizens would achieve much accountability in respect of how the state uses resources, or expect it to start doing so, without further change.[18] In short, the idea that expanding taxation would lead to more accountability cannot be taken for granted in these kinds of elite bargains—a 'fiscal social contract' will not simply emerge.

How can aid then be used to encourage a fiscal social contract, whereby the state taxes and provides services and public goods in an accountable, efficacious way? When it comes to interventions at scale, not least when they involve aid provided by outsiders, there are no silver bullets such as 'decentralisation is the answer' or 'make all development community-led'.[19] So much, then, for the silver bullet approach, but there are three ways of using aid that may be productive.

First, identify, target, and support those individuals and units or organisations within the state that are both influential and committed to change. They may be leading tax authorities, or they may be in charge of aspects of service delivery. Or they may undertake the state's audit functions, such as auditor generals, or have a role in budget management, such as ministers of finance. They may even lead anti-corruption efforts. But this is very different from agreeing with a president to set up an anti-corruption commission or reform a tax authority, unless there is a real commitment to change. Even so, those at the right levels must be willing to act. Helping develop small pockets of excellence within the state can provide examples of what is feasible and an inspiration for those within the state committed to change.[20]

Second, improve the quality of elections. Elections are an obvious path to accountability, allowing those in power to be challenged. Often those with extensive economic power use elections as a means of offering patronage or reaffirming the clientelist affiliations of ethnicity, religion, or region, as highlighted in part II for Nigeria, South Sudan, and Kenya. Yet they are an important route to more accountability and results-based politics; this seems to be true in Ghana and may be emerging in Kenya. For outsiders, using aid in this way will always be something that needs the permission of those in power, but, if allowed, contributing to making elections free and fair, for instance by providing monitors, generally seems sensible.[21]

Access to fair but better-quality information could help make voters more responsive to the issues affecting their well-being. For example, town hall debates in Benin on the issues of concern to voters reduced clientelist behaviours such as promises of jobs and offers of gifts by candidates, and they changed voting behaviour, diminishing support for candidates exercising political control over communities. In São Tomé and Príncipe, voter education reduced the impact of candidates offering cash during the election.[22] These findings suggest that there may be scope for willing politicians, keen on a different way of doing politics, to be rewarded at the ballot box.

Third, strengthen civil society to hold governments to account and to focus more on outcomes than just maintaining power through patronage, clientelism, and corrupt behaviour. Examples would be supporting activism to change laws or policy; detailed public scrutiny of policies or impacts; and enforcing the transparency of budgets, their allocation, and the outcomes. A rich evidence base is emerging on activism, but it points to mixed success. However, one finding stands out: if there is no political will among any of those in power to respond to activists, their interventions don't have much impact.[23]

Spending aid in difficult places

Trying to affect the incentives in the economic and political deals underlying the elite bargain or the accountability of the state does not directly address the huge needs in countries that lag behind. It is hard to ignore these needs, but addressing them in countries where elite bargains are not aligned with development can be difficult The good news is that there are lots of ways of using aid that are not wasteful and that improve people's lives, whether in health, education, sanitation, skills, or safety nets—the menu of options for many development programmes.

One example is cash transfer programmes. High-quality research indicates that such transfers improve well-being. Some beneficiaries will invest the funds in a business, and many spend it on the kind of things they have dreamt of: more and better food, a tin roof to prevent leaks in the rainy season, or schooling for their children. And it works: according to the evidence, recipients are better off and happier with their lives.[24] Other examples are vaccinating children against preventable diseases; implementing an appropriately structured pedagogy to ensure that children learn at the right level; or launching programmes that provide packages of assets such as livestock and other support.[25] Indeed, NGOs and local charities have known for a long time that they can spend money frugally to good effect.

Although there is no doubt that such service delivery programmes perform good deeds, they are not enough, not least for an aid agency that is keen to take a value investor approach. Because aid is a scarce resource, it ought to be spent striving for a high return, impact at scale, and long-term benefits. To spend aid well in difficult places, those doing the spending may wish to keep three principles in mind.

Any aid-funded programme should focus in the first instance on improving people's lives, such as children learning or being vaccinated or families having access to water or new job opportunities. However, too often these programmes are designed in ways that they can never be delivered or sustained at scale; they are too costly, they require far more capability than the country can offer, or they are totally dependent on outside support for their sustainability. So the first principle is to emphasise scale—that is, designs and funding models that are locally feasible and capable of being scaled up.

However, just as in any large-scale organisation or in any public sector, delivery at scale requires systems: a functioning health or education system and accountability structures to ensure delivery. Without them and without understanding how they function, programmes cannot be effectively delivered, let alone at scale. Early work is essential within government channels or at least within locally embedded structures in ways that they can scale and sustain. If not, the opportunity to make a difference is wasted.[26] The challenge in these difficult places is substantial: the state is often more engaged in clientelism and patronage than in delivering better lives for its citizens. A hard-nosed approach to implementation and improving the underlying systems is therefore an important second principle to keep in mind.[27]

Finally, never forget what kind of state one is dealing with, and especially don't give a government an excuse not to take development seriously. This is the hardest part, and most aid programmes appear to give up and just focus on spending their resources as best they can. For every state failing to invest in development in recent decades, there are others where those in charge chose not to go that route. The poor performance of governments and their service delivery structures is not simply based on ignorance that requires a solution dreamt up by a smart McKinsey management consultant or an MIT (or Oxford) researcher. Aid programmes should not simply apply band-aids. They must, as described earlier, be willing to think about how to deliver change as well, working closely with those within and outside the state committed to driving this, thereby helping to shift the incentives in the economic and political deals towards development.

* * *

However straightforward it may seem, it is extremely hard to be as successful as Warren Buffett, as any equity investor in the world knows. The upside one is chasing has to be more than just specific development outcomes: it has to be also about consciously strengthening the systems and structures that can deliver change.

There will be failures. But failures should not be an excuse for a gambler's fallacy: keep on betting in the hope that the odds will change. This leads to more uncomfortable conclusions, such as difficult choices not to spend even if short-term improvements to people may be possible. Even Warren Buffett will regularly withdraw his funds and sell stock when the upside is too low, even in the long term. Over the many years I have followed development spending in many countries, I have asked myself whether the UK or others should not simply close shop in some countries when the upside of spending feels so low. The thought often crossed my mind when dealing at various times with Malawi, South Sudan, Sierra

Leone, Nigeria or the DRC—countries discussed in part II. It's not because of a corruption scandal or a single questionable action by a prime minister or president. Withdrawing aid for such things would be a knee-jerk reaction, more useful for newspaper copy or parliamentary statements in donor countries. Instead, I thought that aid had become counterproductive and was entrenching further the lack of movement towards a long-term agenda of development—even if there was still a lot of need and suffering and a lot of good that probably could be done. It is a question that must be asked regularly, even if for now I consider spending aid in these places still worth the gamble.

The unavoidable part: Aid for humanitarian crises

One never gets used to seeing suffering. I recall the woman I met in 2015 in southern Ethiopia. She had a baby on her back and was exhausted from worrying about whether the drought would kill all her animals in the coming months. The same year, I met a young Syrian farmer, who told me he had to leave everything behind to cross into Jordan to protect his family, but he was now sitting bored and desolate in front of one of the thousands of white tents pitched in straight lines at the Zaatari refugee camp near Mafraq in Jordan. And then there was the frail elderly woman in Ganyiel in South Sudan telling me in 2016 how her family had to walk miles across the front line a few weeks previously, and they were now internally displaced, having just queued patiently, unprotected from the burning sun, to have their identity checked by some aid workers so they could get some cash to buy food.

Helping such people in dire need with aid is a no-brainer. These humanitarian crises usually happen in situations of disarray: conflict, displacement, and where state authorities are unable or unwilling to cope. Outside organisations, often linked to the United Nations, have to step in, not least to protect the most vulnerable. Nevertheless, the structures and systems providing this support at present are far from perfect. Not unlike what I expect from a value investor in development, humanitarian aid providers ought to work towards a greater impact, adopting a long-term perspective and striving for a deeper understanding of the local economic and political context. Meanwhile, the overriding goal is to persuade the local elites to embrace development.

Advocating a long-term perspective for dealing with humanitarian crises may seem illogical. Indeed, these are emergencies: people need help, quickly. Nevertheless, whether the crisis involves a natural disaster such as a flood or an earthquake or displacement after a conflict, what is done with aid well beforehand in preparation for such a disaster is what determines the quality of the crisis response. Later in this section, this approach is applied to natural disasters such as drought or floods, which are intensifying due to climate change. First, however, I look at the crises linked to conflict and displacement.

Long-term responses for long-term crises

A humanitarian crisis typically lasts 9.3 years.[28] The vast majority of people receiving assistance from humanitarian organisations are in protracted crises linked to conflict. And virtually every conflict ends up leading to a long humanitarian crisis. For example, in the last five years Syria and Yemen have been the top two in the statistics of humanitarian funding requirements, accounting in 2020 for about half of the entire needs.[29] The top ten countries barely change from year to year: the DRC, Sudan, South Sudan, Afghanistan, and Somalia are always high on the list, all with conflict at the root of their crises. Long-term crises need longer-term solutions: supporting vulnerable populations and helping them take back control of their lives.

Nevertheless, in practice every crisis seems to be handled as a short-term problem. Responses are often financed and implemented in these protracted settings for at most a year. The goal is usually to provide immediate relief (a band-aid), funded by appeals to donor countries—typically the largest ones such as the US, EU, UK, and Germany. Relief takes the form of transfers of cash or food, or offers of shelter and health care, though little is done to let people take charge of their future.

Finance no doubt accounts for the short-term responses, as it's insufficient for longer-term plans. The United Nations estimated that in 2021 only about half the money needed for humanitarian responses was available. Meanwhile, carrying out relief efforts in these settings is extremely difficult. The states themselves are usually unable or unwilling to support those in need. Warring parties are hostile to outsiders seen as meddling in conflicts, while displaced populations face the hostility of the local communities among whom they end up living. Nevertheless, even in long-lasting crises little effort is expended on building up local structures to handle these crises in more sustainable ways. Instead, large costly parallel structures are constructed, often struggling to function well within the local political and economic context. The result is that these responses are not only less effective, but also expensive in ways that more strategic, long-term approaches from the start could avoid.

How to do this better? Just the nature of these crises calls for the large United Nations organisations, such as the UN Refugee Agency (UNHCR) and UN Office for the Coordination of Humanitarian Affairs (OCHA), as well as outside humanitarian organisations to continue to play their roles as the preservers of humanitarian principles, but they need to keep in mind the following.[30] First, because of the high costs of support and funding gaps, they should not hide behind these principles but pay more attention to how well they are supporting the most vulnerable, even with tight resources.[31] Second, from day one of a crisis they should consider how it might evolve in the long term. There is no point in thinking that these kinds of crises will disappear overnight, and the only role of aid organisations is to protect people in the short term so they can return to their normal lives afterwards. Third, also from the start they should recognise that solutions must work within the local political and economic context. That will require identifying capable pockets of national or local government to work with, even in some of the worst-run places, as well as local organisations connected to those in need. Such groups may not meet the standards of the cavalry-like global response machinery, but at least the result will be a more sustainable and affordable long-term approach to a crisis and, frankly, a help when the UN machinery largely lumbers on to the next crisis.

It is that step of linking to local and national systems that opens the door to the financial sustainability of these systems, such as through funding from development banks. When it works well, collaborating with local and national systems is what more standard development organisations, like the World Bank, are equipped to do, whereas building up local organisations is a most useful role for international humanitarian or development NGOs.

Meanwhile, some governments have found ways to sustainably accommodate large numbers of refugees within the local political and economic reality, working with local organisations. In Uganda, the host of the largest number in Africa, refugees have long been allowed to be more self-reliant, being given rights to work and access to land in ways that fit in with the imperfect local patronage politics, but with broadly beneficial outcomes for those involved.[32] In Jordan, as part of a deal supporting its economy, Syrian refugees were given access to work permits in the context of the Jordan Compact.[33] In Lebanon, when coping with the Syrian refugees,[34] much work went into maintaining municipal services, such as waste collection, thereby benefiting refugees as well as local communities under pressure from the large numbers.

Aid as the scaffolding for responses to natural disasters

The problems with the humanitarian operating model in responses to natural disasters such as drought or floods are even more striking. The room for outsiders to manoeuvre in conflict settings is, of course, limited, and building longer-term solutions may just not be possible. But this defence is hardly possible when it comes to dealing with drought in Ethiopia, Malawi, or southern Africa, or floods in Mozambique.

In this digital age of instant data transmission, satellites, climate modelling, and sophisticated financial instruments, it is surprising that the underlying model for dealing with natural disasters is so old-fashioned. It goes like this: a disaster occurs, the media cover it intensely, support is requested, humanitarian action is mobilised, and an appeal is put out to pay for it. What happens is not fundamentally different from what happens in richer economies, and the explanation for this is largely political. Evidence from India, Mexico, and the US indicates that investing in prevention and preparedness has little electoral gain compared with politicians declaring a disaster and then marching to the microphone to tout their leadership in the response. Aid in response to developing countries during such crises plays a similar role, and it is widely supported by voters.[35] The way this response model is financed is rather medieval, as if begging bowls are the best way to finance public responses. The result is that such aid tends to come late, is less effective, is likely more expensive, and has a limited longer-term positive impact.

In 2015, I saw this in action in Ethiopia during the extensive drought (chapter 10). This Ethiopia, however, was very different from the Ethiopia that dealt with earlier crises. It had the largest safety programme in Africa, covering up to 8 million of the poorest and most vulnerable people, and it had been applauded for its effectiveness. The organisation and structure of the programme were by no means perfect, but they had come a long way. Still, the humanitarian system did what it usually does: it conducted an assessment, made an appeal for funding, and plotted to move in with its vast logistics. It showed little interest at first in the existing safety net, instead setting up parallel systems often targeting the same communities.[36] Valuable time was lost, although in the end the outside agencies and the government worked well together.

It is right to use aid to support people in developing countries during calamities, whether it is in the DRC, Malawi, or Ethiopia. Moreover, because of climate change, largely caused by the richer economies, the number and intensity of extreme events such as storms, floods, and drought will increase in the near future. Meanwhile, as Covid-19 has revealed, with globalisation localised epidemics can become global pandemics. Progress in the quality of the response, however, can be measured by the extent to which the world does not have to depend on the international humanitarian system to respond, relying instead on local and national responses to do the job.

In countries with a shared commitment to development, such as Ethiopia during its drought, the obvious answer to more effective disaster responses is a joint effort by the humanitarian system and government, working together as much as possible. Such collaboration may also be a good way to work in more difficult places, even if the elite bargain is not quite aligned with development. Elites otherwise occupied only with protecting their own interests tend to be moved when natural disasters occur, and they want to be seen responding well in a crisis.

At the moment, these disasters don't tend to be handled well enough by many governments. So what should be done to avoid the pitfalls of the current model? It is all about making the right investments beforehand, and again a value investor approach is helpful. A government needs a system that will work well and is resilient in a crisis—that is, the primary health care system and social protection system can be expanded when needed. Critically, the system must not absolve those with the power to act. If anything, such a system should lock them into action consistent with development progress. And finally, as ever, one needs to pick carefully who will need to act and how.[37]

The value of such systems was rediscovered across the world during the Covid-19 pandemic. For example, in terms of cash transfers it appears that 215 countries had schemes in place, including large numbers of low- and middle-income countries, although their coverage remained limited to those enrolled in these systems, and most people were excluded from the support. Low-income countries disbursed only $6 per capita.[38] In short, these systems were valuable, but they were not set up to be expanded during a crisis. It is nevertheless the kind of investment needed to build a vehicle for reaching people in search of support during crises. In a crisis or, more generally, to alleviate some of the worst suffering, it is simple systems like this that would lead to much more effective responses, thereby limiting the need to bring in outsiders.

Aid can do better

As pointed out often in this book, many countries don't develop because the elite controlling the state are not sufficiently committed to making progress. Instead, they use the state to pursue their own and their supporters' interests or profits. The three final chapters have explored the role of aid in such situations. If no partner is committed to succeeding—'to dance the tango with'—all simple narratives on how to spend aid break down. Indeed, today those extending foreign aid are finding it difficult to have an impact on growth and development. At times, it has become almost impossible to spend well in many places, and this has been the subject of the debates I've had over the years in the corridors of DFID, in the bars at night in Lilongwe or Freetown with colleagues from the World Bank, or, indeed, as recounted in chapter 7, with the Chinese economic counsellor despairing about spending in Kinshasa.

My conclusion: foreign aid can best be spent on countries with a genuine development bargain, or where an elite bargain is emerging. There, without claiming perfection, aid really can then make a difference. This is the easy part. It should also be spent on global endeavours and public goods such as trade access, the transparency of financial markets, or research intended to generate knowledge relevant to developing countries. This is the obvious part. Clearly, these are good investments for aid funders behaving like value investors. Success is not guaranteed, but there are clear upsides, mainly in the long term, and, helpfully, funders don't have to worry too much about a downside because they don't need to invest directly in dodgy or messy countries.

Nevertheless, I don't think one should stop there. Many countries' taxpayers, some philanthropists, and those who give to charities want to help people facing hardship and to protect those suffering. But they also want those entrusted with this money to use it well, which is possible.

As for those who may overstate the case that large volumes of aid are sufficient to lead to real change, humility is essential. I don't think that foreign aid is best used to overcome the failures of the elites, just providing relief, health or other services for the lucky few given the scale of deprivation. Wherever genuine progress has been made in growth and development, aid has always been only a small part of the story. Change will have to come from inside these countries lagging behind, from within the elites who have the power and influence to change the direction of their countries. At best, and when used deliberately, as this chapter has argued, aid can play a supporting role in this.

In the end, more countries, and those with power therein, will have to be willing to gamble on development. Finding ways to improve the odds of such bets is the real prize of aid well spent. In any case, the last thing that ought to happen is that aid, because of the way in which it is used, makes these odds worse, embedding elite bargains not likely favourable to progress. Some will say that using aid in this way is a gamble, but that is precisely the point: without gambling on it, countries may not enjoy the development many so urgently need.

References

Acemoglu, D., and J. A. Robinson. 2013. 'Economics versus Politics: Pitfalls of Policy Advice'. *Journal of Economic Perspectives* 27 (2): 173–92.

Andrews, M., L. Pritchett, and M. Woolcock. 2017. *Building State Capability: Evidence, Analysis, Action*. Oxford: Oxford University Press.

Bandiera, O., R. Burgess, N. Das, S. Gulesci, I. Rasul, and M. Sulaiman. 2017. 'Labor Markets and Poverty in Village Economies'. *Quarterly Journal of Economics* 132 (2): 811–70.

Banerjee, A., R. Banerji, J. Berry, E. Duflo, H. Kannan, S. Mukerji, M. Shotland, and M. Walton. 2017. 'From Proof of Concept to Scalable Policies: Challenges and Solutions, with an Application'. *Journal of Economic Perspectives* 31 (4): 73–102.

Banerjee, A., E. Duflo, N. Goldberg, D. Karlan, R. Osei, W. Parienté, J. Shapiro, B. Thuysbaert, and C. Udry. 2015. 'A Multifaceted Program Causes Lasting Progress for the Very Poor: Evidence from Six Countries'. *Science* 348 (6236).

Banerjee, A., E. Duflo, C. Imbert, S. Mathew, and R. Pande. 2020. 'E-governance, Accountability, and Leakage in Public Programs: Experimental Evidence from a Financial Management Reform in India'. *American Economic Journal: Applied Economics* 12 (4): 39–72.

Bastagli, F., J. Hagen-Zanker, L. Harman, V. Barca, G. Sturge, and T. Schmidt. 2019. 'The Impact of Cash Transfers: A Review of the Evidence from Low- and Middle-Income Countries'. *Journal of Social Policy* 48 (3): 569–94.

Bergeron, A., G. Tourek, and J. Weigel. 2021. 'The State Capacity Ceiling on Tax Rates: Evidence from Randomized Tax Abatements in the DRC'. Harvard University, Cambridge, MA.

Besley, T., and T. Persson. 2009. 'The Origins of State Capacity: Property Rights, Taxation, and Politics'. *American Economic Review* 99 (4): 1218–44.

Betts, A. 2021. 'Refugees and Patronage: A Political History of Uganda's "Progressive" Refugee Policies'. *African Affairs* 120 (479): 243–76.

———, I. Chaara, N. Omata, and O. Sterck. 2019. 'Uganda's Self-reliance Model: Does It Work?' Refugee Studies Centre, University of Oxford.

Clarke, D. J., and S. Dercon. 2016. *Dull Disasters? How Planning Ahead Will Make a Difference*. Oxford: Oxford University Press.

Collier, P., S. Kriticos, S. Logan, and C. Sacchetto, 2021. *Strengthening Development Finance in Fragile Contexts.* London: International Growth Centre.

Deaton, A. 2013. *The Great Escape: Health, Wealth, and the Origins of Inequality*. Princeton, NJ: Princeton University Press.

De Ree, J., K. Muralidharan, M. Pradhan, and H. Rogers. 2018. 'Double for Nothing? Experimental Evidence on an Unconditional Teacher Salary Increase in Indonesia'. *Quarterly Journal of Economics* 133 (2): 993–1039.

Estrin, S., and A. Pelletier. 2018. 'Privatization in Developing Countries: What Are the Lessons of Recent Experience?' *World Bank Research Observer* 33 (1): 65–102.

Evans, W. W., P. J. Evans, A. Grant, A. Pujari, G. Maschhaupt, B., McGillen, C. Mtegha-Gelders, A. Rudge, and S. Roy. 2020. *Best Buys: Governance.* London: UK Department for International Development.

Gentilini, U., M. Almenfi, I. Orton, and P. Dale. 2020. *Social Protection and Jobs Responses to Covid-19.* Washington, DC: World Bank.

Greenwood, B. 2014. 'The Contribution of Vaccination to Global Health: Past, Present and Future'. *Philosophical Transactions of the Royal Society B: Biological Sciences* 369 (1645): 20130433.

Haushofer, J., and J. Shapiro. 2016. 'The Short-Term Impact of Unconditional Cash Transfers to the Poor: Experimental Evidence from Kenya'. *Quarterly Journal of Economics* 131 (4): 1973–2042.

Javorcik, B. S. 2004. 'Does Foreign Direct Investment Increase the Productivity of Domestic Firms? In Search of Spillovers through Backward Linkages'. *American Economic Review* 94 (3): 605–27.

———, A. Lo Turco, and D. Maggioni. 2018. 'New and Improved: Does FDI Boost Production Complexity in Host Countries?' *Economic Journal* 128 (614): 2507–37.

Khan, A. Q., A. I. Khwaja, and B. A. Olken. 2016. 'Tax Farming Redux: Experimental Evidence on Performance Pay for Tax Collectors'. *Quarterly Journal of Economics* 131 (1): 219–71.

Kuteesa, F., E. Tumusiime-Mutebile, A. Whitworth, and T. Williamson, eds. 2010. *Uganda's Economic Reforms: Insider Accounts*. Oxford: Oxford University Press.

Lenner, K., and L. Turner. 2018. 'Learning from the Jordan Compact'. *Forced Migration Review* 57: 48–51.

Mansuri, G., and V. Rao. 2012. 'Localizing Development: Does Participation Work?' Policy Research Report, World Bank, Washington, DC.

McCulloch, N., and L. H. Piron. 2019. 'Thinking and Working Politically: Learning from Practice. Overview to Special Issue'. *Development Policy Review* 37: 1–15.

OCHA (United Nations Office for the Coordination of Humanitarian Affairs). 2012. *OCHA on Message: Humanitarian Principles.* New York: United Nations OCHA.

———. 2021. *Global Humanitarian Overview.* New York: United Nations OCHA.

OECD (Organisation for Economic Co-operation and Development). 2018. *Private Philanthropy for Development: The Development Dimension.* Paris: OECD Publishing.

———. 2020. *Multilateral Development Finance 2020.* Paris: OECD Publishing.

Ogunleye, E. K. 2017. 'The Political Economy of the Nigerian Power Sector Reform'. In *The Political Economy of Clean Energy Transitions*, edited by C. Arndt, M. Miller, F. Tarp, O. Zinaman, and D. Arent. Oxford: Oxford University Press.

Prichard, W. 2015. *Taxation, Responsiveness and Accountability in Sub-Saharan Africa: The Dynamics of Tax Bargaining*. Cambridge: Cambridge University Press.

Pritchett, L., M. Woolcock, and M. Andrews. 2013. 'Looking like a State: Techniques of Persistent Failure in State Capability for Implementation'. *Journal of Development Studies* 49 (1): 1–18.

Remmer, K. L. 2004. 'Does Foreign Aid Promote the Expansion of Government?' *American Journal of Political Science* 48 (1): 77–92.

Roy, P., K. Iwuamadi, and J. Ibrahim. 2020. 'Breaking the Cycle of Corruption in Nigeria's Electricity Sector: A Political Settlements Analysis'. ACE Working Paper 20, SOAS, London.

Vicente, P., and L. Wantchekon. 2009. 'Clientelism and Vote Buying: Lessons from Field Experiments in African Elections'. *Oxford Review of Economic Policy* 25 (2): 292–305.

World Bank. 2015. *Tax Revenue Mobilization: Lessons from World Bank Group Support for Tax Reform (English).* IEG Learning Product. Washington, DC: World Bank.

NOTES

PREFACE

1. Data are from Our World in Data, https://ourworldindata.org/extreme-poverty. This measure is based on poverty calculations from the World Bank using a poverty line of $1.90 in 2011 international dollars—that is, it is comparable among countries as corrected for purchasing power differences.
2. Francis Fukuyama. 1992. *The End of History and the Last Man.* New York: Free Press.
3. Data are from Our World in Data, https://ourworldindata.org/economic-growth, based on the World Bank's World Development Indicators database. All these estimates have been converted into 2011 international dollars so that purchasing power can be compared directly between countries and over time.
4. Data are from Our World in Data, https://ourworldindata.org/extreme-poverty. Poverty is evaluated relative to the benchmark of $1.90 per day per person in 2011 international dollars, as used by the World Bank. The key here is not that this is the right poverty benchmark, but rather that the same benchmark is used to assess progress in all countries (taking inflation into account), making it suitable for comparisons of countries at any moment in time.
5. As implied by data from the World Poverty Clock, https://worldpoverty.io/, which is based on extrapolations from World Bank data. The latest India numbers are not current but are based on survey data from 2011, making the numbers harder to assess at present.

INTRODUCTION

1. 'Building back better' is a slogan frequently used by political leaders in the UK, US, Singapore, and elsewhere, as well as by the World Health Organization and other institutions, to describe their efforts to recover from Covid-19. Its first official use was in official documents of the United Nations, linked to the Sendai Framework for Disaster Risk Reduction, which was endorsed by the UN General Assembly in 2015. Although the phrase was initially closely linked to developing countries, Covid-19 raised its usage across the world.

2. Later in the book, I describe how several more but otherwise diverse countries are taking steps towards achieving such a bargain. To be reasonably successful, a country does not need to follow a simple recipe, especially not the one used by the East Asian economies.

1. DEVELOPMENT THINKERS AND THEIR THOUGHTS

1. https://www.dailymail.co.uk/news/article-2200412/Sacked-Transport-Secretary-Justine-Greening-furious-rant-PM-charge-overseas-aid.html. The original claim was made in the *London Evening Standard*.

2. A more precise discussion can be found in World Bank (2015, ch. 3).

3. https://www.gov.uk/government/publications/civil-service-code/the-civil-service-code.

4. I like to think that I succeeded in this objective because she proved to be a long-serving, enthusiastic, hard-working secretary of state, with a keen interest in economic development as well as in social mobility, not least that of women and girls.

5. The books reviewed were those that at the time were the main books for which these popular writers on development issues were known (all are listed in the reference section of this chapter). Some have written books since then, although they have not revised in any fundamental sense their views on development and how it comes about, which is the main focus of the discussion in this chapter.

6. Abhijit Banerjee, Angus Deaton, Esther Duflo, Amartya Sen, and Joseph Stiglitz.

7. See, for example, Banerjee and Newman (1994) or Stiglitz (1989).

8. For a full exposition, see, for example, Banerjee and Duflo (2011).

9. Romer (1986). He was awarded the Nobel Prize for this research.

10. Krugman (1991); Krugman and Venables (1995). Krugman is another Nobel Prize winner.

11. A well-known example is Acemoglu, Johnson, and Robinson (2005).

12. For a critical review of the empirical contributions to this literature, see Durlauf (2009).

13. For example, some researchers such as Barro and Lee (2015) have argued that education is the key factor, while for others health matters independently (Bloom, Canning, and Fink 2014). Others have questioned both (Acemoglu and Johnson 2007, 2014) and argued for a dominance of institutional explanations (Acemoglu, Johnson, and Robinson 2005).

14. Banerjee and Duflo (2011, 272).

15. This was despite or maybe because of the fact that the UK, led by a centre-right Conservative government, had just agreed to spend 0.7 per cent of its gross national income on development aid, the first G7 country to do so.

16. He used the phrase 'golden thread' as early as 2005, before his election as prime minister. His later, more articulated version can be found here: https://www.gov.uk/government/speeches/david-camerons-speech-to-un.

17. De Soto (2000).

18. Besley and Ghatak (2010); Besley, Burchardi, and Ghatak (2012); Field (2005); Payne et al. (2015).

2.   THE DEVELOPMENT BARGAIN

1. The DRC's growth of 2.4 per cent per year per capita between 2004 and 2019 was actually quite good given its preceding performance: it had shrunk at a rate of 6 per cent per year between 1990 and 2004 (World Bank, World Development Indicators database). GDP per capita is in constant 2010 prices.

2. World Bank (2008).

3. The list also includes Brazil, Malta, and Oman. Brazil's growth largely took place in the 1950s and 1960s and then came to a dramatic end in the 1980s. Its two decades of stagnation were followed by a further growth spurt in the decade before the financial crisis of 2007–8, only to face steep declines since then in per capita GDP. Malta and Oman have idiosyncratic histories. However, Oman appears to have managed its oil wealth to stimulate growth for several decades since the 1960s, but it, too, has faced stagnation over the last two decades.

4. 'Take-off' refers to an acceleration of growth when GDP per capita is low. 'Catch-up' refers to a situation in which the economic growth levels of a poorer country are higher than those of a richer country. For example, China is generally considered to have taken off in the 1980s and has since begun to catch up with Organisation for Economic Co-operation and Development (OECD) countries, a process still ongoing.

5.   Birdsall, Ross, and Sabot (1995); Stiglitz and Yusuf (2001); Rodrik (1994); Chang (2003).

6.   Perkins (2013).

7.   This term is commonly used in works from which I have drawn inspiration, such as those by Burton and Higley (1987), Di John and Putzel (2009), and North, Weingast, and Wallis (2009).

8.   In chapter 3, I discuss in more detail how to judge progress and success empirically. For now, success in development is defined as growth and economic progress, but *also* includes a speedily improving position of the poorest, in terms of their incomes, opportunities, and welfare.

9.   This means there is no need for a 'developmental state' as it is portrayed in today's research and policy literature—that is, a state characterised by a fundamental commitment to economic development, but also where there is strong state intervention, as well as extensive regulation and planning. Although such a state may have been present in East Asia and later Southeast Asia, there were still considerable differences between Japan, Korea, and later China in how extensively the state became involved. Furthermore, later budding successes mentioned in this book were not necessarily using this type of extensive government involvement, but they did succeed in not biting off more than they could chew. For the original discussions of the role of developmental states, see Johnson (1982); Amsden (1989, 2001); and Evans (1995).

10. As I will argue in chapter 10, it does not mean that Ethiopia is a success in the sense of what East Asian countries achieved. However, what was observed for quite a prolonged period had the hallmarks of an emerging development bargain, unlike in the DRC.

11. Nevertheless, by 2020, this development bargain fell apart after years of political tensions within the leadership, followed by conflict, as discussed in chapter 10.

12. This notion is developed in an influential 2009 book, *Violence and Social Orders*, by Douglas North, Barry Weingast, and John Wallis. In it, they formulate a grand framework for how to understand the politics and economics of the state, now and in history, and some of the discussion in this chapter builds on this work. When applied to development settings, the discussion here was also inspired by others, such as Acemoglu and Robinson (2012); Besley and Persson (2011); Di John and Putzel (2009); Pritchett, Sen, and Werker (2017); and Khan (2018); as well as the academic work behind these contributions.

13. See North, Weingast, and Wallis (2009).

14. Olson (2000).

15. North, Weingast, and Wallis (2009) call this a 'limited access order'.

Acemoglu and Robinson (2012) and a host of other authors sympathetic to the importance of an institutional view of development have drawn inspiration from this way of looking at states. See, for example, Pritchett, Sen, and Werker (2017).

16. Recall here the discussion in chapter 1 of the role of market failures when capital markets are left to function in unrestricted ways. In the event of credit market failures, access to some activities and investment may well be limited to the people who have wealth to start with, effectively constraining others in society from taking up economic or political activities.

17. North and his co-authors call this an 'open access order', and they have argued that this order has guaranteed these countries' long-term development success. I cannot help detecting a whiff of Francis Fukuyama's famous *The End of History and the Last Man*, published in 1992, wherein he suggested that liberal democracy as we know it is the end point of the evolution of political systems after the fall of the Soviet Union, and we have achieved this end. Several decades later, this teleological view of history feels surprising and unsatisfactory.

18. This refers to Zhou Enlai's reply to a journalist when in 1971 he mistook a question about what he thought about the French Revolution as referring to events in May 1968 and not 1789.

19. More precisely, he defines a state as a human community that can claim a monopoly on the legitimate use of violence. Legitimacy is not necessarily fair, but it may stem from rational-legal means (the law or constitution), or from tradition, or from the charisma of a leader (Weber 1919).

20. The type of analysis such as in North, Weingast, and Wallis's *Violence and Social Orders* offers good insights into what the state is for and what capability and structures it may need to develop to serve the elite bargain. Besley and Persson (2011) develop this notion further.

21. This is about defined rights in order to provide the right incentives. Fairness never quite enters into discussions on property rights in neoclassical economics (to which North and his co-authors definitely subscribe), as economics students discover early on when learning about the Coase theorem.

22. He continued: 'If you steal a lot to become rich overnight, you'll be caught' (Gould 1980, 485; Van Reybrouck 2014).

23. See, for example, Stokes (2011).

24. See, for example, Fukuyama (2014).

25. Politics organised in this way are often called 'neopatrimonial', even though it is often used to focus strongly on the informal structures as if they, by definition, will dominate the formal ones (Cheeseman, Bertrand, and Husaini 2019).

26. The term 'political settlement' was first used by Melling (1991). Current work on political settlements takes inspiration from Acemoglu and Robinson (2012) and North, Weingast and Wallis (2009), although it does not necessarily like their work (Gray 2016). Leading contributions include Khan (2018) and Whitfield et al. (2015).

27. De Waal (2015). For example, in Sudan President Omar al-Bashir kept his hold on power for decades by accommodating an increasing number of rival political and military entrepreneurs. Finally, however, after thirty years his tenuous grip on power slipped away and he was removed in 2019.

28. Bauer et al. (2016).

29. See, for example, a recent machine learning-based study by Basuchoudhary et al. (2018).

30. In a series of exchanges with Nobelist Gary Becker in 2010, jurist and economist Richard Posner wrote: 'Dictatorship will often be optimal for very poor countries. Such countries tend not only to have simple economies but also to lack the cultural and institutional preconditions to democracy. Dictatorship is much less likely to be optimal for advanced economies. This pattern seems to be broadly observed.' https://www.becker-posner-blog.com/2010/10/autocracy-democracy-and-economic-welfareposner.html.

31. Wrong (2010).

32. https://www.reuters.com/article/us-nigeria-godfather/how-the-godfather-of-lagos-could-shape-nigerias-government-idUSKBN0ND17820150422. See, for example, Olarinmoye (2008).

33. Besley and Kudamatsu (2008) observe that while on average there is little difference between autocratic and democratic regimes in terms of economic performance, growth has lower variance in democracies. The best-performing autocratic regimes are better than the best democracies in terms of growth.

34. Acemoglu et al. (2019).

35. *The Bottom Billion* by Collier (2006) offers a good discussion of this.

36. Myrdal (1968).

3.   DEVELOPMENT TILL TODAY: MOSTLY UPS, SOME DOWNS

1. Rahmato and Kidanu (1999).

2. Sen (1999).

3. I use the most recent estimates from generally reliable and consistent data sources, usually up to 2019. Data from 2020, after the start of the Covid crisis, are not available at the time of writing but some estimates of impacts are presented later in the chapter.

4. Figure 3.1 uses Gapminder, based on the presentation and visualisation work by the great data communicator Hans Rosling, https://www.gapminder. org/tools/#$chart-type=mountain, as downloaded in June 2020. The measure corrects for price differentials over time and between countries, so that each dollar unit can acquire the same level of consumption goods across the world as assessed in 2011. The methods used are controversial, and alternatives, equally controversial, have been proposed, but they are not available with the same frequency and coverage (Deaton 2010; Allen 2017).

5. Even among those keen on poverty measures based on income or consumption, this approach remains controversial because of the methods behind the use of international dollars, and the way in which the $1.90 benchmark was obtained. I vividly recall a closed meeting of a small group of global experts in poverty measurement trying to decide whether and how the World Bank should proceed with the methods behind the calculation of extreme poverty levels relative to the $1.90 benchmark pioneered by Martin Ravallion and critiqued by Angus Deaton (Chen and Ravallion 2010; Deaton 2010). In that heated meeting, opinions were strong. Indeed, some of the language used in critiquing the views of others present cannot be put in print.

6. Sen (1983).

7. The calculation is for a non-working couple in total means-tested benefits per week (based on calculators found on http://entitled.co.uk and http://turn2.us.org.uk), and put first in dollars using international dollars (https://stats.oecd.org/). This is all approximate because benefits are adjusted for individual circumstances, but are unlikely to be ever much lower than this.

8. Approximate inference using data from https://www.gapminder.org/.

9. Taken from https://ourworldindata.org/extreme-poverty. At the time of writing, they provided aggregated updates up to 2017, based on World Bank data.

10. The eighteen countries were Angola, Burkina Faso, Cameroon, Côte d'Ivoire, Democratic Republic of Congo, Ethiopia, Ghana, Kenya, Madagascar, Malawi, Mali, Mozambique, Niger, Nigeria, South Africa, Tanzania, Uganda, Zambia, and Zimbabwe. Calculations here rely on data from the World Bank's PovCal portal (http://iresearch.worldbank.org/PovcalNet). The reported headcount poverty rate closest to 2018 and to 1990 is used. If there are data before and after 1990, but within five years, the average between the two weighted by the proximity to 1990 is used.

11. For example, data from India and China, the world's two largest countries, are essential to any conclusions reached on the scale and rate of change of global poverty. In both cases, their anchoring relative to the rest of the world in terms of their purchasing power, as well as the rate of change since 1990,

is disputed—in China because of limited data in the public domain and in India because no new data have been in the public domain since 2011.

12. For a popular approach, see Alkire and Foster (2011).

13. Data are from https://ourworldindata.org/child-mortality.

14. This is despite the fact that about 50 per cent more children were born in Ethiopia in 2019 than in 1990. In the DRC, live births were estimated for 2019 at more than double for 1990. Data are from Our World in Data.

15. This has been and remains a contentious subject, but the large declines in figure 3.4 before 1979 are hard to ignore. For extensive discussions, see Whyte, Wang, and Cai (2015); Gietel-Basten, Han, and Cheng (2019); *Goodkind* (2019); Harrell et al. (2014).

16. These estimates of GDP per capita are expressed not in actual dollars, but in 2017 constant international dollars, thereby making them comparable over time and between countries in terms of purchasing power.

17. For these figures, I exclude in 1990 the relatively small number of high-income countries in the Middle East, Latin America, and East Asia to highlight the progress of the poorer economies within each of these three regions. Southeast Asia is included in East Asia in the data.

18. Later in this book, I argue it is too easy to reduce this to the so-called natural resource curse. Oil definitely mattered in Nigeria, but it is not a sufficient explanation of Nigeria's lower GDP per capita. Indonesia has oil as well, but that country has managed to be far more successful developmentally.

19. Predictions like these assume typically that the underlying current conditions, such as recent levels and drivers of economic growth and poverty reduction, or the presence of conflict and other sources of instability will persist into the next decade.

20. Such predictions are based on past performance. Ethiopia's current instability challenges may derail this, while other countries may emerge as successes or failures over this period.

21. World Bank (2020).

22. Crespo-Cuaresma et al. (2018).

23. All calculations are based on data on stocks and flows of emissions from https://ourworldindata.org/co2-and-other-greenhouse-gas-emissions.

24. This is even more the case as these data are about the production of emissions within a country's boundaries. The emissions 'consumed' by richer societies are even larger, as they import many goods from high-emitting industries in the developing world, not least from China.

25. To clarify, it is the stock, the cumulative emissions of greenhouses, that is causing climate change, and the annual emissions are adding to this stock.

4. THE DRAGON, THE TIGER CUB, AND THE PEACOCK: CHINA, INDONESIA, AND INDIA

1. An Afrikaans saying, it is apparently used in some West African countries as well.

2. These features are particularly present in what political scientists refer to as neopatrimonial states, discussed in chapter 2. Formal and informal structures coexist, and clientelism and patronage are rife.

3. With its jagged, razor-like teeth and reputation as fierce predators, tigerfish live off eating little fish. They are most commonly found in the Congo River, Lake Tanganyika, the Zambezi River, and lakes across Zimbabwe, Zambia, and Mozambique.

4. A special economic zone is subject to economic regulations that differ from those applied to other areas within the same country, and it usually has better infrastructure—all aimed at attracting business to the zone, including foreign firms.

5. All economic data are calculated based on the World Bank's World Development Indicators, https://datacatalog.worldbank.org/dataset/world-development-indicators.

6. It would be unfair to suggest that the Communist Party itself had had no interest in development. Because of the dramatic famine during the Great Leap Forward in 1960–1, food security has since been at the centre of much policy-making. During the Cultural Revolution, however, it became secondary to politics and ideological purity.

7. No doubt pressure as well as experimentation from below may have forced the hand of party leaders. For example, when a small number of peasants in Anhui Province abolished their commune-based production and began to experiment with land-lease arrangements, their efforts provided the inspiration for the Household Responsibility System. See, for example, Nee and Opper (2012).

8. The focus on the economy rather than ideology did not go unchallenged, most notably around the time of the student protests on Tiananmen Square in 1989. In Beijing, students had initially demonstrated in favour of further economic reforms and against the forces in the party that favoured returning to the communist ideology over economic reforms. However, when the demonstrations increasingly focused on political reforms, Deng, who was by then an important elder in the party, ended up strongly supporting martial law and suppression of the student movement in order to perpetuate the focus on economic reform. His interventions, documented in papers from party meetings later smuggled out of the country, swayed the decision in favour of martial law but also consolidated the development bargain as part

of the underlying deal to suppress the protests. His statement on 2 June, two days before the Square was cleared, said, 'Without [economic] reform and opening, our development work stops and our economy slides down. […] We can't handle chaos while we're busy with construction' (Nathan 2001, 33).

9. For example, Justin Lin suggests that this model could be applicable in other settings, such as Africa. Such settings have a comparative advantage, as China had, in low-skilled labour, with a strong role for the state in offering infrastructure and ensuring that markets function and gradual industrial upgrading occurs (see Lin 2013).

10. How to interpret policy lines from the top remains a challenge today. In the spring of 2018, I was in Beijing at a dinner with a vice minister and some of my academic colleagues. A few months earlier, President Xi had given a well-covered speech at Davos defending free trade, and one of my colleagues asked the vice minister how it would be implemented at multilateral trade forums. He just smiled and said that his government colleagues were still studying the speech to try to understand what Xi may have meant.

11. Yuen Yuen Ang, in her fascinating 2017 book *How China Escaped the Poverty Trap*, calls this directed improvisation. China did not have the perfect technocratic organisations at the local level, nor were bureaucracies free from patronage or corruption. However, scope was given to finding ways of achieving targets and objectives, suggesting improvisation was required because of the relatively weak institutional setting. She suggests that these weaknesses were even an advantage for experimentation. Only later did a more formal institutional set-up appear when the economy became more complex and required it.

12. See Xu (2011) for a discussion of failures.

13. This commitment was never self-evident. A senior Chinese official involved in evaluating the success or failure of experimentation over many decades told me politics always mattered, even today. In principle, leaders at all levels are responsible for delivering on growth and development objectives. If they do not deliver, they have to change their policies, and they may be removed, based on the reports of the powerful Beijing-based unit to which my contact belonged. However, at times local political leaders are too powerful to allow the technocrats to halt programmes or change policies. If so, it is just a matter of waiting until their term in office is finished and programmes can be eliminated or changed.

14. Whether the way China has pursued its development bargain will be enough to guide China to the levels of income attained by, say, Japan, Singapore, Western Europe, or the US is another matter. Some economists such as Acemoglu and Robinson (2012) have questioned whether China will

converge to the living standards found in these Organisation for Economic Co-operation and Development (OECD) countries because of its lack of a more open society and politics, and the challenges for innovation that this brings. This is not a question addressed in this book.

15. See also Dinh (2000) and Vuong (2014).

16. These mechanisms, which are not public but are within the party, are by no means perfect. The party has about 90 million members with about 8 million cadres. Many more people apply to be members than are accepted. Most official positions have fixed time limits. Local offices offer party members an opportunity to prove themselves because day-to-day governance is highly decentralised to the provincial and sub-provincial levels. Rising to the top requires much direct and indirect support from various levels, and also a strong performance, including in economic and developmental matters. That said, the opaque party structures create ample room not only for patronage but also corrupt behaviour, both of which no doubt have long been present and are a more recent matter of concern.

17. Maddison (2001).

18. Data in this section are from the World Bank's World Development Indicators database.

19. GDP per capita (in constant prices) returned only by 2004 to pre-crisis levels.

20. Extreme poverty is calculated using the $1.90 per day benchmark, based on World Bank data and reported by Our World in Data, https://ourworldindata.org/world-population-growth.

21. World Bank (2008).

22. Bevan, Collier, and Gunning (1999).

23. Including through currency undervaluation, a rare feat for a natural resource–rich economy.

24. Beyond growth, commitment of the elite to poverty reduction and broader development appears to have been present as well. This concern with poverty and equity predated the period of fast growth, with roots in the army and the independence struggle. It was present at the time of the country's founding by President Sukarno and remained under President Suharto (Bevan, Collier, and Gunning 1999).

25. Bhagwati (1982). Many suggest Jagdish Bhagwati has been wrongly overlooked for the Nobel Prize, but he did win a fictional one in an episode of *The Simpsons*.

26. Her nickname was particularly well chosen because Tien means 'ten' in Dutch, the language of the former colonial master which the older generation would have studied at school.

27. Another helpful discussion of the early period, which also deals with the

quality of economic policy-making, can be found in Bevan, Collier, and Gunning (1999).

28. See, for example, Lal (1988).

29. Rodrik and Subramanian (2005).

30. Mukherji (2008). See this article as well for a careful discussion of the political economy of this period.

31. Mukherji (2008).

32. Indonesia had more in common with two other countries in the Growth Commission's list—Thailand and Malaysia. In both, a political bargain helped to balance rent-seeking behaviours with moving into export-oriented manufacturing. Meanwhile, the state managed the wealth generated by natural resources in reasonably sensible ways but also left much initiative to private actors, even if mainly those well connected to the political bargain. See Pritchett, Sen, and Werker (2017) for a careful discussion.

5. HIPPOS IN THE LAKE: DEVELOPMENT ON HOLD IN SIERRA LEONE AND MALAWI

1. Political scientists call these neopatrimonial states, alluding to Max Weber's idea of the patrimonial state as discussed in chapter 2, in which the state simply exists to serve the patron, or more broadly the group in power. Excellent discussions of the forms of neopatrimonialism found in sub-Saharan Africa appear in Bratton and Van de Walle (1994) and Clapham (1985). Patronage relates to the ability of those in charge to give favours or privileges at their discretion. Clientelism refers to the presence of individuals or groups who expect favours in return for supporting the 'patron' who is seeking to remain in power. It is thus a societal order based on relations of patronage. See also Cheeseman, Bertrand, and Husaini (2019).

2. See, for example, https://successfulsocieties.princeton.edu/interviews/hans-rosling.

3. Global Fund (2014).

4. See Pieterse and Lodge (2015) and DuBois et al. (2015).

5. In *Dull Disasters*, Clarke and Dercon (2016) discuss this and other examples of the failure of early action.

6. World Bank, World Development Indicators, https://datacatalog.worldbank.org/dataset/world-development-indicators.

7. Security was not an excuse in either Sierra Leone or neighbouring countries, unlike in the DRC in 2018–20 in North Kivu and Ituri Provinces, where the caseload and mortality rate from Ebola were lower, despite a hugely complex security situation with militia activity throughout.

8. The international response to the Ebola crisis had its successes and also its

failings, such as the delayed response by the World Health Organization and the focus on expensive treatment while underestimating the role of cultural practices in containing the epidemic locally. See, for example, DuBois et al. (2015) and references therein.

9. Similar issues were apparently present in Guinea and Liberia prior to the crisis. See, for example, DuBois et al. (2015). Some may suggest that this critical assessment of these states is unfair, not least because all three countries suffered. However, in the years prior to the West African Ebola crisis, other countries had effectively brought Ebola under control, among them Uganda and the DRC.

10. In the end, though, the contraction of the economy in 2016 and 2017 had little to do with Ebola. The collapse of commodity prices was mainly to blame, with declines in GDP in line with price drops, just as in other resource-rich African economies such as Zambia and Nigeria. World Bank, World Development Indicators, https://datacatalog.worldbank.org/dataset/world-development-indicators.

11. *Africa Confidential* (2016b, 12).

12. *Africa Confidential* (2019, 7).

13. Such as US president Donald Trump in 2019. See https://www.washingtonpost.com/politics/2019/07/23/trump-falsely-tells-auditorium-full-teens-constitution-gives-him-right-do-whatever-i-want/.

14. *Africa Confidential* (2016a, 12).

15. *Africa Confidential* (2019, 7–8).

16. *Africa Confidential* (2019, 7–8).

17. *Africa Confidential* (2020, 11–12).

18. *Africa Confidential* (2018, 12). The bridge has been put on hold due to the Covid crisis but is still a commitment. Fighting corruption is a central theme of the current presidency, but real change seems far away.

19. All data in this part are from the World Bank's World Development Indicators database.

20. Among the ten countries with the highest percentage of extremely poor people, Malawi stands out because it has not suffered from conflict since independence, while all the others are conflict-affected states.

21. Crawford (2000).

22. This includes contestation on the streets and in the courts of the 2019 re-election of Peter Mutharika, which led to the ruling that the presidential election had to be repeated in 2020.

23. For a discussion of these challenges, see Dercon and Gollin (2014).

24. For an introduction to the political economy of economic growth in Malawi, see Said and Singini (2014).

25. *Africa Confidential* (2013, 9).

26. *Africa Confidential* (2016c, 4–6).
27. World Bank, World Development Indicators database.
28. It is below the average of sub-Saharan Africa (19 per cent) but above that of neighbouring countries such as Zambia, Uganda, and Tanzania.
29. *Africa Confidential* (2017a, 7–8).
30. Ejeta (2010); Quiñones, Borlaug, and Dowswell (1997).
31. Chirwa and Dorward (2013).
32. *New York Times*, 20 April 2012, https://www.nytimes.com/2012/04/20/opinion/how-malawi-fed-its-own-people.html.
33. Data are from FAO, http://www.fao.org/faostat/en/#data/QC/; latest observation available was 2019.
34. The FAO data suggest Zambia's yields increased by 43 per cent in the same period. In Uganda, they increased by 63 per cent, with support to agriculture but not at this scale nor focusing only on subsidised fertiliser and seeds.
35. Dorward et al. (2008); Denning et al. (2009). Some economists remain big fans of the principles and will point at best at weaknesses in implementation to sustain any of the early gains (Chirwa and Dorward 2013). Some more recent studies have questioned the programme's success, such as whether yield gains really materialised (Messina, Peter, and Snapp 2017). Some caution is then clearly needed in considering this approach. If data concerns prove to be true, it may well be that similar issues also exist with data in neighbouring countries.
36. McArthur and McCord (2017).
37. Jayne and Rashid (2013); Dabalan et al. (2016).
38. Ricker-Gilbert and Jayne (2017).
39. Own calculations from official election returns by the Malawi Electoral Commission.
40. Banik and Chasukwa (2019); Chirwa and Dorward (2013); Chinsinga and Poulton (2013).
41. Since colonial times, extensive intervention in food markets has been used widely in Africa to keep supplies plentiful and prices under control and to deal with actual or perceived failing markets. Most colonies and protectorates adopted marketing boards, which would play a central role as intermediaries buying grain from farmers to supply urban centres. They had extensive powers, often licensing traders or even setting prices. After independence, these boards continued to function in Malawi and other former colonies and protectorates as well as across southern and eastern Africa.
42. Little *appeared* to have changed by then, although it was more an issue of multiple periods of change and reversals of any reforms. See Harrigan (2003) for a discussion.
43. Two rival agencies are involved in managing maize markets. The National

Food Reserve Agency (NFRA), entrusted with managing a strategic food reserve of maize to deal with crises, procures maize from abroad to support supplies in the country. The Agricultural Development and Marketing Cooperation (ADMARC) has played over time various roles as a marketing agent, mainly for maize, buying and selling maize locally. It would be unfair to suggest that their roles have not changed over time, or that their briefs are clear. In fact, NFRA was only set up in 1999 during a period of reform of ADMARC—one of many attempts. In its latest incarnation, ADMARC has since 2003 gradually expanded its role again, but not necessarily for the better and rivalling that of NFRA (Banik and Chasukwa 2019).

44. Gilbert, Christiaensen, and Kaminski (2017).

45. Export bans were in place between 2011 and 2017, as well as earlier intermittently. Prices would then fall to very low levels, below pre-announced prices, and producers could not cut their losses from the low prices by selling abroad. Therefore, few commercial farmers invested in maize because in such years these farmers (who usually had fairly stable yields) would suffer considerable losses.

46. Based on nine countries with complete data (Gilbert, Christiaensen, and Kaminski 2017).

47. For example, see Ochieng, Botha, and Baulch (2019); and Jayne (2012).

48. *Africa Confidential* (2017a, 2017b).

49. Unfortunately—some say conveniently—a fire at his office destroyed all records before the trial. He was duly acquitted because of lack of evidence, despite the cash hoard. Regardless, he was tapped as a possible presidential candidate for his party.

6.   KENYA, UGANDA, AND GHANA: READY FOR TAKE-OFF?

1. See details in Dercon and Gutiérrez-Romero (2012); and Dercon and Bratton (2008).

2. The final results had shown much higher turnout in counties supporting the government. Indeed, in some cases the turnout was higher than the number of registered voters, suggestive of irregularities, including ballot box stuffing.

3. A former UN secretary general, Kofi Annan, led the mediation, assisted by various African presidents. UN Secretary General Ban Ki-Moon, US Secretary of State Condoleezza Rice, and various African presidents paid visits to bring pressure to bear.

4. The National Accord and Reconciliation Act, which was announced on 28 February 2008, by Kofi Annan.

5. Berman (1998).

6. Eifert, Miguel, and Posner (2010).

7. The World Bank's World Development Indicators database shows this not only for extreme poverty, but also for the share of children dying before age one and age five. These indicators of deprivation increased in the late 1980s and early 1990s, only to decline again after the latter part of the 1990s in contrast to those of sub-Saharan Africa, where declines since 1990 have been the norm.

8. The GDP per capita at constant 2010 prices of all these countries was well below the average of sub-Saharan Africa (SSA) in 1980, with Sudan (still pre-oil) having a GDP per capita of about $900, comparable to that of Kenya, and with that of all other countries considerably lower. SSA's GDP then declined between 1980 and 1995 by about 1.5 per cent a year in per capita terms, much more than that of Kenya at 0.3 per cent a year. All of Kenya's neighbours saw significant declines at higher rates than Kenya's in the 1980s.

9. Within the East African Community—the free trade area of this part of Africa—Kenya is no doubt the leading economy and its investment, finance, and trade hub. A quarter of Kenya's exports now go to neighbouring countries.

10. Mwega and Ndung'u (2008) offer a careful discussion of both the economics and the political economy of this period.

11. Measuring manufacturing capabilities is difficult. One such approach is by Hausmann and the Harvard Growth Lab, which constructed an index of complexity based on the nature of the products that economies export (for details, see https://atlas.cid.harvard.edu/). Based on their rankings, Kenya had by 1995 outperformed all sub-Saharan African countries except South Africa, and it was at levels similar to that of Indonesia and well above that of Vietnam. Although for several reasons this finding paints too optimistic a picture, there is no doubt that, relative to its neighbours, Kenya was well ahead in its potential, and that during this period economic policy-makers were not keen to support manufacturing capabilities because they were dominated by Asian interests.

12. Ndulu et al. (2008).

13. For example, the evidence suggests that during Kenyatta's reign road infrastructure investment clearly favoured Kikuyu areas, and during Moi's tenure it favoured Kalenjin areas (Burgess et al. 2015). And it is not just about the president. Educational resources also flow more to the ethnic areas of cabinet ministers and high-level education bureaucrats (Kramon and Posner 2016). See also Barkan and Chege (1989).

14. Wrong (2009). In fact, 'It is our turn to eat' was so widely heard in Raila Odinga's camp during the 2007 election campaign that it was at times assumed to be the official slogan of his campaign. See also Branch, Cheeseman, and Gardner (2010).

15. These areas were part of President Kenyatta's 'Big Four' agenda: food security, affordable housing, manufacturing, and affordable health care.

16. According to the World Bank's World Development Indicators database, private plus public investment as a share of GDP was about 18 per cent in 2018, or less than that of neighbouring countries such as Uganda, Tanzania, Rwanda, and Ethiopia. Kenya had particularly low public investment as a share of GDP—less than 6 per cent, meaning that the government invested relatively little in roads, the port, or other infrastructure. See also IMF (2020).

17. Indeed, the data reveal no structural transformation—the movement of labour from low-productivity to high-productivity sectors, typically from agriculture to the rest of the economy.

18. World Bank (2019).

19. Explaining this persistent dynamism is not self-evident. It may have to do with the fact that several in the political class have roots in and historical links to an entrepreneurial class. In the classic analysis by Harvard's Robert Bates, in Kenya, unlike in many other African countries, the political class post-independence was not just drawn from an urban elite set on capturing rents per se. Instead, it also had its roots in rural productive elites—farmers (Bates 2014). The Kenyatta family embodies such roots (the president's brother runs the highly successful family business, Brookside Dairy Ltd, processing milk products) and highlights the interest of politics in not only not undermining private business but also in valuing good management of the (productive) economy. This is despite the fact that many similar business elite families are closely connected to government and are repeatedly implicated in seemingly dodgy contracts when the government is involved.

20. D'Arcy and Cornell (2016).

21. After Kenyatta was declared the winner with a relatively narrow margin, his opponent challenged the result and the Supreme Court ruled that, because of irregularities, the election had to be rerun.

22. For example, at the time of this writing a Kikuyu–Luo alliance between Kenyatta and Odinga seems likely against President Kenyatta's own vice president, William Ruto, who is Kalenjin but who has fallen out with the president.

23. The mere presence of elections alone is clearly not enough to get real change; how they are fought has to change, too. Studying education, Kramon and Posner (2016) in Kenya and Franck and Rainer (2012) in Africa find that the importance of distributive politics based on ethnicity is unaffected by whether there is democracy or autocratic rule. However, Burgess et al. (2015) dispute this finding.

24. Cheeseman (2018).

25. In Kenya, one in sixteen children died before the age of one.

26. This is extreme poverty based on the international poverty line of $1.90 a day.

27. Hyden (2012).

28. Reuss and Titeca (2017).

29. *Africa Confidential* (2016).

30. Over the years, various contenders to succeed Museveni have emerged or have even been groomed, only to eventually disappear or turn against the president. It may well be that none satisfy Museveni's requirements. Whether this is the cause or consequence of his quest to extend his rule even longer is unclear. See, for example, *Africa Confidential* (2017) about the fate of some contenders.

31. *East African* (2014).

32. Kasekende and Atingi-Ego (2008).

33. Ndulu et al. (2008). This confidence in Uganda's commitment to sensible economic policies also contributed to it receiving substantial aid, although the flow has diminished in recent years because of repeated corruption scandals.

34. 'Washington Consensus' is the term used (often by those critical of international financial institutions) to refer to policies focusing on the liberalisation of all markets, including for trade and capital, privatisation of state-owned enterprises, and a limited role for the state in development, as promoted by the World Bank and the IMF in the 1980s and 1990s. The narrow version of this doctrine has definitely lost its influence within these institutions.

35. Hausmann et al. (2014).

36. Nevertheless, the government makes it hard for opposition parties to raise money from wealthy businesses, including through legal routes (*Africa Confidential* 2018a).

37. On Uganda, in contrast to other experiences, see Patey (2015).

38. All data in this section are from the World Bank's World Development Indicators database.

39. World Bank, World Development Indicators database, and Our World in Data.

40. Cheeseman, Lynch, and Willis (2017). I recall visiting in 2012, not long after elections, and talking to senior leaders linked to the losing NPP. They had disputed the election result, claiming irregularities, and went to the Supreme Court. I asked them what they would do if the Supreme Court rejected their appeal. They looked puzzled by my question, and said, 'Oh, in that case we will just focus on winning the 2016 election.'

41. Whitfield (2018); Aryeetey and Fosu (2008).

42. For example, in 2018 a senior official suggested about $2.8 billion a year was lost in this way (*Africa Confidential* 2018b).

43. Arthur (2009).

44. Cheeseman, Lynch, and Willis (2017), and Lynch (2014) on the Kenyan case as one in which voters trust only a co-ethnic to protect their interests.

45. Cheeseman, Lynch, and Willis (2017).

46. Whitfield (2018).

47. GDP growth per capita ranged between 0.5 per cent in 1985 and 2.6 per cent in 2003. In the 1970s it ranged between 10 and 12 per cent, and it has ranged between –0.2 and 11.3 per cent since 2003 until the Covid crisis. Even so, these numbers should not be interpreted as macroeconomic stability. Although much progress has been achieved as well since the mid-1980s, the range of inflation per year has stayed between 10 and 60 per cent, and only in the last fifteen years has inflation (measured by the consumer price index) never exceeded 10 per cent. Still, all this was much better than in the 1970s, which saw three years of more than 100 per cent inflation.

48. This was not just a cash bonanza, but also part of planned civil service reform to bring parity to grades. However, the way it was done, ultimately the most expensive way possible, raised eyebrows in an election year.

49. IMF (2019).

50. This is overseas development assistance (ODA), as defined by the OECD rules and reported in the World Bank's World Development Indicators database.

51. Whitfield (2018).

52. For example, Williams (2017) shows how one-third of infrastructure projects are never finished, not because of corruption or cost overruns, but because of an inability to keep public expenditure allocations and local stakeholders focused on delivering, when local political imperatives shift to other projects or simply cannot be agreed on. This wastes about 20 per cent of the total capital expenditure involved.

53. Aryeetey and Kanbur (2017); Whitfield (2018).

7.   NIGERIA AND THE DEMOCRATIC REPUBLIC OF CONGO: NOT ENOUGH OIL AND DIAMONDS?

1. Abba Kyari died in 2020 from complications linked to Covid-19.

2. At least when expressed in constant GDP in 2010 prices (World Bank, World Development Indicators database).

3. This share has now fallen—to below half—but largely because oil revenue has collapsed. Non-oil revenue in 2017 was in nominal naira terms below that of 2014 and worth a third less due to inflation. Much has been made

of this re-emergence of the importance of non-oil tax revenue for the Nigerian government. In fact, Burns and Owens (2019) and Usman (2020) suggest that Nigeria is now a non-oil state. However, this has more to do with the collapse of oil prices than any successful attempts by the Nigerian government to increase its pitifully low tax collection levels, let alone change the structure of its economy.

4. Ndulu et al. (2008).
5. Oriakhi and Osaze (2013).
6. Bevan, Collier, and Gunning. (1999).
7. The similarity with Indonesia in the late 1970s and beyond was often pointed out, when technocrats linked with international organisations became more influential, allowing change to become embedded. In Nigeria, Ngozi Okonjo-Iweala, a former World Bank senior official, became minister of finance. For a discussion of the similarities and differences in that period, see Lewis (2009), as well as Bevan, Collier, and Gunning (1999) on earlier periods.
8. For a careful discussion on this period, see Usman (2020).
9. A good example is the way in which exchange rates are managed through busts and booms.
10. See, for example, Kohli (2004), who considers Nigeria fundamentally a neopatrimonial state built on patronage and clientelism, or Joseph (2014), who in the 1980s coined the term 'prebendal politics' to describe how political office was bestowed by powerful groups in the elite on individuals who would be allowed to use it to enrich themselves during their time in office. He wrote in 2014 that little had changed.
11. As a result, several multinationals and large Nigerian firms are able to function and make large profits because they *can* internalise the huge transaction costs and the costly supply chains and can respond to the trade regime incentives, without necessarily being obviously corrupt, and connections to the political elite will help here. Being big, possibly with powerful shareholders, allows such firms to stand up to harassment and signal that they won't pay.
12. The elite bargains that emerged in Thailand and Indonesia were discussed in earlier chapters.
13. The tortuous multiple exchange rate system that emerged since 2013, with exchange rates for specific purposes, was supposedly based on the needs of the economy, but in practice it was providing easy access to connected firms, while others had to go to the parallel market, thereby distorting the economy and fostering corruption through roundtripping. The architect of the exchange rate policy was Central Bank governor Godwin Emefiele, with whom I had some very surprising exchanges. 'Nigeria does not need trade,' he said, when I pointed out that the overvalued exchange rate perpetuated

Nigeria's lack of new export products. 'We could just close all borders and the economy would be fine: in fact I would like to do this.'

14. Data on revenue for government are from OECD (https://stats.oecd. org/), and data on total revenue and population are based on the World Bank's World Development Indicators database. All data are in dollars of that year.

15. There are good reasons to regard the numbers in this section cautiously. Data on the DRC are notoriously weak. However, the scale of the decline in GDP is hardly disputed by most observers. See Marivoet and De Herdt (2014) for a discussion.

16. See Hochschild (1999).

17. Extreme violence was committed by small groups of African sentries of the Force Publique, under the command of small-time colonial agents collecting rubber on behalf of the Crown Domain. The Domain paid its agents only for rubber collected and happily ignored their violence because it delivered profit. A century later, similar methods are followed by the militias roaming the present-day DRC, pilfering minerals often on behalf of others. At least in the early days, the much bigger powers could isolate the leader of a small country responsible for much of the violence to the point that he would leave the scene.

18. That was Jules Cornet, one of the early geologists who discovered copper in Congo—see Lhoest (1995).

19. Currently, the DRC has an urbanisation rate of about 35 per cent, which is about average for Africa. Its rate is similar to that of Mozambique and well above that for Uganda and Ethiopia, but below that of other mining-dominated economies in southern Africa. Its population density, with fast population growth, is creeping up, but it is still among the lower densities in Africa—about 17 per square kilometre—compared with Tanzania's and Kenya's (50 per square kilometre), Ethiopia's (80), and Nigeria's (90). Data are from the World Bank's World Development Indicators database.

20. Booth (2013).

21. The first prime minister, Lumumba (later murdered), probably had the most managerial experience. He was a clerk in beer marketing campaigns for Bracongo, one of the leading breweries.

22. The Belgian prime minister, Gaston Eyskens, dismissed the Congolese economic negotiators, led by the journalist Joseph-Désiré Mobutu, as 'second rank figures'. Mobutu wrote about the negotiations: 'And there I sat, a silly, unmannered journalist, at the same table with the great white sharks of Belgian finance … I became like one of those cowboys in a western who lets himself be bamboozled time and again by professional con men … Our partners in the discussion used a whole series of legal and technical

ruses to successfully safeguard the hold which the multinationals and the Belgian capitalists had on the Congolese pocketbook' (Van Reybrouck 2014, 262–3).

23. For an illuminating account, see Van Reybrouck (2014).

24. An area roughly the size of Britain was handed over to a German private space investor who tried and ultimately failed to develop a cheap rocket.

25 As Mobutu famously observed, 'Half of Zaire has discovered that they could very well be related to me in one way or another, and therefore have a right to my assistance' (Van Reybrouck 2014).

26. Booth (2013).

27. Robinson (2013). See also Acemoglu, Verdier, and Robinson (2004).

28. Robinson (2013).

29. The room where the printing press stood is a highlight of the visit to his ruined villa.

30. Che Guevara wrote famously about the characteristics of a true revolutionary leader and about Kabila in 1965: 'He must also possess a serious attitude concerning the revolution, and ideology that serves to channel his actions, and willingness to make sacrifices that is expressed in his deeds. So far, Kabila has not shown himself to possess any of this … I seriously doubt whether he is capable of winning out over his shortcomings.'

31. An MP's pay rose gradually but persistently during this period, climbing to over $6,000 a month by 2008.

32. *Africa Confidential* (2021).

33. For a careful discussion of structures and practices in the four main markets in Kinshasa of this informal taxation, see Nkuku and Titeca (2018).

34. In practice, the costs are bound to have been much higher. See, for example Laokri, Soelaeman, and Hotchkiss, 2018.

35. Gould (1980).

36. While visiting a soap factory in the east of the country, I was shown a recent letter asking the round sum of $50,000 be paid to a government office in Kinshasa. The letter invoked a set of regulations unknown to the manager and suggested that a visit would be made to enforce payment.

37. For evidence on the inefficiency of tax levels in Congo, see Bergeron, Tourek, and Weigel (2020).

38. Chabal and Daloz (1998) refer to the acute degree of apparent disorder as an instrument of power.

39. Consisting of the North and South Kivu Provinces.

40. *Africa Confidential* (2013, 2020).

41. Congolese Wireless Network sprl. See also chapter 13.

42. Apparently, he had a banknote printing press in his palace in Gbadolite.

When visiting I could see that it was conveniently placed near the swimming pool, where notorious parties were held.

43. Africa Progress Panel (2013). See also *Africa Confidential* (2020).
44. Moore (2007); Besley and Persson (2009).
45. Weigel (2020).
46. The value added tax (VAT) is a charge on the final consumers of goods and services, and not on business. Firms collect these taxes and transfer them to the tax authorities, while receiving refunds on the VAT charged in invoices for inputs used in the supply of these goods and services.
47. This is known as the fictional 15th article of the constitution, alluding to the need in this country to look after oneself as the state won't protect or support you.
48. Scholars on Africa continue to debate the nature of the African state. Some francophone writers tend to emphasise this view of sub-Saharan Africa. For example, Bayart (2009) focuses on the propensity of politicians to hoard and consume resources themselves, using any means other than building states or investing in economies. Chabal and Daloz (1998) focus on the African state in which disorder is used as an instrument of power. In both cases, Zaire and, to a lesser extent, Nigeria are clearly at the back of their minds, and Mobutu is on the cover of the English version of Bayart's book. But others, such as Wiseman (1999), have rightly criticised them for generalising from a few cases.

8. TAMING CLANS OF HYENAS: PEACE AND ECONOMIC DEALS IN SOUTH SUDAN, AFGHANISTAN, NEPAL, LEBANON, AND SOMALILAND

1. Coburn (2015).
2. Bizhan (2018).
3. Ghani and Lockhart (2009).
4. See, for example, Fearon and Laitin (2003); Collier and Hoeffler (2007); and Blattman and Miguel (2010). This work emphasises that the emergence or persistence of civil war more likely stems from economic factors, such as overall low incomes, natural resources, a high poverty rate, or ethnic or other divisions within societies.
5. See chapter 2 and the references therein, such as North, Weingast, and Wallis (2009) and Olson (2000).
6. The SPLA was the Southern People's Liberation Army, and the SPLM was the political wing and later the leading party in the Southern People's Liberation Movement.

7.   World Bank, World Development Indicators database, https://datacatalog. worldbank.org/dataset/world-development-indicators.

8.   This is based on the Integrated Food Security Phase Classification (IPC). For example, it suggested that from May to July 2020, 15 per cent of the population was living under Phase 4 conditions (Emergency), which was just below Phase 5 conditions (Catastrophe). See http://www.ipcinfo.org/.

9.   Other provincial elites perpetually drifting in and out of conflict are those linked to Darfur and Kordofan.

10. See, for example, news reporting from 2011: https://www.bbc.co.uk/ news/world-africa-14050504.

11. This is line with the argument by De Waal (2015) that Sudan's numerous regional conflicts may well be best understood as claims to the rents of those in control of Khartoum. Because the centre is too weak to have a monopoly of violence, uprisings can be successful. Political and military entrepreneurs have then an incentive to use violence to boost their own claim to rents. Peace is ultimately not much more than a settlement of who receives rents. As such, the politics and economics of rent-seeking are at the root of much of the conflict in the recent history of Sudan.

12. The stakes were higher for President Bashir because a peace deal could offer scope for normalising relations with the US.

13. Rolandsen (2015).

14. OECD (2011).

15. See chapter 2 for definitions of these concepts and the relevant references.

16. Guarantees are needed that the Taliban will not allow groups such as foreign fighters from al-Qaida or Islamic State to use Afghanistan as their base for international terror acts. While relevant, it is hardly in the Taliban's interest to do so anyway. However, there are likely other interests at play, such as links with Pakistan and its intelligence services, whose role in Afghanistan has hardly been benign. I do not focus on this regional dimension of the conflict, even though it is hugely important and undermining the possible economics of peace.

17. Rasoly and Chandrashekar (2018).

18. Estimates here are based on averages for 2017 and 2018 from data in Felbab-Brown (2020), which are based in turn on data from the United Nations Office on Drugs and Crime (UNODC). Of course, by its nature these estimates are only approximate, but the highest end of estimates suggests they are about 20–30 per cent of GDP, but because GDP is so low, this is still relatively modest. See also Fishstein (2014), who cites an estimate of 15 per cent for earlier years.

19. See Mansfield (2017) and Felbab-Brown (2020).

20. Mansfield (2016). Not only does the crop offer a higher price, but the well-developed value chains have led to reliable access to inputs and finance.

21. Mansfield (2017).

22. The BBC, quoting Department of Defense sources, has reported that between 2001 and 2019 the US spent $778 billion on the conflict, with a peak of just under $100 billion in 2011 and 2012 (https://www.bbc.co.uk/news/world-47391821). The Afghan Study Group (2021) cites a somewhat higher number based on budget requests from the Department of Defense: $52 billion in both 2018 and 2019 and $952 billion over the period 2001–19, suggesting by 2020 $1 trillion.

23. Bizhan (2018).

24. The data on the United States are from the Borgen Project, with sources (https://borgenproject.org/10-facts-about-u-s-aid-to-afghanistan/).

25. Formerly, they were called the Afghanistan National Security Forces (ANSF), encompassing the army and air force, as well as policy and other security forces.

26. World Bank, World Development Indicators database. Data are for total children in primary education, irrespective of age and vaccination rates for DPT. Other data suggest that between 2001 and 2019 the share of children born alive but not surviving until age five dropped from 12.5 per cent to 6 per cent. All these rates are still double that for Bangladesh but better than those for Sierra Leone and South Sudan.

27. The concept 'hearts and minds' was first used in Britain as part of the strategy in the Malayan Emergency (1948–60), but it became more widely used after President Lyndon B. Johnson embraced it as part of the US Vietnam strategy.

28. Fishstein and Wilder (2012).

29. This echoes evidence from Iraq using careful statistical analysis, where it was found that CEPR (Commander Emergency Response Program) spending led to fewer violent incidents, provided the spending was small-scale (less than $50,000) and government security forces were present, together with development expertise (via Provincial Reconstruction Teams). See Berman et al. (2013).

30. World Bank, World Development Indicators database.

31. Bizhan (2018). This pattern is unlikely to have changed since even data could not be compiled.

32. Although their salaries remain relatively modest, typically about $250 per month, at typical strength this costs about $0.5 billion per year. Moreover, the cost of fielding them had been estimated at about $14,500 per soldier, or about $2.6 billion—all picked up by the US. Data are from 2012 and are cited in Dreazen (2012).

33. These new structures were specific vehicles to deliver projects and services off-budget and outside government using 'parallel' systems, with aid jargon names such as grant management units, programme implementation units, or programme management offices (Bizhan, 2018).

34. In 2002, SIGAR began its focus on US relief and reconstruction funding (about $150 billion). It conducted painstaking investigations into corruption and, more broadly, effectiveness of spending.

35. SIGAR (2020). It stated further, 'The Afghan government often makes paper reforms, such as drafting regulations or holding meetings, rather than taking concrete action that would reduce corruption, such as arresting or enforcing penalties on powerful Afghans.'

36. Jones (2020).

37. Krahmann (2016).

38. Fishstein and Wilder (2012).

39. http://www.theguardian.com/world/2009/nov/13/us-trucks-security-taliban.

40. Transparency International 2020 Ranking (https://www.transparency.org/en/cpi/2020/index/).

41. For a careful discussion of the links between aid and state building in Afghanistan, see Bizhan (2018).

42. Sectors that have emerged on the back of military and other aid are the non-tradables—that is, those products that cannot be traded internationally and don't have much potential for productivity growth, including through exposure to international competition.

43. Even in 2014, firms in Kandahar freely admitted to paying protection money to both Taliban and anti-Taliban groups, largely to avoid kidnapping. One owner told me that the payments had allowed his firm to reduce its security staff from eighty to ten, but security remained expensive. Even if conflict disappears for now, with ISIS becoming stronger, organised crime is bound to grow, responding to the demand for services that in a functioning state would be provided by the government.

44. The Brahmin were historically the scholarly and priestly caste; the Kshatriya, the military caste.

45. Satisfying Maoist demands but also undermining their ability to mobilise.

46. The conflict no doubt accelerated the increase in migration to India and beyond. Happily for Nepal, it has resulted in a vast increase in remittances and is an important factor in the decline in rural poverty. Remittances increased from less than 1 per cent of GDP in 1996 to 16 per cent in 2006. Since then, they have increased further, peaking at 31 per cent of GDP in 2015 (World Bank, World Development Indicators database).

47. This is by no means a complete analysis. In the last two decades, not only has Nepal been able to take advantage of the global demand for migrants, but it also has benefited from the geopolitical rivalry of China and India, neither keen to let the other control Nepal but remaining cautious in its interference.

48. The foundations of that deal are older, going back to 1943 National Pact that agreed to the sectarian division of power. In 1989, the Taif Agreement essentially restructured some of the balance between groups but still reaffirmed the sectarian basis of politics.

49. Lebanon is the only country in the world that by convention stipulates the religion of its central bank governor as part of a long-standing elite power-sharing deal.

50. http://news.bbc.co.uk/1/hi/world/middle_east/7764657.stm.

51. A Ponzi scheme is a form of fraud that lures investors and pays profits to earlier investors with funds from more recent investors.

52. Within a week of its independence from Britain in 1960, British Somaliland formed a union with Italian Somaliland to the south to constitute the Somali Republic, which is present-day Somalia.

53. The peace deal emerged from the 1993 Boroma Conference.

54. The main northern clan and subclans—the Isaq, Dir (Ise and Gudabursi), and Harti Darod (Dolbahunte and Warsengeli)—have long histories of interaction, through intermarriage, competition, and cooperation over resources. The Isaq constitute about 70 per cent of the population.

55. Elder is not an inherited role or a formal position, even though elders may be chosen to represent subclans based on factors such as age, knowledge, piety, wealth, political acumen, and negotiation skills (Kaplan 2008).

56. Kaplan (2008).

57. In 2020, the hajj was restricted due to Covid-19, leading to a slump in sales.

58. Balthasar (2013). There were other attacks as well, such as on the airport, and the emergent state launched some of them to ensure it could secure revenue by controlling the airport.

59. Musa and Horst (2019) shed light on how the business community shaped the peace.

60. Renders and Terlinden (2010).

61. De Waal (2015). At the Boroma Conference the entire elite were in the room to choose a president. They rejected a candidate with massive Saudi Arabian finance offering ample short-run rent-seeking opportunities. Instead, they chose someone who would likely be more accepted by businesses, politicians, and elders.

62. https://www.worldbank.org/en/news/press-release/2016/06/10/world-bank-makes-progress-to-support-remittance-flows-to-somalia.

63. Musa and Horst (2019); Stepputat and Hagmann (2019).

64. See, for example, Kaplan (2008).

65. International donors have continually pressed for more democratic accountability through elections, and while presidential elections have been held (albeit late) in 2017, parliamentary elections for the House of Representatives have been delayed repeatedly since 2005. One could argue, though, that peace is central here, and that it only can be obtained effectively as a power-sharing deal between clans. Elections leading to majority rule or winner-take-all patronage opportunities may then be more disruptive here than not holding them, at least for now.

66. World Bank (2019) finds a very high incidence of poverty and other deprivation in Somaliland as part of an analysis of Somalia as a whole.

9.   BANGLADESH: THE BENGAL TIGER CUB

1. I was in Bangladesh in early February 2020, before it was clear that Covid-19 had just begun to spread across the world. I was visiting as a researcher at that time.

2. Bandiera et al. (2017); Banerjee et al. (2015).

3. In constant 2010 prices, taken from World Bank's World Development Indicators database, https://datacatalog.worldbank.org/dataset/world-development-indicators. Data reported here are for 1972–1989, 1989–1999, and 1999–2019.

4. Data are from the World Bank, based on poverty at the international poverty line of $1.90 in 2011 international dollars.

5. World Bank, World Development Indicators database.

6. See chapter 3. Data are from the World Bank's World Development Indicators database.

7. Alamgir (1980).

8. The trade restrictions were linked to the Multi-Fibre Agreement of 1974, which aimed to restrict imports from emerging and developing economies, including Korea, through quotas in Europe and the US.

9. Rhee (1990); Mostafa and Klepper (2018).

10. Data are from Bangladesh Garment Manufacturers and Exporters Association (BGMEA), https://www.bgmea.com.bd/page/Export_Performance.

11. Overseas development assistance was initially relevant in the economy as a whole, peaking at 8 per cent of the gross national income (GNI) in 1977. Since then, however, it has declined to 1 per cent of GDP, or $3 billion by 2018 (World Bank, World Development Indicators database).

12. Raihan and Khan (2020). Export-oriented manufacturing was the main source of the increase from 21 to 30 per cent in the overall industrial share

of GDP between 1991 and 2019, whereas agriculture declined from 32 to 13 per cent of GDP, and services increased from 44 to 53 per cent of GDP during this period.

13. Agriculture now accounts for about 38 per cent of active workers, almost halving since 1991. More than one in five are employed in the industrial sector, and more than 40 per cent in the services sector. Bangladesh urbanised rapidly, with the share of the population living in urban areas doubling to almost 40 per cent over the last thirty years. Non-agricultural activity is not just taking place in urban areas; far more make a living outside agriculture in rural areas. The engine has been garments and remittances. The income and jobs multipliers worked via services and other non-agricultural activities.

14. Kabeer, Huq, and Suleiman (2020).

15. The International Organization for Migration (IOM) puts this number at about 8 million, of which around 70 per cent are most likely migrant workers (IOM 2019). However, it most likely underestimates those on relatively shorter contracts of a few years, not least in the Gulf, although it would also count permanent migrants such as those to the UK who left a long time ago.

16. Marx said: 'at the other [pole of society] are grouped masses of men, who have nothing to sell but their labour-power' (Marx 1990, vol. I, ch. 28).

17. Robinson (1962).

18. This finding is adjusted for cost-of-living increases. Real rice prices fell in this period. Data are calculated based on Hassan and Kornher (2019, table 1). Rural incomes were also boosted by rising rice yields. According to Food and Agriculture Organization (FAO) data (http://www.fao.org/faostat), rice yields increased between 1990 and 2019 by 85 per cent, outpacing India, which earlier had been at similar levels.

19. By 1995, rural wages were still only about half those for industrial jobs, suggesting that labour was not scarce in rural areas; indeed, there was even 'surplus' labour. Since then, the gap between farm wages and (low-skilled) industrial wages seems to have effectively closed (Hassan and Kornher 2019, table 1, using data from Mymensingh, Rangpur, Dhaka, and Chittagong for 2014). The Lewis model, the workhorse of the basic economics of structural transformation, suggests a turning point has been reached: surplus labour in agriculture has disappeared, and labour is increasingly scarce across the economy (Lewis 1954). In recent decades, labour demand has slowly begun to outpace labour supply, pushing wages up further (Zhang et al. 2014).

20. El Arifeen et al. (2013).

21. Hossain (2017); BRAC (2019).

22. See Roodman (2012) on the role of microcredit within Bangladeshi society.

23. Yunus (2009); Roodman (2012); Banerjee, Karlan, and Zinman (2015).

24. Collins et al. (2009).
25. Bandiera et al. (2017); Banerjee et al. (2015).
26. These are nominal dollars of net overseas development assistance (ODA) received between 1971 until 2019, as reported in in the World Bank's World Development Indicators database.
27. Definitions of a fragile state are varied. OECD characterises fragility 'as the combination of exposure to risk and insufficient coping capacity of the state, systems and/or communities to manage, absorb or mitigate those risks. Fragility can lead to negative outcomes including violence, poverty, inequality, displacement, and environmental and political degradation' (OECD 2020). Others suggest 'fragility' reflects lack of a monopoly of violence, weak state legitimacy, or weak state capacity to provide for its citizens (Mcloughlin 2009).
28. Khan (2013).
29. Mahmood (2010); Zafarullah and Siddiquee (2001); Khan (2017).
30. Khan (2013); Hossain (2017).
31. Khan (2013).
32. Asadullah and Chakravorty (2019, table 3).
33. Hossain (2017); Khan (2013).
34. President Zia Rahman made the initial contacts between Daewoo and Desh and was helpful in supporting some of the early facilitating actions—see Khan (2013) for a discussion—but he hardly offered a full-fledged industrial policy of protection and other support, based on demands from industrialists.
35. Hassan and Raihan (2017); Jahan (2015). The BGMEA is a powerful association that lobbies the government to maintain support for the garment industry. Without such an inside track, other business sectors find it hard to receive the same kind of political support, which contributes to the persistent dominance of garments and to the problems faced by new export sectors.
36. Asadullah and Chakravorty (2019). Foreign direct investment (FDI) was less than 1 per cent of GDP in 2019—lower than that of India, Indonesia, and Sri Lanka (World Bank, World Development Indicators. database).
37. Hossain (2017).
38. Hossain (2017); Hassan (2013). For many observers at the time, and probably even today, the overriding focus was on the 'Malthusian' disaster waiting to happen, whereby food production could not keep up with population growth. The proposed answer: control population growth through family planning. But this was always the wrong answer, as was shown subsequently. Family planning options definitely had a role, but they were only one factor relative to female empowerment through opportunities, such as jobs, as well as broader health care and especially education. For a recent reassessment, see Bora, Saikia, and Lutz (2019).

39. As discussed in chapter 2, a 'developmental state' is a state characterised by a fundamental commitment to economic development, with strong state intervention, as well as extensive regulation and planning. Johnson (1982), Amsden (1989), and others have argued that in Korea and other East Asian and later Southeast Asian countries, this was a defining feature.

40. Christensen and Weinstein (2013).

41. Or at least mostly—or until the last decade. Increasingly vocal in politics, Yunus became a thorn in the side of Prime Minister Sheikh Hasina. Politically motivated cases were brought against Yunus in an effort to remove him from his role at Grameen.

42. During a visit to rural Bangladesh in 2014, a group of women told me that to enrol in one of the many government welfare schemes, they first had to pay a bribe of about $60, which meant they could not afford to join. Even the state recognised that its own structures could hardly deliver, so it has set up its own parallel systems outside government through non-profit organisations. For example, the Palli Karma-Sahayak Foundation (PKSF) operates just like an NGO, delivering targeted credit and services, seemingly quite effectively, even though it was initially fully endowed by the government itself.

43. Hossain (2017).

44. This is in nominal US dollars (World Bank, World Development Indicators database). The highest level ever in Bangladesh was in 2019, at $27 per capita.

45. Hossain (2017).

46. Hossain (2017) goes further and suggests in her fascinating discussion that Bangladesh was an 'aid lab': 'When aid officials and diplomats come to Bangladesh they seek not minerals or land or geopolitical advantage, but to demonstrate that the social, economic, and political model they promote works.'

47. Grameen has been more defensive about its approach, and rigorous impact evaluations conducted with its support remain limited, contributing to the debate on the effectiveness of its programmes. However, philanthropists and some aid agencies continue to find the notion that all poor people can escape poverty through entrepreneurship attractive, despite gaps in the evidence base.

10. ETHIOPIA AND RWANDA: AFRICAN LIONS?

1. De Waal, Taffesse, and Carruth (2006).

2. Dercon and Porter (2014). The crisis ended up playing out in front of the media, and the coverage of the Korem refugee camp by the BBC became one of the most haunting news reports ever (https://www.youtube.com/watch?v=XYOj_6OYuJc&ab_channel=LiveAid1).

3. De Waal, Taffesse, and Carruth (2006).

4. See Sabates-Wheeler et al. (2020) for a recent review of the programme. It has succeeded in protecting people, but it is less clear that it has been sufficient to 'graduate' people out of poverty in a sustained way. Even during the Covid-19 pandemic, those in the programme were successfully protected. See Abay et al. (2020).

5. NDRMC (2016); Hirvonen, Sohnesen, and Bundervoet (2020). Child undernutrition includes stunting (low height for a given age) and wasting (low weight for a given age).

6. In the final line of his Gettysburg Address, President Abraham Lincoln described democracy as 'government of the people, by the people, and for the people'.

7. The height of state terror was in 1976–7, as part of the Red Terror in which the military leadership encouraged the persecution and often summary execution of possibly half a million alleged sympathisers of a rival political party, the Ethiopian People's Revolutionary Party (EPRP) and associated groups. For a detailed discussion of this period, see Ottaway and Ottaway (1978) and Clapham (2017).

8. World Bank, World Development Indicators database, in constant 2010 dollars.

9. Data on gross enrolment and on child mortality from the World Bank's World Development Indicators database.

10. World Bank, World Development Indicators database, in constant 2010 dollars. The scale of growth has at times been questioned (such as by Lefort 2013) because across much of Africa the data are not always reliable. For example, agricultural growth may have been lower in the early period since 2004, as I argued in Dercon, Hill, and Zeitin (2009). However, I would not dispute that growth has been sustained and is for Africa at exceptionally high levels.

11. World Bank, World Development Indicators data on share of the population below the international poverty line of $1.90 in 2011 prices, corrected for purchasing power. In 1999, the estimate was 57.8 per cent, and in 2015, 30.8 per cent of the population was below this line.

12. Dercon and Gollin (2019).

13. This is based on net enrolment rate figures—that is, children in primary school of primary school age relative to the number of all children of primary school age. Allowing for older children still in primary school, this figure would reach close to 100 per cent.

14. I am using the Ethiopian naming convention of referring to figures by their first name, as this is the person's name. The second (and third) name is their

father's (and grandfather's). Thus I refer to Meles rather than Zenawi and Abiy rather than Ahmed in later references to the prime minister in 2021.

15. Ministry of Planning and Economic Development (1993). For a detailed discussion of its success and failings, see Dercon and Gollin (2019).

16. SDPRP = Sustainable Development and Poverty Reduction Program; PASDEP = Plan for Sustained Development and the Elimination of Poverty; GTP = Growth and Transformation Plan (numbered as GTP1 and GTP2).

17. See the discussion of the developmental state in chapter 2. In Korea and other East Asian and later Southeast Asian countries the developmental state was a defining feature of their development—see Johnson (1982), Amsden (1989), and others. Unlike in India, Indonesia, and Bangladesh later on, the state was seen as central in delivering progress. Senior Ethiopian officials travelled to Korea and other places to learn about the way they achieved this.

18. This is net overseas development assistance (ODA) received in current US dollars, totals and per capita, based on data from the World Bank's World Development Indicators database.

19. Incomplete drafts of his thesis are available online and are worth reading (Zenawi 2009). See also De Waal (2013) and Lefort (2013) for heated discussions on the content.

20. See also Oqubay (2015).

21. Dercon, Hill, and Zeitin (2009).

22. Bachewe et al. (2018).

23. Clapham (2017). There is no better articulation to help understand Ethiopia and the region than Clapham's. To be precise, Ethiopia was briefly occupied by Fascist Italy from 1936 to 1941. Eritrea was a formal colony of Italy from 1890 until 1941, after which it fell under British military administration until 1951. In 1952, it became part of Ethiopia. All data in the rest of this chapter, such as on composition of the population, do not include Eritrea.

24. Clapham (2017).

25. The idea of a 'competent' bureaucracy is hard to prove, but historians have described the spread of local administrators with political ties across Menelik's empire and the quest to 'modernise' Ethiopia during the reign of Haile Selassie. Compared with other African states, Ethiopia had a head start in building a state—its interwoven but hierarchical informal and formal networks. See, for example, Levine (1965); Keller (1981); and Marcus (2002). The perceived importance of this bureaucratic class until recently is illustrated by the fact that until the 1990s all university graduates were entitled to a public sector position (Krishnan 1996).

26. This term used by Marxist writer Rosa Luxemburg features extensively in debates on this subject in Ethiopia.

27. Other groups include the Somali (6 per cent), Sidama (4 per cent), and the Gurage, Welayta, Afari, and Hadiya (with a few per cent each). In total, Ethiopia has about eighty recognised ethnicities and nationalities.

28. Data on urbanisation are from the World Bank's World Development Indicators database. Data on ethnicity are from the Central Statistical Agency (2010).

29. This is in constant 2010 dollars (World Bank, World Development Indicators database).

30. This tension between de facto centralisation and de jure decentralisation never went away, as today's conflict between the TPLF and its former brethren in the EPRDF illustrates. This is discussed in more detail later in this chapter.

31. The government argued that food security was at the core the country's national security (Federal Democratic Republic of Ethiopia 2002). Meles is credited as the author of this statement (De Waal 2013).

32. The border claims were a reflection of much deeper tensions and distrust, between the TPLF and the Eritrean regime. See Lata (2003).

33. Zenawi (2009).

34. Meles said this at a closed event organised in Manchester, UK, at which I was present.

35. Abiy's intellectual roots are less Marxist-Leninist than those of his former comrades. Much inspiration appears to come from his Pentecostal Christian beliefs, as well as aspects of the prosperity gospel common in charismatic beliefs, which asserts that prosperity is a sign of God's blessing.

36. Over the last decades, the voices arguing for political opening and democracy were loud, and in principle they were right. Meles's tight hold on security was brutal and ruthless. Nevertheless, it limited some of the widespread conflict now observed, in which most tensions are interpreted as stemming from some injustice towards an ethnic group. This counterfactual is now reality, with politics, like a can of worms, opened up. The opening up need not be criticised, but the transition does seem to be full of potholes.

37. It is often argued in political discourse on Ethiopia that the core Tigrayan group around the leadership was also engaged in large-scale political corruption—their own form of rent-seeking. There is no doubt that key positions in 'private' firms with good government connections were often occupied by former military and other leaders of the main political groups in the EPRDF, thereby helping them to enrich themselves. However, I have never seen credible evidence that this practice ever resulted in the kind of large-scale procurement and other fraud typical of many other African countries, or the excessively opulent lifestyles accompanying it.

38. The IMF ranked Ethiopia as at high risk of debt distress, the second worst

category (data from February 2021, https://www.imf.org/external/Pubs/ft/dsa/DSAlist.pdf). The level of gross government debt relative to GDP was 57 per cent in 2019, which is lower than that of Ghana or Kenya and just above the mean for sub-Saharan Africa (51 per cent).

39. Dorn and Matloff (2000) have argued that genocide could have been foreseen and prevented. Africa Watch (1993) documented large-scale human rights abuses by the government, including the killing of 300 Tutsi and other members of political parties, and some by the rebels of the Rwandan Patriotic Front.

40. This is in dollars at constant 2011 prices (World Bank, World Development Indicators database).

41. To be precise, this is based on the percentage of children born alive who do not survive past age five (under-five mortality) as reported in the World Bank's World Development Indicators database. For Rwanda, this stood at 34 deaths per 1,000 live births in 2019, the lowest number across mainland sub-Saharan Africa—better than far richer South Africa or well-performing Ghana and Ethiopia. Only the Seychelles, Cabo Verde, Mauritius, and São Tomé and Príncipe fare better in sub-Saharan Africa. In 2000, child mortality stood at 179 per 1,000 live births, worse than average for sub-Saharan Africa, where it was 151 deaths per 1,000 live births.

42. According to the World Bank's World Development Indicators database using the latest (2016) estimate, extreme poverty is 56 per cent, based on the 2011 international poverty line of $1.90 per capita, down from 63 per cent in 2010. These numbers are much debated, but even these official numbers suggest a relatively slow decline.

43. Jones, De Oliveira, and Verhoeven (2012).

44. Vansina (2004); Lemarchand (1970).

45. Prunier (1995). According to Heldring (2021), obedience to a central authority helps explain variation in violence during the genocide as well.

46. Based on the World Bank's World Governance Indicators, more specifically the Government Effectiveness Index capturing perceptions of the quality of public services, of the civil service, of policy formulation and implementation, and of the credibility of the government's commitment to such policies.

47. Transparency International Perceptions of Corruption Index 2020.

48. See, for example, *Africa Confidential* (2021).

49. Net overseas development assistance in current dollars (World Bank, World Development Indicators database).

50. The World Bank put a halt to these rankings in 2021 after finding irregularities and political interference, but these had nothing to do with any African countries.

51. See Sutton (2012).

11. THE SWEDISH AND OTHER MODELS

1. The United Nations Millennium Declaration, https://undocs.org/A/ RES/55/2. Photograph from UN Photo Library, https://www.flickr.com/ photos/un_photo/43208152355.

2. The Millennium Development Goals comprised 7 goals and 21 targets. The goals were (1) to eradicate extreme poverty and hunger; (2) to achieve universal primary education; (3) to promote gender equality and empower women; (4) to reduce child mortality; (5) to improve maternal health; (6) to combat HIV/AIDS, malaria, and other diseases; (7) to ensure environmental sustainability; and (8) to develop a global partnership for development.

3. The Sustainable Development Goals comprise 17 goals and 169 targets, much broader than the MDGs, and are applicable to all countries. They cover again goals on poverty and hunger, good health and quality education, but also different dimensions of sustainability linked to climate and environment, as well as the broader economy, including cities, employment and infrastructure, and commitments to peace and justice.

4. Sweden also tends to stand for an open, liberal society with a well-functioning state and moral, decent politicians, along with impressive gender equality. It is a tolerant society for immigrants, too. In the twentieth century, Sweden always stood out as a peace-loving country, promoting benign international policy positions and seemingly holding the moral high ground, in the Cold War as well.

5. Salonen (2009) offers a thoughtful introduction. He highlights the undoubted achievements of the Swedish model, but to some extent he debunks the notion that it has been an *exceptional* success throughout the last century beyond more recent times. Sweden experienced no wars or revolutions in the last two centuries, perhaps because it is, in common with other Nordic countries, homogeneous in language, religion, and ethnicity. Despite this useful precondition, it was a late industrialiser, and it remained deeply poor well into the twentieth century, with up to a million Swedes migrating in search of a better life overseas. Generalised suffrage, including for all workers and women, came only after World War I, as elsewhere. The notion of a welfare state slowly became a reality in the 1930s, but it was only until the 1970s that social spending and even measures for gender equalisation outpaced those of other Organisation for Economic Co-operation and Development (OECD) countries and the Swedish model was properly established.

6. In common with other Nordic countries, Sweden tends to be ranked among the happiest countries, with low inequality in outcomes such as health, even though in recent years income inequality has increased rapidly (see data from Our World in Data).

7.   Collier and Dercon (2006).

8.   The standard World Bank threshold for a high-income country was first used in 1987. It was set at a gross national income of US$6,000 per capita. See Edvinsson (2013) for historical GDP per capita for Sweden. Based on any reasonable inflation estimate and extrapolation of this classification, Sweden was no doubt a high-income country soon after World War II or even earlier.

9.   Carl Göran Andræ, as quoted in Sturfelt (2019). However, Sturfelt points out that not all historians agree that there was no struggle and disruption.

10. See also Clemens, Kenny, and Moss (2007). The SDG list of goals and targets is vast and, in practice, too expansive. It is therefore impossible for a committed poor country to prioritise all of these goals.

11. For a useful overview, see OECD (2020).

12. Examples of what is not included are non-concessional loans by governments to other governments, export finance (supporting firms to sell in other countries), non-concessional loans by multilateral development banks such as the World Bank's International Bank for Reconstruction and Development (IBRD) beyond the capital paid by countries that this bank leverages, and commercial lending to countries that may be used to finance development activity. The grant equivalent of the World Bank's International Development Assistance (IDA) loans is included.

13. OECD   data,   http://www.oecd.org/dac/financing-sustainable-development/development-finance-data/.

14. Despite Covid-19 and large aid commitments to fight it worldwide, total official development assistance has remained broadly unchanged in recent years, implying that resources committed to development were reallocated to focus on Covid-19 and its consequences.

15. In the UK, the MDGs helped forge a broad commitment across political parties to development spending. The emphasis was on development spending delivering 'results' and the accountability opportunity that stems from it, as well as boosting aid spending to the commonly held aid target of 0.7 per cent of the UK's gross national income, which it achieved between 2013 and 2020. This consensus was short-lived, and in 2021 UK fiscal policy shifts meant that it is unlikely to achieve this level of spending at least in the near future. For a fascinating discussion of the origins of the 0.7 target, see Clemens and Moss (2007).

16. For example, see Zedillo (2001) or Sachs (2019) on the calculations.

17. The $5–$7 trillion figure is based on figures in UNCTAD (2014). In 2019, $6 trillion was about 0.74 per cent of the global GDP of about $81 trillion. Since the 1970s, various UN events have affirmed a norm of 0.7 per cent of gross national income as the sum that countries who can afford it should spend on international development.

18. I was in good company. Soon after the Millennium Summit, Shanta Devarajan, a senior official and researcher at the World Bank, calculated with co-authors in 2002 that it would cost an additional $50 billion to achieve the MDGs (Devarajan, Miller, and Swanson 2002). 'Shame on me,' he wrote in a blog in 2015, as he explained it was an answer to the wrong question, but also the wrong way to approach the problem of development (https://www. brookings.edu/blog/future-development/2015/03/02/shame-on-me-why-it-was-wrong-to-cost-the-millennium-development-goals/).

19. One of the best-known studies is that by Alesina and Dollar (2000).

20. There are exceptions. When contributing to the review of the performance of SIDA, the Swedish aid agency, more than twenty years ago, I was struck when a very senior official stated that for Sweden it did not matter whether aid was spent well and had an impact. It was more important for Sweden to do the morally right thing and give aid to poor countries (and for politicians to be *seen* giving aid). But I still do not know whether this was the official policy line or just the view of a cynical official.

21. Probably the most careful paper on this using cross-country and time series data is that by Clemens et al. (2012). Studies focusing on the overall macro-level impact of aid on poverty or other deprivations exist, but they do not tend to meet the methodological threshold for statistical validity. In any case, these studies cannot claim likely large impacts, on average, across countries.

22. The problem is how to establish the counterfactual in a convincing way: what would have happened without aid in these specific places, which is the problem bedevilling the literature on aid effectiveness. See Clemens et al. (2012).

23. Note the direction of the logic: budget support is an effective route to spending foreign aid when there is a development bargain. That does not mean budget support is always a good instrument. On the contrary, providing such support simply based on a principle of ownership by countries is counterproductive in countries where the rulers could not care less about what happens to development.

24. Such countries would no doubt welcome the approaches suggested by Banerjee and Duflo (2011)—testing what works and improving how it is delivered.

25. It is the kind of setting in which William Easterly or Angus Deaton would most likely encourage halting aid because it is counterproductive. Such countries lack the institutions to start with, and that is where change will have to come first, with almost no role for outsiders.

26. At the regular meetings of FOCAC, China announces new funding targets. They are, however, cumulative since the first of these conferences. So the

latest offer in 2018, $60 billion in loans, was not all new money but included all that had been pledged before.

27. China does not follow the DAC rules for reporting foreign aid, so all these numbers are estimates. They are based on communications with Naohiro Kitano for 2018, using methods as in Kitano and Harada (2016). About half of this is bilateral aid—that is, not through international organisations. Other sources such as Strange et al. (2017) estimate this level of aid to be even lower.

28. Loan data are from http://www.sais-cari.org/data. It is likely that the 2020 figures will be much lower with a debt crisis emerging and China reluctant to lend more.

29. These are the same types of finance Western export finance agencies use to promote their own economies through their firms abroad.

30. Morris, Parks, and Gardner (2020).

31. OECD DAC calls these 'other official flows'.

32. *Africa Confidential* (2020).

33. As part of the G20 Common Framework, Chinese banks are now, for the first time, part of debt-rescheduling arrangements in countries such as Chad, Zambia, and Ethiopia.

34. Still, not all members have equal power, and shareholdings are skewed towards richer countries, the US being the largest shareholder with 17.25 per cent of the shares.

35. Spearing (2019).

36. Cormier and Manger (2020). The actual reform conditions, preconditions, or milestones are broader now than what in the 1990s would have been an agenda around small government, with limited involvement in the economy. They have to be approved by the World Bank's Board, where voting power is based on shareholdings, giving the richer Western countries in the world a majority of the votes. As a result, the policies are more orthodox than the rather broader and varied set used by successful, fast-growing developing countries in recent decades, as discussed in parts I and II of this book.

37. What is now old literature helped to establish this consensus, such as Collier et al. (1997) as well as the suggestive empirical evidence by Dollar and Svensson (2000).

38. Dollar and Svensson (2000) analyse structural reform programmes and find that political factors were strongest in correlating with successfully completed programmes.

39. Much of this echoes what the research on conditionality two decades ago was noticing: some countries were using aid effectively and progressing at the same time, while others were not, despite aid. It found correlates of

economic growth with packages of policies more focused on growth, but these correlations were not strong. Dollar and Svensson (2000), among others, asserted that donors should identify reformers to support, not try to create them. But it appears that this advice has not been followed.

12. ABOUT WARREN BUFFETT AND THE OBVIOUS USES OF AID

1. Value investment in development should not be confused with impact investment in development. The latter is investing that combines financial returns, but also with outcomes in terms of development, such as jobs or reducing poverty. Value investing is also not simply spending on development with results in mind, such as boosting education or health outcomes in the short run, but it aims to consciously seek out opportunities with long-term outcomes, such as systemic change in the economy or health and education systems or, indeed, in the political and economic deals of countries.

2. Unless otherwise stated, all data are from World Bank's World Development Indicators. This is a decline from about 1.5 per cent of their GNI in 1990, but GNI also increased by 140 per cent over this period.

3. For example, see Besley and Persson (2009).

4. Besley and Persson (2009); Prichard (2015).

5. This alludes as well to promising ways to measure the presence of certain dimensions of a development bargain, using metrics that capture the fiscal contract, state capability and investment climate. Measurements should be made *de facto* and not just *de jure*—that is, not simply the rules or laws (such as investment, tax or anti-corruption laws) but how in practice they are applied and used. Similarly, it would involve assessing how effectively limited resources are used and not simply noting finance levels or shares of budgets.

6. See Ang (2016) and the discussion in chapter 4.

7. Banerjee and Duflo (2011).

8. This is undeniably a challenge: aid providers are outsiders, and their ability to champion institutional development and accountability—such as pushing for political openness and democratic values—is limited, as well as deeply political and at times ideological. Multilateral organisations and banks are notoriously weak at such efforts because of the nature of their mandates. Bilateral donor agencies or international NGOs funded by them may find it easier to be more political.

9. Persson, Rothstein, and Teorell (2013).

10. Marquette and Peiffer (2015). Chapter 13 has some ideas about interventions that may be effective, but they require a serious political commitment to succeed.

11. Multilateral development banks will offer loans at non-concessional rates

to middle-income countries (that is, those with a GNI exceeding $1,026 in 2011 prices), but at lower-than-commercial rates through the global risk pooling across the loan portfolios of these banks. Because there is no direct subsidy by richer countries, these loans are not counted as ODA. As discussed in chapter 11, the World Bank's International Development Association can offer loans at concessional rates because of the grants it receives from rich countries.

12. See chapter 3 for a further discussion of the data, and the case studies in part II for more details.

13. The aid and GDP figures are in nominal terms because of how ODA figures are reported. Data are from the World Bank's World Development Indicators.

14. Codifying this selectivity, such as in the World Bank's International Development Association, would require a (daring) move to include more political economy analysis in tools such as the Country Policy and Institutional Assessment, one of the indicators used to determine how much IDA lending a country may get.

15. This is not the same as being able to prove scientifically that development bargains were at the root of the improvements. For one thing, measuring the constituent parts of elite bargains is not self-evident, while quantitatively establishing the causal links is likely to remain problematic, as with most work on the 'causes' of economic growth.

16. See chapters 4 and 9.

17. For example, see Milanovic (2016) for some of the arguments. See Ravallion (2018) for a critique.

18. Sometimes even less. Just a landing strip, some guns, and satellite phones proved enough for diamond mines to operate under the control of local militias for a few months during the height of conflict in the DRC in the early 2000s.

19. Some natural resources, such as copper or coal, may need more investment, but even then, to keep the rents flowing, the infrastructure needed is limited to linking a mine with a port, without much need for sensible economic policies to be globally competitive.

20. Our World in Data, https://ourworldindata.org/trade-and-globalization.

21. Capital flight estimates are from UNCTAD (2020). GDP and FDI of sub-Saharan Africa plus Egypt, Algeria, Tunisia, Libya, and Morocco are from the World Bank's World Development Indicators database.

22. Zucman (2015) delves into the subject of lost taxation linked to offshore centres. In some of the types of countries I am concerned with here, it is not self-evident that public resources are well spent on development or growth anyway, so this is not my primary focus.

23. Luanda Leaks are a series of investigations conducted by the International Consortium of Investigative Journalists (ICIJ).

24. Transparency International, Perceptions of Corruption Index 2020.

25. https://www.transparency.org/en/news/25-corruption-scandals.

26. OECD is an international organisation whose members are mainly high-income countries. One of its roles is coordination on issues related to taxation and its evasion by multinational corporations as well as work on anti-bribery and transparency. The Financial Action Task Force is the global monitoring body on money-laundering and terrorist finance, setting international standards that its global membership is committed to implementing.

27. Transparency International (2018a).

28. Based on the World Bank's World Development Indicators database.

29. Data from 2018. Transparency International (2018b).

30. Jones, Temouri, and Cobham (2018).

31. The Gupta brothers were involved in large-scale corruption linked to President Zuma. Dan Gertler is an Israeli mining billionaire with notorious dealings in Africa, including with Joseph Kabila in the DRC (*Africa Confidential* 2020, 2021). The support by audit or PR companies in these cases was not obviously illegal.

32. The strict definition of public goods is that they are non-excludable—it is impossible to exclude anyone from benefiting—as well as nonrival—using the good does not prevent anyone else from benefiting.

33. Data are from Our World in Data, https://ourworldindata.org/cheap-renewables-growth. In 2009, solar photovoltaic and onshore wind were 223 per cent and 22 per cent, respectively, more expensive than coal. By 2019, both were more than 60 per cent cheaper than coal.

34. I have sympathy for the argument that ridding countries of the worst elite bargains may require some degree of instability and violence, but agnostic on how outsiders really can help here.

35. The stresses of environmental hardships and climate change no doubt contribute to the risks of conflict, but they are but one of many factors. Limiting climate change will have a positive impact on those risks, but that is not the same as directing large-scale climate finance to those countries at risk of conflict because such an effort could further fuel conflict by strengthening the kind of elite bargains that will not act on these stresses.

36. For knowledge and research to be useful for poorer countries, it does not have to be provided as a public good. Vaccines (just like other medical treatments) involve patents and other international property rights protection, and they can be made excludable and rival, the features of a private good. The key is to find ways to make them affordable and widely available, so that the actual

public good—high vaccination rates—can be achieved, despite the vaccine being produced as a private good.

37. One way to make this research more worthwhile is for researchers and implementers to work closely together in target settings.

13. AID IN MESSY PLACES

1. There are similarities here to the approach proposed by Acemoglu and Robinson (2013).

2. In 2018 US dollars, GDP per capita is about $2,200. All data are for 2018 and are from the World Bank's World Development Indicators database.

3. Much worse outcomes for Nigeria are also found in terms of the maternal mortality rate, use of safe water sources, and child malnutrition. These data are from the World Bank's World Development Indicators database, and usually 2017.

4. Ghana also has four times as many nurses or midwives per 100,000 people as Nigeria. However, Nigeria and Ghana have similar numbers of physicians per 100,000 persons, which suggests that the health system in Ghana is more focused on primary health care for the broader population than the system in Nigeria.

5. There is no evidence that the Nigerian government is systematically fiddling away foreign aid provided for health, nor are the aid programmes in Nigeria ineffective. Most foreign aid in Nigeria is not handed directly to the government, and current design and monitoring practices have made it increasingly difficult for aid to disappear in someone's pockets. However, because foreign aid donors do not trust government systems, parallel structures must be set up to deliver aid, some within federal or local government systems but more often simply using contractors that mimic government systems. Within them, it is possible to set up services using the best practice and evidence. The widespread inefficiencies in government and the extensive monitoring needed to address the valid concerns about bribery and corruption make foreign aid systems costly.

6. This may seem suggestive of fungibility effects, whereby offering aid to particular programmes leads to the withdrawal of government resources. As a result, the net benefit is smaller than the total aid provided (Remmer 2004). I am not claiming that the presence of aid leads to a reduction in spending by government in general. Ghana's government health spending is much higher than Nigeria's despite both countries having similar aid levels. In both countries, the total and external health expenditures per capita have evolved similarly, but the government expenditure in Nigeria has systematically lagged behind Ghana's.

7. In the jargon of development practitioners, this calls for 'political economy analysis' and 'thinking politically' when designing development aid programmes. See, for example, McCulloch and Piron (2019), starting from a clear understanding of the way specific states function (Andrews, Pritchett and Woolcock 2017).

8. Pritchett, Woolcock, and Andrews (2013) referred to this as systemic isomorphic mimicry, wherein the outward forms (appearances, structures) of functional states and organisations elsewhere are adopted to camouflage a persistent lack of function.

9. Definition of 'capitalism' from the *Oxford Dictionary of Current English*.

10. The structures involved were complicated, but much of the privatisation of the electricity sector launched in 2010 involved connected businesses. This was obviously not surprising. See Ogunleye (2017) and Roy, Iwuamadi, and Ibrahim (2020) for a discussion of political interference and corruption in the Nigerian privatisation of the energy sector. International agencies are aware of these challenges, and they have learned over the years that they must take a more cautious approach to privatisation and similar programmes, ensuring that an appropriate regulatory framework and other aspects of competition policy are preconditions, although it is not clear how much they have learned in practice (Estrin and Pelletier 2018).

11. See an account of this from Uganda in Kuteesa et al. (2010).

12. See for example, Andrews, Pritchett and Woolcock (2017).

13. For example, see Javorcik, Lo Turco, and Maggioni (2018).

14. This political economy impact is not attained by foreign direct investors simply setting up foreign affiliates without any domestic counterparts. The evidence also suggests that the local spillovers and benefits are in any case less clearly proven in such investments. See, for example, Javorcik (2004).

15. Collier et al. (2021).

16. See Besley and Persson (2009).

17. World Bank (2015). For an example from Pakistan, see Khan, Khwaja, and Olken (2016). For the DRC, see Bergeron, Tourek, and Weigel (2021).

18. Prichard (2015).

19. Mansuri and Rao (2012) were highly critical of World Bank programmes that focused on decentralisation in the form of community-led development.

20. There is evidence that certain tools put in the hands of such individuals and their organisations may work. For example, simple financial information systems would allow them to track finance, while performance-based budgeting in which expected outcomes are matched to budgets could be a step towards more accountability. See Evans et al. (2020) for a careful review. One example is from Bihar; see Banerjee et al. (2020).

21. Evans et al. (2020).

22. Vicente and Wantchekon (2009).
23. Evans et al. (2020).
24. Haushofer and Shapiro (2016); Bastagli et al. (2019).
25. Greenwood (2014); Deaton (2013); Banerjee et al. (2017); Bandiera et al. (2017).
26. Often, because of the problems encountered in working in these countries, development funders prefer to outsource delivery to large, specialised contractors. Such a strategy may help improve some lives for some people now, but it is never sustainable. Instead, it breeds aid dependence and little change.
27. Andrews, Pritchett, and Woolcock (2017) and Banerjee et al. (2017) look at different ways to think about this. It remains an under-researched area.
28. Estimate from the United Nations Office for the Coordination of Humanitarian Affairs (UN OCHA) for a humanitarian response plan in 2019.
29. Data are from UN OCHA's financial tracking service, https://fts.unocha.org/appeals/overview/.
30. The humanitarian principles are a set of commitments on how to provide humanitarian action, such as independence and only basing support on need.
31. For example, more attention should be given to critically assessing whether health or nutrition was genuinely protected rather than on the number of beneficiaries helped or the value of support given. The humanitarian aid sector is a surprisingly evidence-free zone in which impact is assumed as long as support is provided. Too rarely do organisations involved in humanitarian support invite in-depth evaluation not just of their ways of working, but whether the work was cost-effective or had an actual impact.
32. Betts (2021); Betts et al. (2019).
33. Lenner and Turner (2018). In 2015, while I was contributing to the design and preparation of the Jordan Compact, a very senior member of the royal family confided in me that 'Jordan needed a different way to deal with refugees than it had done in the past'. In the conversation that followed within the royal palace, the focus on job opportunities took shape.
34. In 2016, refugees were estimated to be about 25 per cent of the population.
35. In Clarke and Dercon (2016), we analysed this in greater detail, and references to various studies can be found there.
36. In November 2015, I recall sitting in the smartest hotel in Addis Ababa, talking to a senior international humanitarian official, and asking, 'Why don't you work with the government, building at least on what it has in the drought areas that works well?' He looked bemused, clearly not knowing much about the country and its existing systems, and I was lectured on the principle of humanity, and how humanitarian agencies did what was best for the people.

37. They also need the finance in place beforehand to call on when needed. See Clarke and Dercon (2016) for details on how to build the financial systems for this.

38. Gentilini et al. (2020). Still, only 7 per cent were extended to new recipients beyond those that had been registered in the system pre-crisis.

INDEX

Note: Page numbers followed by "*n*" refer to notes, "*f*" refer to figures.